Rainforest Politics

Ecological Destruction in South-East Asia

Philip Hurst

Zed Books Ltd
London and New Jersey

Rainforest politics: Ecological Destruction in South-East Asia was
first published by Zed Books Ltd, 57 Caledonian Road, London
N1 9BU and 171 First Avenue, Atlantic Highlands, New Jersey
07716, USA, in 1990

Copyright © Philip Hurst, 1990

Cover designed by Andrew Corbett
Cover picture by Mark Edwards
Typeset by EMS Photosetters, Thorpe Bay, Essex
Printed and bound in the United Kingdom
by Biddles Ltd, Guildford and King's Lynn

British Library Cataloguing in Publication Data

Hurst, Philip
  Rainforest politics: forest destruction in South-
  East Asia.
  1. Asia. South-East Asia. Tropical rainforests.
  Conservation. Management.
  I. Title.
  333.750959

  ISBN 0-86232-838-1
  ISBN 0-86232-839-X pbk

Library of Congress Cataloging-in-Publication Data

Hurst, Philip
  Rainforest politics: ecological destruction in South-
East Asia/Philip Hurst.
      p.   cm.
  Includes bibliographical references.
  ISBN 0-86232-838-1. – ISBN 0-86232-839-X (pbk.)
  1. Deforestation – Control – Asia, Southeastern. 2.
Forest conservation – Asia, Southeastern. 3. Deforestation – Asia, Southeastern – Case studies. 4. Forest
policy – Asia, Southeastern – Case studies. 5. Rain
forests – Asia, Southeastern – Case studies. 6. Lumber
trade – Asia, Southeastern – Case studies. I. Title.
  SD418.3.A785H87   1989   89-35865
  333.75'137'0959–dc20   CIP
                                          Rev.

Contents

Tables

*To Kim
and the Dayaks*

Acknowledgements

All the staff at Sahabat Alam Malaysia, my parents for their patience and encouragement, Anna Gourlay for patience with my writing style, Delphin Ganapin, Harrison Gnau, Thomas Jalong, Anderson Mutang, FoE PNG, Thavivongse Sriburi, SKEPHI, Marcus Colchester, Charles Secrett, Jonathon Porritt and the people of South-East Asia for the best hospitality and food on earth.

Wasting Away
Beneath a burning sun,
Between starvation,
And the rule of the gun,
All the sorrow, tears and pain,
Isn't worth the price of grain.

Mark Burgess
The Sun and the Moon
1908

Foreword

On the one hand, the loss of the world's remaining rainforest seems to be such a devastatingly simple issue: through a combination of different pressures, 100 acres a minute are destroyed, and about 1.8 per cent of the total rainforest area is lost every year.

On the other hand, behind these very simple statistics, one finds an immensely complex situation, differing not just from country to country, but region to region. Some of the pressures on the rainforest are very similar throughout the world; others are unique to certain specific areas.

There is an understandable but dangerous tendency amongst Western environmentalists to generalize about 'the rainforest', in a way that often angers people from the rainforest countries themselves. There may well be some 'solutions' to rainforest destruction that would prove to be viable in all countries, but for the most part, any solutions will need to be specific to the individual country concerned.

Rainforest Politics is an important book simply because it goes behind the truisms of rainforest destruction to consider the historical, cultural and political contexts in which it is taking place. Five South-East Asian countries (Indonesia, Malaysia, Papua New Guinea, The Philippines and Thailand) are profiled in some detail, with particular attention to traditional forms of cultivation and land use.

Much of the author's analysis is based on personal experience in the different countries. He clearly feels the deepest sense of anger and sadness at the utterly wanton wastage involved in current forestry policy, but has kept his feelings well under control. His case is the stronger for such rigour, and will be of benefit to all those seeking the actual *facts* behind the myths.

But the average reader will be hard pressed *not* to be angered by the picture that emerges. For instance, it is bad enough to know that as much as one-third of the forests in Sarawak (in the eastern half of Malaysia) has been destroyed in just 20 years. It is even worse to discover the extent to which political corruption within Sarawak has contributed to that pattern of destruction.

The power of vested interests, be they unscrupulous politicians or unaccountable multinational companies, provides many such stumbling blocks to the emergence of genuinely sustainable forestry policies in South-East Asia. Both economically and socially, let alone ecologically, it would make so much sense to develop the practice of extractive reserves, concentrating on non-timber products as an alternative to unsustainable timber extraction.

We already know this works: the value of such products to Indonesia already amounts to around $120 million every year. And the expertise is already there amongst the indigenous people of these countries, who know more about the real wealth of the rainforest than generations of foresters and professors will ever be able to absorb.

But the notion of 'harvesting' the rainforests in this way depends on the rainforests still being there, and in their blind pursuit of short-term gain through highly damaging logging, South-East Asian countries are in the process of destroying the natural capital from which such a lucrative form of interest could be drawn from here to the end of time. Some, of course, have already destroyed that capital.

At a time when more and more people are realizing the crucial importance of *genuine* sustainability, there are plenty of hopeful, viable alternatives to current patterns of deforestation. The future of the rainforests and their people depends on the skilful advocacy of these alternatives. *Rainforest Politics* has an important part to play in that process.

Jonathon Porritt
May 1990

Author's Preface

May I urge the readers who normally 'skip' prefaces to read this one as it may help with an understanding of the chapters that follow.

This book includes reports covering five countries, only three of which are technically in South-East Asia: Indonesia, Malaysia and Thailand, while Papua New Guinea and the Philippines are frequently regarded as part of the Pacific region. These two countries are included here, however, because of the geographical and cultural similarities between them and their South-East Asian neighbours. I have attempted to create a general picture of the current situation in each country and to explain how this condition arose. The Forest Futures sections are, as their title suggests, speculation on what may happen in the foreseeable future.

Between November 1985 and May 1987 I visited each of the countries covered except for Papua New Guinea. For this country my research is based on a library search and talking to people from that country. This lack of on-the-spot experience may be apparent from the text, but I have endeavoured to provide an overall analysis of the situation from the information at my disposal.

Within each of the countries visited I initially carried out library research at universities and government departments as well as contacting people known to the Asia–Pacific Peoples Environmental Network (APPEN). I then travelled around each country, visiting the forests and the people who live and work in them.

There are major problems in attempting this type of research in Asia. The political situation in certain countries means that many people are suspicious of a foreigner asking questions. This same problem also leads to many texts remaining anonymous and I have tried to avoid using such texts wherever possible. It is even more difficult to get the real views of the people one meets in the towns or countryside. People are very friendly, but they may in fact try to be too helpful and frequently tell you what they think you want to hear, which is often far from what they may really think about a subject. One can only begin to understand the way people are thinking by spending time with them and gaining their confidence. This can take months or even years, a luxury I could not afford. To overcome this somewhat intractable problem I expended much of my efforts talking to researchers who specialized in particular areas and had spent an appropriate length of time with the people concerned.

My conclusions are therefore based on a cumulative knowledge that is already present in the region, but, as far as I have been able to ascertain, is not widely available outside these countries.

The final chapter attempts to bring together the common factors identified in each country. The presentation of the arguments is my own, but the underlying concepts are those of the people whom I talked with. In the final chapter, therefore, there are no attributed references as many of the points raised orginated from a number of people, as well as, obviously, my own assessment and analyses of the problems.

The original idea for this book emerged out of my time with Sahabat Alam Malaysia, and I extend my thanks for the help and advice all the staff in the organization gave me while in South-East Asia.

This book presents a personal view of deforestation in South-East Asia and any errors are, therefore, the responsibility of the author.

London, 1990

Introduction

World wide, our planet is losing 100 acres of tropical forest every minute. In Latin America an estimated 76,300 square kilometres (sq. km) are lost each year; in Africa approximately 16,000, Asia (not including SE Asia) 17,000 and in South-East Asia 25,000 sq. km. The scale of this destruction has consequences for the entire human race, not only for those living in the tropical regions.

This introduction briefly outlines the consequences of tropical forest destruction on a global scale, why these forests are so important, and who is responsible for their loss. The following chapters give details of the situation in five countries: Indonesia, Malaysia, Papua New Guinea, Philippines and Thailand, which together contain 23% of the world's tropical forest. The final chapter summarizes the situation in the region and suggests ways in which the problems can be tackled. Some of the suggestions may be applied to any developing country, but significant differences between the causes of forest destruction in South-East Asia, in Africa and in Latin America mean that direct comparisons are not valid.

On a global level, tropical forest destruction is not only resulting in the greatest loss of species ever experienced in the planet's history, but also contributing to changes in the world's climate.

Tropical forests are the genetic storehouses of the planet. Some estimates claim that tropical forest destruction is resulting in one species becoming extinct every hour. Even using conservative estimates, approximately 25% of all species known to humankind will be extinct by the turn of the century, not including the thousands yet to be discovered by science. The net result of this loss will be to impoverish our options for developing new drugs for medicine, new crops for food, and new materials that could prove invaluable in the future. There is also a justified concern for the conservation of true wilderness, where nature has a right to flourish, where humankind must adapt its conduct to co-operate with the environment, not dominate it.

Tropical forest produce has been of vital importance to the development of Western industrial culture. In the late 1970s it was estimated that the active ingredient in 40% of prescribed drugs in the United States (US) originated from tropical forest flora. Malaysian forests are believed to support more than 200 potentially important medicinal plants that have yet to be scientifically analysed. The future development of Western medicine is clearly heavily dependent on the tropical forests. Rice and potatoes also originated from tropical forests, as did many fruits such as bananas and pineapple. The development of disease resistant, or more productive, or more adaptable strains, is dependent on the availability of fresh genetic material and, for the few plants mentioned above, and for many more, tropical forests are the sole source of such material. Industrial production is similarly dependent: rubber, tropical timber, and a wide range of oils, resins and waxes, originate from tropical forests, and, too, potential substitutes for a variety of non-renewable resources, such as oil, have already been found in the tropical forests.

The scientific community has taken a random and limited look at perhaps one in ten known tropical forest plants, and a more detailed analysis for the industrial potential of these has been carried out on less than one in one hundred. The potential is clearly vast. The Malaysian and Indonesian forests are frequently cited as having the greatest diversity of species found on earth.

The effects of tropical forest destruction on global weather patterns are less well defined. Many tropical forests are cleared by burning and this undoubtedly contributes to the build-up of carbon in the atmosphere, the 'Greenhouse' effect. The climatic effects at a regional level are, however, better understood. Tropical forests act as a sponge, sheltering fragile tropical soils from the extremes of torrential rain in the wet seasons and searing heat in the dry seasons. In each country covered in this book there is ample evidence that the removal of trees creates flooding followed by drought. In short, to remove trees intensifies the extremes of the tropical climate, initiating a flood/drought cycle which is proving disastrous for agriculture throughout rural Asia. This may eventually result in the creation of deserts, areas where land is incapable of supporting any form of agriculture. Large tracts of Thailand and Indonesia already show symptoms of desertification.

This book, however, is essentially about forest destruction, not trees, and therefore takes an integrated approach in an attempt to explain the present situation and what may be done. Tropical forests are being destroyed through four major processes: shifting agriculture, tropical timber extraction, government sponsored transmigration schemes, and large-scale development projects, such as dams and mining operations. All of these threats exist, to a greter or lesser extent, in each of the countries in South-East Asia.

Poverty underlies all these causes. The destruction of forests is a symptom of the development path chosen by poor nations as they strive, by whatever means, to improve the living standards of their populations. Politics and ecological poverty can no longer be regarded as separate issues.

Government response to deforestation is frequently contradictory and uncoordinated, as land development policy is generally geared to meet demands from export markets rather than the needs of the rural poor. Replanting efforts have also tended to take the same approach, meeting the demands of timber or paper industries rather than the needs of the rural poor directly. The highly publicized Tropical Forest Action Plan promoted by the United Nations, the World Bank and others, broadly follows this path, and has aroused much criticism from Non-Government Organizations (NGOs) working at the grass roots level. In the 1980s, however, NGOs have promoted a new approach, known as social forestry, in which replanting efforts are controlled by the rural poor, ensuring that their basic needs are met. These small-scale projects have proved far more effective than commercial replanting efforts, but they face strong resistance from commercial interests vying for the same land. In these rural economies, the root of many problems is who controls land. Land reform is therefore seen by many NGOs as the only viable solution to relieving poverty and its deleterious effect on the forests.

The following chapters have many similarities between them as the process of what is happening is remarkably similar in each country. There is, however, a different emphasis in each chapter depending on the major causes of the problem.

The aim of this book is to inform the reader of what is happening in the forests, illustrate some possible solutions and hopefully instil an urge to become actively involved in addressing the problem.

Note

Many figures given in the following pages are large and difficult to imagine; therefore, as a guide:

The volume of Wembley Stadium in London, England is approximately one million cubic metres with a capacity for 100,000 people.

One hectare equals 2.47 acres; 100 hectares equals one square kilometre; eight square kilometres equals three square miles.

1. Indonesia

Introduction

Indonesia is a collection of more than 13,000 islands straddling the equator between Asia and Australia. The total land area of 1,475,000 sq. km stretches 5,100 km from North Sumatra to Eastern Irian Jaya and is the home of one-fifth of the world's population. Within this vast area is a wide variety of ecosystems and cultures.

The population distribution is by no means even: the island of Java, although accounting for only 7% of the land area, is inhabited by more than 60% of Indonesia's population of 165m[1] – a population growing at 2.3% per year and estimated to exceed 230m in the 1990s.[2]

Most people continue to live off the land, but the agricultural sector accounts for less than 30% of the Gross National Product (GNP).[3] Oil and natural gas are the major earners of the foreign capital needed to service a national debt estimated at US$16,600m.[4] On the outer islands the huge mineral reserves have been exploited only since the 1970s. Timber products are the second most valuable export after oil. Much of Indonesia's development has, however, been dogged by almost institutionalized corruption. It is probably the only country in the world where the nationalized oil industry went bankrupt in the mid-1970s after the oil price boom.[5]

Most Indonesians are Muslim, although outside Java there are significant religious minorities including: Christians on Sumatra and Sulawesi, an ancient Hindu culture on Bali, and a wide variety of animist societies on outer islands. This diversity has inhibited the development process in more remote areas as Muslim Java is often regarded as unrepresentative of the nation as a whole.

Java is the site of one of the earliest human settlements and historically the major populations of Indonesia have been located on its fertile volcanic lowlands. Much of the lowland has for centuries been cleared of forest but major agricultural expansion into the hills and other islands is a new phenomenon.

The Portuguese, in their search for spices during the 16th century, were the first colonial power to show an interest in the islands. Full colonial control, however, was not established until the mid-18th century, when the Dutch claimed Java and Bali. Despite vigorous resistance the Dutch gained control over the most fertile lands and forced local farmers off their lands to make way for Dutch cash crops, thus initiating the first major agricultural expansion into the hills.[6] Throughout the 18th and early 19th centuries the Dutch imported slaves from Sulawesi to work on the Java coffee, sugar, tobacco and tea estates.[7] The Indonesian author, Pramoedya Ananta Toer, describes, in a novel set in the beginning of the 20th century, how the Dutch maintained political control over dissident farmers who 'courted disaster; the factory also controlled the Civil Service right down to the village officials.'[8]

In 1905, considering that Java was becoming dangerously overcrowded, the Dutch initiated the first transmigration programme to move people off the island. They were keenly aware of the build-up of resistance in the population and regarded transmigration primarily as a means of relieving political pressure on Java itself. Once on alien land they thought the Javanese would be less likely to cause trouble.[9] The Dutch moved more than 200,000 people in this way before leaving Indonesia during World War Two.[10]

The Japanese briefly took control of the archipelago but the Dutch returned after the war and vainly attempted to regain their former position. In 1949, after a long and fierce campaign, the Indonesians finally gained independence.

For the first decade of independence the country was in a state of constant turmoil. The chaos rapidly declined after the military coup of 1957 brought President Sukarno to power. Today the military is still very much in command under the leadership of President Suharto and his 'New Order' government. Compared to the early days of independence, Indonesia is relatively stable and has shown strong economic growth.

Before the 1960s major clearance of forest was restricted to Java. The change since then is illustrated by the development of the timber industry. In 1961 Java accounted for 89% of timber production with 10% of the total being exported; by 1971, 65% came from Kalimantan and 75% of the total was exported.[11]

Towards the end of the 19th century teak was in great demand and the Dutch established their first plantation in 1897. A formal management system was established based on the Burmese *taungya* system, known locally as '*tumpangsari*'; this involved intercropping teak seedlings with food or cash crops. In total, 82,000 ha of teak plantations were established before the Dutch left.[12] Javanese teak plantations dominated the Indonesian timber industry until well into the 1960s.

Ten percent of the world's tropical rainforests are in Indonesia, described by Robert Goodland of the World Bank as 'one of the biologically most significant areas of the world'.[13] Scientists still classify this huge area of forest into three major ecosystem types: tropical moist forest, monsoon forest and small areas of tropical dry forest.

The figures on how much forest is left vary tremendously. In 1983 the government estimated that there were 147m ha of forest, but most independent experts claim it was nearer 94m.[14] The government admits, however, that of the total, 30m ha are in some stage of conversion into another land use.[15] Indonesia does not apply the United Nations 10% minimum tree cover to identify forested land; officially, forests simply refer to areas that, in the opinion of the forest department, should have trees on them. If the UN standard were applied, 1978 estimates range from 120m ha to 80m ha.[16] More recently the government estimated forest cover to be around 113m ha.[17]

The last ground level survey was undertaken in 1950 and a current analysis is unlikely to be available until the early 1990s. There is, however, more general agreement on past rates of forest destruction. Between 1950 and 1981 approximately 49m ha of forest were cleared across the archipelago; well over one million hectares per annum.[18] The FAO estimated that between 1976 and 1980, 550,000 ha were cleared annually.[19] In contrast, current estimates, including the conversion of primary forest to other uses, range from 600,000 to 1,500,000 ha per annum.[20] At present the island of Kalimantan is suffering the greatest forest loss.

Mangrove forests warrant a special mention. In 1982 official sources estimated the country had 4.2m ha, although this figure is widely disputed.[21] By 1985 this had been reduced to around one million hectares, most of which has been designated as logging concessions or is due for conversion into fishponds.[22] In the typically chaotic fashion of forest statistics 500,000 ha are officially protected.[23] The figures do not add up.

Legislation exists that requires most timber concessions to replace trees they fell, but replanting is minimal and concentrated almost exclusively on Java. At present Java has approximately 1.4m ha of plantations, of which 875,000 are under hardwoods such as teak, the remainder under softwoods.[24] Despite being established for many years, teak now plays only a minor role in timber exports. The modern trend in the few concessions that do replant is to establish fast-growing softwoods such as eucalyptus and pine. Of the country's more than 4,000 tree species only four account for more than 75% of exports.[25]

Government sponsored and spontaneous transmigration to the outer islands, logging, mining, general agricultural expansion and population growth on Java all contribute to forest loss. In addition, there are numerous secondary factors forcing Indonesia into its present situation, for example, international debts, trade tariffs and the self-interests of multinational corporations.

The effects of forest loss

Environmental consequences

The tremendous variations between the ecology and soils of Java and those of the outer islands exacerbate the country's deforestation problems. The imposition of an inappropriate farming system on the outer islands, a logging industry out of control and highly corrupt, and a callous disregard for the wishes of indigenous tribal groups, all contribute to the present environmental and social degradation. Even the fertile soils of Java are not immune to these problems.

Indonesia has more than 8.6m ha of 'critical land', areas the government describes as: 'Land which is generally unable to fulfil any of the normal soil functions, including water absorption or the production of even a meagre subsistence crop'.[26] A further 12m ha is classified as having 'serious erosion' problems. These areas' problems are the direct result of forest destruction.[27]

Java's one million hectares of critical land are spreading at a rate of 200,000 each year.[28] The island was already losing 770m tons of topsoil annually by the late 1970s.[29] Even the government admits that soil erosion in Java's upper river catchments is so serious that crop yields are falling by up to 5% per annum.[30]

Conditions outside Java are even more precarious. Sumatra has more than two million hectares of critical land.[31] A main feature of such land is the dominance of *alang-alang* (*Imperata*) grass. This tough, tall grass, useless for fodder and extremely difficult to eradicate, now covers more than 20m ha of Indonesia, mostly on the outer islands which, since their soils are old and thin, are more susceptible to the problem.[32] Less than 2% of Kalimantan, for example, is suitable for permanent agriculture.[33] Duncan Poore of the International Union for the Conservation of Nature (IUCN), commenting on the transmigration programme to the outer islands, estimates that: 'The resettlement of over half of the 250,000 families moved from Java has been a failure due to poor soils, flood, or soil damage caused by mechanical land clearance.' As a result, 'yields of rice and other annual crops become lower and lower, planned agricultural incomes were never attained.'[34]

Soil loss also results in siltation of major rivers, ports and dams. Java's second largest port at Surabaya is threatened with excessive siltation[35] and, on the Barito river, port authorities claim silt is being deposited faster than they can dredge it out.[36] The projected lifespan of the Solorajo dam in East Java has now been reduced from 100 to 33 years, due to excessive siltation in its reservoir.[37]

Flash flooding is another characteristic of critical lands. Since the late 1970s the Barito river has become increasingly prone to flooding, with waters rising by up to 15 metres, regularly leaving tens of thousands homeless and destroying thousands of hectares of crops.[38] Similar problems are occurring on Sumatra and in Sulawesi where, in recent years, the

Banggai river floods have already claimed four lives and destroyed thousands of homes.[39] The siltation in the port of Surabaya has also intensified the flooding problems. In late 1984 flooding swept away 137 villages leaving 39,000 people homeless. Indonesia has 69 watersheds in this condition.[40]

There is little doubt that local changes in climate have occurred where forest cover has been removed. The net result has been to intensify the extremes, as one study found measuring monthly temperature ranges in an area before and after selective logging. The original temperature range (before logging) in the forest was between 23°C and 26°C. After logging, temperatures of 40°C were recorded regularly.[41]

In 1982 and 1983 Kalimantan experienced the worst droughts for a century. Drought is not new to this region, but the intensity of this one was extreme. Scientists are now linking it with a change in the Pacific air current known as the El Nino Southern Oscillation Event. A team from the University of Hamburg think forest destruction may play a central role because it affects the turbidity of the South China Sea, which in turn may affect the intensity of El Nino.[42] This drought proved disastrous for farmers in East Kalimantan, as 80% of rainfed fields and 30% of wet rice paddies yielded no crops.[43] Massive forest fires also destroyed millions of hectares of forest.

The most detailed study on the cause and effects of the Kalimantan fire carried out by the German Agency for Technical Co-operation states:

> The considerable decrease of foliage and related changes in the stand structure, increase of albedo, horizontal and vertical air movements, may produce significant and lasting effects on the regional climate.[44]

Indonesia's geographical location and structure creates a mosaic of natural habitats. As one report put it, this 'created the world's richest assemblage of species, many of which still remain unknown to science'.[45] The result is that a large proportion of Indonesia's fauna and flora is endemic. Of the 1,480 bird species found (16% of the world's total) 370 are endemic.[46] One hundred of the 500 mammal species identified are unique to the archipelago.[47] The Worldwide Fund for Nature (WFN – previously the World Wildlife Fund) classifies 30 species as threatened or endangered, including tiger, cloud leopard, orang-utan and the Sumatra and Javanese rhinos; only 61 Java rhinos survive.[48]

The variety of plants is equally vast, with more than 4,000 tree species already identified.[49] Dr Kartawinata of the National Biological Institute claims that no more than 50% of Indonesia's flora is known to science.[50] On one 1.6 ha plot in Kalimantan, he and his colleagues found 203 plant species, of which 40 were trees that provided edible fruit or some useful material other than timber.[51]

The potential value of these plants to science is immense, as a recent WFN report from the Gunung Leuser National Park in North Sumatra revealed. In ten weeks of studies, Drs Elliot and Brimacombe, staying with the Gayo tribe, recorded the use of more than 200 medicinal remedies from 171 plants.[52] The area inhabited by the Gayo is under threat from logging interests, despite being located in a national park.

With such a diversity of species there are few individual representatives of each plant or animal in any one area. As a result the loss of species is proportional to the loss of individuals.[53] Indonesia undoubtedly warrants special attention for the preservation of the world's genetic resources.

Economic and social costs

As deforestation progresses, social and economic conditions in Indonesia's forests have deteriorated significantly. One of the most contentious issues has been land rights for indigenous tribal groups. Present policies on forest development have not improved people's lifestyle on the outer islands. The net effects of the timber industry and the government's transmigration programme have proved disastrous for many indigenous and migrant groups.

Commenting on the timber industry, the President of Survival International, Robin Hanbury-Tenison, claims that, 'far from bringing benefits to the people, the eventual effect of the lumber business has been to lower the standard of living and remove their ability to be self-supporting.'[54]

The Indonesian timber industry in its present form does not provide significant employment in rural areas. A recent government report noted that: 'In 1982 the logging industry employed only 70,000 people; it is probably one of the least labour intensive of all the major productive sectors in Indonesia.'[55] This figure accounts for approximately 0.2% of Indonesia's total labour force. Between 1972 and 1985 employment in the timber industry grew by a mere 1.72% despite a massive growth in output.[56] The few who do get work in the Indonesian timber industry are frequently migrants from the Philippines or Malaysia.

These figures hide the true loss of employment as large-scale interests force smaller operators out of the forests. In the 1970s the southern provincial government in Kalimantan took over the rights for exploiting the ironwood trees, denying a cash income to an estimated 10,000 tribesmen.[57] In central Sulawesi, a similar number of indigenous people lost their livelihood when a Japanese logging company refused them access to the trees they traditionally tapped for resin.[58] In the early 1980s 11,000 workers involved in small-scale teak production on the island of Muma lost their jobs when the provincial government took over exploitation rights.[59] These three examples account for almost 50% of the total employment provided by large timber companies during the early 1980s.

Forest destruction further hampers sustainable development in that it undermines Indonesia's considerable industry in minor forest products – a term that applies to any forest product other than timber. The classification as 'minor' is a misnomer as Indonesia's exports of these products in 1987 alone was worth more than US$238m.[60] As tables 2.1 and 2.2 show, these products range from rattans (the cane used in furniture) to resins. In the early 1980s Indonesia produced approximately 90% of the world's rattan traded.[61] The trade was deemed sufficiently important for the government to place an immediate ban on raw rattan exports in late 1986 in an attempt to gain more revenue through processing.[62] Despite the export value of these products local minor forest produce collectors are continually ousted in favour of timber production.

Most significantly for the Indonesian economy the value of trade in minor forest produce increased by 198% between 1977 and 1981.[63] Despite an expanding world demand for these products the government is unwilling to consider allocating specific areas for the exploitation of minor products rather than for timber. The two forest industries are at present totally incompatible: timber extraction causes irreparable damage to the forests so that few minor forest products can survive in the new environment. By contrast, the collection of minor forest produce generally has a minimal effect on the forest environment, requires little capital investment and is labour intensive. It meets the needs of Indonesia's rural population far better than the timber industry.

Loss of cash income has obvious social consequences but the effect on forest-based tribal societies can be even more dramatic. Officially classified as '*suku suki* terracing', (isolated and alien) tribal groups are subject to a government policy of integration into mainstream Indonesian society. Most tribal people regard this as the imposition of Javanese Islamic culture.[64] The Department of Social Affairs, which co-ordinates tribal development policy, notes that:

> The problem is no longer one for the isolated groups themselves to tackle, or for the Department of Social Affairs alone, but a social one at the government and national levels. . . . It is called a national problem because it involves national and humanitarian prestige. The fact that there are still isolated and remote peoples, developing at too slow a pace, can affect the prestige and dignity of men in that country. Therefore the problem must be tackled.[65]

The 'problem' is tackled by refusal to recognize traditional land rights and declaring their traditional shifting farming methods (swidden farming) as illegal and damaging to the environment. The Dayak longhouse communities in Kalimantan are seen as a particular problem. A longhouse is a single large dwelling, comprising rows of rooms, each family having one room facing on to a common veranda; the whole structure is supported on stilts.

The veranda accommodates intimate social interaction and debate and undoubtedly helps maintain social cohesion. In the more remote region the authorities regard these buildings as a security threat and force communities to abandon them for government villages with single family dwellings.[66]

Tribal society is further undermined when all forms of shifting cultivation are held responsible for forest destruction, and Javanese wet rice paddy is promoted as the most advanced farming method in Indonesia. This policy is mainly implemented through the transmigration programme whereby landless farmers from Java are given land on the outer islands. The forest is usually cleared to make way for wet rice paddy even if the area is unsuitable for such permanent agriculture or already supports a significant tribal population. Local indigenous groups are rarely included in transmigration projects and there are frequent cases of violent clashes between settlers and tribal groups. In Irian Jaya, for example, there is an increasing security problem involving the Free Papua Movement (OPM). An estimated 10,000 refugees fled to Papua New Guinea in 1984 as troubles flared up in the North-East of the province over land rights and natural resource issues.[67]

Individual logging companies have also come under attack. In South Kalimantan during the early 1980s the Indo-Philippine company Yayanbg Aya decided to temporarily dam the upper reaches of the Tabalong river and release the waters to help the logs flow downstream faster. The subsequent wave killed two people and washed away numerous homes. Three years later the same company attempted to evict all Dayak longhouse communities from the concession, but the police were not enthusiastic as most of them were Dayaks themselves; the company was forced to withdraw.[68] Environmental and human rights groups active in Indonesia claim there are many unrecorded cases in which the companies have been successful in such actions.

In Irian Jaya the government has designated huge areas for logging and mining, many of which have been attacked. One of the best recorded examples involved the Freeport Incorporated Mining Consortium. Their 10,000 ha concession encompasses the traditional land claims of the Amungme people who received minimal compensation for the loss of their land. A series of small attacks culminated in blowing-up a pipeline that transported the gold, silver and copper slurry down to the coast.[69] Government troops retaliated with indiscriminate attacks on the Amungme, forcing entire villages down to the coast, where, according to Marcos Colchester of Survival International: 'they have suffered starvation, epidemics and cultural collapse.'[70]

'Cultural collapse' denotes a dislocated population, loss of all sense of identity, and the emergence of frontier towns with severe alcohol, drug and prostitution problems. Even small towns of less than 50,000 can have several hundred full-time prostitutes.[71]

New words have evolved to describe some of the new social phenomena in the outer islands. *Kawin Kontrak* is a marriage that lasts as long as the loggers or miners are contracted with the local company; when this ends, so does the marriage. *Bayi Asean* is a baby born out of such a contract marriage. Many workers come from other countries and it is almost impossible for local mothers to contact their 'husbands' once they have left.

In a report from East Kalimantan, SKEPHI (Indonesia's leading independent environmental group) concluded: 'Complaints of elders, parents and teachers are the cry of a people who are at a wits' end in facing the destruction of their culture and community.'[72]

Development of present forestry policy

The national Constitution of 1945 continues to form the philosophical base for Indonesia's development aims. Known as the Pancasila, Article 33 notes that: 'Land and water and the natural riches therein shall be controlled by the State and shall be made use of for the greatest welfare of the people.'[73]

The philosophy underlying the Constitution is based on consensus rather than majority rule. The International Institute for Environment and Development (IIED) describes it as a:

System of compromise and joint agreement [which] is significantly different from a strictly democratic process ... Consequently, in Indonesia, 'Dynamic protection', i.e. policing actions to prevent illegal activities, is not the preferred method of protecting natural resources. If it is deemed necessary to take certain action such as protecting forests, then a management system which deters or deflects destructive elements, is much the preferred path.[74]

In this way social justice is seen as central to forest conservation and development. Despite much rhetoric, the goal of social justice seems as far away today as it was 30 years ago. The IIED accepts this analysis by claiming that until 'socio-economic conditions are improved with some measure of equity, there will continue to be certain elements in society which will not heed the message of forest protection.'[75]

Current government policies are outlined in five-year plans known as Repelitas. The Repelitas have undoubtedly been a success in improving the country's GNP but there has been no major shift in the distribution of wealth and control over natural resources. Thus the middle and upper income groups gain more from forest exploitation than have the rural poor.

In the late 1960s Indonesia faced a major economic crisis with 85% inflation and a rapidly increasing foreign debt. As a result development policy during Repelita I (1969–74) centred on improving agriculture and expanding agribusiness. Processing in all land-based sectors was encouraged and timber concession holders were required to carry out some form of value enhancement to their product. Timber resources on Sumatra were running low and Kalimantan was identified as the main area for expansion. By 1974 approximately 11m ha of Kalimantan had been designated as logging concessions. Indonesia's foreign earnings from timber rose 2,800% between 1969 and 1974.

Following the relative success of Repelita I, a reorganization of industrial production and consumption was envisaged during Repelita 2 (1975–79). The role played by plantation crops in earning foreign capital was reduced and timber was promoted as the major export earner (after oil). The plan displayed much rhetoric on how the forests could be exploited in perpetuity, if managed properly, but it provided no regulations on how this was to be achieved. In keeping with the Constitution there were no laws forcing companies to replant or manage their forests.

The overriding goal of Repelita 3 (1980–84) was self-sufficiency in basic food needs. Oil and natural gas revenues were ploughed back into agriculture. Only now did the government make any attempts to regulate the timber trade through a ban on log exports in 1980. Regulations on timber extraction and forest management, however, continued to be voluntary.

Self-sufficiency in basic foods continued to be a major policy in Repelita 4 (1985–89) in which industrial expansion was linked to promoting greater processing of timber products. Expansion of the minor forest products sector was envisaged along with the development of social forestry programmes. Repelita 4 notes that: 'Exploitation of . . . natural resources should not destroy environmental living conditions, and should be executed by an overall policy which takes into account the needs of future generations.'

The effectiveness of these policies, however, continues to rest on two major land-use laws: the Basic Agrarian Law of 1960 and the Basic Forestry Law 1967.

Forest legislation

The Basic Agrarian Law (1960) concentrates on land-use rights and notes that all forested land and natural resources are ultimately owned by the state as: 'an Authoritative Organisation of the Whole People'. Other sections involving forestry include:

'In order not to harm the public interest, excessive ownership and control of land are not permitted.'
There is no definition of the word 'excessive' in this clause.

'The right of [timber] exploitation is granted for a period of no longer than 25 years.'

Concessions may be annulled for a number of reasons including neglect, abandonment and even 'the destruction of the land.'

'The right of opening up land and collecting forest products may only be possessed by Indonesian citizens.'
As most tribal people are classified as 'isolated and alien' their status as citizens is not always clear.

'As long as the . . . right of ownership . . . has not yet been established the provisions of the local Adat [customary] law . . . apply, as long as they are not in conflict with the spirit and the provisions of this law.'
Traditional land claims are therefore recognized, but only if they do not conflict with the interests of the government.

The first official recognition of forests as an integrated resource was represented by the Basic Forestry Law (1967), which classified all forests into production, protection, wildlife and other reserves. Production forest is sub-divided into the permanent forest estate, that is, land that should remain as forest but be open for timber exploitation; and conversion forest, meaning land that has potential for agriculture.

Protection forest should remain untouched in order to provide general environmental services, such as soil retention and flood alleviation. These areas are found mainly on steep slopes and in critical watersheds. Wildlife and other reserves are protected for their genetic resources or to save a particularly rare species.

This Law describes its overall goal as: 'obtaining the highest possible benefits . . . on a sustained yield basis . . . to develop a prosperous and just Indonesian society.' Thus forest management accepted the social nature of the resource.

This Law strengthened previous legislation on Indonesian control of timber rights in an attempt to keep timber profits within Indonesia. Concession holders must produce annual and five-year plans as well as an overall strategy covering the period of the concession. They must also make some attempt to establish a processing plant, such as a saw- or plywood-mill. Provisions for replanting, sustainable yield and for greater research by individual concession holders are also included. Failure to comply with any of the above could result in confiscation of equipment and harvested forest produce, fines and/or imprisonment.

As a general policy statement it is fairly comprehensive but it lacks detail. This is reflected in the 217 amendments the government had applied by 1984. Even now, the Law makes no mention of environmental impact assessments for projects in forest areas, public participation in replanting schemes or the influence of the transmigration programme.

Despite classifying forested areas the system is applied only by the

Forestry Department. Other government departments frequently override these classifications for their own ends. This frequently results in dual purpose sites and also creates great confusion over natural resources data. Such inconsistencies and contradictions within the establishment have not helped create respect for the Basic Forestry Law. The result is that the Forestry Department is mainly concerned with timber production and has little influence over more general forest development. For example, government policy on shifting agriculture in forest areas is implemented through three departments: Agriculture, Social Affairs, and Interior; control of National Parks falls to the Department of the Environment.

Government policy on shifting agriculture
The government regards shifting agriculture as a problem it attempts to counteract through its Population Resettlement, Development of Isolated Communities, and Village Resettlement programmes. These have proved highly controversial; opponents claim they violate basic human rights and actively force Javanese cultural values upon other societies. Underlying these programmes is a more general government policy of creating: 'one Indonesian nation and people.'

The Population Resettlement Programme, under the control of the Department of Agriculture, aims to prevent damage to commercial forest resources, protect forests in general and develop forest areas. All forms of shifting agriculture are regarded as a threat to these aims, and many tribal groups are forced into settled farm sites. The authorities claim this is in order to help provide better welfare and services. A report for UNESCO on this Programme, however, notes:

> Evaluation of this project revealed that participation in religious activities is the most successful. Education is almost a complete failure. What is more disappointing is that most of the settlers practise their previous farming system which is shifting agriculture . . . This failure is probably due to the fact that social activities take priority over running their farms [and] supporting systems have not been developed.[76]

The Development of Isolated Communities Programme is run under the Department of Social Affairs with the goal of 'improving' the 'social function' of tribal groups. This is a social integration programme that promotes settled agriculture and discourages longhouse communities. The Village Resettlement Programme under the Department of the Interior, is also involved in gathering together scattered groups, especially in remote or unstable areas. Under the guise of promoting general development opportunities by providing infrastructure, schools, and so on, it is frequently regarded as a means of political repression. Development programmes for remote communities are wanted by many tribal groups but it is the manner in which they are carried out that angers them.

Collectively, these schemes have been compared to the military repression of tribal groups in the Philippines under the Marcos dictatorship. These projects are generally unpopular with the people they are designed to help.

Conservation areas and national parks

Indonesia has an impressive number of forest reservations and national parks that in 1985 covered almost 18m ha.[77] The government has even proposed that 40% of Irian Jaya be designated as protected forest.[78] These statistics look impressive but the reality does not bear close scrutiny. The most worrying aspect of the present system is that central government frequently permits major land use changes in these protected areas. Logging in national parks is common, with little or no monitoring of its effects. Examples of government-sanctioned forest destruction within conservation areas can be found on all the major islands.

Sumatra: The Sikundur Nature Reserve lost 10,000 ha to logging concessions in 1977.[79] In the Padang–Sugihan Reserve, a survey of logs at the local sawmill found 96% smaller than the regulation minimum diameter. Logging in this reserve is supposed to be severely restricted and sustainable.[80]

Kalimantan: The 303,750 ha East Kutai reserve is one of only two lowland rain forest reserves in Kalimantan. In 1968 more than 100,000 ha were leased out to logging and mining interests. In the mid-1970s a further 60,750 ha were given over to logging.[81] Professor Tim Whitmore of the Oxford Forestry Institute in England described this reserve as containing one of the most 'biologically important' forests in the Asean region.[82]

Irian Jaya: The government has stopped logging and suspended the introduction of transmigration sites in many protected areas, but such activities are frequently located just beyond a park's boundaries. The Kumbe–Merauke reserve has 108,000 ha set aside for settlement schemes around its borders.[83] Many settlement sites have been abandoned due to poor soils, and settlers move on to cut down adjacent forest for more farm land. Illegal logging and wildlife hunting also tend to develop near new settlements. Similar problems face the Wasuar Wildlife Reserve near Merauke, the Arfak Mountain Nature Reserve near Oransbari and the Cyclops Mountain Nature Reserve near Jayapura. The Danau–Bian Reserve, an important wetland site near Merauke, is threatened by drainage schemes just outside its boundaries.[84]

Despite this lack of commitment to fully protect forest areas, the government has more recently initiated a number of social forestry projects. Social Forestry is based on the concept of combining the needs of the local population with forest conservation or the establishment of forest areas. Most originate from a Burmese model known as the *taungya* system, in which agriculture and forestry are combined.

The Burmese *taungya* forestry system was developed during the early part of the 20th century but was not widely used until the 1950s. Almost all modern agro-forestry systems promoted in South-East Asia are based on this system. It operates as follows.

Teak seedlings are grown alongside normal food crops. As the trees develop the food crops are changed to fit the conditions created by the young trees. The local population care for both the crops and the young teak trees, thus ensuring almost individual attention for the trees. This intercropping continues for 40 years, when the trees are sufficiently mature to be harvested; local farmers then move to another site and start the process again. Only when the trees are mature are areas under this system classified as 'Forest Estate' and open for felling. The forest is then left to grow unmanaged until the loggers move in.

The *taungya* system is successful because it makes full use of the local population who have an interest in establishing and maintaining the forest. By 1980 Burma had more than 100,000 ha managed under this system. Although developed as an intensive means of producing teak the principles of intercropping can be applied to a wide variety of trees, not only those good for timber.

In Indonesia, most social forestry programmes are integrated with other projects that provide clean water, schools, medical help, and developing infrastructure and small-scale industries. The state-owned Perum Perhutari Corporation co-ordinates these projects, which are initiated as a 'two-way' process in which it is made clear that the villagers can enter the forest to make use of its resources, and the corporation is entitled to enter the village and encourage people to plant trees.

Fast-growing trees are planted between the village and the forest, creating fuel-wood groves, which act as a buffer zone around the forests. Within the state-owned forest, cash crops are planted between young teak trees and villagers are given full rights to anything they produce. There is an emphasis on yield improvement through the use of pesticides and fertilizers. The corporation claims that the costs of such inputs are offset by the value of produce and they contribute to faster growth of the teak trees. Bee-keeping and sericulture (farming silk worms) are promoted as alternative cash crops that do not compete with subsistence crops for ground space. The corporation buys the produce and employs about 250,000 labourers and 13,000 officials.

There is also a programme in which social forestry is concentrated near or even within national parks. Twenty-four projects are envisaged, of which the most advanced is on the Mount Cyclops reserve in Irian Jaya;[85] this 31,000 ha reserve has suffered encroachment from loggers, migrant farmers and land speculators. The project aims to stabilize this situation and develop a sustainable land-use pattern. Local government officials, academics, NGOs and the Forestry Department were all involved with the project's initiation;

sponsorship came from the WWF, the Ford Foundation and the Department of Forestry. By using aerial photographs and maps, the project workers and villages involved managed to assess present land claims and use. Two land-use zones were established, one accommodating intensive agriculture, the other with a less demanding system. The low intensity area permits the local population to use forest resources and cut trees for domestic needs. Complete clearance for agriculture, however, is restricted to the intensive use zone.

There are plans to develop tourism to the park and thus produce another source of income. The local tribe involved are the Ormu and they now enjoy the most secure land rights of almost any tribal group in Indonesia. The current land-use agreements will run for 25 years if the three other tribal groups approached also take up the programme.

The project workers claimed that using aerial photographs was a crucial factor in arousing the interest of the local populations. This need not be expensive and is a useful technique that other land-use projects might employ. Another innovation was to define certain forest boundaries with a brightly coloured local shrub traditionally used for this purpose. This makes a clearly definable marker that, once established, would be difficult to move and costs very little.

The social forestry projects are generally perceived as successful, both by those involved and the authorities, but in terms of addressing Indonesia's forest problems they must be expanded.

Present causes of forest destruction

The transmigration programmes, the timber industry and, to a lesser extent, shifting cultivation are the dominant factors in Indonesia's forest loss.

The timber industry

Timber has played a significant role in Indonesia's economic development and, as was noted in the introduction, continues to be the country's second most valuable export after oil.[86] In 1987 Indonesia exported more than US$1.7 billion worth of plywood.[87] Timber exports as a whole, however, have been declining since the ban on logs in 1980, when revenues exceeded two billion US dollars.[88]

During the boom of the 1970s the industry was characterized by large multinational corporations linking with local firms to export logs. Today the emphasis is on plywood, with foreign joint ventures accounting for only 16% of production.[89]

In 1985 the Forest Department classified 64m ha as production forest, of which 53.4m ha was designated under timber concessions. Only 521 companies hold these concession rights, creating an intense concentration of political control over more than 25% of Indonesia's land area.[90] The World Bank estimate that: 'At the current annual level of earning from commercial production, Indonesia's forests will be exhausted in about 40 years. The factors causing this trend include careless logging practices.'[91]

Building the boom: In Repelita I the government's aim to induce foreign investment resulted in the Domestic and Foreign Capital Investment Laws (1967). Entering the world timber trade for the first time Indonesia had to woo foreign expertise and investment if their timber was to be competitive on the world markets. As the IIED note, however, this brought in individuals and companies looking for 'the quickest possible return on their investment'.[92] Japan became a major investor, expanding from nine companies active in the country in 1968 to more than 200 a decade later.[93]

Weyerhauser, and Georgia Pacific came from the United States, Mitsui, Itoh, Sumitomo and Mitsubushi from Japan. Mitsubushi held controlling shares in 11 Indonesian companies, two with large concessions on East Kalimantan. By 1980 Mitsui and Co. had interests in at least 28 Indonesian companies involved in a huge range of products including agricultural estates, insecticides, automobiles, shipping companies and timber. To maintain control over timber investments many retired military and government personnel became involved with logging companies. There is little doubt that political favours were involved in the allocation of many timber concessions.

The decline in timber export earnings during the 1980s was in part due to the government's change of policy, banning log exports in favour of plywood. It was hoped that more revenue would accrue by exporting a processed product. The present Forestry Minister summed up current policy on timber resources as 'based on the principle of sustained yield and domestic conversion. The objective is to maintain the supply of raw materials for [the] forestry industry as well as to enhance the value of forest products through local processing.'[94]

Timber extraction and management

The Indonesian government regulates timber extraction by demanding that any logging in areas that should remain forest must adhere to the TPI (Tebang Polih Indonesia) selective felling system. The regulations are a guideline, and companies must also conform to the laws outlined earlier. Only trees over 50 cm at breast height can be cut. At least 25 trees of 25–49 cm at breast height must be left intact on each hectare logged. If less than 25 trees are left, enrichment planting should take place, otherwise natural regeneration was relied upon. The cutting cycle was stipulated as 35 years, by which time the forest should, in theory, have fully recovered. This system, even if applied, which it was not, has some basic weaknesses, as an IIED report noted:

There now appears good reason to believe that many of the assumptions which form the basis of this system may be incorrect, e.g. many trees do not continue to grow or become stimulated to enhanced growth as a result of opening of the forest canopy through harvesting. In addition, scientists do not understand fully the role and effectiveness of 'mother' trees and the need to conserve untouched areas of forest within the production forest. It also assumes that the forest physiology and response to disturbance is similar throughout the forests of Indonesia, whereas, in fact, there are many different forest types.[95]

Dr Kartawinata, head of the National Biological Institute, goes further and argues that in tropical moist forest, 'no sound ecological basis for any selection system has yet been established.'[96]

Despite the regulations, the government applied the system in the spirit of the Pancasila principles, and concession holders were rarely checked to see if they conformed to the regulations. When it became clear that they were not conforming the authorities established a levy of US$4 for every cubic metre of timber extracted, returnable if they stayed within the system. They hoped this would attract reinvestment in the industry.

It is now clear that most foreign companies regarded the levy as a direct cost rather than an incentive for reinvestment. The result of this relaxed approach by the government is that approximately 23m ha of Indonesian forests have been seriously damaged through timber extraction.[97] Indonesia's largest environmental group, SKEPHI, estimate the area of seriously degraded forest to be nearer 43m ha if transmigration sites are included.[98]

The TPI at ground level: There is ample evidence that the system was blatantly abused. In the early 1980s two scientists for the Weyerhauser corporation studied nine concessions in East Kalimantan and noted that, 'none was leaving the required 25 select crop trees per hectare and indeed, on much of the area there were not sufficient trees at the start to comply with the regulations.'[99]

Of Indonesia's 4,000 tree species just four, Meranti, Ramin, Keruing and Agathis, account for 75% of exports by volume.[100] Pressure on these species is considerable and if a dense stand is found there is a great temptation to over-cut. In Sumatra a recent spot survey by WWF on the Padang–Sulihan reserve found that 96% of logs measured outside local timber mills were smaller than the legal minimum.[101] The Forest Research Institute in Java recently reported that on logging sites for Meranti in Sumatra up to 70% of the non-target trees were damaged during extraction.[102] They also noted that 52% of those trees damaged were commercial species, that is, the next crop.

Logging in East Kalimantan is even more intense, with up to 20 trees being extracted per hectare.[103] SKEPHI report that in this state, where bulldozers are used, 50% of the forest is totally destroyed during selective timber extraction.[104] One site they studied had 70% of the forest canopy open 15 years after extraction.

Even logs felled are wasted. The same SKEPHI report estimates that 50% of the logs felled never reached the sawmill.[105] The Forestry Research Institute (FRI) estimate that more than 30% of Meranti logs felled in Sumatra have 'serious damage' such as cracking or other defects. Despite this, 80% of these damaged logs are dragged to the depots where they were left to rot.[106] They estimate 5.6m cubic metres of timber were wasted in this fashion each year throughout the 1970s.[107]

The damage and waste caused by careless logging has a permanent effect on many areas, as Dr Kartawinata recorded on one logging site in East Kalimantan: 'Even in the selectively logged forests, 40 years after logging, the flora still includes a large number of secondary forest species'.[108] He also noted that the commercially valuable dipterocarp species regenerate very poorly. In table 2.3 his results are outlined in more detail.

George Adittondro of the Pedanan Development Project Information Centre in Jayapura, Irian Jaya, in an article for the Tokyo-based magazine *Kogui*,[109] wrote an excellent description of logging on the outer islands. Following is an extract from that article.

Based on observations in Kalimantan, you can easily say that the very initial steps for preparing the logging operation already destroy a substantial part of the forest. This is because most companies in Kalimantan, or you can safely speak of the whole of the country since the Minister for Environmental Control discovered the same practice widespread in Sumatra, prefer the yarding technique. By locating the highest point on the banks of a valley the loggers can easily cut all the mature commercial trees around it and then pull up the logs to the highest hill by means of a steel cable network.

They first have to locate the valley with the most valuable trees and the hill to serve as the log terminal. This cruising operation is done by tractors just pushing their way through the dense forests. After the cruising team has located the right hill close to the right valley, the road building team start to build semi-permanent logging roads according to the landscape but sometimes not hesitating to explode a hill or a mountain slope to make the roads shorter or easier. These roads are just sandy, hardened with gravel to enable the heavy-duty logging trucks to pass. Tree planting is usually avoided along the roadside so that the sunshine can dry it up after heavy showers, which are very common. Sometimes, as a way of window-dressing, logging companies plant quick-yielding trees along the road to give a 'good impression' to the inspector.

Once the suitable hill has been found all trees and shrubs will be cut to leave a tall, big tree to serve as a fulcrum pole to pull up the logs cut all around the valley banks. The trees are cut down by chainsaws and then attached to the steel cables and pulled up to the log pool, swinging and striking other trees along their path. Using the yarding technique loggers can easily cut trees on slopes with a more than 25% inclination, which is actually prohibited.

With this popular technique logging can be done very fast and extensively. In the Soriano Brothers timber concession in East Kalimantan with an area of 1.2 million hectares, I once saw a double-pole yarding process going on. After ten years adopting this technique all over the archipelago, the Minister for Environmental Control has declared it to be just 'harmful' but no regulation to prohibit yarding has been issued up to this moment.

It is the same case with helicoper logging. Indonesia is maybe the first South-East Asian country to use helicopters to transport the felled logs from the jungles to the log terminals. The first company to carry out this operation was Jayanti Jaya, a big timber company closely related with forestry and other high ranking officials, managed by a Kalimantan-born Chinese businessman, Iurhan Uray, nicknaming himself the 'timber king'. This company, operating a cluster of timber concessions covering a total of 2 million hectares in Central Kalimantan, rented helicopters in 1977 to transport the dipterocarp logs out of the forest. But this experiment only lasted for several weeks. Some said that the helicopter's rent was too high compared to the price of dipterocarp logs at that time. (*Tempo* 21 October 1978). But others told the writer that it was just a publicity stunt to impress the state banks in order to squeeze more loans for the timber group's operations.

Another reckless fellow tried to do the same thing in Central Sulawesi when the price of ebony logs in the Japanese market was at its peak. Sakura Abadi, a Japanese-supported company which suddenly got a monopoly on ebony logging, thanks to a letter from the Director General of Forestry, rented two Bell 205 helicopters to transport the ebony logs from the jungles to the floating log ponds along the sea coast. They did that, not only because the price of ebony could allow them to pay the US$850 per hour rent of the helicopters, but also because the government had put January 31st, 1979 as the deadline for the export of ebony logs. They did not have to do much logging due to the Director's memo which gave them immediate rights over 150,000 hectares of ebony forests which had been logged but the timber not taken out of the area. More than a dozen local entrepreneurs had to leave 40,000 tons of ebony logs for Sakura Abadi. (*Tempo* 21 October 1978).

This government-backed take-over aroused some friction between Sakura Abadi and the local entrepreneurs who were pushed aside without any compensation. Besides that, the concession area assigned to Sakura Abadi actually included some protection forests and areas inhabited by local people. That is why when once a 2-ton ebony log slipped loose from the helicopter's sling cables and crushed down on somebody's garden below, the people's antipathy towards Sakura increased more and more, although no victim had fallen yet. But the tension rapidly increased when in less than two months 2 helicopters crashed. One pilot was killed in the first crash, but the other pilot survived until the second crash in which the helicopter's blade broke loose and smashed into a mosque's dome. (*Tempo* 28 October 1979). After these 2 accidents, helicopter logging was abruptly stopped. Good enough, because by using helicopters, the loggers would also be able to fell down trees on the prohibited slopes, thereby increasing the danger of erosion and landslides.

That report from 1979 is still relevant because the situation at ground level has remained the same.

Timber industry developments: In 1978 the export tax on logs rose from 10% to 20% as the government tried to encourage more timber processing within Indonesia.[110] The following year a new export tax of 5% was placed on sawn timber. The most significant government intervention, however, came in 1980 with the 'Three Ministers Decree', which called for a complete ban on log exports within three years. This deadline was extended to 1984 but the trade in logs declined sharply after 1980. In contrast, plywood exports increased from 283,000 cubic metres in 1980 to 3.5m by 1987.[111]

Most foreign investors' immediate reaction was to pull out of the Indonesian timber industry. The log export ban, however, was not the sole factor to shift foreign corporate investment. The most valuable timber resources were already running low. By 1980 most Sumatran forests had been logged over, and the average log size was regarded as too small for the international market. There was no room for expansion within Kalimantan since most forest had already been designated to logging companies. Irian Jaya has a much lower ratio of dipterocarps and, with difficult terrain, these are frequently regarded as too expensive to exploit. Many foreign investors moved to East Malaysia over this period. As those reserves become depleted the same corporations are now investing in the Brazilian Amazon.

Indonesian timber companies rushed into plywood production and by 1985 the country's 108 plywood mills had a capacity exceeding six million cubic metres, more than the total world trade in tropical plywood;[112] 80% of these mills came into existence after 1981.[113] Plywood processors tried to retain the level of profits yielded by raw log exports by producing ever larger quantities of plywood. This resulted in over-production, which flooded the world market, and the price of tropical plywood dropped to the point at which many Indonesians sell their plywood below cost price. Indonesia currently accounts for approximately 70% of the world's plywood traded on international markets.[114]

This fall in plywood prices had catastrophic effects throughout the Far East. By 1986, of the 100 plywood mills in Taiwan active in the early 1980s only eight were still in production.[115] Even the Japanese plywood industry closed two-thirds of its mills by 1986.[116] In 1984 the Malaysian Timber Industries Board commented that the Indonesians were a 'new but resolute bunch of competitors, who by force of circumstances have little regard for market sentiments and have little choice but to sell at any price'.[117]

The future for Indonesia's timber industry is projected to meet a considerable growth in domestic demand (see table 2.4). By the late 1990s domestic consumption is scheduled to have increased by 54% but exports by only 45%. According to the World Bank, however, 'Many plywood producers have faced difficulty in obtaining a regular supply of logs'.[118] This is due to a combination of over-exploitation of certain species, and poor infrastructure on the outer islands.

A Plywood Export Joint Marketing Board has been formed that hopes to establish minimum export prices, but many companies are willing to transgress these regulations. The Board is also lobbying Japan, Taiwan, the United States and other major timber importers to lower their tariffs on plywood. They also consider the European Economic Community quota system on plywood to be unfair, in that it gives all suppliers an equal volume of tax-free exports. Understandably, Indonesia wants a greater share of tax-free exports due to its production capacity.

Increasing plywood prices and stabilizing the industry will not create a sustainable timber industry, but could relieve much of the pressure on logging companies. These trade relations play a key role in creating a financial balance sheet that discourages any attempts at sustainable logging.

Transmigration
The Indonesian Transmigration programme has caused a major international controversy. Transmigration is not new; the Dutch started to move people off Java in the early part of the 20th century as a political device to diffuse resistance to land acquisition by the colonial power. Access to the most fertile soils is still a problem for the Javanese poor, but population pressure is the dominant factor at present.

With 690 people per sq. km Java is far more densely populated than the outer islands. In Irian Jaya there are three people per sq. km and twelve in Kalimantan.[119] Java's population of almost 100 million continues to expand at 2% per year despite a vigorous family planning campaign.[120] Transmigration is seen as a means of redressing this uneven population distribution and relieving poverty in Java itself. The present five-year plan proposes to move almost 700,000 families, more than three million people, by 1990.[121] The authorities originally hoped to move one million families but this proved too ambitious. Table 2.5 provides an outline of the problem. The government sees the programme as having a range of advantages for the country as a whole. It improves population distribution, provides land for the landless of Java, helps foster development on the outer islands and is seen as a 'vehicle to promote national stability and integration'.[122]

In total, 40 transmigration sites are planned on forest land, mainly in Kalimantan, although Irian Jaya is due to become the main recipient of transmigrants in the 1990s.[123] The population of East Kalimantan has risen by 46% since 1983 and that of Irian Jaya by 52%.[124]

The figures may look impressive but they must be seen in the context of the situation in Java. Between 1985 and 1989 Java's population will have increased by almost ten million but the transmigration programme will involve less than three million.[125] Dr Arndt of the Australian National University notes: 'The population imbalance in Indonesia is an irremediable fact of life. The question is only whether whatever economic or other disadvantage it may entail can be remedied *within* Java.'[126]

The transmigration programme, however, does focus on some of the very poorest people in Java and this accords with the goal of poverty alleviation, but the major questions are: is this an efficient strategy, considering the great financial costs? And are projects implemented in such a way that the needs of the rural poor take precedence? Could the money be better spent on Java itself?

Organization and goals: The Ministry of Transmigration co-ordinates the programme as a whole, although individual sites may be more locally organized or under different Ministries. To attain the general aims of the programme the government promotes it by providing the following for those taking part:

- A two to four hectare plot of farmland on freshly cleared forest. The size depends on the location and type of project site.
- A basic wooden house.
- A supply of basic foodstuffs for one year, to bridge the gap between arrival and the first crops.
- Basic tools for the farming model chosen.
- Seed supplies for the first harvest.
- Fertilizers and pesticides for the first three years, if required.
- Free transport to the sites.
- The provision of infrastructure for the new community as a whole, such as roads, schools and clinics.

For a landless farmer or slum dweller on Java these are strong incentives to participate in the programme. There can be little doubt that for many participation has led to a genuine improvement in their welfare. For others, however, the promises have not materialized and in a number of cases the environmental problems threaten the sustainability of the entire programme.

Site choice: Previous experience of site choice has not only destroyed large tracts of forest but jeopardized the agricultural potential of the outer islands as a whole. The policy of using forested areas for sedentary agriculture was so widely disputed that, in 1979, President Suharto temporarily banned the clearing of forests for transmigration sites.[127]

Six scheduled sites were cancelled immediately, but pressures have increased and now 80% of new sites are in the primary forests, resulting in clearance of at least 3.3m ha by 1990.[128] In a report by the Land Resources Development Centre (LRDC) of the UK and the Coordinating Agency for National Survey and Mapping (BAKOSURTANAL), however, they note that: 'The amount of land converted into farm plots for the government-sponsored transmigration settlers is, in fact, the minimum amount lost from the forest estate.'[129]

The sites chosen are classified as conversion forest and therefore theoretically suitable for agriculture. As the programme progresses, the Ministry of Transmigration has demanded more land be made available from the forests. As a result, land the Forestry Department regarded as unsuitable for clearance, is now given over to transmigration sites. The Ministry of Transmigration holds more political power than the Forest Department. Despite numerous warnings from soil experts and development consultants, the Transmigration Department continues to clear sites as large as 15 to 20,000 ha that are unsuitable for permanent agriculture.[130]

The LRDC estimate that only 75,000 ha of East Kalimantan is suitable for permanent agriculture. The Transmigration Ministry hopes to have opened up 17 times that area by 1990.[131] Across Indonesia as a whole an estimated 500,000 ha of transmigration sites are located on inappropriate forest soils.[132] Many critics claim the choice of sites is based on the 'least unsuitable' rather than the most viable.[133]

Site clearance and farming models: These problems have been exacerbated by the methods used to clear forests and by the farming models chosen. The scale and tight time schedule of many transmigration sites exclude the possibility of manual forest clearance. Large bulldozers are used; a capital-intensive approach that not only costs the country foreign currency but also creates serious environmental degradation. The use of such heavy machinery compacts and destroys the soil structure. Since the majority of nutrients are found in the top two to three centimetres of the old soils found on Indonesia's outer islands, a bulldozer can destroy this layer by simply driving over it. By the time contractors start to pull out the trees and push over the stumps the soil has been thoroughly churned, mixed and compacted. The timber debris is then burnt, destroying nutrients such as nitrogen and sulphur. Burning frequently renders other nutrients more soluble and in normal conditions they would seep into the soil, but on these sites rain washes over the hard clay-like pan that bulldozers frequently leave behind.

The hapless transmigrants are then brought from the rich fertile soils of Java and told to establish wet rice paddy farming on these poor soils. This has not helped these people adapt to the new situation and in many cases the farming methods promoted by the department have been a complete failure.

Abandoned transmigration sites: The Indonesian government has kept very quiet on this issue, but independent reports have filtered into the press. Between 1984 and 1986, on Irian Jaya, an estimated 1,500 transmigration plots and houses were abandoned.[134] On Sulawesi, the newspaper *Merdeka* reported in 1984, that more than 400 out of a total 1,000 families deserted two major sites near the provincial capital Kendari.[135] In Southern Sumatra, the huge projects around Air Sugihan, involving some 80,000 people, have been officially declared failures due to persistent crop failures in the swampy soils, lack of potable water and a cholera epidemic.[136] The list of failures is significant for the programme as a whole and these are by no means isolated examples.

The government has started to change its policy of swamp reclamation in favour of more stable sites. This strategy has been a limited success, the soils may be less boggy but they are thin and old. At the same time the authorities admit that *alang-alang* is spreading at the rate of 150–200,000 ha per year on the outer islands, but no figures are available on how much of this is associated with deserted transmigration sites. Farmers who abandon their sites tend to practise a very crude version of the local swidden farming, which undoubtedly destroys significant areas of forest. The government, however, consistently blames the tribal groups for the environmental havoc caused by wandering transmigrants.

In 1984 the government announced a change of policy on the farm model promoted and now hopes to establish cash crop estates. This has proved slightly more successful than wet rice paddy but it will rely heavily on developing infrastructure. Provision of these basic services has been a problem for the authorities.

Corruption in the programme: In a country where bribery is almost an accepted part of the political scene the transmigration programme is extremely vulnerable to corruption. Forest clearance is carried out by private contractors who frequently have no experience in this field. Contracts can be so lucrative that companies frequently offer project officials as much as 17% of the contract price in order to secure the job.[137] It is estimated that on average 40% of foreign aid to Indonesia is 'lost'.[138]

Government spending on the programme between 1986–90 will exceed US$10 billion.[139] In 1985 the Minister for Transmigration admitted that, 'the contractors who are [supposed to be] partners of the government, only look for their own profits and do not implement their job with a sense of responsibility.'[140] In early 1986 the Ministry announced that it had settled 818 cases of: 'irregularities involving state funds . . . committed by suppliers, contractors and agencies under its authority.'[141] The Minister also announced that his Department had taken action against 30 ministry officials and struck 14 major contractors off their lists.

While contractors and the Ministry argue over who gains the major contracts, transmigrants are brought on to sites with the utmost haste, in many cases before proper infrastructural works are completed. There are numerous instances of projects having no access roads, of inadequate housing, even incomplete drainage systems on swamp land sites. On the Way Seputik site in Southern Sumatra transmigrants had to wait 14 years for their irrigation and drainage canals to be completed.[142] In an attempt to divert attention from the administrative problems of the scheme the authorities began to suggest that transmigrants were lazy and wanted to be spoon-fed, which according to the government, explained why so many sites had been abandoned.

A new farming model: In 1984 a drastic change of policy on the farm models to be used was announced, breaking away from the rice-based subsistence model to cash crop estates. Without the provision of proper infrastructure the possibility of cash crops reaching the markets at which they are aimed seems somewhat fanciful. But it is not only the environment that suffers from the transmigration programme.

Traditional land rights: Almost all transmigration sites have 'owners' under the traditional *adat* law system. Tribal groups have no secure land rights that provide them with any protection if their forests are designated as transmigration sites. As Joseph Weinstock of Cornell University notes:

> From a legal standpoint, the Basic Agrarian Law is a masterpiece of legislation in that it appears to protect and preserve the traditional adat system of land tenure while being couched in sufficiently vague terminology enabling the government to do as it pleases.[143]

More than 700,000 ha of tribal land has been annexed by the government on Irian Jaya alone.[144] Government methods of obtaining the co-operation of the tribal peoples to relinquish land has been severely criticized. Marcus Colchester of Survival International notes that on Irian Jaya, 'by the early 1970s, evictions of local peoples by trickery and at gunpoint, to make way for transmigrants, had already become the established practice'.[145]

Violent confrontations between tribal groups and government forces or settlers have been recorded on Irian Jaya, Sulawesi, Kalimantan and Sumatra. Few dare talk of these issues but the Association for Legal Aid Institute in Jakarta claims the worst cases are in Irian Jaya.[146] Here, in 1981 the Indonesian army engaged in 'Operation Clean Sweep' under the slogan: 'Let the rats run into the jungle so the chickens can breed in the coop'.[147]

Trouble is not restricted to occasions when transmigrant sites are cleared. In 1985, starving migrants in the Donggala region of Southern Sulawesi stole livestock from the local tribes; in the ensuing battle one transmigrant was killed. As retaliation the settlers burned 27 tribal houses before the army moved in to prevent further trouble.[148]

Much criticism also arises from a more subtle process of attempting to Javanize the outer islands and force the populations into a Muslim society. One of the original goals for the programme was 'national stabilization and integration'. The ideal of creating an Indonesian identity incorporating all the cultures sounds plausible but the domination of the Javanese makes its achievement highly unlikely. More than 60% of the population live on Java and it is unlikely that the remaining 40%, scattered across a vast area, will make a significant contribution to this new identity because the non-Muslims are not a homogeneous group. In addition, central government is very much in control and based on Java, where all major decisions on development are taken.

In 1986 the government attempted to silence its critics by announcing that 25% of transmigrants to Irian Jaya would be from Bali and other non-Muslim centres.[149] There is also a change of transmigrant selection policy within Irian Jaya as more Irianese are offered places on projects. But the attraction for local farmers is limited, as they can see that many sites are ecological disasters.

Resistance by tribal groups has resulted in the emergence of another aspect of the programme: security. There are accusations that a large percentage of transmigrants to the less stable areas, particularly Irian Jaya, are retired army personnel.[150] The Indonesian government has used this tactic before, the best-known case being the Sapta Marga villages in Southern Sulawesi, established in 'troublesome' areas.[151] Many regard the large concentration of sites along the border areas of Irian Jaya, and the development of the OPM (Free Papua Movement) in the same area, as more than coincidental. It is not clear whether the transmigration sites prompted the development of the OPM or whether this was a rebellious area in the first place. Whatever the reasons, the programme is generally running a long way behind schedule and insurgency problems do not help the Indonesian authorities.

International funding: In 1982–3, the government was spending, on average, upwards of US$12,000 per family.[152] For more remote locations government's spending is in excess of US$15,000 per family.[153]

Indonesia had to borrow US$637 million between 1972 and 1985 to fund transmigration; two-thirds came from the World Bank.[154] The World Bank, however, also provides funding for rehabilitating deforested areas adjacent to failed transmigration sites.[155] The IIED describes these as loans for: 'activities which contribute significantly to the destruction of forests as a result of the establishment of poorly planned agricultural settlements. Thus an unfortunate cycle of destruction and rehabilitation is becoming institutionalised.'[156]

The World Bank claims that its involvement has 'contributed substantially to improvements in the Programme'.[157] Charles Secrett of Friends of the Earth, however, commenting on the Bank's own reports on Indonesia noted that: 'there is virtually no recognition of any of the past environmental, agricultural or human failures so carefully analysed by the Forest Review Team.'[158] At the international level, the World Bank has developed significantly better policies since the mid-1980s and these are noted in the final chapter.

The Bank continues to fund the programme without calling for a major review of its goals and implementation, which is surprising considering the range of criticisms levelled at the programme in general. The IIED report ended noting that it: 'leads one to conclude that the Programme as it presently is implemented, does not support sustainable development of Indonesia's forest lands or for that matter, the settlements themselves.'[159] The Environmental Minister, Emil Salim, went further and compared the programme to: 'sailing on a boat that is still under construction. Some of the passengers are nailing down the timber, others are ladling out water, while yet others are still trying to decide where the boat is supposed to be going.'[160]

Shifting cultivation

No one is certain how many people are practising some form of shifting agriculture in Indonesia. The official estimate for 1980 was around one million families throughout Indonesia, although estimates of up to 1.5m are accepted.[161]

The government claims that shifting cultivators clear around 400–500,000 ha of forest each year; conveniently more than the 200–300,000 ha lost to transmigration. This implies that shifting agriculturalists bear the major responsibility for forest loss in Indonesia. But this is an over-simplification as the Land Resources Development Centre (LRDC) and BAKOSURTANAL (the Coordinating Agency for National Survey and Mapping) note:

It is very doubtful whether there are one million families of genuine shifting cultivators in Indonesia. The probability is that a significant proportion are in fact shifted cultivators, the unfortunate victims of transmigration which has misfired, and small farmers who have been dispossessed.[162]

Traditional swidden cultivation: With 300 different ethnic groups in the country, a correspondingly large variety of traditional swidden agricultural systems are found, each based on its particular forest type. Major subsistence crops vary from rice in the highlands of Sumatra and Kalimantan, and sweet potato in interior of Irian Jaya, to sago in its coastal lowlands.

The majority of established swidden-based societies use only secondary forest. Tribal populations are increasing but this does not imply that there is a proportional increase in forest clearance.[163] To monitor migration patterns of the more nomadic groups is frequently complex, as it is often not clear to an observer whether the changes are permanent or part of a long-term cycle. As a result, as populations increase, details on social and agricultural adaptations within swidden-based societies are rare. There are, however, extremely small numbers of people involved in comparison to the populations of Java. In short, the population increase in tribal groups is a minor factor in Indonesia's forest destruction.

The Mimika of South-West Irian Jaya is one group that has been blamed for forest destruction. They live in semi-permanent villages and divide their time between tending forest gardens and hunting and gathering. The older members of the community work in the subsistence crop gardens producing a wide variety of vegetables, bananas and tobacco; no large trees are felled to make way for these crops. Most protein is obtained from wild game while sago palm forms the basis of the diet with wild stands being cultivated in the forest. The sago groves may be some distance from the village so that when large quantities are needed the younger family members stay in temporary huts near these sites. Each year entire villages migrate to the coast, to catch fish in the season, staying until the sago they have brought with them runs out and then returning to their original sites. The Mimika undoubtedly have an effect on the forest but more as a part of the ecosystem rather than as a destructive force.

Some of the Dayak communities along the Telan river in Kalimantan have a more profound effect on the forest; they clear small areas of forest and burn the debris. Most plots are in secondary forest that has previously been cleared for agriculture. Burning is done at the end of the dry season with a three to five metre strip around the site cleared as a fire break; even if the fire gets out of control the rains will soon come. Their rotation system comprises two fields under cultivation and four left fallow at any one time. One cultivated field will always be near the river, in case of drought. Originally the fallow period for each field was ten years but with restricted access to the forests it has become as little as three years.

Subsistence crops such as rice and corn are grown on freshly cleared sites, cash crops are grown only after the land has been cultivated for some time. The local *adat* laws allow exclusive use rights over all cleared land. As a result, a family has the right to evict anyone trying to farm their fallow land.

SKEPHI note that the local Dayaks are experiencing increasing problems from migrant farmers cultivating land that should be lying fallow.[164] Direct eviction from logging concessions is another factor that has restricted access to traditional agricultural sites. It is not the swidden system that is at fault in many areas, but denial of access to forest that forces a more intensive use of the land than would normally occur.

The authorities, however, regard shifting cultivation of all kinds as a problem and attempt to stop it through three major schemes: Population Resettlement projects; the Village Resettlement scheme; and the Development of Isolated Communities project. All three programmes are aimed at getting tribal groups to practise settled farming methods.

Modern shifting cultivation: While responsibility for forest destruction has centred around indigenous groups, voluntary migrant farmers have largely escaped attention. The World Bank estimates that 170,000 families have moved from Java on to the outer islands without any government assistance.[165] Many are middle-class speculators growing cash crops. Pepper is the main harvest and many regard shifting agriculture as a more profitable way of growing such crops. They rarely practise any of the traditional restraints used by swidden farmers and instead grow crops until the soil is totally exhausted. There is a greater financial profit in abandoning an area than investing in its future by terracing, or maintaining tree cover. Not all migrants from Java fit the popular image of desperately poor landless farmers.[166]

The primary causes of forest destruction can be separated but it is unwise to regard them in isolation. In any one area the forests may face all of the above threats.

The Dumoga Valley in northern Sulawesi provides a good example of combined pressures.[167] In the 1970s the area was opened-up by a road that connected a transmigration site, a World Bank funded irrigation scheme, and the regional capital.

The irrigation scheme made possible wet rice paddy cultivation and entrepreneurs quickly started to clear the Valley's forest; land claims can be made only on cleared land. By 1980 the Dumoga and Bone Forest reserves were consolidated into a protected area to save the river's catchment area, as deforestation threatened the irrigation scheme. The establishment of this reserve was also funded by the World Bank and more than 400 families were moved out to other sites.

In financial terms the irrigation project is a success, the area now exports rice. Rather than benefiting the Valley's original inhabitants as it was hoped, the major benefits have been shared between speculators and wages for foreign experts who provided advice at all stages of the development. As Gradwohl and Greenberg note:

> Unfortunately, the original inhabitants of the valley have benefited least from the switch from dry-land to wet-land cultivation. Having sold their holdings and moved to the hills, most were unable to be part of the development programme and were more likely to be living on the reserve, and therefore to be evicted from the park, or resettled.[168]

The park cannot be considered a complete failure in that the forest is intact but it does represent a rather crude method of saving forests.

Forest futures in Indonesia

Indonesia is in no immediate danger of losing all its forest cover. The spread of its 'critical lands', however, can no longer be regarded in isolation from the severe degradation of forests from whatever cause. The future of the country's agriculture and rural economy lies within the forests and despite the problems, much more could be done to safeguard their future. In terms of area the transmigration programme probably poses the greatest single threat although logging still affects large areas.

Transmigration: This practice is here to stay. Even if the World Bank were to cease its funding the Indonesian government would continue the programme. But this does not mean that there is little chance of dramatic changes in key aspects of its implementation. While some NGOs outside Indonesia are calling for an end to the programme, those within the country are taking a more pragmatic approach.

It is widely believed within Indonesia that something has to be done about population pressure on Java and, since the birth control programme has had a limited effect, transmigration provides an option. This may be so, but transmigration has a very limited effect on Java's population growth. The authorities are beginning to realize the limitations of this strategy but, as yet, there has been no major shift in allocating resources to other poverty alleviation schemes within Java. In citing Java as over-populated, the fact that industrialized countries are capable of supporting dense populations must be recognized; Java's problem is thus one of development as well as numbers.

The government's continued determination to pour resources into transmigration may even have been influenced by widespread criticism from outside Indonesia. The country fought hard for independence and obviously wants to retain it. Despite a forgivable reaction to what is often seen as foreign meddling, the implementation of the programme clearly requires an extensive overhaul. At present the government is intent on following the present path for the foreseeable future. The following suggestions are based on local ideas of what could be implemented without completely abandoning the programme. A starting point for reform could be the choice of sites.

Changing site choice: When, in 1979, the President banned the expansion into forests, research was started on rehabilitating the ever-growing areas of *alang-alang* grasslands. The studies were based around the use of leguminous crops as an aid to fix nitrogen in the soils and thus contribute to the general fertility of the land.[169] Opinion differs on how effective these projects may be but little effort is put into developing this alternative. Robert Goodland of the World Bank, however, claims that using *alang-alang* sites is actually 20% cheaper than clearing forests in that heavy machinery is not required.[170]

This option has widespread support amongst Indonesia's NGOs who rightly claim that these sites could be developed with a greater human input, a resource Indonesia has in abundance. Money spent on capital-intensive machinery could be diverted to paying manual labour, which would not only provide employment but also cause less damage to the environment.

There are also calls for the basic agricultural model to be changed to a more complex and sustainable farming system. Shifting cultivation *per se* need not be abandoned as a possible farming method for transmigrants, provided it is properly managed. In addition, all project sites, not only the social forestry projects on Java, should have agro-forestry buffer zones. If this is regarded as necessary on Java, with its rich soils, why is it not applied to the outer islands?

In addition to what actually happens on the chosen sites, planning controls over independent migrants are desperately needed. They have cleared large tracts of forests in certain areas and as these migrants are not starving peasants simply trying to survive, there can be no humanitarian plea against such control.

Corruption within the programme is another aspect that central authorities can influence. That the authorities have attempted to stamp out this corruption should be recognized, but there is clear need for a much stronger policy. If the corruption were eliminated the money saved could be spent on the migrants, but resources are needed to eradicate corruption in the first place. In the longer term, money used to end massive corruption will have a direct effect on lives of Indonesia's rural poor.

Much foreign criticism of transmigration has been aimed at the unjustifiable treatment of indigenous people who live in or near areas cleared. This is an extremely delicate issue within Indonesia, even within the environmental movement. At present land rights are rarely recognized and compensation for loss of forest is unknown. The inclusion of tribal population in transmigration projects is a new policy that has yet to become widespread. This might placate some tribal groups but will do little to reduce the loss of forest.

Giving land rights to tribal groups and providing adequate compensation may relieve some of the social conflicts that have emerged from the programme. But in future the wishes of local populations could be included at the initial stages of proposals for transmigration sites. Unfortunately, local populations' valuable knowledge, acquired through experience of their environment and what it is capable of supporting, is at present ignored.

Integrating transmigration: With overemphasis on transmigration, poverty alleviation programmes within Java have suffered from a lack of large-scale commitment. Development of local market economies within Java could evolve if efforts similar to those expended on transmigration were applied to such projects on this central island; for example by providing cheap loans for small-scale entrepreneurs and the rural poor at the 'ground level'. With this kind of development of local economies employment opportunities would increase, thus relieving much pressure on marginal lands that at present support Java's rural unemployed. Such programmes could be concentrated in areas where there have been numerous applicants to go on transmigration schemes, thereby attempting to solve the problem at its root.

The same principle could be applied to the rather limited social forestry programmes on Java which, although imaginative, need expansion. By intensifying these programmes the demand for transmigration could well decrease.

Whether any of these possibilities may be explored is open to speculation. The current political atmosphere, however, does not facilitate widespread debate on transmigration within Indonesia. Herein lies the tragedy, since it is the transmigrants themselves who will suffer most as the programme in its present form proves unsustainable.

Timber production: Even with the reduction of exports the timber industry will continue to have a detrimental effect on the country's forests. Domestic demand is predicted to increase dramatically over the next decade and this will compensate for any loss of exports as far as forests are concerned. Despite being an unmitigated failure, in terms of conserving the country's forests, the policy of self-policing timber concession is to continue. Tougher laws backed up by strong enforcement on forest management, extraction methods and replanting are now essential.

A start could be made by making enrichment planting, which is central to the TPI forestry system, applicable to all concessions. Licences should be renewable subject to satisfactory inspection of sites on the ground and from the air. One way in which the government could ensure replanting is to make a charge on all timber cut sufficient to cover the costs of forest rehabilitation. Alternatively, concession fees should reflect rehabilitation costs. This would be successful only if there was a possibility of imposing fines in the event of over-cutting.

The allocation of concession licences should include stipulations on minimum investment periods. Legislation could be enacted whereby the government may seize company assets – whether or not the company is working the concession area – if concession agreements have not been fulfilled. This principle has been applied to companies dumping toxic wastes in the US, why not in tropical forests?

The Indonesian timber industry is capital intensive rather than labour intensive and this trend needs to be reversed. This would provide more employment, better distribution of the benefits from foreign exchange earnings, development of the local economy and contribute substantially to saving the forest.

The minor forest produce industry is one forestry sector that does need capital investment. This sector has shown considerable growth over the last decade yet has failed to attract anything approaching the scale of investment in timber. The development of basic infrastructure would greatly assist this sector to expand. In addition, more research is required if the full potential of this industry is to be recognized.

Minor forest produce operations should, however, remain small-scale and be actively promoted in or near logging concessions. Two groups of people could then earn a living from the forest, and logging interests would have to accommodate themselves to the needs of the minor forest product industry. The best policeman is often a local company concerned with its own resource.

On the international scene it is crucial that Indonesia plays an active role in the International Tropical Timber Trade Organization (ITTO). Only by restricting its output of plywood and other semi-processed wood materials will Indonesia benefit from the advantages of stable world markets.

Rapid expansion of the timber or pulpwood plantation sector should be regarded with caution. Industrial plantations could be established on the 'critical lands' but there is no justification for any forest to be cleared to make way for them. On Java the preference for planting teak could be extended to reafforestation on the outer islands. The time is now ripe for Indonesia to apply the knowledge acquired from its social forestry programmes throughout the archipelago.

Case studies

Logging in East Kalimantan
East Kalimantan occupies 211,000 sq. km of Borneo. In 1981 there were an

estimated 173,000 sq. km of forest, of which 130,000 had been designated for logging.[171] This area is divided between 100 concession and even fewer companies, since many investors have interests in a number of operations.[172] Kalimantan as a whole supplies almost one-third of the country's timber exports,[173] earning, in 1984, US$443m.[174] Despite this contribution to the economy the profits accrue to a small minority and have not generally improved the living standards of the local people.[175] By 1984 Kalimantan had more than 10,000 sq. km of 'critical lands', a dangerous situation for an agricultural region.[176]

In the late 1970s major foreign concession holders in East Kalimantan included: Weyerhauser (USA); Georgia Pacific (USA); Mitsubushi (Japan); Sumitomo (Japan); Shin Asahigawa (Japan); and Ataka and Co. (Japan). The Weyerhauser corporation provides a good example of logging concession politics in this region.

Weyerhauser and the Generals: By the late 1960s Weyerhauser's logging concessions in the Philippines were becoming unprofitable.[177] Wishing to expand operations Weyerhauser went into partnership with an Indonesian company: the International Timber Corporation of Indonesia (ITCI). In 1971 ITCI gained rights to 386,000 ha of primary hill forest in East Kalimantan.[178]

Weyerhauser could never buy out its partner because ITCI was a trust set up personally by President Suharto.[179] On paper, Weyerhauser owned only 65% of ITCI but they provided the operations' total investment of US$32m.[180] Both parties gained: Weyerhauser had financial control over ITCI and ITCI acquired a large working capital with no investment. ITCI's major shareholders were the top 73 Generals in Suharto's 'New Order' government.[181] In effect the partnership was a form of pay-off from Suharto for the loyalty of Indonesia's military elite. Over the first seven years ITCI's log sales averaged US$37m annually.[182] In 1977, output from this one concession reached 1.6m tons of logs worth US$66m.[183]

How much of this figure was straight profit for Weyerhauser is not clear. The forest expert, Norman Myers, estimated that for a similarly funded operation the foreign shareholder gained more than US$3m profit per year.[184]

The Three Ministers Decree of 1980 put pressure on all logging operations to reinvest profits in processing facilities, but this did not suit Weyerhauser who pulled out of ITCI in 1984.[185] In short, Weyerhauser was not interested in timber processing or managing the forest after they had extracted the highest value timber, an attitude typical of foreign investment in Indonesia's timber industry at this time.

Logging and the environment: In 1985 SKEPHI carried out research on a similarly large concession in East Kalimantan, owned by PT Kiani

Lestari.[186] In 1960, when the concession was granted, Kiani Lestari was controlled by Georgia-Pacific Indonesia (GPI). GPI was a joint venture between Georgia-Pacific Canada and Bob Hasan, a wealthy Chinese business man, reportedly a close ally of President Suharto.[187] The concession covered 357,000 ha of primary hill dipterocarp forest, of which approximately 10,000 was to become a transmigration site and thus justified clear felling. By the time SKEPHI surveyed the concession 69,000 ha had been logged over.[188] GPI had little direct involvement with the company in 1985, but the concession has been managed under the theoretically sustainable TPI Select Fell system since its inception.

Kiani Lestari opens up about 75 km of logging roads per year, not including skidder tracks. To construct these roads complete hills are blown-up to provide crushed rock. Approximately 25 ha of forest is selectively felled each day. SKEPHI report that:

> About 50% of the surrounding forest was completely destroyed by bulldozer movement in the logged-over areas. Areas where bulldozers turned around, cleared roads and dragged logs over 15 years ago still have not recovered . . . We found that the number of 25–49 centimetre trees per hectare was often smaller than the required 25. We also found less than 10 trees over 50 cm. in diameter per hectare. Visual observation of logged-over areas from past years, even 15 years ago, revealed about 60%–70% of the canopy was open. Worse conditions were encountered in collection sites and along roads.[189]

SKEPHI also estimate that 50% of the trees felled never reach the mill and are left to rot. Of those taken, the maximum size of log used is 14 metres as Kiani Lestari require straight wood with no blemishes or knots. As a result, a lot of debris is left on the felling site, crushing seedlings, inhibiting sapling growth and creating a major fire hazard. That no attempt is made to utilize this waste wood was undoubtedly a factor in the 50,000 ha of logged forest lost to fire in 1982–83.

Reafforestation on this concession started in 1980. By 1985, 6,000 ha of fast-growing monocultures had been established, less than one tenth of the area logged. Despite this ratio, SKEPHI described Kiani Lestari as 'one of the few companies which is undertaking to reafforest some of its logging areas'.[190]

Logging and the Dayaks: Logging concessions in East Kalimantan now extend right up to the border with East Malaysia, denying official access to the forests for the majority of the local population. There has been almost no independent research on the effects of logging on these communities. The government claims that loss of access rights to traditional farming and hunting areas has been offset by new employment opportunities in the timber industry. The reality is that working conditions are dangerous, employment is usually seasonal, and pay low and infrequent, because this often relies on the timber being sold. The long-term effects of the destruction of indigenous rights to harvest forest produce has probably denied a cash income to more people than the timber companies employ.

All the social consequences of forest loss noted earlier are found in East Kalimantan. Tribal resistance, however, has been sporadic and inconsistent. The Dayaks of Kalimantan are less highly organized than those in Sarawak. This is probably due to Indonesia's internal politics rather than to satisfaction with the present situation. The promotion of the plywood industry has provided more employment opportunities but these are quickly taken up by the huge influx of migrants. Few profits from timber have entered the local economies and least of all have filtered down to the indigenous groups.

Fires: During 1982 and 1983 fires swept through 3.5m ha of East Kalimantan.[191] An estimated 20 million cu. metres of timber from primary forests and a further 35 million from secondary forest were destroyed in Kalimantan as a whole.[192] The export value of this timber was estimated to be worth US$5.5 billion to Indonesia.[193] There is increasing evidence that careless logging was responsible for intensifying the fire.

From July 1982 to April 1983 East Kalimantan faced a serious drought, with rainfall down 68% on average levels in the last four months.[194] Major droughts are not unknown on Borneo and were the cause of widespread starvation among the Dayak tribes in the 1880s. Significantly, however, travellers at that time made no mention of widespread fires, despite the dominance of traditional slash and burn agriculture.[195]

The most thorough study on the fire was commissioned by the German Agency for Technical Co-operation. The authors wrote a vivid description of the pre-fire conditions:

> Agricultural production virtually came to a halt, fresh vegetables became scarce, many fruit trees and root crops died as the drought continued. With dropping water levels, navigation on major rivers became increasingly difficult and many rafts of logs destined for down-river plywood mills got stuck in small rivers. In peat swamps and swamp forests the organic matter dried up to a depth exceeding 0.5m. In the forests, dry leaves accumulated on the ground, the top layer of organic material dried out while tree tops and wood residues provided additional fuel in logged-over areas; a critical situation.[196]

Exactly why the drought occurred is not clear. As noted earlier, El Nino was very active but this may have been in response to the deforestation process. Whatever the cause, the resultant fires consumed almost 3,500 sq. km in this one state, of which 1,400 sq. km was logged-over forest – an exceptionally high proportion. The fire was most intense in these areas because they were drier and more open than primary forest. The waste timber provided ideal fuel, the lack of canopy dried out the leaves and, with fewer trees, the wind speed increased. Any rivers that may have acted as fire breaks were spanned by wood debris bridges used by the loggers. By comparison, the German report noted that, 'due to the closed forest structure, fire in primary forest has been less intensive'.[197] They go on to comment that so conducive to fires is the physical structure of logged-over forests that, 'a dry spell of only 10 to 15 days may create a situation more dangerous than that in February 1983'.[198]

In 1984 the Forestry Minister, Sudjurmo, claimed there was 'no conclusive proof' of how the fires started, but drought and 'nomadic cultivators who used outdated [slash and burn] techniques' were the major factors. He made no mention of the role played by the logging industry.[199]

There is little doubt that the initial spark was provided by slash and burn farmers but to blame them *en masse* is simplistic. The number of shifting cultivators in East Kalimantan has increased dramatically since the 1970s, when it was the main destination for transmigrants and freelance settlers. As a local researcher Cynthia Mackie notes:

> While subsistence farmers account for some of the forest clearing and burning occurring, an undetermined proportion also results from entrepreneurs such as peppercorn growers and middle class land speculators.[200]

Pioneer settlements are generally located along logging roads or near timber camps, in the heart of the logged-over forest. By comparison, traditional Dayak farmers cultivate near rivers and generally avoid logging concession land if possible. They also have a detailed knowledge of how to control fires.

The authorities took a very relaxed view of the fire, as an extract from an interview with Minister Sudjurmo illustrates:

> Much of the area that was burnt was conversion forest [for transmigration sites]. So what you have is land clearing for free. The forest fire was the natural way of clearing the land.[201]

According to the German study, however, these potential transmigration sites have soils that are experiencing: 'rapid mineralization and increased rates of leaching of nutrients . . . increased erosion and . . . irreversible physical, chemical and morphological changes.'[202]

To summarize, the forests of East Kalimantan have been exploited in an uncontrolled and destructive manner. The TPI selective felling system proved to be a failure in that it took no account of the widespread environmental destruction caused by modern logging methods. In addition, it was based on a 35 year cycle but implemented by corporations who never had the remotest intention of staying that length of time. They left behind not only a grossly over-cut forest but also a tinderbox waiting for a match. The drought intensified the situation and the initial flames of the fire were probably set by migrant farmers.

Underlying all this is the fact that the major decisions affecting this area were imposed from outside. There is no one cause for the problems, but many different contributory factors. The authorities, however, failed to recognize the cumulative effects of their policies on the forests and the local populations.

Saving Siberut

Siberut island is part of the tiny Mentawi group off the coast of Sumatra; it is the largest island covering 4,500 sq. km, with a population of 18,000.[203] The island has a rather unusual forest structure in which the ridges are dominated by dipterocarp species while the lower areas have no single tree family in abundance;[204] there are also freshwater-swamp forests and mangroves. For an island of this size its wildlife is unique: 25 of the island's mammals are endemic and this includes all four primates.[205] Siberut is the smallest island in the world to have its own primates.

The island has been populated for more than 2,000 years but until recently this has had little impact on the forests. Traditional society in the islands is based on shifting agriculture, fishing and hunting. The social group is the longhouse, similar to those found in Kalimantan.

Major crops are sago palm, bananas and taro, intercropped with fruit trees. The island's people relied heavily on the forest for their other needs. They shifted their small fields or *ladangs* regularly, before crop yields dropped. *Ladangs* rarely exceeded half a hectare and little or no burning took place. The crops chosen enjoyed shade, so there was no need to clear large trees; they also demanded few nutrients. Instead of burning debris, undergrowth was left to provide an *in situ* source of compost. Once abandoned, the forest quickly recovered and the fruit groves are a popular source of food for the island's mammals.[206]

According to the WWF the island has five grades of forest:

1) *Undisturbed*: virgin forest that has experienced no major human activity apart from hunting and the removal of occasional *sal* trees, which are ideal for making canoes. This forest type covers 291,300 ha, but most is leased out for future logging.

2) *Moderately disturbed*: noticeable human influence where timber has been extracted for local use or has been partially cleared for traditional agriculture. This accounts for 71,700 ha.

3) *Very disturbed*: a more intense version of type two and includes areas

adjacent to villages or currently under traditional agriculture.

4) *Totally disturbed*: areas under newly imposed permanent agriculture schemes, mostly as government development projects.

5) *Logged over*: areas that have been disturbed by the timber industry.

The government estimates that 35,700 ha have been converted to permanent agriculture and 10,000 are officially protected;[207] the remainder of the islands' forests they regard as viable for logging.

Since the 1960s most longhouse communities have been moved into the 50 government style villages.[208] Although not admitted officially, this can be seen as a move to make way for the timber industry that became established on Siberut during the 1970s. Having the power to use forest land for the 'welfare' of the people the Forest Department gave logging rights for almost 90% of the island to four timber companies.[209] The local population had land rights, but the authorities were empowered to claim rights over the timber, not the land. By not claiming actual ownership the government avoided paying compensation.

As logging became established, forced relocation of entire villages became commonplace.[210] Many of the present villages on the coasts were established by this means; farmers are 'encouraged' to practise wet rice paddy cultivation. As Catherine Caufield notes:

> Rice, a more 'civilised' crop is replacing sago palm though rice requires more labour input for a lower yield. There is less time for hunting and, because the villages are concentrated, the hunting area is smaller and overexploited. The traditional taboos that prevented over-hunting are being forgotten. Due to poor rice harvests the villagers depend more and more on store-bought goods.[211]

Bananas, sugar cane, cassava and cloves are grown in addition to rice. Cloves, needing well-drained, fertile soils and unable to tolerate shade, have proved to be a particularly damaging crop. They are promoted as a cash crop to provide the local population with an income, but the gains are minimal, since planting the crop requires total clearance of the forest. The trade in rattans from the island exceeded US$165,000 (175 rupees) between 1975 and 1977, even with severely restricted access to forest areas;[212] this considerable income is now denied to villagers. The loss might have been cushioned if the logging companies had provided employment, but less than 5% of the timber workforce is from Siberut,[213] most is from the Philippines.

This lack of employment is partly because companies regard the locals as unreliable, and partly because many villagers do not wish to work in the industry.[214] For the local population the timber industry provides limited seasonal employment and they will work only to earn enough money for some item they particularly want; once the necessary sum has been earned they see no reason to continue with the job; furthermore they also regard the work as very poorly paid. There has also been widespread opposition to companies refusing local workers time to carry out religious ceremonies to appease the spirits of the trees before they cut them down. And antagonism between the two groups has been increased by logging companies destroying fruit groves and *ladang* sites.

The environmental damage has been considerable, as the President of Survival International noted:

> I visited one of the Filipino [Philippine] camps walking inland from a beach where my friends wept to see the total destruction of a place they said had once been the most beautiful spot on the island. An idyllic coral reef and sandy beach had been totally destroyed by bulldozers and dynamite to make a landing stage. We made our way for mile after mile through a nightmare landscape that looked as though it had been hit by a bomb.[215]

A WWF report notes that 'logging on Siberut with its . . . mining approach ensures that the forest becomes a non-renewable resource.' They continue:

> Maps of concession boundaries are plentiful but no two are the same and they are rarely followed closely. In one company for example, the concession map in the manager's office shows an allocation of 40,000 hectares, not the published 35,000 hectares. This company has also logged outside their concession to the north accounting for an estimated 6,000 hectares.[216]

Despite the obvious exploitation, the timber companies have been running at a loss and during the late 1970s, 25% of felled timber was left to rot.[217]

Future prospects: The Indonesian government asked the WWF and Survival International to produce an alternative development plan for the island. The resultant plan divided the island into a 1,000 sq. mile development zone; a 400 sq. mile traditional land use zone; and a 200 sq. mile nature reserve.[218] The project was launched, but the government agreed only to the nature reserve. A number of research projects were initiated in the non-designated traditional land use zone but the project manager claims: 'the minute our full-time person left the loggers came in again. They are in a hurry to destroy as much as possible before we get our act together.'[219]

References

1. *Asiaweek*, 1986, 4 May.
2. Government of Indonesia (GOI), and International Institute for Environment and Development (IIED), 1985.
3. Astbury, S. 1984.
4. UNESCO, 1983.
5. Wheller, T. 1985.
6. GOI and IIED, Vol. 3, p. 4.
7. Hayter, T. 1985.
8. Pramoedya Ananta Tuer, quoted in Osborne, R. 1985.
9. Osborne, R. 1985.
10. Ibid.
11. FAO, 1981.
12. GOI and IIED, 1985.
13. Goodland, R. 1981.
14. Haeruman, H. 1983.
15. Ibid.
16. Goodland, R. 1981(a).
17. GOI and IIED, 1985.
18. Secrett, C. 1986.
19. FAO, 1981.
20. GOI and IIED, 1985.
21. Jhamtani, H. and E. Hafield, 1986.
22. Ibid.
23. Ibid.
24. GOI and IIED, 1985.
25. Ibid.
26. GOI and IIED, op. cit.
27. FAO, 1981.
28. Caufield, C. 1985; and GOI and IIED, 1985.
29. Myers, N. 1984.
30. GOI and IIED, 1985.
31. Ibid.
32. Hafield, N. 1986.
33. Guppy, N. 1984.
34. Poore, D. 1984.
35. Bird, E. and O. Owgkosongo, 1981.
36. Adittondro, G. no date.
37. GOI and IIED, 1985.
38. Adittondro, G. no date.
39. Secrett, C. 1986.
40. GOI and IIED, 1985.
41. Kartawinata, K. no date.
42. *Asiaweek*, 1984, 13 July.
43. Mackie, C. 1984.
44. Lennertz, R. and K. Panzer, 1983.
45. Goodland, R. 1981.
46. Caufield, C. 1985.
47. Secrett, C. 1986.
48. World Wildlife Fund (WWF) 1984.
49. Hafield, N. 1986.
50. Kartawinata, K. no date.

51. Ibid.
52. WWF (Indonesia) 1984.
53. Kartawinata, K. no date.
54. Hanbury-Tenison, R. 1975.
55. GOI and IIED, 1985.
56. Ibid.
57. Adittondro, G. 1979.
58. Ibid.
59. Ibid.
60. De Beer, J. and M. McDermott, 1989.
61. Myers, N. 1984.
62. *Sarawak Tribune*, 1986, 11 October
63. GOI and IIED, 1985.
64. Colchester, M. 1986(a).
65. Ibid. (Quoted from Achemidi).
66. Plumwood, V. and R. Routley, 1982.
67. Osborne, R. 1985.
68. Adittondro, G. 1979.
69. Colchester, M. 1986(b).
70. Ibid.
71. Adittondro, G. 1979.
72. SKEPHI, 1985.
73. GOI and IIED, op. cit.
74. Ibid.
75. Ibid.
76. Soewardi, B. 1983.
77. Jhamtani, H. and E. Hafield, 1986.
78. Secrett, C. 1986.
79. Plumwood, V. and R. Routley, 1982.
80. Nash, S. and A. Nash, 1985.
81. Caufield, C. 1985.
82. Whitmore, T. ibid.
83. Secrett, C. 1986.
84. Ibid.
85. FAO, 1986.
86. GOI and IIED, 1985.
87. Warner, K. 1988.
88. World Bank, 1988.
89. Ibid., 1986.
90. GOI and IIED, 1985.
91. World Bank, 1986.
92. GOI and IIED, 1985.
93. *AMPO*, 198, Vol. 12, No. 4.
94. Soedjarwo, 1985.
95. GOI and IIED, 1985.
96. Kartawinata, K. and A. P. Vayda, 1986.
97. Goodland, R. no date.
98. Hafield, N. 1986.
99. Eckholm, E. 1979.
100. GOI and IIED, 1985.
101. Nash, S. and A. Nash, 1985.
102. Soenarso, R. and Sampe Radja, 1979.
103. Kartawinata, K. et. al., 1981.

104. SKEPHI, 1985.
105. Ibid.
106. Soenarso, R. and Sampe Radja, 1979.
107. Ibid.
108. Kartawinata, K. et al, no date.
109. Adittondro, G. 1979.
110. World Bank, 1986.
111. GOI and IIED, 1985.
112. World Bank, 1986.
113. Ibid.
114. World Bank, 1988; Repeto, R. 1986.
115. World Bank, 1986.
116. Ibid.
117. *Timber Trade Review*, 1984, Vol. 13, No. 3.
118. World Bank, 1986.
119. Repeto, R.
120. Arndt, H. 1983.
121. GOI and IIED, op. cit.
122. Osborne, R. op. cit, quotes 5-Year National Development Plan 1984–89.
123. Osborne, R. op. cit.
124. Secrett, C. op. cit.
125. Arndt, H. op. cit.
126. Ibid.
127. Secrett, C. op. cit.
128. Ibid.
129. GOI and IIED, op. cit.
130. Johnson, B. 1985; and Secrett, C. op. cit.
131. Secrett, C. op. cit.
132. Ibid.
133. *Far Eastern Economic Review*, 1985, 7 February.
134. Adittondro, G. 1986.
135. Budiardjo, C. in Otten, M. 1986.
136. Secrett, C. op. cit.
137. Adittondro, G. 1986.
138. Bonner, R. 1988.
139. Arndt, H. op. cit.
140. Martono, quoted in G. Adittondro, 1986.
141. *Jakarta Post*, 1986, 11 January.
142. Otten, M. 1986.
143. Wienstock, J. 1979.
144. Colchester, M. 1986(b).
145. Ibid.
146. Ibid.
147. Ibid.
148. *Jakarta Post*, 1985, 5 July.
149. Adittondro, G. 1986.
150. Osborne, R. op. cit.
151. Adittondro, G. 1986.
152. Arndt, H. op. cit.
153. Ibid.
154. Secrett, C. op. cit.
155. Ibid.
156. GOI and IIED, op. cit.

157. World Bank, 1985.
158. Secrett, C. op. cit.
159. GOI and IIED, op. cit.
160. Emil Salim, quoted in M. Otten. 1986.
161. Soewardi, B. op. cit.
162. Westoby, J. quoted in Secrett, C., op. cit.
163. Kartawinata, K. and A. Vayda, op. cit.
164. SKEPHI, op. cit.
165. World Bank, 1988.
166. Mackie, C. op. cit.
167. Gradwohl, J. et al, 1988.
168. Ibid.
169. Goodland, R. op. cit.
170. Ibid.
171. Kartawinata, K. et. al., op. cit.
172. Ibid.
173. Romm, J. 1980; GOI and IIED, op. cit.
174. GOI and IIED, op. cit.
175. Kartawinata, K. et. al., op. cit.
176. GOI and IIED, op. cit.
177. Plumwood, V. and R. Routley, op. cit.
178. Myers, N. 1980.
179. Guppy, N. op. cit.
180. Myers, N. 1980.
181. Guppy N. op. cit.
182. Myers, N. 1980.
183. Ibid.
184. Ibid.
185. Guppy, N. op. cit.
186. SKEPHI, op. cit.
187. Adittondro, G. 1979.
188. SKEPHI, op. cit.
189. Ibid.
190. Ibid.
191. Lennertz, R. and K. Panzer, op. cit.
192. Ibid.
193. Ibid.
194. Ibid.
195. Klaverkamp, R. 1984.
196. Lennertz, R. and K. Panzer, op. cit.
197. Ibid.
198. Ibid.
199. Klaverkamp, R. op. cit.
200. Mackie, C. op. cit.
201. Klaverkamp, R. op. cit.
202. Lennertz, R. and K. Panzer, op. cit.
203. WWF, 1980.
204. Ibid.
205. Myers, N. 1984.
206. WWF, 1980.
207. Ibid.
208. Caufield, C. op. cit.
209. WWF, 1980.

210. Plumwood, V. and R. Routley, op. cit.
211. Caufield, C. op. cit.
212. WWF, 1980.
213. Ibid.
214. Agusing. quoted in WWF, 1980.
215. Hanbury-Tenison, R. op. cit.
216. WWF, 1980.
217. Ibid.
218. Caufield, C. op. cit.
219. Fernhaut, A. quoted in Caufield, C. op. cit.

2. Malaysia: West Malaysia

Malaysia is divided into two distinct regions, West Malaysia, covering the Malay Peninsular, and East Malaysia, occupying North Borneo. Together they cover a land area of 330,000 sq. km.

Politically, Malaysia is structured as a federation of eleven states with a constitutional monarchy, but individual state governments have a high degree of autonomy, particularly on forestry issues. Apart from very basic political similarities East and West Malaysia can be regarded as separate entities. The cultures and the economies of the two areas vary significantly, and geographically they are separated by 600 km of the South China Sea.

Introduction

From its northern borders with Thailand to those of the island republic of Singapore in the south, West Malaysia occupies 131,700 sq. km. In its natural state much of this area is swampy lowland, although the Barisan Titiwangsa mountains form a backbone.

With a population of 15m, West Malaysia is unique to Asia in that the government has a positive population expansion programme. The more children a family has the greater the financial help from the federal government. The stated goal is to reach a population of 70m. Nobody is certain why this figure was chosen or what its long-term economic implications may be.

West Malaysia has the highest standard of living in South-East Asia. This is primarily due to rich natural resources, a small population and a rapidly expanding economy. Replacing natural forest with oil palm and rubber estates undoubtedly played a significant role in its development. Today, however, these estates are maintained more for political and social rather than economic aims. The international rubber and palm oil markets have collapsed and West Malaysia is basing its economic future on hi-tech industries; already it is the largest producer of computer micro-chips in the Far East. With the urban population comprising 37% of the total, West Malaysia is rapidly developing into an industrial society.[1]

In cultural terms, West Malaysia has extremely large minorities of Chinese and Indians, with Malays making up 60% of the population. This mixture has proved volatile, despite an outward appearance of calm. A major factor is that the Chinese are very much in control of the economy, while the Malays, or *Bumiputeras* (translated as 'sons of the earth') control the political arena. The Malay-dominated government has tried to redress this financial imbalance with its highly controversial New Economic Policy, which gives *Bumiputeras* great advantages in education and business that are regarded by many Chinese as unfair. Within the Malay political scene a power struggle is developing between those wishing to follow the growing trend towards a more fundamentalist Muslim state and those seeking a more Western style development. The result is a bizarre mixture of magnificent mosques alongside MacDonald hamburger bars.

Traditionally, West Malaysia was a seafaring society, relying more on trade than on opening up the interior for agriculture. This was in part due to its geographical location, separating the Indian Ocean and the South China Sea. Another factor was perhaps the absence of broad rivers with fertile flood plains, similar to those that supplied the needs of the Thai and Javanese rice cultures.

In common with other seafaring societies, West Malaysia was strongly influenced by a constant stream of traders from other cultures. Both the Hindu and Buddhist religions came to West Malaysia before being superseded by the Muslim faith in the 13th century. The original Muslim stronghold of Malacca emerged as the centre of a new trading empire stretching from Sumatra to Borneo and comprising a loose affiliation of sultanates that remained intact until the second half of the 18th century. The Portuguese took control of Malacca in the 16th century but had little immediate effect over the empire as a whole. In the longer term, however, the European arrival heralded the slow decay of the Malacca Empire. In the early 19th century the British and Dutch intervened, and Malaya, as it was known then, became a colony. The political organization through sultanate states, however, continues to dominate West Malaysia.

In the early 19th century the British gained control of the ports of Penang and Malacca, before establishing Singapore. The peninsula had been claimed by the Dutch but it was exchanged for Sumatra. The British showed little interest in the interior until the latter half of the 19th century, when the Malacca empire collapsed and the sultans resorted to piracy – an activity not tolerated by the British as it affected trade. To stabilize an unruly sultanate the British moved into any area in which piracy was taking place and restored law and order by force. In return they demanded that the sultan concerned should have a 'Resident' as an adviser. Once appointed, the sultan could pass laws and judgements only with the Resident's approval, except for strictly Muslim affairs, which were left in the hands of the sultans. With the all-embracing aspects of Islam this effectively kept the Muslim

Malays out of the British colonial system.

The Malay Peninsula already had a significant Chinese population that expanded rapidly under the British. General trade and tin exports formed the backbone of the Malaysian eocnomy during early colonial times. The British worked closely with the Chinese in developing tin and rubber, thus establishing a typical divide and rule system between the Malays and the Chinese.

Rubber: The expansion of rubber plantations marked the first mass clearance of forest in Malyasia. Rubber was introduced in 1884 by Sir Huw Low, Resident with the Sultan of Perak,[2] beginning with twelve rubber seeds brought in from their native Brazil, via London. Sir Huw Low's experiment proved a success and the tree rapidly emerged as a major cash crop. The British encouraged sultanate states to sell their land, and provided considerable tax incentives if the new owners planted rubber. Since the concept of large-scale land ownership was alien to the Malay culture, selling something one did not own must have seemed very profitable. With the Residents giving advice on such matters the expansion of rubber was dramatic. By the 1950s tin and rubber accounted for more than 85% of Malaysia's exports and the crop covered more than 15,000 sq. km of the Peninsula.[3]

At one point, however, the British almost abandoned rubber. The rapid clearance of forest created an ideal habitat for mosquitoes and thousands of plantation workers died of malaria. The problem became so serious that the London School of Tropical Medicine was established primarily to solve the problem of this new epidemic.

Throughout the first half of the 20th century there was a shortage of labour, so immigrants from Tamil Nadu in southern India were encouraged to come and work on the plantations. Escaping what many regarded as an oppressive system in India they were willing to work for pitifully meagre wages.

The British attitude to managing the Malay economy was to keep down the cost of raw material for the British consumer. To this end, individual states were not allowed to tax rubber, but if the end consumer of any product was Asian, the British enforced heavy taxation. Opium, a drug actively encouraged by the British throughout the Far East, was thus heavily taxed; if a state wanted to raise cash it did so by increasing the tax on opium. Thus, local development not associated with rubber had to rely on tax revenues from opium addicts. West Malaysia continues to have major heroin and opium addiction problems despite severe penalties for smuggling or use of these drugs.

With independence, in 1957, West Malaysia continued to follow the economic pattern initiated by the British. Rubber plantations continued to dominate the economy until the emergence of the international timber trade in the 1960s.

Present forest resources
In 1984, the government classified 48% of West Malaysia as 'Forested Land'.[4] The major forest types include mangrove, swamp, lowland and hill dipterocarp and montane. West Malaysian forests, like those in parts of Indonesia, are regarded as possibly among the most diverse found anywhere on earth.

The present classification of forests in Malaysia as a whole is confusing as a new system is being introduced. Eventually all land with forest, including plantations, will be classed as part of the 'Permanent forest estate'. This is a rather misleading term since it includes forest areas that may be cleared for agricultural projects or plantations. There is nothing permanent about their status.

Within the permanent forest estate are three major classifications: forest reserve; stateland forest; and wildlife and other reserves. The forest reserve covers areas that should remain as forest and are unsuitable for other land uses. This ensures that forest cover is maintained, but reclassification is a simple process. Stateland forests are areas still owned by the individual states which, eventually, will be classified as either land suitable for conversion to agriculture, part of the forest reserve or as wildlife areas of some kind. In other words it is a temporary classification left over from the old system. Wildlife and other reserves are generally safe from commercial exploitation, although their protected status can also be changed extremely quickly. According to the Forestry Department's Annual Report for 1984, the relative areas of classification are as follows: Permanent forest estate: forest reserve, 29,996 sq. km; stateland forest, 20,500 sq. km; wildlife and other reserves, 5,497 sq. km; awaiting classification (old stateland), 6,827 sq. km; making a total of 62,820 sq. km of forest in West Malaysia.

The forest reserve is split into 'productive', that is open to logging, and 'protective', which should remain intact as it encompasses vital water catchment areas or steep slopes. West Malaysia has 21,159 sq. km of 'productive' forest and 8,837 sq. km designated as 'protective'.[5]

How large an area of virgin or untouched forest remains is the centre of a hot debate. Most foresters classify any area that has not had significant human activity for at least 80 years as virgin. Many ecologists would not agree, but the authorities cannot reach agreement even with this liberal classification. In 1978 Dr Salleh Nor, Director of the Forestry Research Institute claimed that the total area of 'virgin forest' in West Malaysia was 1,800 sq. km.[6] By 1981, the same Institute, in their promotional literature, claimed that West Malaysia had 2,900 sq. km of virgin forest.[7] The logging industry cuts 149,000 ha of forest annually of which half could be classified as 'virgin'.[8]

Deforestation
West Malaysia has probably the most reliable forest loss figures in Asia,

because most forest destruction is government controlled. Government agricultural development projects, co-ordinated by the Federal Land Development Agency (FELDA), cleared approximately 100,000 ha annually throughout the 1970s.[9] The FAO estimated that an additional 10,000 ha per year were lost to roads and mining.[10] Between 1980 and 1985 a further 417,000 ha were cleared, mainly for agricultural expansion.[11]

FELDA continues clearance at an annual rate of 60,000 ha for the 1986–90 five year plan.[12] Whether or not this target will be achieved is open to debate, since the agency underwent a crisis in late 1986 and its future is uncertain.

Replanting

There is very little replanting of timber species at present. By 1984 fast-growing softwood plantations covered 6,750 ha.[13] The timber industry practises enrichment planting to sustain supplies but on a small scale. From 1971 to 1980 some 47,000 ha had enrichment planting of chosen species.[14] With logging affecting approximately 300,000 ha each year throughout the 1970s and 200,000 ha during the early 1980s, replanting is clearly not a high priority with the Malaysian timber industry.[15] Logging is now restricted to 149,000 ha per year, but the replanting programme has little chance of compensating for the damage.

In the mid-1980s the government became desperately anxious about the continued existence of timber supplies for the future and proposed to establish 188,183 ha of timber plantation by 1995.[16] If this is to be implemented a major change in attitude is required within the West Malaysian timber industry.

Despite this gloomy outlook, forest destruction in West Malaysia is not as bad as it is in many other countries, because most agricultural expansion replaces natural forest with oil palm or rubber trees. These tree crops may be regarded as a type of forest as they are able to provide some of the environmental functions that natural forests perform. This is a great improvement on replacing forest with other cash crops but it justifies little of the present destruction.

In terms of silviculture and developing sustainable timber supplies, the Malaysian timber industry is one of the most advanced in the region. There is, however, a great disparity between the considerable research work carried out by government bodies and the activities of loggers at the ground level.

Effects of forest loss

Environmental costs

Due to the policy of replacing natural forest with tree plantations West

Malaysia's experience of environmental problems has been less intense than that of its neighbours. In addition, the effect of these changes on the population as a whole has been softened by increasing urbanization.

Research into what follows clearance of natural forest for plantations is, however, clearly lacking. Limited studies have been carried out since the 1950s but none on a national scale, and Malaysia has no classification system for the condition of its vital watersheds.

Soil loss and erosion: The Klang river passes through Kuala Lumpur, the capital city of Malaysia, and urban expansion into its catchment area has led to a massive increase in the silt load as forests are cleared. The Environmental Protection Society of Malaysia (EPSM) found that between 1975 and 1977, the silt load of the river doubled.[17] Each year the river carries approximately 10m tons of silt through the capital, but EPSM are quick to point out that this probably accounts for only 10% to 20% of the total soil loss from the catchment slopes.[18] A comparative study, also by EPSM, on the forested Sungei Cerul river in Kelantan revealed that sediment loads in the Sungei Cerul were approximately 625 times less than in the Klang.[19] A similar study by the University of Malaysia measured soil loss from an area totally cleared of trees: the land had a 17% slope and, after clearance, lost 43,500 kg of soil per ha during the 60 days of the study.[20]

Total clearance of forest may be regarded as atypical as replacement with plantations is more usual. Table 3.1, however, illustrates that, even under mature tree plantations, soil loss can more than double that in forested areas. Conversion to non-tree crops increases soil erosion dramatically, as Shallow recorded in the Cameroon Highlands where, on land converted into tea plantation, soil loss increased 20 fold, and 30 fold if converted to vegetable cultivation.[21]

Sedimentation: The other main land-use is selective logging. The effect from this industry is of particular interest since it is now concentrated in the hills and encompasses many vital water catchment areas. Studies in Kelantan found that selective logging of 35% of the catchment area increased sediment loads in the rivers three-fold and 25-fold when the entire area was selectively felled.[22]

The Klang river, a major trade route for barges transporting tin during colonial times, is now so shallow that even small craft can no longer reach the old quays upstream.[23] Further up-river the capacity of the Klang Gates Dam reservoir has also been reduced through excessive sedimentation.[24]

Sedimentation also increases the likelihood of flooding due to reducing the volume of water the river banks can effectively contain. In 1979 the Kelantan river burst its banks, flooding a large area including the city of Kota Baru. The river mouth was so clogged that the floods subsided only when the army blasted the channel clear.[25]

The problem of flash flooding is such that the government has established more than 1,200 evacuation centres capable of housing 411,000 flood victims at any one time.[26] In December 1986 all the major rivers in the states of Terenganu and Kelantan flooded,[27] with the result that ten people died, 20,000 were evacuated and more than 500 homes were destroyed. Damage to the general infrastructure of schools, roads and so on, was estimated at more than M$10m (US$4m);[28] the total cost in terms of crops and housing destroyed was considerably more. Along the Sungai Terenganu, one village lost most of its housing in the November floods and the remaining 50 were washed away in December.[29]

Flash flooding outside the rainy season can be equally devastating. In May 1986 farmers around Malacca lost an estimated M$2m worth of tobacco crops and more than M$200,000 worth of market vegetables to unseasonal flash floods.[30] Even in the major cities, flooding is accepted as part of everyday life; the poorer districts of all the major cities experience regular flooding, causing untold damage to property. West Malaysia also experiences the other extreme: drought.

Drought: Due to its geographical position West Malaysia can experience unusual contrasts in weather conditions between its east and west coasts. These, however, have become more extreme with the clearance of forests. While the front page headlines of the *Daily Star* (Malaysia) newspaper reported the 1986 flooding (mentioned above) page 12 carried an article on how the Mada Agricultural Development Agency was about to artificially induce rain, at great expense, to relieve the drought in Kedah and Peralis.[31] Rice farmers in these two states were about to lose M$100m worth of crops.[32] The Kedah state government had just begun to construct 13 major water supply and irrigation projects costing more than M$100m.[33] The irony is more apparent when it is remembered that Malaysia is one of the wettest countries in the world.

These problems are not new and the media has commented on the lack of any long-term proposals to eliminate the root cause of these cycles. As an editorial in the *New Straits Times* noted, in 1977:

> Our water problem is usually one of too much or too little. . . . Dry spells are fairly common in Malaysia. Yet each time they happen we never fail to go through the well rehearsed responses that just barely serve to keep the problem within endurable limits without in any way helping us towards a long term solution.[34]

Climate: West Malaysian weather is difficult to predict but Dr Goh Kim Chum of the University Sams Malaysia claims that the Peninsular has experienced a general decline in rainfall since the mid-1960s.[35] Studies from the same University also indicate that between 1975 and 1979, rainfall in the

Klang Gate reservoir catchment decreased by 30%[36] – coinciding exactly with forest clearance in the area.

Even when forest is converted into rubber plantation changes in rainfall patterns have been recorded. As far back as 1969 a UNESCO report on climactic changes in West Malaysian rubber plantations noted: 'While the total annual rainfall appeared to remain unaffected, the number of rainfall incidents decreased and the intensity per rainfall increased.'[37]

With rubber and oil palm plantations covering 17,000 sq. km of West Malaysia, the conditions for producing this flood/drought cycle have been established over an extremely large area.

Wildlife loss: The forests of the Malay Peninsula are frequently cited as the most biologically diverse on earth. The following figures indicate what has been classified to date: West Malaysia has at least 7,900 species of flowering plants,[38] of which 2,500 are trees.[39] More than 5,000 species of algae have been identified, almost one-third of the world's total. The Peninsula can claim more than 207 species of mammals, 495 of birds and 250 of fresh-water fish. To date 150,000 insect species have been classified and 25,000 other invertebrates.[40]

With such diversity the density of individuals of any one species is generally low. On an average 20 ha site in the state of Pahang one study found 375 tree species that reached the canopy,[41] that is, excluding smaller species or young trees that had not reached such heights.

Lowland forest is particularly rich and is the exclusive habitat for 80% of the Peninsula's mammals and 70% of its birds.[42] This forest type has suffered greatly with the expansion of agriculture and the Malaysian Nature Society recently noted that 61 species of mammals and 16 of birds were on the verge of extinction. A further 130 mammal and 148 bird species are considered 'vulnerable'; that is, having a total world population of less than 3,000 individuals.[43] The best-known species under severe threat of extinction are perhaps the Sumatran rhino, with only 50–80 individuals remaining, and the tiger, down to 250 in 1982.[44]

Logging and wildlife: Many species do not survive in forest that has been logged. The rhino and tiger are two examples, along with the Malaysian honey bear.

The numbers of primates also tend to decline after logging. Table 3.2 outlines the results from a comparative primate survey in one area prior to it being selectively logged in 1958 and then in 1975. Despite the area having had minimal human activity between these dates an estimated 50% of the forest canopy was still open in 1975.[45] Resilience to logging varies between primates. The white-handed gibbon population dropped by 50%; these primates are strongly territorial and usually refuse to move out of an area; their decline was probably due to increasing numbers of young dying as a result of falls as their mothers attempted to leap increasing distances from tree to tree.[46] Siamang monkeys declined by 56% and dusky-leaf monkeys by 49%; but long-tailed macaques declined by only 23%.

Hunting increases the problems faced by wildlife as logging roads open up new areas. One of the world's largest markets for wildlife produce is Singapore, and this increases the pressure on rare species still further.

Social and economic costs

Environmental degradation affects a large proportion of West Malaysian society; for a few it threatens their way of life. Still living in the forests is a small population of indigenous tribal groups, known collectively as the Orang Asli, comprising three major groups: the Senoi; the Melayu Asli; and the Negritos. In 1980 their populations were estimated as: Senoi 36,000; Melayu 24,000 and Negritos 2,000.[47]

The Senoi practise swidden farming under a long-cycle system. Forest is cut and burned, a large variety of crops is grown and the area is then abandoned for as long as possible. The Negritos are more nomadic, cultivating forest gardens and relying mainly on hunting and gathering. Both groups have considerable knowledge of forest produce, and various anthropological studies have found that they use more than 1,280 forest plants as well as timber.[48] The Melayu practise wet rice paddy farming and are thus slightly more removed from the forests than the other two groups.

All three groups have always been in contact with the lowland Muslim populations although not always on a peaceful basis. The Muslim Malays established a thriving slave trade in Orang Asli that continued until the end of the 19th century. Reportedly, the Orang Asli were very much in favour of British colonialism since it liberated them from enslavement; upon emancipation many returned to their more traditional way of life.[49] The relationship between Malays and the Orang Asli has not always been based on a slave and master race, both groups have traded in forest produce for centuries. Even today, if the Orang Asli have access to intact forest resoures they can maintain a reasonable cash income.

The old attitude of slave and master, however, dies hard and Orang Asli are undoubtedly regarded by many as a liability to modern Malaysia. In legal terms they are not considered *Bumiputeras* since they do not follow the Muslim faith. As a result they cannot own land and have no access to the development benefits enjoyed by many poor Muslim Malays. They have no representation within the Federal Government. Responsibility for their well-being and development lies with state ministers, who usually have a wide variety of other tasks to carry out. They are the forgotten people of West Malaysia.

The denial of any rights to the land they have traditionally inhabited has had a profoundly damaging effect on these people. Conditions among the Batek De Negritos in south-east Kelantan have been studied in some detail. In their area logging became established in the 1970s but they have never been offered compensation. Despite the timber industry's claim to practise sustainable selective felling, the damage to the environment in this area has been considerable, as Professor Endicot notes:

> While logging companies agree to undertake a certain amount of reafforestation on their concession areas it is well known in Kelantan that compliance is minimal. In general the logging is done clear cutting rather than selective cutting and no attention is paid to preventing erosion or removing the debris after the forest is destroyed.[50]

Rather than confront the logging companies, the Batek have moved uphill. With reduced access to forests their cash income declined and many of their forest gardens were destroyed. At present the group is in a stage of transition: some have moved into Taman Negara national park, others have abandoned their nomadic lifestyle and live in settlements provided by the Malaysian Department of Aboriginal Affairs. The settled lifestyle is not popular with the Batek and, in order to survive, they are clearing forest around the site at Post Lebir to plant rice and other crops. With no source of cash they have to wait for department hand-outs and have thus become a burden on the state. The Batek undoubtedly regard the quality of life on the settlements as being lower than they had enjoyed in the forests. Most of the young men are leaving Post Lebir for the towns or to join the army.

Evidence for this decline in living standards is confirmed by a recent survey by the Faculty of Medicine at the University Kebangsaan Malaysia, which concluded that: 'Resettlement of the Orang Asli has not improved, or may even retard, their nutritional status.'[51] The survey covered 24 settled Orang Asli villages throughout West Malaysia. Of the 500 children under the age of ten who were monitored it was found that: 57% were underweight and a further 21% 'severely undernourished' (according to WHO criteria)[52] and that: 'The prevalence of severe malnutrition is still very high, even higher than the poverty in Malay villages.'[53]

For those who wish to retain a more traditional lifestyle, moving out of their traditional areas is only a temporary solution. Taman Negara national park and the few other wildlife areas on the Malay peninsula are coming under increasing pressure with the recent influx of tribal groups. The population densities in these areas are rapidly becoming too high to support the traditional lifestyle of these people. The Orang Asli, however, are not the only social group reliant on forests for their livelihood. West Malaysia's forests have become so depleted that the economic base of the timber industry is also under threat.

Timber job losses: The West Malaysian timber industry is in a serious decline. The general world recession has been held responsible for the decrease in exports but there is also a shortage of commercial timbers due to over-exploitation. The problems are perhaps best illustrated by looking at the recent history of the timber industry in the state of Johore.

In 1981, Johore produced 21% of the Peninsula's timber, making it the most productive state in West Malaysia.[54] The Malaysian Timber Industries Board reported that in 1982 Johore's saw-mills 'were operating in excess of their capacity'.[55] In 1983 the state suspended the issue of new saw-mill licences, foreseeing a future timber shortage if cutting continued as its then current pace.[56] By 1985 the Malaysian *Business Times* reported that, 'at least 40 of the 80 mills in the state have closed down with losses running into millions of ringit [Malaysian dollars].'[57] More than 4,000 jobs were lost. The authorities admit that almost all the remaining saw-mills are working well below capacity[58] and, despite a slight recovery in early 1986, this trend has continued. The decline also hit Johore's timber export traders and by 1986 only 35 of the state's 360 registered exporters were still in business.[59]

A similar recession occurred throughout West Malaysia, with the closure of 200 saw-mills in 1984 alone.[60] A survey by the Malaysian Timber Industries Board on problems the industry faced in 1983 concluded that: 'The problem in securing raw materials which the saw-milling industry is facing at the present was also again the major problem anticipated in future.'[61] Since the early 1980s, tens of thousands of jobs in the industry have been lost.[62]

Log poaching between states has also been increasing as mills vie with one another for supplies. This became such a widespread problem that the Malaysians even developed a name for this new phenomenon, *pajak*.[63]

West Malaysia has been importing timber since 1978, mainly from East Malaysia and Indonesia. The Forestry Department estimates that by 1990 the Peninsula will be a net importer of logs.[64] In 1986 West Malaysia had a production deficit of more than 600,000 cu metres. A sorry state of affairs for an area in which timber exports in 1984 earned them more than M$4.2 billion (US$1.7 billion).[65]

The loss of export revenue from timber has disturbing implications for a country that already has a considerable national debt. The economic costs, however, extend beyond the loss of export earnings. The Forestry Department has launched a massive replanting programme estimated to cost M$571m (US$225m) to initiate, and an annual M$10m (US$4m) to maintain.[66] This money, borrowed from the Asian Development Bank, further increases Malaysia's foreign debts. For many years the West Malaysian timber industry took pride in having few of the problems faced by its contemporaries in Asia, but recent developments now suggest otherwise.

Mangroves and fishermen: An estimated 110,000 ha of mangrove remain around the coasts of West Malaysia. Over the 1970s and 1980s approximately 1,000 ha have been cleared each year for industrial expansion.[67] More recently, however, timber companies have expanded into mangrove exploitation. In Perak 40,000 ha are leased out as a timber concession.[68] The company is clear-felling approximately 1,000 ha per year on what it claims is a sustained yield basis. (That is, the growth rate of the forest as a whole equals the quantity of timber cut. In this way the timber yield can be sustained indefinitely.) Regeneration looks promising as the felling is in small patches and properly managed. The company employs 1,400 people and supports a further 1,000 indirectly. The timber is mainly used to produce charcoal and in 1982 sales exceeded M$9m (US$3.5m).[69] Superficially, the people of Perak are making the best use of these mangroves, but even on a sustained yield basis there is a viable alternative.

The logging operation is putting pressure on the local fishing industry, which is based on prawns and cockles. These invertebrates are dependent on intact mangroves at vital periods in their life cycles. An estimated 2,500 fishermen work the area and the industry indirectly supports an extra 7,500.[70] In 1979 the prawn and cockle harvest earned an estimated M$30m (US$12m).[71] The effect on the fishing industry of felling the mangroves for charcoal is not clear, but there are indications that these mangroves should be harvested with extreme caution if the two industries are to be sustained.

Mangroves in other areas have been cleared to establish rice paddy. This has generally failed because the soils under mangroves are fragile, highly acidic and tend to form solid impermeable pans when exposed to the tropical sun.[72]

West Malaysia earned a considerable income from timber exploitation in the past but those days are clearly over. Relatively few Malaysians benefited significantly from this industry but it is now clear that the costs of over-exploitation must be borne by most of the population.

Development of current forest policy

Forests, and all land development policy, have always been in the hands of the individual states and remain so today. During the first half of the 20th century forests were generally regarded as obstacles to the expansion of rubber plantations. In West Malaysia, even in the 1960s, an average 17,500 ha of forest was cleared annually to establish this crop.[73] But it was during the 1920s and 1930s, when the proliferation of rubber planting was at its height, that states developed their own forestry legislation. These individual forest enactments form the basis of current Malaysian forest law and policy.

State forestry laws: Between 1921 and 1940 all individual states enacted some form of forestry legislation. These enactments are very similar and those passed in five states in 1934 provide a typical example.

The Malays States Forest Enactments provide no definition of precisely what comprises a forest but compensate for this with an exhaustive list of forest products. At the time there seemed little need to define forest types as forest was abundant, but the result was the establishment of a vague classification system: forest that had been surveyed became part of the 'Forest Reserve'; all other forested land was 'Stateland'. Forest Reserve meant simply that the area had been surveyed and found to hold trees, there was no implication that it would be managed, or excluded from agricultural or mining developments. Stateland meant that the state still controlled the land, if no individuals had made any written claim over it, and it was probably forest.

Land-use classifications within the forest reserve were left to the individual state departments. The result was a chaotic system, with different departments planning land development in isolation.

The Forest Reserve was frequently claimed by individuals or companies wishing to clear the land for plantation. Local inhabitants could oppose these plans by complaining to the District Forestry Officer, who was obliged to notify all the villages under his jurisdiction of any changes in land use or classification. The Officer also had to take note of any objections and hand them over to the state minister for consideration. The minister, however, was under no obligation to take into account local opposition when deciding on projects.

The concept of land rights for the forest-dwelling Orang Asli was not tolerated, as the policy on traditional forest farming notes: 'No right to practise Ladang [swidden] cultivation should be recorded, as such right is not recognised by the government.' Niether do they have any right to collect forest produce, unless they receive permits, a 'privilege' that may be withdrawn at any time. These permits, however, stipulate that no forest produce may leave the boundaries of the forest reserve, thus eliminating the possibility of any cash income the local population could obtain from the forests. The Orang Asli, who had been involved in bartering forest produce with coastal Malays for centuries, now found that if this trade continued they were breaking the law.

The highest official created under the legislation is the State Forester. This individual co-ordinates all forestry matters including issuing logging licences. No guidelines on who should receive licences were provided, with the result that the logging industry developed around the interests of the State Forester rather than development needs. Most concessions were to run for between 20 and 30 years and included a number of stipulations relating to timber extraction and forest management. The general impression is that there was a vague attempt to establish sustainable forestry in the minds of those involved but no means of enforcing this goal. The enactments were concerned more with consolidating political power over forests than with timber management.

There were, however, rules forbidding any forestry officers having any direct financial interests in the timber trade. This was an enlightened inclusion but difficult to impose since it was not applicable to these officers' family and close friends.

Penalties for transgression of enactments were established and continue today. One of the main goals of the acts was to prevent illegal logging; a system was introduced whereby those caught were fined twice the value of the logs felled. This volume was calculated by the number and size of stumps at the cutting sites, not the timber seized; the confiscated logs were used in state-funded public projects. One problem to emerge was to find the original felling area, as logs may come from several sites or be adjacent to legal concessions. To this day concession boundaries are not always well-defined at ground level.

These enactments were geared towards forest administration rather than providing the basis of a policy. They were quite comprehensive in that they took account of a variety of forest uses but promptly banned most of them. With each state working in isolation and trying to gain its share of the international timber market, not surprisingly no national policy developed until the 1980s. These enactments were still enforced during the early 1980s and have been absorbed into the new forestry legislation.

Colonial federal forest laws
As the British administration was preparing Malaysia for independence they enacted a number of federal laws concerning forests. The first of these was the Aboriginal Peoples' Act of 1954 that described itself as: 'An act to provide for the protection, well-being and advancement of the aboriginal people of West Malaysia.' Still in power today, it defines 'aboriginal' in order to ensure other groups may not claim its supposed benefits.

Each state is required to appoint a Commissioner for Aboriginal Affairs. Aboriginals, that is, the Orang Asli, can obtain rights over the forest land they are inhabiting, but only at the discretion of the Commissioner. He retains the power to evict entire villages from stateland or the forest reserve if he wishes. The state may also set up 'aboriginal reserves' in which Orang Asli have full rights over forests and their resources, excluding timber extraction; but the state can revoke an aboriginal reserve at any time. Reserves are established through a complex system of licences ensuring that non-aborignals are excluded from gaining access to these privileges. These restrictions, however, fail to provide any security to the Orang Asli because the Act states that the Commissioner may grant timber or other collection licences to non-aboriginals.

The fact that the system is based on a set of privileges rather than on recognized rights, means that compensation for loss of these resources or for reclassification of these lands is not compulsory. The compensation process, like all other aspects of the legislation, is at the discretion of the Commissioner.

The Act is based on a British concept of land ownership that is inappropriate when applied to nomadic and semi-nomadic forest societies. Reserves are established with the idea of creating settled villages that can then be provided with medical aid and schools. Despite an outward appearance of benevolence, it must be remembered that the Act established discretionary reserves that provided little security for the Orang Asli, while other aspects of forest legislation banned almost all aboriginal activities.

Today, an Orang Asli not in a reserve is a trespasser. Few collecting licences are issued; the application procedure is a lengthy process, resulting in time spent away from the forests, families and friends. Even though this legislation was slightly revised in 1974, it continues to reflect a colonial attitude of paternalistic repression over the Orang Asli. Responsibility for establishing the legislation lies with the British, but it should be noted that successive Malaysian administrations have done nothing to change the principles upon which it is based.

Independence

With independence in 1957 the federation of states became formally known as Malaysia. It was a time of great social upheaval and a Constitution, based on Muslim principles, was hastily established. The new national government inherited a growing insurgency problem that was known as 'the emergency'. Communist rebels were to be found throughout the Peninsula as the most violent campaign since the Japanese invasion during World War Two was fought out in the forests. The bitterness of this conflict was heightened by the fact that many rebels were Chinese. A few pockets of rebels still exist in the more remote areas along the Thai border.

The new Federal authorities still regarded forests as a state government affair and as such they were not mentioned in the Constitution. The British, however, established a number of government agencies concerned with land development, including the Federal Land Development Agency (FELDA), which continues to be the main federal body involved with forest clearance. Within months of independence the National Land Council was established as the other major rural development agency. The original goals of FELDA were to solve the landless farmer problem, relieve rural poverty and continue to develop the plantation sector.

In the mid-1960s the International Bank for Reconstruction and Development (IBRD) recommended that Malaysia should industrialize, diversify the cash crop economy and expand the timber trade. Timber exploitation and industrialization were developed but agricultural diversification went only as far as promoting one more crop, oil palm.

By the time of the first Malaysia Plan in 1966, the then Prime Minister,

Tunku Abdul Raman, was calling for, 'All Malaysians to redouble their efforts to sustain economic growth and development.'[74] Malaysia was to invest more than M$10 billion (US$4 billion) between 1966 and 1970 to achieve this economic growth.[75] Borrowing from foreign banks was becoming fashionable and, in 1966, Malaysia's foreign debts already exceeded M$750m (US$296m).

The rapid development of an industrial sector resulted in significant migration from the countryside into the towns. This prompted a labour shortage in the plantations that continues today. The plantation sector continues to increase under FELDA but is seen more as a poverty alleviation programme than as a basis for national economic growth.

In contrast, the timber industry experienced rapid growth from the mid-1960s until the early 1980s. All the major international development agencies, not only the IBRD, promoted the exploitation of the forests for timber. The first Malaysia plan did, however, note the dangers of over-exploiting the forests:

> Such exploitation, however, cannot be allowed to be excessive as a portion of the country's forests must be reserved to avoid the danger of sudden climatic changes in the country, safeguard water supplies and soil fertility, and prevent flooding and erosion.[76]

But no legislation was introduced to ensure appropriate management of the forests, despite the fact that large machinery, capable of extracting more timber than ever before, was introduced.

By the early 1970s an awareness of the value of wildlife and the natural environment was developing and, in 1972, the Wildlife Act was passed. This Act emerged from a confusing history of state laws attempting to protect individual species. In consolidating these laws a system of establishing protected areas was standardized. States could establish two kinds of protected forests: wildlife reserves; and/or wildlife sanctuaries. Wildlife reserves apply to areas in which general environmental protection is required, such as in critical watersheds or in areas suitable for recreation. Wildlife sanctuaries encompass areas set aside to protect rare or endangered species and, therefore, are subject to strict laws on hunting and collecting.

In wildlife sanctuaries all species are protected, while in reserves only certain ones are. Entry into both types of area is restricted, although permits may be granted. Permits for entry into reserves may cover any kind of exploitation, including logging. One of the best-known abuses of this legislation was in the Endau-Rompin wildlife reserve on the borders of the Johore and Pahang. Since the early 1970s, environmentalists had been campaigning for the area to be made a national park due to the extremely rare wildlife found there. In 1976 the Third Malaysia Plan recommended that 20,000 ha of the wildlife reserve be made a national park. The states concerned refused, and were under no obligation to provide any justification for their objections. In 1977, the state government of Pahang granted a logging permit covering 6,000 ha of the core area.[77] The loggers selectively felled more than 25 ha per day, working the area out in less than eight months. The state governments concerned also gave FELDA 4,000 ha within the proposed park. Since FELDA is a federal agency the agricultural project has not yet gone ahead. Endau-Rompin, however, is still not a national park and its core has suffered severe damage from the logging.

This example exposes the fundamental weakness of all Malaysian forestry legislation. Designed to protect an area of national importance it continues to permit local or even individual interests to dominate. If an area is of importance to both the nation and the international community then these interests should take priority over those of individuals involved in logging. One of the most basic concepts of democracy is that the wishes of the wider community should take preference over those of particular individuals. Current legislation on national parks is subject to similar problems.

The National Parks Act (1980) aimed to establish a series of national parks that would protect key wildlife areas and sites of historical and cultural significance. This Act, however, has never been applied in West Malaysia. The only national park, Taman Negara, was established in 1939 under the British administration.

The narrow base that sustained the Malaysian economy since colonial days has not fared well in the 1980s despite the development of its microchip industry. The rubber, tin and palm oil markets have all collapsed, and timber prices continue to decline. To maintain economic growth Malaysia has been obliged to borrow more money from the international lending banks. In 1980 the national debt was approximately at M$10 billion (US$4 billion); by 1985 it was estimated to exceed M$41 billion (US$16 billion).[78]

The collapse of these markets has had a dramatic effect on the rural poor and, as a result, there has been much debate over the direction rural development should take. Corruption within the Malaysian tin market was exposed in the mid-1980s when government officials were accused of trying to maintain false price levels. In contrast, the timber industry continued to be an individual state matter, with no national strategy, until the adoption of the National Forestry Act in 1984.

The National Forestry Policy

Proposed in 1972 the National Forestry Policy was accepted by the National Land Council, itself a federal body, only in 1978. The states' independence *vis-à-vis* forestry issues has been vigorously defended. At the time of writing, not all the state forestry departments have been signatories to the Policy, most notably Sarawak in East Malaysia.

The overall aim of the Policy is to establish a sustainable forestry industry throughout Malaysia. Previously, the concept of sustainable logging was not a stated policy. Numerous regulations on replanting, enrichment planting, extraction methods and proper planning schedules for concessions are outlined in the Policy. It goes beyond what many foresters regard as their responsibility and includes schemes whereby local communities obtain control of exploitation rights, and trade in non-timber forest produce is restricted. Stronger protection for water courses, the issues over aboriginal rights to use forest resources, urban expansion policy and national parks are all covered. This far-reaching Policy takes an integrated view of forest development, and for this reason, opposition has extended beyond the forestry departments as other state departments see it as encroaching on their territory.

The major opposition, however, has centred around the Policy's wider political implications rather than the exact rules and regulations within it. Despite these problems the 1984 National Forestry Act attempts to give some legal footing to the Policy.

The National Forestry Act aims to standardize the development policies of various state forestry departments. It reiterates that forestry is a national rather than a state matter and that forest management should, therefore, be on this basis. The Act calls for a reclassification of forests into four major categories: production; protection; wildlife, recreation and research; and federal forests. If a forested area has not been classified it falls into the productive class, which implies it is open for timber exploitation unless otherwise stated. Since state governments have much to gain from the timber industry, there is little incentive for them to reclassify the forests into the new system.

Under this Act a Forest Development Fund was established as a federal research and co-ordinating body on timber management and production. The Fund also researches watershed rehabilitation projects but it has little power as it cannot overrule state forestry policy.

State forestry departments are encouraged to widen their scope of influence in an attempt to integrate forestry and general land development. The Act, however, provides no clear guidelines as to how such integration should occur and there is still no policy on which department holds ultimate responsibility for development on forested land.

This Act falls far short of the proposals in the National Forestry Policy but does provide an initial framework for future legislation. Notably absent from the Act are aboriginal land rights and any reference to tightening rules on timber extraction methods.

In summary, Malaysia has enacted some comprehensive legislation on forestry. On closer examination, however, the federal authorities have found themselves relatively powerless over state government interests. Only when this basic problem is addressed will Malaysia develop a more coherent policy for its forests. The only area in which the federal authorities have had influence over forestry management is that of replanting and rehabilitation;

state governments have willingly relinquished responsibility for these tasks to the federal government.

Replanting timber

During the 1970s replanting was minimal in comparison to the scale of logging and cash crop expansion. Timber management was essentially based on the natural regeneration of forest and occasional enrichment planting. Thus, during the 1970s only 47,000 ha of West Malaysian logged forests had any form of enrichment planting.[79] Timber plantations were established over less than 16,000 ha.[80] With the logging of more than 3.5m ha in the 1970s less than 2% was replanted in any form.[81]

In 1982, the federal government realized that the Peninsula's timber industry was in jeopardy and hastily launched a major replanting initiative. The Compensatory Plantation Programme planned to establish more than 188,000 ha by 1995.[82] The cost is estimated to exceed M$517m (US$204m) most of which will be loaned from the Asian Development Bank (ADB).[83] The costs to the federal government will be higher, as the ADB charges interest on such loans. The programme will be implemented by the individual state forestry departments.

Three species are to be planted: Acacia *magnum*, Gmelina *arborea* and Albizia *falcatia*. Acacia *magnum* originates from Indonesia and is a fast-growing timber useful for general construction. Gmelina *arborea* is found throughout northern and central Asia and is suitable for producing finished furniture. Albizia *falcatia* is from the Philippines and is fast-growing but very poor quality. It is hoped that these species will replace red meranti, the all-purpose timber that forms the basis of the present Malaysian timber industry.

But the programme has not kept to schedule. While the government estimated they would plant 26,300 ha by 1985, only 7,000 ha were established.[84] To compensate for this poor start the second phase, 1985 to 1990, called for the establishment of 74,000 ha rather than the planned 60,000 ha.[85]

The forestry departments are under no illusions that the programme will sustain the forestry industry at its present levels of production. These trees are aimed to meet an expanding domestic demand rather than replace the present export trade. How the present phase of planting is proceeding is not clear as this extract from the Federal Forestry Department's 1984 annual report shows:

> The achievement for the Disturbed Forest Inventory and forest treatment programme, which includes the treatments of enrichment planting and forest plantation, was very satisfactory. However, the enrichment planting and forest plantation projects achieved very low rates of success.[86]

Present causes of forest destruction

In West Malaysia there is only one major cause of forest clearance: government-sponsored agricultural expansion. A much larger area of forest, however, is degraded by the timber industry and therefore also warrants attention.

Land development projects

Forest clearance for agricultural development has been co-ordinated by federal government agencies since independence. A number of schemes and departments have been involved but today only the largest, the Federal Land Development Agency (FELDA), is still active.

FELDA was established in 1956, ostensibly to help provide land for the landless. The rapid expansion of rubber estates had pushed some people off the land and also contributed to the growing insurgency problem. Communist rebels were present throughout the Peninsula, and opening-up forest with new communities was initiated as a security measure. From the outset FELDA projects therefore had a political goal as well as a welfare role. As the first general meeting of FELDA in 1956 noted, the broader political aim was: 'to give opportunities to those who have initiative rather than charity to those who have not . . . the best land for the best people.'[87]

Since eligibility for the programme was based on political rather than social grounds active membership of the Malay 'Home Guard', a voluntary army unit that fought the communists, greatly enhanced the chances of selection. Only in the late 1960s did the official basis for selection change from political allegiance to one of meeting basic needs.

The FELDA model: Rubber, and later oil palm, formed the basis for the new wealth that participants could expect from the schemes. Each family was designated 4.5 ha of cleared land planted with one of the two crops. Settlers were given a basic house, and infrastructure such as schools, medical facilities and roads was provided. Participants had to pay for the house and crops on a loan basis with 6.5% interest annually. FELDA worked on the assumption that the cost of an average house would be paid off within 15 years; the family would then own the house and the land.

In an attempt to prevent fragmentation of such small, individual estates the 1960 Land Act stipulated that FELDA plots could not be divided or sub-let. The original model, however, proved too clumsy and, as mechanizaton became more readily available, a block system was developed. This involved communal control by 20 families harvesting and planting the area in blocks rather than individual plots.

In 1986 the most radical changes were introduced when FELDA established new projects as working co-operatives. Individual land claims were abolished and settlers drew wages from the co-operative. Individuals may no longer buy the land since it is owned by the co-operative. The irony of the new system is that it is remarkably close to a communist management plan. There has been fierce opposition to the new scheme because many people feel they are estate workers rather than independent landlords.

By late 1986 FELDA projects covered more than one million hectares of West Malaysia.[88] Almost 500,000 people had been relocated in more than 100,000 family units.[89] From the participants' point of view the programme can be regarded as a success; only 4,000 families have left since FELDA's inception.[90] Table 3.3 outlines the areas of forest cleared for such projects since the mid-1960s. In the 1986–90 five year plan FELDA is due to open up 286,700 ha across Malaysia as a whole.

By 1985 it was costing FELDA M$53,000 (US$21,000) to resettle each family and up to M$76,000 (US$30,000) if the project was based on cocoa rather than rubber or oil palm.[91] These sums should be repaid by the participants but this is highly unlikely to happen. Palm oil prices crashed by more than 50% between September 1985 and February 1986, primarily due to over-production.[92] Many participants have severe financial problems because they relied almost exclusively on these crops for their income. Despite this economic collapse, FELDA continues to promote the same narrow range of cash crops: under the 1986–90 five-year plan 65% oil palm, 13% rubber and 16% cocoa will be planted.[93] In the mid-1980s all repayment of loans was suspended until these markets improve. During 1986 FELDA was spending an estimated M$7m (US$2.7m) per month on food relief for settlers.[94]

These problems may be resolved with a more diverse planting policy but the long-term sustainability of the programme is being questioned. One study by the University of Malaya in Kuala Lumpur found an almost universal ambition amongst the young to move away from these schemes, reporting that:

> The recurrent impression given in their answers is that the second generation does not have anything remotely like the rural pioneering spirit of their parents. . . . Instead they apparently want to be pioneers in the new Malaysian frontier – the cities.[95]

This should come as no surprise as the government has centred much development effort on urban industrial expansion. FELDA villages clearly hold no attraction for many of the young.

Despite these problems there is a waiting list for participation in FELDA schemes. Between 1981 and 1985 approximately 150,000 people were resettled under the programme, while the rural population of West Malaysia grew by more than one million.[96] Although FELDA has changed the lives of many people, poverty continues to dominate many rural areas. The Institute of Medical Research in Kuala Lumpur, using WHO criteria, estimate that

42% of rural children suffer from malnutrition.[97] They also claim that the calorie intake in the daily diet of 66% of rural families is inadequate, and that 34% of family diets are short on protein.[98]

These estimates indicate that more people need assistance than FELDA can hope to include in their projects and that a selection process is required. Selection for such a programme is a thankless task and despite claims by the authorities that there is no political bias in this process, many disagree. Professor Rokiah Talib notes that:

> The applicants may be scrutinised for their political affiliations. . . . Politicians can and do exert their influence for selecting their own supporters from grass roots level, that is the village unit, thus ensuring that party cadres are selected and extra votes assured in the next election.[99]

Since FELDA projects are expensive the money may be better spent on *in situ* development, improving general infrastructure and local markets rather than moving people; an option that is being pursued through the Integrated Agricultural Development Projects. The rapid expansion of this programme may indicate a change in strategy or, as some government officials claim, it is due to West Malaysia running out of land suitable for plantation projects. Whatever the case, it can no longer be assumed that West Malaysian land development will be based solely on cutting down forest.

The timber industry

Logging has been established on the Peninsula since the 19th century but developed most rapidly in the 1970s; timber production peaked in 1979 and has since been declining.[100] In 1970 the government issued new logging licences over 60,000 ha of the Peninsula's forests; in 1972 approximately 424,000 ha was similarly designated.[101] These figures however, give little indication of the scale of logging. In the early 1970s approximately 373,000 ha of West Malaysia's forests were logged each year.[102] A peak was reached in 1976 with 411,000 ha being selectively felled, but this has since declined to the present 149,000 ha.[103]

Output from the Peninsula's timber industry continued to increase after 1976, despite a decline in the size of the areas affected, indicating more intensive logging. In the 1970s West Malaysia had one of the most intensive timber industries in Asia.

Timber management: According to the Ministry of Primary Industries:

> The forest resources of Malaysia have been systematically managed from the beginning of this century when the first forestry officer was appointed in 1901. Over the years, ecologically and environmentally sound forest conservation and management have been developed to ensure forest renewal and sustained yield.[104]

There is little doubt that West Malaysia is a leader in the field of silviculture and timber management. The Malayan Uniform System (MUS) of selective logging, developed in the 1950s, is widely respected by foresters throughout the world. The reality in the forest, however, is that the system is implemented only in a small minority of logging areas. By 1975 the MUS had been applied to just 80,000 ha of logged-over forest; less than one quarter of the concession area felled in that year alone.[105] By 1987, 764,000 ha of the Peninsula's forests had had some kind of silvicultural treatment applied; approximately 14% of the area logged since 1970.[106] The lack of enthusiasm to implement the MUS has caused the FAO to describe it as a 'so called selective management system'.[107]

The MUS is based on selectively felling all desirable trees with a trunk diameter of more than 46 cm at breast height. Non-commercial species above this size may also be cut if the individual tree is considered to be over-mature (trees that have passed their peak growth stage) and are hindering the growth of more valuable species. Clearing them allows desirable young trees access to the light they need for maximum growth. After selective felling has been accomplished the forest is left to regenerate naturally. The end result was a more uniform growth of trees in the Shorea genus, a variety of the most valuable commercial timbers. The MUS also involves surveying each area logged to assess if enrichment planting (planting seedlings of desired species) is required. As the pace of logging developed in Malaysia the forestry departments failed to carry out this task due to a lack of manpower, and enthusiasm.

Such a management system can be successful only if it is combined with environmentally sensitive extraction methods. West Malaysia uses bulldozers and skidding tracks to get timber out of the forests. On average only 30% of the standing timber is actually removed but most studies agree that 50% to 70% of the forest canopy is destroyed in the process.[108] As the loggers have moved further into the hills the damage has intensified. The average logging track is four metres wide with up to 20 metres cleared on either side in an attempt to prevent forest growth reclaiming the path. Even on gentle slopes, each square kilometre of logged forest has an average of 13 km of logging roads, not including skid tracks.[109]

A more recent development in West Malaysia is an attempt to diversify the number of tree species marketed. In the late 1970s only 63 of Malaysia's 2,500 tree species had any commercial value and just eight accounted for almost all exports.[110] Creating a market for a wider variety of timbers could prove a mixed blessing: extraction may become even more intensive. One great improvement, however, is the present effort to promote rubber wood, a resource that West Malaysia has in abundance. Most rubber trees are felled and burnt after their useful latex-producing life is over. This is a waste of a valuable resource, about which the timber industry is quite rightly very concerned. Rubber wood may emerge as one of the major timber exports from Malaysia in the 21st century.

A considerable portion of the timber that reaches the mills is wasted, due to poor quality logs, and foreign customers' very specific demands for consistencey. The timber industry is aware of this problem, as the chairman of the Malaysian Timber Industries Board put it in 1983: 'There has been too much wastage for far too long in the exploitation of our forests.'[111] Exactly how a more efficient industry will be created, however, is still not clear.

Timber exports: At present, West Malaysia is concentrating on supplying a growing domestic timber market. By 1984 only 25% of the ten million cubic metres produced was exported.[112] Although considerably less than previous years the income this derived is still vital for many individual state economies. As the volume of timber exported has decreased the forestry department has encouraged more processing in order to maintain income; at present raw logs account for only 0.5% of exports.[113] Twenty-seven tree species can no longer be exported as logs and as West Malaysia's processing sector remains limited, rough sawn timber dominates exports.[114] Table 3.4 shows the mix of exports in more detail.

The major export markets for West Malaysian sawn timber and plywoods are Europe, Japan, Australia, and the USA, with Singapore acting as a major clearing house.[115] Attempts to follow the trade path from the saw-mill to the finished product in a European or American high street are frustrating. Timber can pass through a large variety of dealers and processors before reaching the end customer. Figure 3.1 shows a flow diagram illustrating the most common routes within Malaysia, even before export. This complex structure makes it extremely difficult to gauge the influence of foreign buyers on the West Malaysian industry.

The British agribusiness conglomerate, Harrison Crossfield, provides some indication of the tortuous paths of influence. Harrison Crossfield wholly own the Sabah Timber Company which has a controlling interest in Perkayuan Tengara Sdn Bdh. Perkayuan is currently logging 48,000 ha in the state of Pahang.[116] Malaysia has complex laws on foreign control of timber concessions and as such the influence at this level is severely limited. Foreign influence comes through the trading houses in Singapore; approximately 68% of West Malaysia's log exports pass through this island state.[117]

West Malaysia will continue to export timbers, despite becoming a net importer of logs in 1990. Given a chance, the industry claims it wants to develop as a major furniture exporter but suitable conditions for the adoption of this option are unlikely to occur. The furniture trade is dominated by the major customers of Malaysian timbers and, in view of Indonesia's dominance, even expansion into the plywood trade is limited. Any expansion in these two sectors will concentrate on the domestic market. There can be little argument that West Malaysia's timber industry has passed its peak. Whether it can establish itself on a more sustainable footing in the future depends on developments within the 1990s.

Other causes of forest loss
West Malaysia has a well-developed road network. The only major road project that has opened up new areas in recent years is the East–West Highway. Crossing rugged terrain, however, it has not heralded a new era of agricultural expansion and many claim it was built for political prestige rather than regional development. Expansion of the road network has no significant effect on West Malaysia's forests. The same can be said for the mining industry; tin mining is in decline and no expansion is envisaged. In the past, significant areas of forest were cleared for mining and the devastation was total. Around Ipoh and towards the west coast large areas of wasteland dominate a moon-like landscape. Most sites, however, have been abandoned and mining can no longer be regarded as a significant factor contributing to West Malaysia's forest destruction.

West Malaysian forest futures

West Malaysian forests will soon become a drain on the nation's economy rather than sources of an income. It has taken West Malaysia a long time to accept that forest loss could have serious environmental consequences. The massive replanting schemes are evidence of a serious concern for the future of the forests within the government, particularly regarding the collapse of timber exports. Reaction to the more general decline of the environment is, however, still limited and few believe that areas like Indonesia's critical lands are likely to develop in West Malaysia – a complacency based more on the attitude to land management than any major physical differences between the two countries.

This is borne out by the Federal Land Development Agency's minimal regard for forest conservation, both in site choice and farming models developed. FELDA is planning to concentrate more of its efforts in East Malaysia. The current levels of forest clearance in Malaysia may diminish, but the impact on remaining forests will be more intense as more remote areas are opened up.

The influx of people into the cities has created a significant area of abandoned farmland in West Malaysia. This is usually composed of individual holdings and as such are not used by FELDA, who prefer larger schemes.

The forestry department and timber industry, however, seem more intent on sending delegations around the world to assure everybody that everything is fine rather than to sustain the resource. The virtual abandonment of the Malayan Uniform System throughout the late 1970s and early 1980s was a particularly short-sighted policy. The Compensatory Replanting Programme may result in a partial recovery of forest in certain areas but it is no substitute for the proposals within the National Forest Policy. This programme, by ignoring the social context of replanting, simply meets the needs of an industry that has wilfully over-exploited a renewable resource.

The other area of major concern is the lack of national parks. There can be little doubt that Endau Rompin needs further protection and that other areas should be established. This is perhaps the least developed aspect of conservation in West Malaysia. In brief, the authorities are not providing adequate protection, and this does not reflect well on their commitment to conservation. West Malaysia has been one area in South-East Asia where the establishment of fully protected conservation forests has been woefully neglected.

In more general terms, a much wider debate is needed if the authorities are to be dissuaded from their present position of considering that timber must dominate all forest development. Possibilities for such discussion, however, look more uncertain as the present authorities consolidate power. Government critics, including anyone critical of the timber industry, face long gaol sentences without trial under the infamous Internal Security Act. In addition, recent developments in the Official Secrets Act have put great pressures on reporting malpractices within government, further restricting public debate on development issues that may affect the national economy.

As inhabitants of one of the most industrialized areas in South-East Asia, the West Malaysian population is generally more remote from the forests than other populations in the region. This has undoubtedly been a factor in forming the present lax attitude to forest loss. Those most directly affected, such as the Orang Asli, have little or no political voice and their opinions are rarely heard. The hard work done by groups such as Sahabat Alam Malaysia and the Consumers Association of Penang is forcing the issue on to the public agenda but it is frequently overshadowed by party politics. The fear of communism, remaining from the time of the emergencies, has stifled debate as critics of development policy are branded traitors or eccentrics who want to restrain progress. Public attitude is changing but official policy is slow to react, which may explain why any radical changes from present policy within West Malaysia are unlikely.

This is reflected by the lack of any social forestry programme and a severely underutilized potential for minor forest product industries. In the longer term these industries could develop; West Malaysia is in an ideal situation with a well-developed infrastructure and key trading cities on its coasts. If the national forestry policy can be enforced the possibilities for sustainable forestry will be greatly increased. The rather weak framework provided by the National Forestry Act fails to reflect the concerns highlighted in the initial policy.

West Malaysia is not about to lose all its forest but unless certain areas are immediately designated as national parks and the original National Forestry Policy is taken up more positively, there is little room for complacency.

Case study

Taman Negara: West Malaysia's only national park[118]
Taman Negara was designated a national park in 1939 to be: 'reserved in perpetuity for the protection and preservation of the indigenous flora and fauna.' The park covers 4,340 sq. km of the central mountain range on Peninsular Malaysia and consequently can lay claim to being the site of one of the most diverse rain forests on earth. All of West Malaysia's 254 bird species are found here, alongside the rare Sumatran rhino, tiger and barking deer. One study within the park boundaries found more than 200 species of flowering plants in a single hectare. Despite the area's obvious scientific and cultural value West Malaysia's sole national park has had a turbulent history. The two most well-known development proposals have been the Tembeling Dam and the construction of a road to the peak of Gunung Tahan, West Malaysia's highest peak.

The Tembeling dam: The Tembeling hydroelectric project was initially proposed in 1972, scrapped in 1978, revived in 1982 and abandoned in 1983.
   In the late 1960s Malaysia embarked on a programme of rapid industrial expansion that required new sources of energy. The National Electricity Board (NEB) looked into a variety of sources, including developing West Malaysia's hydroelectric potential. In October 1971 the NEB published a report recommending the harnessing of the upper Tembeling river.
   In June 1972 the Malaysian government asked an Australian agency to study the serious flood problems in the Pahang river basin. The Tembeling constituted part of the upper reaches of this area and dams were regarded as an effective means of reducing flooding. The NEB signed a contract with a Russian consultancy in early 1973 to carry out a feasibility study into a Tembeling dam. This study came out at the same time as the Australian study, in late 1974.
   The Russian report was based soley on the technical feasibility of building the Tembeling dam; the Australian report covered the wider issues. Four other viable dam sites, besides the one on the Tembeling, were identified by the Australians. They also recommended that a more detailed environmental impact assessment be carried out on the Russian proposals. No action was taken and two years later the government announced that the Tembeling project was temporarily postponed.
   In 1978 it was reported that the project had been shelved indefinitely. No

reasons were given. During this time the environmental movement in Malaysia was small and relatively ineffective. Little debate took place and there were few open challenges to such government proposals. When, in January 1982, the Deputy Premier Datuk Musa Hitam announced that the project was to be revived opposition was more immediate. Letters appeared in the national press openly condemning the project, and a heated debate ensued.

Throughout 1982 Tembeling became a rallying point for Malaysia's environmental groups. SAM, the largest, collected a 45,000 signature petition against the proposals. The Malayan Nature Society had letter and postcard campaigns to the Premier; the Environmental Protection Society of Malaysia also collected signatures for their own petition. The issue caught the imagination of the public and by deft campaigning managed to steer clear of being labelled an anti-development issue. This was a major achievement, as most environmental groups in Asia are frequently accused of opposing development.

Criticism emerged on almost every aspect of the project, from the social and environmental costs to the NEB's predictions on electricity demand.

The site, on the Trenganu river, formed part of the southern limit of the park. The surface area of the reservoir would be 250 sq. km and flood almost 70% of the park's lowland rain forest; very few areas of lowland rain forest are left in West Malaysia.

Even access for construction would have opened up the area to the logging industry. As present there are few illegal logging problems in West Malaysia, but the chance to harvest such a rich area may prove too great a temptation for some. Any further clearance would increase flooding in Pahang, thus exacerbating one of the problems the dam was intended to eliminate. SAM claimed that up to 5,000 people would have to be relocated and that the social costs, excluded from the feasibility studies, would be considerable.

To counteract the campaign opposing the dam the NEB had predicted a massive growth in the demand for electricity as the basis of the need for its construction. Electricity demand was increasing in West Malaysia but at nothing like the rates predicted, primarily due to the general world recession during the early 1980s. But the NEB's argument was further undermined by the Australian study from the 1970s that identified three alternative sites outside the national park, all capable of supplying even more electricity while flooding a smaller area.

If the Bersia and Kenering options were considered, 30 sq. km of reservoir would provide more electricity than the 250 sq. km of Tembeling.

In January 1983, one year after the project's resurrection, Datuk Musa Hitam announced that the scheme had again been shelved because the expected electricity demand could be met by existing power sources. But the project has still not been officially abandoned. Other development proposals for Taman Negara have, however, kept environmental groups busy since 1983.

A road to nowhere: In January 1986 the Federal Government announced plans to construct two roads into the park as part of a long-term strategy to develop tourism; at present the only access into Taman Negara is by river. In total 80 km of road are proposed, from Kuala Tembeling outside the park to the foot of Gunung Tahan via the park headquarters at Kuala Tahan. The first section to the park headquarters opens up an old logging track; the second cuts through virgin forest. Construction of the road would cost an estimated M$2.9m (US$1.1m).

The main opposition is directed against the second section, from the park headquarters to the foot of Gunung Tehan. This section would follow the track to the salt licks at Jenut Tabing and Jenut Kumbang thus destroying their isolation and observation value. A major attraction of Taman Negara is the possibility of observing wildlife from hides close to the park headquarters. Construction of the road and its daily use would undoubtedly result in certain species abandoning the area.

Even though the road would be no more than a hard core dirt track it would cause considerable environmental damage. More than 40 bridges would be needed and foundation stone would have to be mined on site. Bulldozers need to turn and, due to the steep terrain, screes are easily formed on the downhill side of the track. Combine these factors and clearly a small track can affect a large area.

Physical destruction of the area is only one side of the argument raised against this road; the psychological effect on tourists to the park is also relevant. One of Taman Negara's main attractions is the sense of remoteness and adventure it imparts. As West Malaysia becomes increasingly industrialized so does the need for wilderness areas. The road might reduce the present ten days needed to climb and return from the summit of Gunung Tahan to five days, but the sense of achievement of this journey would be lost. Does Taman Negara need this type of development?

Developing tourism: Taman Negara is undoubtedly a great asset to West Malaysia and in many ways is also greatly underdeveloped. There is only one residential centre within its boundaries and accommodation is severely limited. A single access route is used and the eastern end of the park is extremely remote.

It would be possible, however, to develop the area and retain its sense of remoteness. The park has an extensive river system for communications and there have been suggestions of four possible visitor centres: at Kuala Kenyam, Sungai Balak, Kuala Koh and Merepoh. The park has few guides, few well maintained jungle trails and a small education centre. All could be improved in ways that enhance people's use of the park much more than a bulldozed road. There is also a much greater chance that the new centres would be cost effective. The road proposals, particularly the one to the foot of Gunug Tahan, illustrate a lack of understanding of how the park works and why people go there. There is undoubtedly great potential at Taman Negara but these roads will probably not provide what future visitors will be seeking.

Table 2.1
Production of non-timber forest products, 1977–1981

Product	Units	Total Production 1977	1979	1981	Change '77/'81
1. Damar resin	tons	2,027	2,867	7,179	+254%
2. Gomdorukem resin	tons	2,893	8,483	9,310	+245%
3. Turpentine	litres	441,741	698,822	813,966	+ 84%
4. Silk thread	kg.	3,831	6,986	6,299	+ 73%
5. Fuel, wood	m³	377,319	356,220	364,711	– 3%
6. Rattan*	tons	37,884	70,476	28,921	– 24%
7. Kayuputhi oil	litres	160,661	264,253	113,833	– 29%
8. Charcoal*	tons	34,280	28,540	3,875	– 89%
9. Shingles	000's	24,616	29,982	1,198	–95%
10. Bamboo	tons	**	**	12,438	—
	stalks	108,328	111,134	*nd	—

Notes: *   Production and export data show some inconsistency,
      **   No data available.
Source: Derived from Table II.2.12 (p. 75) Statistik Kehutanan Indonesia. 1982/ 1983. Department Kehutanen, 1984.

Table 2.2
Export of major non-timber forest products, 1977–1981

Product	Total Exports				Change	
	1977		1981		1977–81	
	Volume	Earnings	Volume	Earnings	Volume	Earnings
	000 tons	mill.$	000 tons	mill.$	%	%
1. Rattan	75	15.5	75	70.4	0	+354
2. Cassia bark	5	4.4	9	10.2	+ 80	+132
3. Tangkawang*	6	4.1	1	0.3	– 83	– 93
4. Charcoal	47	1.5	39	3.9	– 17	+160
5. Jalutong**	5	1.1	3	8.2	– 40	+645
6. Damar resin	4	0.4	10	4.3	+150	+975
7. Copal resin	2	0.4	2	0.9	0	+125
8. Other	20	22.1	57	93.5	+185	+323
Total	*164*	*49.5*	*196*	*191.7*	*– 20*	*+287*

Notes: *   Edible fat from tree seeds.
        ** Type of latex.
Source: Derived from Table II.3.13 (p. 97), Statistik Kehutanan Indonesia, 1982/
        1983, Department Kehutanan, 1984.

Table 2.3
Structure and composition of plots of primary forest (1.6 ha.) and 30-year-old secondary forest (0.3 ha.)

Characteristics	Primary Forest	Secondary Forest
Number of species:		
a. dipterocarp	12	1
b. non-dipterocarp	197	118
Number of genera	125	89
Number of families	44	39
Number of trees/ha.		
a. dipterocarp	29	1
b. non-dipterocarp	446	578
Basal area/ha.		
a. dipterocarp	26.35	0.04
b. non-dipterocarp	41.13	21.90

Source: Ambio, vol. 10 No. 2-3, 1981 'The Impact of Man on a Tropical Forest in
        Indonesia'.

Table 2.4
Projected production and marketing of forest products 1984/1999

Type of product	Units	Pelita IV '84/5–'88/9	Pelita V '88/9–'93/4	Pelita VI '94/5–'98/9
A. EXPORT MARKET				
Sawn Wood	000 cu.m.	3,700	4,207	4,782
Plywood	,,	4,500	5,798	7,469
Wood Panels	,,	800	883	975
Non-timber Products	000 tons	310	396	505
Sub Total	*000 cu.m.*	*9,000*	*10,888*	*13,226*
	000 tons	*310*	*396*	*505*
B. DOMESTIC MARKET				
Sawn Wood	000 cu.m.	8,400	10,225	12,440
Plywood	,,	2,500	3,346	4,478
Wood Panels	,,	200	221	244
Pulp & Paper	000 tons	600	996	1,556
Non-timber Products	,,	20	26	33
Sub Total	*000 cu.m.*	*11,100*	*13,792*	*17,162*
	000 tons	*620*	*1,022*	*1,589*
TOTAL	*000 cu.m.*	*20,100*	*24,680*	*30,388*
	000 tons	*930*	*1,418*	*2,094*

Source: Draft Long-Term Forestry Plan of Government of Indonesia.

Table 2.5
Transmigration programmes 1969–1989

Repelita I 1969–1974	Repelita II 1974–1979	Repelita III 1979–1984	Repelita IV 1984–1989	Total a
		(Number of families)		
		Sponsored Transmigration		
46,000	83,000	366,000	450,000	929,000
	Spontaneous transmigration with limited or no government assistance			
17,000	35,000	169,000	300,000	529,000
Total 63,000	*118,000*	*535,000*	*750,000*	*1,458,000*

a = Targets
Source: GOI and IIED, 1985.

References

1. Karim, G. (ed.) 1986.
2. Li Dun Jen, 1982.
3. Karim, G. (ed.), 1986.
4. Ministry of Primary Industries, 1985.
5. Ministry of Primary Industries, 1984.
6. Consumers Association of Penang, 1979.
7. Ministry of Primary Industries, 1984.
8. Karim, G. (ed.), 1986.
9. Government of Malaysia, 4th Malysia Plan, 1981.
10. FAO, 1981.
11. Government of Malaysia, 5th Malaysia Plan, 1986.
12. Ibid.
13. Ministry of Primary Industries, 1985.
14. Government of Malaysia, 5th Malaysia Plan, 1986.
15. Ibid.
16. Yong Chai Ting, 1984.
17. Lim Ching Hing, 1978.
18. Ibid.
19. Ibid.
20. Goh Kim Chung, 1983.
21. Shallow, P. 1956.
22. Pushparajah, E. 1985.
23. Ibid.
24. Ramayah, J. 1977.
25. Sahabat Alam Malaysia, 1982.
26. *Sunday Mail*, 1977, 17 October.
27. *New Straits Times*, 1986, 2 December.
28. *The Star*, 1986, 8 December.
29. Ibid.
30. Ibid., 15 and 25 May.
31. Ibid., 8 December.
32. Ibid., 1986, 9 December.
33. *New Straits Times on Sunday*, 1986, 6 April.
34. *New Straits Times*, 1977, 11 April.
35. Goh Kim Chum, 1979.
36. Ibid.
37. Khoo, G. 1977.
38. Aiken, R. and C. Leigh, 1985.
39. Shelton, N. 1983.
40. Aiken, R. and C. Leigh, 1985.
41. Shelton, N. 1985.
42. Shelton, N. 1983.
43. Kew Bong Heang, 1982.
44. Aiken, R. and C. Leigh, 1985.
45. Khan, M. 1978.
46. Shelton, N. 1985.
47. Karim, G. (ed.) 1985.
48. Myers, N. 1984.
49. Hood Saleh, 1984.
50. Endicot, K. 1982.
51. Mohd Sham Bin Kasim, 1986.

52. Ibid.
53. Ibid.
54. Malaysian Timber Industries Board, 1983.
55. Ibid.
56. *New Straits Times*, 1983, 8 December.
57. *Malaysian Business Times*, 1985, 29 November.
58. *The Star*, 1986, 28 March.
59. Norzita Samad, 1986.
60. Azam Aris, 1985.
61. Malaysian Timber Industries Board, op. cit.
62. Lim, K.H. and Manan Osman, 1984.
63. Syed Abu Bakar, 1984.
64. *Malaysian Business Times*, 1986, 15 September, quotes H. C. Thang, Director of Forestry Management, Forestry Department of Malaysia.
65. Ministry of Primary Industries, op. cit.
66. Ibid.
67. *Malaysian Business Times*, 1986, 15 September.
68. Jin Eong Ong, 1982.
69. Ibid.
70. Ibid.
71. Ibid.
72. Ibid.
73. United Planting Association of Malaya, 1984.
74. Government of Malaysia, 1st Malaysia Plan, 1966.
75. Ibid.
76. Ibid.
77. Flynn, R. 1978.
78. Jaffar Mussein, Y. B. 1986.
79. Government of Malaysia, 5th Malaysia Plan, 1985.
80. Government of Malaysia, 4th Malaysia Plan, 1981.
81. Sothi Rachagan and Shamsul Bahrin, 1983.
82. Yong Chai Ting, 1984.
83. Ibid.
84. Government of Malaysia, 5th Malaysia Plan, 1985.
85. Ibid.
86. Ministry of Primary Industries, 1984.
87. Federal Land Development Agency, 1956.
88. Government of Malaysia, Five-year Plans (various).
89. Government of Malaysia, 5th Malaysia Plan, 1986.
90. Rajeswary, I. and H. Rohiman, 1986.
91. Ibid.
92. *The Star*, 1986, 27 February.
93. Government of Malaysia, 5th Malaysia Plan, 1986.
94. Rajeswary, I. and H. Rohiman, 1986.
95. Shamsul Bahrin et. al., 1986.
96. Government of Malaysia, 5th Malaysia Plan, 1986.
97. Narinder Kaur, 1985.
98. Ibid.
99. Rokiah Talib, 1986.
100. Ministry of Primary Industries, 1985.
101. Sothi Rachagan and Shamsul Bahrin, 1983.
102. Ibid.
103. Government of Malaysia, 5th Malaysia Plan, 1986.
104. Ministry of Primary Industries, 1985.

105. FAO, 1981.
106. Forestry Department of Malaysia, 1988.
107. FAO, 1981.
108. Sothi Rachagan and Shamsul Bahrin, 1983.
109. Ibid.
110. Leong Khee Seon, 1983.
111. Tan Sri Rama Lyer, 1983.
112. Ministry of Primary Industries, 1985.
113. Ibid.
114. Ibid.
115. Baharuddin Ghazali, 1983.
116. Secrett, C. 1984, personal communication, April.
117. Ministry of Primary Industries, 1985.
118. Sahabat Alam Malaysia, various reports.

3. Malaysia: East Malaysia

Introduction

The two largest states in the Malaysian Federation are Sarawak and Sabah, on the northern half of the island of Borneo. Sandwiched between them is the tiny oil state of Brunei with, after Kuwait, the second richest population in the world. At present East Malaysia has the dubious distinction of being the world's largest exporter of tropical logs. Forests therefore play a central role in the economy.

Sabah: Sabah covers 73,700 sq. km to the north-east of Sarawak, with rolling hills leading up to the Croker mountain range inland. Here, Mount Kinabalu, the highest peak between the Himalayas and Papua New Guinea, reaches 4,000 metres above sea level. The population of little more than one million, mostly inhabiting the western lowlands around the capital, Kota Kinabalu, is growing at 3% per year.

Culturally Sabah has more in common with Mindanao in the Philippines than with West Malaysia. An unknown number of illegal immigrants from the Philippines and Indonesia work in the state, but native tribal groups, known collectively as the Dayaks, form the majority (most Dayaks approve of the term 'native' since it distinguishes them from the *Bumiputeras* of West Malaysia). Sabah joined the Malaysian Federation in 1963, after emancipation from the British North Borneo Company, which had run the state as a limited company since the 19th century.

The economy is based on forestry, agriculture and fishing. The FAO estimate that up to 30% of Sabah is suitable for agriculture but less than 10% of the state is under permanent cultivation;[1] as a result, Sabah is about to be the major area for FELDA projects in the 1990s.

Sarawak: Sarawak occupies 124,450 sq. km of north-west Borneo. A belt of lowland peat swamp forests along its coast leads to a hilly interior gradually rising to more than 600 metres along its borders with Kalimantan. The coastal swamps account for 20% of the land area, 70% of the remainder has slopes of 30° or more.

Two major rivers, the Rejang and the Baram, both navigable for more than 150 km, drain into the South China Sea. Rivers continue to form the major transport routes, although the logging road network now extends far inland.

Sarawak had a population of 1.5m in 1985, growing at 2.7% per year.[2] The Dayak tribal groups account for 44%, making them the single largest group in Sarawak; Chinese constitute 29%; Muslim Malays 20%; and the remainder are Melanu or Indian.[3] Many tribal people have been converted to Christianity, although traditional beliefs continue to permeate the daily life of most people. Unlike West Malaysia, those following the Muslim faith are in a minority in both East Malaysian states.

Sarawak's economy, like Sabah's, is rural with 81% of the population living outside the towns. Oil and timber form the backbone of the cash economy. Oil is Sarawak's most valuable export but the considerable revenues accrue to the federal government in Kuala Lumpur; this has created a certain degree of animosity between a strongly independent Sarawak and West Malaysia. Log exports continue to dominate state income and account for at least 20% to 30% of total export value each year.[5] In 1985 logs to the value of M$1.4 billion left the shores of Sarawak.[6]

History

The caves of Niah National Park in Sarawak confirm the existence of human habitation on Borneo for 50,000 years, but very little is known about these early times. The Chinese have been trading with the Dayaks for several centuries; Buddhist and Hindu artefacts have been found at various sites.

Sarawak has a colourful colonial history. In the mid-19th century the British adventurer, James Brooke, came to Borneo looking for trade. At that time Sarawak was part of the Brunei empire. Based more on piracy than actual rule from the capital, Brunei Dareselam, the empire was in a highly unstable state with much in-fighting as various tribal groups were in rebellion against Brunei. Because Brooke's boat was attacked by tribal rebels he decided to take sides with the Brunei powers. In recognition of his help the Brunei governor gave him 11,200 sq. km of what is now Sarawak and declared him the first white 'rajah' on Borneo. By building forts on all major river mouths, and through various battles and clever political manoeuvring, Brooke extended his sphere of control to cover most of present day Sarawak.

Brooke ruled with a mixture of enlightened Victorian liberalism and a typical British divide and rule policy. With the coast as his stronghold he exploited the old rivalry between the coastal Malays and Chinese and the inland Dayaks. The Sarawak army was built up of members of the Iban tribe, the largest tribal group in this part of Borneo. The Iban were denied access to schooling and colonial economic activity in the early days of the Brooke 'empire' because they were of more use as soldiers than traders. In more enlightened mode, however, Brooke abolished the slave class in Sarawak society. Slaves were rarely of the same tribe as their masters, most were prisoners-of-war, but Brooke's legislation liberated many.

Brooke followed the general British colonial policy in Malaysia of not interfering with tribal customs and religion but concentrating on trade. In 1842 his Land Code forbade any immigrant group claiming rights to settle on customary Dayak land. In 1863 the Land Order gave Brooke control over all 'unoccupied and wastelands', which were automatically the property of the government. Brooke clearly saw the great financial advantage of claiming rights over all 'unused' forest, for timber exploitation. The legislation thus also included restrictions on clearing forests for agricultural expansion without permission from the authorities.

A number of amended Land Orders and Codes, along similar lines, formed the basis for rural development before World War Two. The state was ruled by the Brooke family until 1947 when they finally ceded power to the British authorities. The memory of Brooke provokes a variety of reactions in Sarawak, particularly within the tribal groups. Many feel that the Brooke family would have been more accessible and more likely to listen to their current problems than are the present authorities; others are glad of the independence from foreign colonial rule.

In contrast, Sabah, once also part of the Brunei empire, had a relatively prosaic colonial master, the North Borneo Company. Established in 1863, the company managed Sabah as a limited business in much the same way that India had been managed by the East India Company.

Forest resources

East Malaysia has four major forest types: peat swamp; mixed dipterocarp; heath and montane. Mixed dipterocarp forest covers the largest area in both Sabah and Sarawak.

According to the state's Forest Department there are more than 4.5m ha of forest in Sabah.[7] This accounts for approximately 60% of the land area, but the figure is based on projections from old surveys. Until the new survey is completed it is advisable to assume that government figures are probably optimistic. The Forest Reserve covers 3.4m ha of which 2.7m is productive.[8] The remaining forest area is on 'stateland'. One forestry department official recently claimed that Sabah now has only 2.8m ha of commercially viable forest; a stark contrast to the 6.3m ha thought to be exploitable in 1973.[9]

Data on forests in Sarawak are equally unreliable since current figures are projections from a survey completed in the 1960s. The FAO notes that: 'According to the official land use of the mid-sixties 76.5% (9.4 million hectares) of the total land area was forested.'[10] The Forest Department still claimed to have 9.4m. ha of forest in 1985;[11] it is difficult to believe that in 1985 Sarawak's forest cover remained the same as had existed 20 years previously.

Forest destruction rates

According to the state departments, Sarawak is losing 41,000 ha of forest per year, and Sabah 59,000 ha, although these can be regarded only as rough estimates.[12] The authorities frequently cite shifting agriculture as the major cause of forest loss in East Malaysia, but Tony Hatch, of Sarawak's Department of Agriculture, who carried out one of the most thorough surveys in recent years, claims that this is not so.[13] He estimates that approximately 2.4m ha of Sarawak is under some stage of shifting cultivation with 150,000 ha planted annually. Most of this, however, is in a long cycle and he concludes that the area of new land taken up each year is 'modest' and has probably not increased significantly since the early 1970s. This analysis reduces Sarawak's forest cover from 9.4m ha to seven million. But as FELDA becomes more active in both East Malaysian states the annual clearance rate is due to increase rapidly.

With seven million hectares of forest it may be concluded that Sarawak has no serious problems in this respect, but this is too simplistic for practical analysis as it takes no account of the effects of the timber industry. No official figures are available for the total area of forest logged in Sarawak to date. The most comprehensive study on Sarawak's timber industry and its effects on the Dayak groups there is by Evelyne Hong of the Institut Masyarakat in West Malaysia. She estimates that between 1962 and 1985 approximately 2.82m ha of Sarawak's forests had been logged through. She reaches this figure by using annual log production figures and multiplying by an average yield of 45 cubic metres per hectare. This is a reasonable assumption, as yields were averaging 70 to 80 cubic metres per hectare in the lowland swamp forest but have dropped to 33 in the hills. Thus, in 22 years, 30% of Sarawak's forests have been logged and, at the current annual rates of 270,000 ha a further 30% will be severely degraded by the mid-1990s.

The forests of Sabah have consistently yielded more timber than those of Sarawak, but again estimates of how much is logged over vary. In 1987, the specialist journal *Flora Malesiana Bulletin* reported:

> The facts are that within another five years or so all the lowland forests of Sabah will have been logged except for a few small Virgin Jungle Reserves. . . . The time is already late for botanical research in the primary forests of Sabah.[15]

In 1982–83, in addition to logging, between one and 3.5m ha of the state's forests were reportedly burnt in major fires in Sabah.[16]

Replanting

By late 1986 Sabah had established 45,000 ha of timber plantation and planned an additional 210,000 ha. Sabah Softwoods, a joint venture between North Borneo Timbers and the Sabah Foundation, is leading the replanting effort and so far have established 25,000 ha of fast-growing hardwoods.[17]

The effects of forest loss

Environmental

Environmental degradation directly affects the lives of rural populations. In comparison to West Malaysia, there is little scientific data on the effects of forest clearance in East Malaysia. The remoteness of many areas undoubtedly accounts for this dearth of information.

Timber extraction is, however, cited by SAM and many Dayaks as the primary cause of environmental problems in East Malaysia, although swidden agriculture also plays a part. As one senior forester in Sarawak put it, 'if millions of trees are felled without replacement, Sarawak's climatic conditions, its soil condition and its forest will surely and certainly degrade to the detriment of its inhabitants.'[18]

Erosion and siltation: No thorough soil erosion survey has been carried out in East Malaysia, nor has any classification system been developed. Seen from the air, the coasts of Sabah and Sarawak reveal wide fans of red silt spilling from all the river mouths into the South China seas. Two dredgers work daily at the mouths of the Igan and Oya rivers in Sarawak, (the major transport route between the towns of Sibu and Mubah) to keep the channels open.[19] The *Borneo Post* reports that they are 'fighting a losing battle'; and the state government estimates it will cost at least M$3m (US$1.2m) to maintain the deeper channels.

One of the clearest indications of erosion is the decline in fresh water fish stocks as siltation increases. No thorough study has been carried out on the region as a whole but a WWF survey of opinions in almost 100 longhouse communities found that 76% of those interviewed perceived a serious decline in fish stocks in recent years.[20] The survey notes that 'a catastrophic decline in fish stocks' is perceived in areas affected by logging.[21] Siltation also reaches the few coral reefs and mangroves found in East Malaysia. WWF report that the coral reefs around Pulay Satang Besar 'have already been killed by siltation and others nearby are likely to be killed off in the near future.'[22]

Sabah had 130,000 ha of rough grassland by the early 1970s, but more recent figures are not available.[23] There has been no overall study on soil erosion from these areas but they can be compared to Indonesia's critical areas.

The most thorough soil survey completed in Sarawak is by Tony Hatch of the Sarawak Department of Agriculture.[24] Although his study was geared towards assessing the agricultural potential of many soils he clearly states: 'there is little doubt in this writer's mind that the soil erosion created by timber extraction is far in excess of that created by shifting cultivation.'[25] Shifting agriculture cannot be exonerated from contributing to soil erosion, but its role has been over-emphasized.

Flooding and drought: There is a general perception amongst the Dayaks that floods and droughts are becoming more intense in East Malaysia, although again there are no long-term scientific data to support this. Its location near the Philippines results in East Malaysia experiencing some of the more extreme weather fluctuations, which may account for occasional floods but forest destruction has probably intensified them.

Flooding along the Baram river has increased significantly since logging was established in the area; major floods occurred in 1979 and in 1981, when 30 people were drowned.[26] Wong Leong Do, then co-ordinator of flood relief operations, claimed that excessing logging had exacerbated the problem.[27] Flooding along the Baram in January 1984 claimed four lives and left hundreds homeless,[28] and in 1985 the area was again subject to flooding. In early 1986 flash flooding in Sabah claimed five lives and forced an estimated 10,000 people to flee to higher ground.[29]

Like Kalimantan in Indonesia, East Malaysia experienced serious droughts in the early 1980s and water had to be delivered into many areas in both states.[30] In 1981, as water supplies dwindled, more than 100 cases of cholera were reported, resulting in 16 deaths.[31] Research into possible causes of this major drought have been restricted to Indonesia, despite the problems experienced in Sabah. The sequence of droughts continues and similar conditions were developing in 1986.[32]

Wildlife loss: East Malaysia's fauna and flora differ significantly from that of West Malaysia. Clearance of virgin forest, particularly by the logging industry, is starting to take a toll on East Malaysia's wildlife. In Sarawak the endangered species list includes the proboscis monkey, the Sumatran rhino, silvered and banded langur and the dugong.[33] In Sabah the orang utan survives only in limited numbers, and even the hornbills, the state symbol of Sarawak, are becoming increasingly rare.

The importance of genetic resources has been noted previously, but one study on wildlife in Sarawak places a new emphasis on their value. This study, by Julian Caldecott, originates from a WWF project to assess the wild pig population of Sarawak.[34] Caldecott estimates that at least one million bearded pigs, 31,000 Hijang deer and 23,000 Rusa deer are caught by the Dayak population each year. This amounts to more than 35,000 tons of wild meat, only a small fraction of which enters the cash economy. The economic value of this food source is considerable, as Caldecott notes:

At ordinary rural prices the annual wild pig and deer harvest would cost nearly MS$210m [US$100m]; if it was replaced by domestic pork, and for venison or beef, at current prices, the harvest would cost more than MS$320m [US$150m] each year. It can easily be seen that somewhere along the line the availability of wild meat is effectively liberating the state's development budget many tens of millions of dollars annually.[35]

A combination of forest disturbance and greater access to firearms in longhouses had led to an overall decline in the size of catches. In the lowlands, where little virgin forest remains, bearded pigs average 30 kg; in the more remote areas they average 100 kg.

A similar situation prevails with estimates for the value of fresh water fish to the economy. Along the lower reaches of the Baram an estimated MS\$190,000-worth of fresh water fish caught in one section of this river was traded annually.[36]

Sarawak also has a sizeable in-shore fishing trade. Crabs and prawns to an estimated value of MS\$65m (US\$30m) are traded annually; this industry is almost totally dependent on intact mangroves. Mangroves, however, are being cut for woodchipping in both Sarawak and Sabah. The WWF estimate that, if left intact, the mangroves would provide between two and five times more employment and cash revenue than the woodchipping operations do at present.[37]

For many Dayaks wild food will continue to play a major role in the daily diet for many years. This value of forests as a food source is rarely considered in development proposals, not only in East Malaysia but throughout Asia. As Caldecott concludes, 'even a massive investment in wildlife management in Sarawak should remain firmly and indefinitely on the side of good economic sense.'[38]

Social costs

Dayak culture is closely linked to the land. The rapid expansion of the timber industry has had a profoundly damaging effect on almost every tribal community in East Malaysia, in so far as timber extraction not only causes great environmental damage but also severely restricts access to forest areas and swidden sites.

Despite the extent of Sarawak's rural population averaging only 2.4 inhabitants per square kilometre there is a shortage of farm land.[39] This is because the fallow periods for the swidden fields are declining and the soils becoming exhausted. Traditionally, swidden land would be left fallow for between ten and 20 years; this is now reduced to three to seven years.[40] In 1970, rice production from hill paddy sites was estimated to be 60,000 tons, by 1980 this had dropped to 47,000 tons.[41] Sarawak is now a net importer of rice.[42]

A major survey by the Sarawak Medical Services in 1979 found that 72% of rural Dayak children were moderately malnourished (20–39% under-weight) and 8.4% severely malnourished (40%+ underweight).[43] In comparison, the average percentage of severe malnutrition in Latin America is 1.6%; in Asia as a whole 3.2%; and in Africa 4.4%.[44] As a result, many tribal people drift into the coastal towns and settle in the squatter areas, hoping to find casual labour. Despite being part of a Muslim-dominated Malaysia, Sarawak and Sabah have a large number of prostitutes, nearly all of whom are Dayak women, forced into prostitution as a means of survival.

These problems stem from three roots: lack of access rights to the majority of the forests; a general contempt for tribal society; and a capital-intensive timber industry that provides little, poorly-paid and dangerous employment.

Malaysian law enables the state governments to claim all forest land and develop it as they see fit. Most longhouse communities are trespassers in the permanent forest estate and have few or no land rights. Frequently no warning is given to the local population that their lands have been leased out as a timber concession; they discover this only when the bulldozers move in. In 1981 the Baram District Officer in his annual report noted:

> Extraction of timber in fact has caused extensive and irreparable damage to the natural land surface and vegetation. It has frightened and threatened the life and habitation of wild, rare and precious birds and animals, depriving the local people of their hunting grounds. . . . Complaints of water pollution by timber camps and damage to jetties by tug boats, barges and floating logs have often been received from the longhouse people. . . . In the past two [1979–81] years the Baram District has experienced successive severe flooding causing extensive damage to crops and livestock, cutting communications for weeks and causing hardship to people from all walks of life.[45]

In *Natives of Sarawak*, Evelyne Hong describes the gradual escalation of conflicts between logging companies and longhouse communities throughout the state. There are numerous cases in which local communities have tried to obtain compensation for damage to their environment, but very few have had any degree of success. Longhouses attempting to secure rights over Communal Forest areas frequently have their applications rejected. Between 1974 and 1985 the area of communal forests decreased from 303 to 56 sq. km.[46] At present it takes between six and 12 years for communal forest applications to be heard in court.[47]

The case study for East Malaysia outlines the events leading up to the 'timber blockades' of 1987 and 1988 in the Fourth Division of Sarawak. At this point the case of logging in the Belaga area in the Seventh Division provides an adequate example.

The Belaga area lies towards the upper reaches of Sarawak's largest river, the Rejang. Logging was established there in 1976, and by 1985 12 concessions were operating. In 1982 several longhouses began to voice opposition to logging because of the damage it caused. The longhouses had submitted more than 30 applications for the status of Communal Forest to be conferred on the areas around their longhouses in the hope that they could control the logging; all 30 were rejected. In 1982 the Chief Police

Officer for the Division is reported to have, 'stressed that all applications for Communal Forest should be automatically turned down and the local population informed of this promptly so that they would not hold up logging operations in those areas.'[48] In 1983, this position was reaffirmed by the Sarawak Resident.[49]

As Evelyne Hong notes: 'This clearly reflects a negative stance towards the natives in their application for Communal Forests (a right upheld in the Sarawak Forest Ordinance).'[50] She recalls one Kenyah (a particular Dayak tribe) telling her, 'We were never informed that the timber companies were operating on our land. We only knew when we saw the big tractor coming.'[51] In another case, also in the Belaga area, Evelyne Hong notes:

> According to the headman, sometime in early 1985, a man came to the longhouse and delivered him a letter and a map. The map showed the location of the Danum Protected Forest. Eighteen longhouses will be affected by this conversion. This means that natives are now forbidden to exercise customary land tenure in this area. . . . When I asked him if he understood the contents of the letter and the map, he said he did not know. He showed them to me as if he wanted me to explain the contents to him.[52]

Logging companies are neither compelled to announce their intentions in local newspapers nor to use local languages, everything is written in English.

Once logging became established numerous cases were reported in which valuable fruit trees were destroyed, sacred burial sites bulldozed and the rivers polluted.[53] In early 1983 six longhouses formed a company whose aim was to approach all the logging operations in the area to obtain compensation for this damage through a levy system based on the timber extracted. The money would be used for the general welfare of the people in the six longhouses. They originally asked for MS$10 (US$4) for every ton extracted but soon reduced this to MS$0.5 (US$0.20 cents); the logging companies, however, still refused to negotiate.

Later that year (1983) an entire longhouse approached Lua Timber, a contractor working for Delapan, the largest concession holder in the area, seeking compensation for damage to their boats due to a low bridge the contractor had built across the river. Siltation had increased in the river, and the local longhouse claimed many people had developed diarrhoea after using water from it. According to those involved, the police were flown in and produced a threatening letter which they claimed six headmen had sent to the logging company. The police maintained that the threats in the letter were illegal, as was the assembly of the longhouse people on company land.

After hours of fruitless negotiations a few tribesmen approached the bridge threatening to cut it down; others from the longhouse talked them out of this. Soon, however, according to eye witnesses:

They took all the discarded tyres; carried them to the bridge intending to burn it. Then the police went down and told them, 'Don't'. They did not listen to the police. Some of the policemen said; 'if you don't stop we will shoot.' Then some [tribesmen] said 'Police can shoot us, never mind if we are all killed'. They stood in front of the police, stuck out their chests, some took off their shirts. . . . They then stopped and we went back to the camp.[54]

The next day a large crowd from several longhouses went to Lua Timber's logging camp. Eighty 'fieldforce parapolice' had been flown in to keep order. Representatives of the local community were invited to talks but again these were unsuccessful. The following day 13 of these representatives were arrested on ludicrously vague charges; a local councillor had to put up MS$2,000 (US$800) bail for each of the accused. In 1984, the case was brought to court four times, until all the charges were finally dropped. The bridge that was the focus of the trouble still stands.

It is no surprise that as contractor to the licensee, Delapan, Lua Timber can override the interests of the local population. Major shareholders in Delapan at that time included: Datuk Tajang Laing (Parti Pesoka Bumiputera Bersatu [PBB], statesman for the Belaga district. PBB is the senior party in the state's four-party National Front coalition); Haji Zainuddin Satem (senior PBB member); Haji Idris Abdullah (personal secretary to the Chief Minister); Norlia Abdul Rahman (daughter of the previous Chief Minister); and Kupa Kayan (a community leader in Belaga).[55]

Before 1987, in Sarawak alone, the police were called to intervene in 20 to 40 similar cases each year.[56] Most disputes, however, do not involve the police, as some form of compensation is usually agreed upon between the logging camp manager and the longhouses concerned. But this does nothing to prevent the damage, and negotiations begin only if the local population blockade the logging road. There has been an unknown number of small blockades in recent years, mostly due to the destruction of sacred burial sites. In early 1987 Harrison Gnau of Sahabat Alam Malaysia in Sarawak estimated that the average compensation for the destruction of a site was MS$300 (US$125).[57] For a culture in which ancestor worship is common this sum does not reflect a realistic value, it simply indicates how much the Dayaks think they can get.

Since 1987 a more militant stand has been developing, particularly in the upper catchment area of the Baram and Limbang rivers. In late 1986 a statement by eight Penan headmen, through Sahabat Alam Malaysia in Sarawak, illustrated the increasing frustration of many Dayak communities:

We cannot wait any longer as everyday our livelihood is continually besieged by the threatening activities of the logging companies. And if we are continually ignored, we take it that you are no longer interested in our problems; and shall take appropriate actions to defend ourselves, our future generations, our land, our crops, our properties and so forth, from further and continued destruction.[58]

Despite the reactions of those people adversely affected, timber exploitation has, on one level, helped East Malaysia to develop: a few people have made a lot of money. For the population as a whole, however, including those directly employed in the timber trade, the problems frequently outweigh the advantages. It cannot be denied that there is a demand for Western consumer items in most Dayak longhouses, and consequently a need to earn a cash income from the forests. But there are other, less destructive means for them to do this. At present, however, most Dayaks have little choice.

In 1977 logging in Sarawak employed 27,800 workers, approximately 57% of whom were local people.[59] Most skilled work, however, is carried out by imported labour from the Philippines, with the result that the Dayaks are generally restricted to poorly paid and dangerous seasonal, manual labour; pay is usually based upon how much the worker produces. Fleet engineers, employed on a more permanent basis, may be paid as little as MS$8 (US$3) per day. The timber camp has accommodation but most workers must provide their own food, which they usually buy from the camp shop, as the nearest town may be many miles down river. The Sarawak Timber Industries Development Corporation (STIDC) notes that:

> Poor accommodation and living conditions prevail in most logging camps. Poor housing conditions can be the reason for the spread of certain insect-borne diseases like malaria and typhus. . . . Medical supervision and care is non-existent in the logging camps.[60]

Wages are frequently withheld until the timber has been sold. In 1985 SAM surveyed five randomly selected logging camps in Sarawak and found that in only two were workers paid regularly, and in many cases individual workers had not been paid for three months or more.[61]

It is common for seasonal labourers to work a 16 hour day in order to maximize their income over the year. But perhaps the major problem is the danger involved; the timber trade has the highest incidence of accidents and death of any of East Malaysia's industries. In 1983 Sabah recorded 153 fatalities and Sarawak 81.[62] By 1984 the industry in Sarawak claimed seven lives for every one million cubic metres of timber produced. In comparison the Canadian logging industry recorded one death for every three million cubic metres of logs produced.[63] Serious accidents, usually involving the loss of a limb, are also recorded in East Malaysia. In Sarawak in 1984, there were 1,553 non-fatal logging accidents.[64] These statistics illustrate management's disregard of the need to implement proper safety measures, as the Ministry of Forestry put it: 'Even fatal accidents are soon forgotten in places where labour is cheap and abundant.'[65]

The timber workers' plight is compounded by the minimal compensation they or their families receive in cases of injury or death. Two compensation schemes are available, the Workmen's Compensation Scheme (WCS under the Workmen's Compensation Act 1977) and SOSCO (under the Social Security Act 1969). The maximum compensation for the death of a worker is MS$14,400 (US$5,700) under the WCS, or 70% of the average monthly earnings under SOSCO.

Compensation for permanent disablement is also considerably lower than the courts award for injuries sustained in accidents outside the forestry industry. SAM cite numerous cases including that of Lutau, a chainsaw operator in Sarawak who lost his right leg due to a falling tree and was awarded MS$14,400 (US$5,700) compensation under the WCS.[66] Under SOSCO he would have received MS$190 (US$75) per month. Whereas the courts awarded shop owner, Soon Song Lee, who was knocked down by a lorry and disabled due to a shortening of his right leg MS$64,000 (US$25,300).[67]

In addition, there is no provision for the rehabilitation of injured workers in the timber industry in Malaysia. Workers are not even allowed to appeal against any compensation decision under WCS or SOSCO and are also forbidden to sue their employers for injuries sustained while working. There is no legislation covering workers' safety specific to the timber industry, despite the high rate of injuries and death. Logging in Malaysia is one of the most hazardous jobs in the world.

Forced relocation: Although timber extraction affects almost every longhouse community in East Malaysia, forced relocation to make way for dams and resettlement schemes is also prevalent. The Batang Ai dam in the Lubok Antu district of Sarawak's second division provides a good example.[68] The dam across the Ai river was completed in 1985 with a projected operational lifetime of 50 years, at a cost of more than MS$520m (US$204m); the main contractor was Maeda-Okumura of Japan. The project covered 16,000 ha of which 8,500 was to be flooded. In total, 29 longhouses upstream and four downstream, had to be relocated, involving the provision of compensation and new land for more than 3,000 Iban people.

According to a survey by the Sarawak Museum, before the dam was built the majority of the local communities affected did not fully understand the project and its implications. The Museum's report concluded:

> Unless proper regard and due consideration are given for their social and
> economic interests the evacuated Iban will suffer from the experience of
> moving, as it would uproot them from their traditional life patterns;

upset their productivity and income; and deprive them of their most important assets – land. In short, they may see it as a direct threat to their very existence.[69]

Opposition grew as the scale of the project became clear to the Iban. In 1982 ignition keys for more than 30 large vehicles were confiscated by a small group of Iban and, soon after, a Japanese worker was killed. The authorities issued stern warnings to anyone opposing the dam. In 1985 the official opening of the dam was marred by police breaking up a demonstration of relocated Iban demanding their compensation money; of the MS$35m promised to those relocated, MS$10m was still outstanding in 1986.[70]

Many Iban claimed to have been told they would be provided with free housing, water and electricity when they moved. The reality, however, was different, as one headman explained in 1984:

We were told that when we arrive at our new longhouses we would be given 11 acres of cleared land. The land was also to have been planted with five acres of rubber, three acres of cocoa and two acres of paddi. At present we have no steady income. The cocoa, when planted, will take three or four years before it is ready for harvesting and the rubber trees will take seven or eight years. In the mean time how are we supposed to pay for our homes, our electricity and water supply?[71]

There were also complaints that the water taps never worked, roofs leaked and the electricity supply was sporadic. Those who received compensation, between MS$30,000 (US$11,800) and MS$100,000 (US$39,500) per family, faced problems on how to adjust to this sudden wealth. Most of the money went on spending sprees, some on gambling and some to the flood of conmen promising land and company shares. The following extract from Evelyne Hong's book *Natives of Sarawak* illustrates what happened to one Iban family.

I met an old Iban who happened to be the head of the longhouse so I introduced myself to him. I asked him a question. I called him father as a way of respect. 'Father, how is the life after the dam, how is your life now after you've been resettled?' He said, 'It is lovely, it is fantastic. I have a lot of money in the bank. I have a good house. I have a big car, brand new. And now we have roads to go to town.' He asked me: 'Son, what do you want to drink?' I told him: 'I want only a cup of coffee'. He was so disappointed. . . . He told me: 'I don't drink coffee here. I've only brandy, whisky, Bacardi and the expensive brands of liquor. Why do you want to drink coffee? Why do you look down on me? You are not a good boy and I'm sorry we have no coffee here.' So I had to get drunk because I forced myself to drink. And I started to wonder how beautiful their life was because at that time I still had very little knowledge about them.

After ten months in the Batang Ai I came back home. I went again to Batang Ai to see my old father and his face smiled when he saw me. He said to me: 'Oh you're here again' and I asked him: 'Father, how is life now, it has been so long since I left you and we have not seen each other.' And he answered me slowly 'Son, to say that it is good will be bad, I should say here that the life here is good because I have a house, I have electricity, I have water supply and I have a car, I have roads. But I say it is bad because I have to pay for the water bill, I'm going to pay for the electricity. I'm surprised that I have to pay MS$27,000 for this house and I'm paying it monthly and last month my electricity bill was very high, because I had opened it for 24 hours with the refrigerator on, with the tv on, ironing clothes, using the rice cooker and the heater and the lights. I thought it was free at the beginning. So it was a burden to me to have to pay the very high bills last month. And I have to maintain this house with my own money. And I have to buy the petrol for the car and maintain this car. I'm going to buy the vegetables and fish in the town because hardly anything is found around here. No crops are available to us here although the government promised to give crops to us before we came. That's why I tell you it is bad and the life is bad here.'

I went back to my own district. After I returned I read about the problems of the Batang Ai people in the newspapers and that the people in the resettlement areas were blaming their politicians for many of the problems they were facing in the resettlement scheme. I wanted to know what had happened to my rich father so I met him again for the third time and I asked him again, 'Father I have come, how is life now? After reading a lot of news about you all here I am anxious to know.' With his sad face, I should say, he never smiled again. He spoke to me in a low voice that had no life in it at all. 'Son, we are going to die.' But I said 'Why? I'm not satisfied with the answer.' He said, after a long pause, 'No money. The money in the bank has finished. I can't afford to pay the electric bill so I cut off the meter, maybe I will cut off the water meter later on if I can't afford to pay that too. The house is leaking, I have to pay for the maintenance.' I asked him: 'Father, where is the big car?' And he answered me: 'I have sold it, son.' I said 'Why, it's a good car, it is brand new, it is only over a year old.' He said: 'I have no money.' I asked him how much did he sell it for and he answered: '500.' 'And how much did you buy it for?' and he told me '25,000.' And that car is a Galant Sigma, a big car. I shook my head. 'So what will happen father?' He told me: 'We are going to fight for our rights because we have been cheated. We thought the authorities were sincere, but they are not.' I told him: 'It's too late to struggle now.'

He never answered me and brought me a cup of water. I thought it was expensive brandy which they were offering me again. But it was only plain water and it was not boiled and he gave it to me with a very sad voice: 'I have only this son, I've nothing to offer you, it is only plain water.' I was so sad to drink this. They were laughing at the beginning but now they are crying, and I believe they will cry forever and forever because they have lost their lovely land.[72]

Even the promises that the dam would bring employment were never fulfilled. At the peak of construction, in the early 1980s, the dam employed 1,500 local Ibans.[73] By early 1985 this had been reduced by half and now the dam is fully operational and managed by 40 to 50 people, nearly all of whom are skilled workers from outside the area.[74]

The mistrust of the local Iban population was compounded when the Prime Minister, upon opening the dam, stated that the compensation provided was 'completely ridiculous' and that Sarawak would 'have to pay the price' of this extra expense with higher electric bills.[75] (The Malaysian authorities plan to construct a much larger dam at Bakun on the upper reaches of the Rejang river. This more extensive project is outlined in the case studies.)

Similar problems in connection with compensation for loss of land have occurred in general land development schemes. Those who can claim compensation are fortunate; proof of ownership of land is essential in order to qualify, and many have none.

Development of forestry policy

The Brooke family's influence on Sarawak was as strong as any colonial administration. Despite a rather liberal image the family gradually undermined the traditional *adat* law system with successive pieces of legislation. For example, the 1875 Land Code called for leniency when dealing with 'squatters' on government forest land, but permitted others to claim cleared areas. These cleared areas were the land left fallow in the swidden farming system, which could thus be legally claimed by anybody, despite individual families possessing full *adat* rights over it. In 1899 the Fruit Trees Order further curtailed the power for natives to establish customary rights, and forbade disposal of land even within their own community.

No comprehensive land development system had been developed by the end of the century and the legislation was dominated by a confusion of land orders. In 1920, Land Orders Eight and Nine consolidated all previous laws and decreed that state land included all areas not 'leased or granted or lawfully occupied by any person'. In other words, customary land rights were recognized only if they were registered with the authorities; most Dayaks were now living on 'stateland'. In addition, 'Rajah' Brooke was empowered to lease out or to grant ownership over any state land. A new classification system was developed, dividing state lands into town and suburban lands, country lands and native holdings. Dayaks were given some rights over forest areas under 'native holdings' which later became 'Native Land Reserves'. These reserves were divided into three-acre family plots but took no account of communal forest areas.

Cash crop expansion was becoming established in East Malaysia during the 1920s and the financial value of land was increasing. State legislation in the 1930s reflected this development, as the government consolidated its powers to claim ownership over any non-registered land. For example, the 1933 Land Settlement Order gave the state powers of compulsory purchase over any native customary land.

Sarawak was handed over to the British government in 1946. The new authorities established another land classification system that is maintained under the present legislation, the 1958 Land Code. At present Sarawak is divided into four tenure categories: Mixed Zone, 7.9%; Native Area, 7.4%; Reserved Land, 15.7%; and Native Customary Right and Interior Land, 69%.[76] Mixed zone land may be owned by any individual. Native area land is supposed to be held only by the indigenous population but others can acquire mineral or forest produce (timber) rights over it. Individuals may also acquire this land if they enter into any deal with a native who has legal title. In legal terms the purchaser then becomes 'native'. Institutions may acquire this 'native' status; the Sarawak Timber Industry Development Corporation is one such body. Reserved land refers to areas such as national parks, wildlife sanctuaries and so on, all of which can supersede native land rights.

Native customary land may be claimed by local people only if the authorities were notified of such claims before 1958. After this date customary rights can be claimed only with written authority from the chief minister; if granted, the area becomes a 'communal reserve'. In most cases, however, a permit system is employed, conferring temporary use rights over state-owned interior land. But as Evelyne Hong notes:

> The Minister can simply declare by order in the Gazette that such Native Communal Reserve will cease to be one and the government is free to dispose of the land. Although in degazetting . . . the Minister must be satisfied that it will not cause 'injustice or oppression', there is nothing in the provision that allows for an appeal to the courts about the decision.[77]

Customary rights may be granted over Interior Land but, as the authorities admit, such rights are 'no greater than a bare licence',[79] and the government may retract them at any time, without even publicizing their decision. As a result natives' customary rights may be rescinded without their knowledge.

In the eyes of the authorities, despite these considerable powers, swidden agriculture has hindered the development of cash crops in East Malaysia.[79]

During the 1960s East Malaysia followed a similar development path to that of the Peninsula's, with timber playing a central role in the economy. Timber exploitation was perceived as the source of the state's wealth, as oil revenues accrued to the Federal Government. Native claims over large areas of land were regarded as an obstacle to economic development and, in 1974, an amendment to the Land Code empowered the Chief Minister to make changes to any land tenure rights for a 'public purpose'. A further amendment in 1979 stated that to erect any buildings, to plough, dig, enclose or cultivate 'any state land' was an offence. This amendment also empowered land and survey officers to arrest any 'trespassers' and to remove buildings and crops from these areas; previously such powers were restricted to the police.

These laws helped implement general land development policy, but East Malaysia also had more specific Forest Ordinances, similar to those in West Malaysia. The 1953 Sarawak Forest Ordinance forms the legal basis for today's forest policy. Only minor differences exist between the ordinances in East and West Malaysia, but it is worth noting some of the details in order to provide some idea of forest policy.

Sarawak has two major forest classifications: the Permanent Forest Estate (32,800 sq. km) and Stateland Forests (62,400 sq. km). The Permanent Forest Estate is sub-divided into: Forest Reserves; Protected forest; and Communal forest. Restrictions applying to Forest Reserves are the most stringent as these areas are designated as a permanent source of timber. Entry into Forest Reserves is forbidden without a licence, and the local population is banned from hunting, farming or collecting forest produce. By 1984 Forest Reserves covered almost 8,500 sq. km of Sarawak's forests.[80] In Protected forest, customary land tenure is forbidden but the local population is allowed to hunt, fish and collect non-timber forest produce, if they have the authorities' permission. Protected forests cover 24,000 sq. km of the state.[81] Communal forests are established near longhouses in a convenient area that may provide for the community's needs. The Ordinance notes that: 'Communal forests will normally be large enough to supply permanently the domestic needs of the community specified, allowing for a reasonable increase in population.'[82] In 1985, of Sarawak's 32,800 sq. km of Permanent Forest, 56 sq. km were designated as Communal forests.[83]

The Ordinance provides details on timber extraction and general forest management in the same way as its counterparts in West Malaysia. Amendments in 1979 enable forest officers to evict anyone breaking the code and to confiscate their belongings. Prior to the amendment, forestry officers could repossess or destroy housing and crops only with a court order. In addition, no forestry or police officer may be held liable for any loss or damage to the property of anyone trespassing or breaking this law.

The official view is that the Land Code and the Forest Ordinance are there to protect the forests for the good of the state as a whole, while simultaneously retaining native rights. Although the laws recognize the existence of native land rights, they contain so many provisions for their removal that they offer little protection. Control of forest land in East Malaysia is thus concentrated in the hands of a few individuals. The concept of land ownership is, however, alien to Dayak culture, as one elder put it:

> The land belongs to the countless numbers who are dead, the few who are living and the multitudes of those yet to be born. How then, can the government say that all untitled land belongs to itself when there have been people using the land even before the government itself existed?[84]

Present causes of forest loss

East Malaysia is the site of South-East Asia's most active timber industry; logging is therefore largely cited as the primary cause of forest loss by most observers. Shifting cultivation is also held responsible, along with agricultural development projects and large dams.

Before the 1980s the authorities' view that swidden agriculture was the primary cause of forest destruction was rarely questioned. Today, however, many environmentalists in the region regard swidden as perhaps the only viable agricultural system for many areas. It is perhaps relevant here to outline some of the fundamental concepts underlying swidden cultivation and *adat* law in East Malaysia.

Adat as a way of life

In many texts *adat* is used to describe a traditional legal system, but it is much more, encompassing a set of beliefs and values that affect all aspects of tribal life. *Adat* is a set of unwritten rules and principles that extends to everything and to relationships in both the physical and the spirit world. Everything is inhabited by a spirit of some kind and there is a proper way to conduct relationships with them. Everything is in balance and any disturbance in the spiritual world may well affect other members of the earthly family or community.

Each longhouse has a number of elders, men well versed in *adat* and its rituals, and others, who command great respect within the community. Most village elders are members of the higher social strata, although this is not a stipulation for the position; the traditional social hierarchy within many Dayak groups has declined since slavery was abolished. These elders form a council that takes collective decisions on important matters and also preside over village courts in which all longhouse disputes are settled.

The concepts of *adat* are also embedded in the agricultural systems developed. There is a wealth of ritual involved with the swidden system that aims to redress the balance of nature that agriculture temporarily interrupts. Spirit worship is practised through these ceremonies rather than in specific places or at regular intervals. The whole process of work thus brings individuals into contact with the spirit world, and if that work should cause conflict between the spirits the consequences may be felt by the whole community. This factor undoubtedly encourages communal work, in so far as responsibility for any project that may adversely affect the spirit world is shared by all.

In common with other tribal societies in the region, land is not owned, but each generation in turn acts as custodians over it. Individual families have well-defined farming sites of which they enjoy exclusive use, in effect a temporary resident with protected rights. The forest, however, is almost always communal property, although individual trees may be claimed by one family. Most areas of forest will be claimed by a longhouse community, but boundaries, particularly to general hunting grounds, are often vaguely defined.

This basic social structure survives in the upper reaches of East Malaysia's rivers although few unadulterated examples exist. Modern political, economic and cultural forces have infiltrated the vast majority of longhouse communities. The result is a curious mixture of the traditional, alongside 'pop' music and great enthusiasm for American wrestling. Christian missionaries have also been very active in East Malaysia but old beliefs are often incorporated into this newly introduced faith. A general mistrust of West Malaysian Muslim society undoubtedly enhances the attraction of Christianity for the Dayaks.

All these factors have modified and transformed the *adat* system, and consequently agricultural methods and forest use. Traditional swidden agriculture is a manifestation of the Dayak concept of a world of balance and renewal, which is rapidly eroding under modern conditions and circumstances.

Swidden agriculture

The swidden system is based on rotation: land is cultivated and then left fallow until its fertility is restored; the cycle then begins again. The duration of a complete cycle depends on local ecological conditions and the availability of land.

The basic model may seem crude, but traditional swidden cultivation is a highly developed, sustainable means of farming on poor, tropical forest soils. According to Erik Eckholm of the Worldwatch Institute, swidden farmers, 'usually carry in their heads an extraordinary fund of scientifically sound knowledge about plant species and soil qualities'.[85] Spencer, commenting on their knowledge of soil types, noted that: 'Such awareness is indicative of a people who are far advanced technologically from the very beginnings of crop-growing practice.'[86]

In the swidden cycle the initial process is slashing and burning a new site, hence it is also known as 'slash and burn' agriculture. Secondary forest sites are preferred, as it takes much more energy to cut down primary forest. Burning the resultant debris releases potash and phosphates into the soils immediately prior to planting crops that will need them. It also increases the potential acidity of soils, a useful development in the old laterite soils that dominate much of this region.[87] The burning is fast – affecting only the top few centimetres of the soil – and controlled. Many trees survive these fires and, as Watters notes, it 'also leads to an improvement in certain properties of the soil which in some areas makes cultivation possible and generally leads to increased yields during the period of cultivation.'[88] Other studies confirm this and claim that soil nutrient levels increase dramatically after burning but drop to initial pre-burn levels after the harvest.[89]

In Sarawak, the average size of a swidden plot for a family of five varies from 1.3 to 2.5 ha, although traditionally the latter is not common;[90] the size is usually restricted to an area that one family can weed properly. In this way only small areas are cultivated, leaving most of the land in the cycle fallow. Clearing only small areas is a major contribution to reducing soil erosion. Tony Hatch recently claimed that 'erosion and run off occurring during the hill paddy cropping cycle is very low and does not differ significantly from that under either primary or well grown secondary jungle.'[91] Even on slopes of more than 25° erosion under traditional crops is minimal. But cultivating pepper, which is promoted as a modern cash crop, commonly causes serious erosion;[92] this is because pepper grown for cash is not planted with other crops and it does not provide adequate ground cover.

The other major factor that reduces soil erosion is the variety of crops grown on any one site. Different crops are planted throughout the year, providing the farmer with a steady supply of food. Inter-cropping looks 'messy' to those accustomed to the neat rows in Western-style farming, but it has distinct advantages in the tropical forest environment. The field structure frequently mimics the surrounding forest, with a top or canopy layer, perhaps banana or sago palm, a middle layer of maize or beans, and a bottom layer of root vegetables. Multiple cropping reduces pest infestation as there is not enough of any one plant for the pest population to expand indefinitely. Inter-cropping also reduces soil erosion, as the ground is never totally cleared at any one time.

The staple crop is usually rice, but other common crops include: pumpkins, various beans, maize, cassava, banana, sugar cane, pineapple, sweet potato, tapioca, tobacco, chillies, ginger, betel leaf, and mustard. This variety of plants also helps the forest to reclaim these areas, as certain crops provide shade, enabling forest species to germinate. Even after the rice harvest and during the fallow period, swidden sites continue to yield a variety of crops.

Swidden agriculture requires relatively large tracts of land but is labour intensive and requires few tools. In East Malaysian conditions it is more appropriate to measure the system's efficiency not by output per unit labour but yield per unit area. To this end, swidden is remarkably efficient. According to Tony Hatch swidden farms frequently produce more than 1,000 kg of rice per ha and up to 2,000 kg in some areas.[93] As Spencer comments:

> Shifting cultivation is still practised in sections of the Asian tropics because there has been developed no other system of greater efficiency, effectively suited to the rather poor physical environments and specific ecological situations in which shifting cultivation is still employed.[94]

This description is based on the traditional system that over the millennia has proved to be sustainable.[95] Today, however, there are serious restrictions that have caused problems for swidden farmers. The system needs access to land, a right that has been strenuously denied to swidden farmers for the last two decades. This loss has reduced the fallow periods and placed further burdens on the swidden sites. These problems are compounded by the lack of access to forest for collecting other sources of food. According to Dr Chin See Chung, fish provide up to one third of the average food intake, wild meat approximately 20% and wild plants, such as mushrooms, bananas, and various shoots and such like, from 10 to 25% of daily needs.[96] The cumulative result of these problems is that when swidden farming is severely restricted and the fallow periods reduced or even abandoned, the forest and the soils can no longer survive. This is not the fault of the initial farming system, but of political control over forests and land. Despite its contribution to long-term forest clearance, swidden farming in East Malaysia must be placed in context with the timber industry and the needs of the local population.

The most severe critics of swidden agriculture in East Malaysia are those involved in the timber industry. This is no surprise – the two sides are competing for the same land. The anti-swidden lobby frequently quotes the estimates for forest destruction in Sarawak from Lau Buong Tiing, a senior executive forester. In his paper, 'The effects of shifting cultivation on sustained yield management for Sarawak national forests', Lau claims that approximately 61,000 ha of virgin forest are 'destroyed by shifting cultivators every year'.[97] He also claims a further 40,000 ha of secondary forest is cleared by the 36,000 swidden households in Sarawak.[98] This gives a total 100,000 ha of forest cleared by swidden agriculturalists every year.

These figures are based on some rather unscientific assumptions. First, they are estimated from aerial photographs taken in certain parts of Sarawak between 1966 and 1976. Whether these areas were truly representative of the state as a whole is open to debate. The second assumption is that each family uses an average of seven acres (2.8 ha) each year. As noted above, this can be regarded as an overestimate of the accepted norm in Sarawak. Even taking Tony Hatch's upper figure of 2.5 ha per family the total area affected already drops to 90,000 ha. Lau's figures also ignore the widely acccepted fact that swidden farmers frequently prefer secondary forest sites. Taking this into account Evelyne Hong notes, 'it is likely that much less than 18,000 ha of new primary forests are cleared by swidden farmers each year.'[99] By comparison, Hong estimates that more than 270,000 ha of forest is logged annually.

Whatever the role of swidden farming in forest destruction the reality is that there may be little alternative, as Erik Eckholm puts it: 'The unpleasant truth is that, for many tropical areas of Africa, Latin America and South East Asia, no alternative food production system to shifting cultivation has yet proved both biologically and economically workable.'[100]

East Malaysia, as already noted, is the site of the most intensive timber industry in South-East Asia. It is a region where, according to ESCAP (the UN's Economic and Social Commission for Asia and the Pacific), 'Logging is undoubtedly the primary cause of degradation and indirectly of deforestation too.'[101] Timber extraction, in contrast to swidden farming, is concerned more with economic gain than with providing a basis for survival. Nobody will starve if logging is stopped in East Malaysia.

The timber industry

Despite the significant contribution the timber industry has made to the East Malaysian economy there is widespread criticism of its management and implementation. One former Member of Parliament recently claimed that:

> Sabah's regal mountains and valleys, once lush with tropical forests resembling an endless green carpet from the air, is now very badly pock-marked by huge patches of bare, pitted earth studded by stumps of once mighty and stately trees. Timber companies in Sabah have been raping thousands of acres of forest.[102]

Sahabat Alam Malaysia claim that: 'Nowhere in the world are the forests being chopped with such ferocity and speed as in Sarawak.'[103]

The resource base: In 1986, Sabah's Forestry Department claimed to have 3.4m ha of commercially viable forest.[104] This figure is widely disputed and other qualified sources within the department admit it may be as low as 2.8m ha.[105] According to a recent report in the *Far Eastern Economic Review*, Sabah's forests are capable of yielding only three million cubic metres of timber annually if there is to be any chance of recovery;[106] in 1986 production exceeded ten million cubic metres.[107] Despite the disparity between these figures the timber industry continues to encroach on inadequately stocked forests. As Mr Cassels, Director of the Sabah Foundation in 1986 explained: 'Already there are pressures to go back in and cut faster. There are pressures from government, individuals, politicians, everybody. I don't know if we will be able to withstand them.'[108]

Forest figures for Sarawak are equally unreliable. According to official sources there were 9.4m ha of forest in Sarawak in 1985.[109] As noted earlier, this same figure was given in the mid-1960s and, therefore, is unlikely to be realistic.[110] There are no official figures for how much forest has been logged but Evelyne Hong estimates that 28,000 sq. km (2.8m ha) have been logged since the early 1960s. In 1985 more than 270,000 ha of the 6.7m ha of concession forest were logged; 60% of Sarawak is under logging concessions. At current levels a further 28% of Sarawak's forest will be logged by the year 2000.[111]

The timber industry in Sarawak today is restricted mainly to the hill forests, as most lowland areas are recovering from previous logging. The wood extracted from the lowland 'peat swamp' forests was chiefly *ramin*, a slow growing and valuable hardwood. As far back as 1974 the FAO noted that, 'the next cutting cycle [of peat swamp forest] will be long, due to the fact that a low minimum girth limit has resulted in overcutting of this extremely slow growing species.'[112] In short, too many small trees were cut and the forests are unlikely to recover for many years.

Unlike West Malaysia, logging in both Sabah and Sarawak has continued to increase during the 1980s; Tables 3.5 and 3.6 provide details for both states. In 1984 Sabah exported timber to the value of MS$1.6 billion (US$650m), mainly in the form of logs.[113] Sarawak's timber exports exceeded MS$1.3 billion (US$513m) in 1985, again, almost exclusively derived from logs.[114] State tax on timber exports is 34% of export value, a significant sum indicating direct government interest in the industry.[115]

This interest frequently extends to personal involvement. It is an open secret that timber concessions are handed out in East Malaysia as a means of strengthening political allegiances or as rewards for favours. Timber concessions in Sarawak cost nothing; they may be distributed by the Chief Forester or Chief Minister. Concessions may also be revoked by these individuals who thus have tremendous influence over development policy within each state.

In 1985 political rivalry prompted numerous accusations of corruption within Sabah's timber industry. Datuk Harris Saleh, an ex-Chief Minister with the Berjaya party, claimed that the new Chief Minister with PBS had 'already farmed out over 4,000 acres [1,618 ha] of timber land to its leaders'.[116] Datuk Joseph Pairin, the new Chief Minister, responded by claiming that: 'The leaders of the previous ruling party were so thorough in carving up timber land for the ultimate benefit of their associates and themselves that there is little left.'[117] He went on to accuse them of revoking concessions over huge areas and transferring the rights to their own interests when they came into power in 1976.[118] He also added that the concessions he personally had transferred were all secondary forest and therefore contained limited supplies of timber.

In the run-up to Sarawak's state elections in 1987 the question of who controlled timber concessions became a major issue. Extensive lists were published showing that leading politicians, their families and numerous associates, controlled millions of hectares of concessions. Like Sabah, a change of political party controlling the state initiated a flood of accusations of corruption. Within months of the election the new Chief Minister, Datuk Patanggi Taib Mohamed, froze activity on 25 concessions in the state, covering 1.2m ha and worth an estimated MS$22.5 billion (US$8.8 billion).[119] He claimed that these concessions had been given to friends and relatives of his political rival, Tuan Rahman, the former Chief Minister, during his term in office. With such influential contestants, longhouse communities lose out in the political squabbling, as Sahabat Alam Malaysia have commented:

> The web of economic and political interests enveloping the lucrative timber industry helps explain why the many requests of indigenous communities for communal land to be allocated to them have been rejected.[120]

Timber concessions: Despite these factors, the East Malaysian timber industry regards itself as sustainable and well managed.

Sabah has three types of concession: Full Concession; Special Licences; and Form 1 Licences. A Full Concession is valid for 21 years and enables the holder to carry out one selective harvest under a fixed annual quota system; harvesting must fall within an approved felling plan and follow state logging policy. A Special Licence is valid for ten years under the same conditions as a Full Concession. The Form 1 Licence is valid for only one year and has few restrictions. In 1980 Sabah's productive forest was divided into: 8,690 sq. km under Full Licence; 7,820 sq. km under Special Licences; and 770 sq. km under Form 1 Licences; with allocation pending on a further 3,000 sq. km.[121] During the 1980s an average of 176,000 ha of forest was logged annually in this state.[122]

Sarawak has only one concession category, but management periods vary between Stateland and the Permanent Forest Estate. Concessions in the Permanent Forest Estate are managed under a Working Plan, with a fixed area selectively felled annually. Working Plans must obtain state approval, and include restrictions on road development and the size and species of trees that may be felled. On Stateland, Felling Plans similar to Working Plans are required, but with far fewer restrictions. Both systems are used in hill and swamp forests, but concessions over hilly areas are generally of longer duration than those in the lowlands. At the end of 1984, 38,673 sq. km of Sarawak's forests were under Working Plans and 18,856 sq. km under Felling Plans.[123]

Having gained their concession, the holder sub-contracts the felling. Few concessionaires have either the equipment or expertise to manage their holdings and this system has the added advantage of relieving a concessionaire of the need to make a capital investment. Several sub-contracting arrangements may take place before actual management at the site is identified and, as a result, few workers know who owns the concessions they work on.

Concession holders in Sarawak frequently delegate the job of selling the timber to the contractor. Concessionaires usually receive either a percentage or a fixed sum based on the timber sold. This can be as low as 5–10% or MS$15 per ton (approximately 1.8 cubic metres hardwood.)[124] This may seem a low return but revenues quickly build up and involve the concessionaire in almost no financial risk. The greatest part of the selling price may accrue to the sub-contractor, but he also has major costs, investing in plant and manpower as well as finding buyers. The concession holder frequently does nothing.

Timber extraction and management: The two major commercial forest types, peat swamp and hill dipterocarp, require two different management systems. Both states claim that their timber extraction is 'sustainable', although there is little evidence to support this. As W. Meyer of Kentucky University in the US, himself involved in setting up East Malaysia's National Park system, recently commented: 'The official line is that everything is under control, that a sustained yield policy is being followed. The facts speak a different language.'[125]

Peat-swamp timber extraction was originally based on a 60-year cycle with the forest recovering naturally; no intensive management system was applied and felling was selective. This might have worked if the original recovery period had been adhered to. By the early 1970s, however, this was reduced to the present 45 years. Few, if any, areas have passed through even one rotation of the cycle and many forests are logged with a much shorter recovery time.

The major factor that gives some hope for these swamp forests is that the use of heavy machinery is extremely limited. Instead of bulldozers, small rail tracks are used because heavy plant sticks in the swampy soils. This has radically reduced the damage to residual stands, although there has been overcutting of commercial species in many areas. The *ramin* and *alan* species both grow too slowly for contractors to risk missing their one opportunity to harvest the trees.

In contrast, by the early 1960s, timber extraction in the hill dipterocarp forests was already heavily mechanized in Sabah. Here, the British authorities established an 80-year logging cycle based on extracting trees with a minimum six foot girth at breast height, and using limited machinery; natural regeneration was relied upon. By the early 1970s, both East Malaysian states began to apply the Malayan Uniform System (MUS) developed in West Malaysia under a 25 to 30 year cycle.[126] The practice of silviculture was always limited and today is applied to approximately 12,000 ha of logged forest annually in Sabah.[127]

The FAO, commenting on results from Sarawak's experimental hill dipterocarp logging site in the Niah forest reserve, notes:

> Growth measurements showed that typical stands cut . . . and left without silvicultural treatment would, after 55 years, yield 4 mature (commercial) trees per hectare. It is apparent that an even longer period of wait would be needed for a third economic crop.[128]

The present cycle has not been properly tested and is clearly inadequate according to current research.

The most successful, or least harmful, silvicultural method developed in East Malaysia is 'liberation thinning'. In essence this is a less intensive form of the MUS system described earlier. It has been applied to several experimental sites, and preliminary results led the FAO to claim that after 30 years of recovery timber production is 'probably comparable with present yields'.[129] By 1985 liberation thinning had been applied to only 29,000 ha (approximately 1%) of Sarawak's logged forest.[130] This is due to a combination of severe shortages of staff and resources in the Forest Departments, and to official lethargy. One example was the attitude of the Tourism Minister for Sarawak in 1987, Datuk Amar James Wong, owner of the 100,000 ha Limbang concession. He recently claimed that there is no need for intensive management, commenting that: 'Nature is very resilient and five years after an area is logged, one would not be able to tell the difference between it and primary forest.'[131] In contrast, Mr Cassels, General Manager of North Borneo Timbers, recently stated: 'It is crazy to think you can keep nice managed natural forest and rely on natural regeneration. It is a bunch of baloney because of the population pressures for land and the pressures for cash.'[132]

At the cutting site: Despite the number of regulations controlling logging operations, timber extraction in East Malaysia is dominated by economic considerations. As one State Assemblyman in Sarawak put it: 'A man given a small concession of say 40,000 hectares, will take all the timber he can out of it . . . nobody gives a damn about regulations.'[133] Both contractors and concessionaires want to work an area as fast as possible; the former because they have to pay off debts and sell the timber before they make a profit, the latter because their concession may be revoked if they lose favour with certain politicians. With these economic and political realities there is little chance that extraction will be restrained. One forester in Sarawak blamed it on contractors, claiming: 'Their primary objective was to get into the logging area quickly without spending too much money and taking out as many merchantable logs as possible.'[134] He went on to comment:

> The logging operators showed little concern for the need to reduce soil erosion and stream sedimentation and did not appreciate that a healthy residual stand would be necessary to ensure the continuity of harvesting operations in the next cutting cycle. Tree fellers just cut down the merchantable trees in a haphazard manner and tractor drivers simply bulldoze their way through the forest to skid the logs to the landing.[135]

This lack of proper management at ground level was graphically described by Marn and Jonkers at an International Forestry Seminar in 1980:

> After arriving with his tractor and mobile living quarters at the logging block, the tractor operator makes a brief reconnaissance to decide where to locate his landing (ie. river landing site). Once this decision is made felling begins at the landing and proceeds into the logging block. After clearing the landing the tractor follows behind the feller, proceeding from log to log and skidding them one at a time, extending his skid trail as he follows the felling operation.
>
> Trees are felled in the direction convenient to the feller and are thus scattered at random over the block. Extending as they do from log to log, skid trails are usually long, steep and winding, sometimes completing a full circle: curves are often very sharp. As a result the skidding tends to be slow and damage to both logs and the remaining stand is excessive. The tractor operator has one assistant known as a hookman, who works with the machine at all times, proceeding back and forth between forest and landing. Thus, the tractor operator must spend some time searching for each log or lose valuable tractor time while his assistant searches and locates it. Frequently, however, the tractor driver moves aimlessly around with his tractor until he eventually locates a log, destroying many trees in the remaining stand during his search.
>
> Once a log is located the tractor operator turns his machine and the hookman then attaches the cable. If this operation proves difficult from the original position, the tractor may be moved again to a better position or the log pushed or lifted to a better position with the dozer blade. During all this activity many more trees of the remaining stand may be destroyed or damaged. At times the tractor may even completely circumnavigate the whole log, resulting in even greater destruction.[136]

The Sarawak Forestry Department's own experimental sites confirm the damage caused to the forest by timber extraction. In their Niah Forest Reserve, where only seven trees per hectare were removed using 'normal' extraction methods, 34% of the land was totally cleared for skid tracks and roads and 45% of the residual trees were damaged.[137] As many as 40% of the trees left standing may die due to their injuries.[138] In East Malaysia the removal of seven commercial trees per hectare is usually a minimum, many sites extract as many as 20.[139]

The situation is far removed from Datuk Amar Wong's claim that 'logging is harvesting the forest and nothing more'.[140] Similar realities dominate Sabah's timber industry, where the rate of extraction is thought to be roughly four times the current rate of regeneration.[141]

Timber exports: At present, East Malaysia is the world's largest exporter of tropical hardwood logs. Sarawak exported 11.4m cubic metres of logs in 1985, of which 5.8m cubic metres went to Japan.[142] Sabah exported 10m cubic metres in 1987, most of which also went to Japan. The structure of the export trade between the two states is, however, significantly different. In Sarawak a large number of producers compete for the major buyers. Foreign interests are not allowed to buy into Malaysian companies but they retain a great influence over prices for logs. The major Japanese trading houses provide credit for contractors in order to have first refusal on the timber produced. The Federal Minister for Sarawak, Datuk Leo Moggie, recently commented that, 'the marketing of Sarawak timber is still very much controlled by the Japanese trading houses as Sarawak timber companies are largely dependent on these trading houses for their intricate line of credit.'[143] The major trading companies are very particular about the quality of timber required and as a result have few fixed contracts with logging operations. Felled timber is floated down to the river mouths where it awaits a buyer, if the price is not right the logs will be left to rot. Millions of cubic metres of timber are wasted in this way.

With Japan as the major buyer of East Malaysian timber there is little incentive to process logs before they are exported. Japanese import duties on plywood continue to be high, reduced from 20% to the current 17% only in 1984.[144] The Japanese market is thus virtually closed to plywood imports, the tariffs for which were reduced only under extreme pressure from the USA. Japan has a considerable plywood industry and its forest cover is almost comparable to that in East Malaysia. Japan's own timber industry, however, has strict extraction regulations, harvests fast-growing softwoods on a 60-year cycle and has reduced its cutting area by more than 50% since the mid-1960s.[145] As one British timber expert suggested: 'Japan has a very clear strategy to exhaust the south-east Asian forests before turning to its own sizeable resources of timber.'[146]

In 1981, Sabah's Chief Minister stated that, 'the vicious circle – lack of processing and manufacturing facilities, which necessitated log exports, which in turn discouraged the establishment of processing and manufacturing facilities – has been broken.'[147] In 1987, however, Sabah still exported ten million cubic metres of logs.[148]

The East Malaysian timber industry has been split since the Philippines announced their log export ban in 1986 and called on Malaysia to do the same. Resistance within the industry has been very strong and the pro-log export lobby claim the problem is not one of no processing, but too much red tape. Some want even further deregulation, as, according to one exporter: 'If we are not fast enough we will lose our competitive edge and our markets.'[149] Others see the rationale and advantage in processing timber but cannot afford to invest while competitors continue to export logs.

How much East Malaysia's 'competitive edge' is based on blatant over-exploitation is open to debate. One 'insider', however, was recently quoted as claiming that, 'illegal logging is now the only way to make a profit: two out of every five ships leaving here [Sabah] have not paid duty.'[150] By contrast, the Malaysian Timber Industries Board has been trying to promote timber processing for many years. In 1986 Nik Mohamed, Director of General Lumber in Sarawak stated that: 'if the present adverse situation is not corrected the future of the Malaysian timber industry will be bleak . . . we are helping these countries [Japan, Taiwan, and so on] to prop up their timber industry while our own [is] in the doldrums.'[151] For the present, however, it is highly unlikely that East Malaysia will stop exporting logs, because the short-term profits available dominate a more viable, long-term approach.

Despite these considerable profits for minimal investment, instances of tax evasion and general corruption within the industry have begun to emerge. In 1984 one of the largest concession holders sued the contractors for M$35m (US$14m). Newspaper reports stated that, 'two timber tycoons are alleged to have committed frauds, criminal breach of trust and gross mismanagement of the licence company'.[152] Even the Sabah Foundation, a partially state-funded venture, has had major problems. Established in 1966 the Foundation's aim was to raise income for the state to aid development projects. As capital it was given rights to log 10,000 sq. km of primary forest. By 1985 it had logged more than 4,000 sq. km but its debts exceeded M$170m (US$67m).[153] One major logging partner of the Sabah Foundation is the US Weyerhauser Corporation. The foundation invested between M$60–80m (US$24–31m) in processing plants that economic analysts claim should have cost no more than M$10m (US$4m). The Foundation also had a shipping company, designed for exporting logs, which collapsed after losing an estimated M$9m (US$3m) per year since 1971. In 1986 a major upheaval took place within the Foundation and new management was brought in. The Foundation's corporate investment department was cited as the root cause of these heavy losses, an area in which, according to the new director, a lot of 'hanky-panky' went on.[154]

Illegal logging: Log-poaching in East Malaysia does not occur on the same scale as that experienced in the Philippines or Thailand but it is on the increase. There are two types of illegal logging: that practised by the local population, who may cut down a few trees in order to buy specific consumer goods such as a television or motor bike; and that practised by organized gangs. Nobody is willing to talk about the scale of the problem. The Forest Department publish figures of 'forest offences', but these will include prosecutions for minor offences, even down to swidden farming, so they are of little use.

The strongest indication that organized gangs are on the increase has been forestry officers' frequent calls for armed protection. Even in 1979 one forester stated that 'many staff in the past few months have been threatened with death when they encounter those well organized tree fellers.'[155] In 1986, on the east coast of Sabah, one illegal logging operation was found with 6,000 cubic metres of logs ready for export.[156] A similar operation was discovered in 1983, when logs to the value of MS$200,000 (US$79,000) and five tractors were confiscated.[157]

The development of the local timber market has led to the smuggling of sawn timber from Kalimantan into Sarawak's capital, Kuching. In 1985 it was estimated that 5,000 tons of sawn timber was reaching Kuching each month.[158] There is a local tax on sawn timber, smuggled planks can therefore be sold more cheaply or at greater profit.

Illegal felling is a problem in East Malaysia, but it is on a relatively small scale and the damage caused is not significant when compared to the area selectively felled by legitimate operations.

Major development projects

The authorities have initiated a number of agricultural development schemes and large dam projects. The two state governments have made land development a high priority as a means of general economic development. By 1984 some 593,000 ha of land had been developed in Sarawak through a mixture of state and private enterprises.[159] According to Sarawak's Chief Minister, the state has approximately 500,000 ha of land available for further agricultural development.[160] This will involve establishing agricultural estates, integrated development projects and resettlement schemes, mainly on Interior Area land and Native Customary Land.[161] A similar land development policy is being pursued in Sabah where approximately 2.2m ha is thought to be suitable for permanent agriculture.[162]

In Sarawak, between 1986 and 1990, the state will have invested MS$100m (US$40m) in such schemes; the aim is also to invite foreign investment, particularly in estate development. Four main bodies are implementing Sarawak's land development policy: FELDA, the Sarawak Land Development Board (SLDB), the Sarawak Land Consolidation and Rehabilitation Authority (SALCRA) and the Land Custody and Development Authority (LCDA).

FELDA has been given permission to establish 200,000 ha of oil palm plantation in Sarawak, involving more than 50,000 people.[163] To expedite this development the rate of land surveys has been increased. Legitimate claims are noted but the net effect is that Native Customary Land will be further restricted. One aim of the survey is to identify 'idle' land that could become part of the plantation sector. Most of these 'idle' lands are fallow swidden sites. In conjuction with this is the policy of regrouping native longhouses into model villages of 5,000 and more that are to be created in which settlers will work on communal estates, in a similar way to FELDA participants in West Malaysia.

By 1980, the SLDB, established in 1972, had schemes covering more than 100,000 ha.[164] They promoted cash crop expansion and livestock rearing and also established plantations, but the projects are generally regarded as failures because few wish to take part. By the late 1970s more than one-third of the participants were contract workers from Indonesia, brought in to maintain the estates. Most Ibans involved had been forced to participate as they were resettled, either for security reasons or because they had lost their traditional lands to the projects themselves; the only compensation offered was a place on the estate. The programme incurred large debts, totalling MS$200m (US$80m) by 1983, and there have since been numerous calls for its abolition.[165]

SALCRA was created in 1976 specifically to develop Native Customary Land. Its role is to discourage swidden agriculture, which it regards as unproductive and uneconomic. Cash crop and sedentary agriculture are promoted through the creation of 'Development Areas', in which natives lose all land rights during the development period. SALCRA assumes responsibility for all farming, and land ownership titles are issued only when SALCRA has recovered all its costs. By 1985, SALCRA had developed more than 12,000 ha of Native Customary Land.[166] The authorities regard SALCRA as a success and its projects are to be expanded in the 1990s.

The LCDA works in a similar fashion but creates 'Development Areas' on any category of land. This is achieved by developing plantation estates on a proposed 80,000 ha of Native Customary Land and bringing in private investors to provide the capital required.[167] Since, ultimately, ownership of the land lies with the authority, there is no guarantee that it may not be sold to outside interests.

Obviously, the longhouse communities view most land development schemes with mistrust. If a longhouse does not wish to participate in a scheme that claims rights over its land it must move. The result is that land development schemes may actually create forest destruction by forcing off their traditional lands those who do not want to become estate workers. One Iban spokesman summed up the sentiments of the people when, in disputing a state government reclassification of Native Customary Land and giving it to non-natives, he said:

Being ordinary farmers it is unfortunate that we do not know anything about the Land Code or Land Law or whatever name you call it. We Ibans are poor these days and our livelihood lies much on farming. . . . The Land Code or Land Laws are man-made and they appear to be designed in such a way as to rob the Iban of their land. As you know, land is our last resort to live on. Why cannot we Ibans express our own sentiments when we are being deprived of our land? Where is justice? Where is humanity? Above all, what's wrong with us? Why should we be called 'agitators, trouble makers and pseudo-champions'? What we want is our land.[168]

Proposals for building large-scale dams represent the other major threat to East Malaysia's forests. Although the areas involved are small in comparison to those affected by timber or agricultural development, at a local level the effects are equally devastating. Problems associated with the Batang Ai dam have already been outlined, the only other proposal was for a major dam at Bakun, on the upper reaches of the Rejang river.

The Bakun dam was to have been the largest in South-East Asia, creating a 695 sq. km reservoir flooding land inhabited by more than 5,000 Dayaks. Almost one-third of the 2,400 mega-watts they hoped to produce would have been transmitted by cable to West Malaysia.[169] The project, if it had proceeded, would have cost at least M$20 billion (US$8 billion), but it was shelved in the late 1980s as being too expensive.[170]

East Malaysian forest futures

Currently, forest policy is geared totally towards meeting the demands of the timber industry. Within the present political scene it is highly unlikely that minor forest produce industries will be developed, or that tribal land rights will be recognized. There are neither plans to reform the timber industry nor laws concerning Dayak land-ownership issues. The late 1980s saw the consolidation of current laws in favour of the timber industry and further undermining tribal land claims.

There is, however, no immediate danger that East Malaysia will become a barren wasteland unsuitable for agriculture. The tragedy, however, is one of lost opportunity. Most sources project that if current trends continue, East Malaysia will exhaust its timber for export in the mid to late 1990s.[171] In East Malaysia, therefore, there is still an opportunity to develop sustainable forestry and minor forest produce industries; an option most of East Malaysia's neighbours lack.

For the immediate future the complacency that marked the West Malaysian timber industry during the 1970s is even more pronounced in East Malaysia. The government has no plans to reform the timber industry and the views of the indigenous population on deforestation are low on the political agenda.

There is, however, widespread criticism of the timber industry, from both within and outside East Malaysia. Evelyne Hong and SAM are currently calling for the government to freeze the issuance of new concessions.[172] In addition, Hong considers that all timber concessions which have not started operations should be cancelled.[173] Such action, they see as an initial step to avert a more critical situation developing in the early 1990s.

The moratorium on logging, however, is only an initial step. As Hong notes: 'The issue of land [rights] is so central to the Sarawak natives because land lies at the heart of their cultural, spiritual and economic life.'[174] Environmentalists envisage a two stage process involving land development and the timber industry. The first is to use current legislation and increase the area of Communal Forest Reserves; the second is to secure more general land rights for the Dayak population as a whole.

Even with the pitifully small area of Communal Forest Reserves in East Malaysia, these sites have been taken over by logging companies. The communities have rarely received compensation for the loss of this land, despite the Federal Constitution (Article 13) noting: 'No law shall provide for the compulsory acquisition or use of property without adequate compensation.'[175] Evelyne Hong argues, quite rightly, that such protection should apply equally to Communal Forest Reserves as to private property. Because the state authorities issue the timber licences, compensation for damage caused by logging should come from both the state and the timber companies.[176]

It is unlikely that a wider interpretation of the Malaysian Federal Constitution will be applied without government documentation of the true grievances of the tribal groups affected. SAM is therefore calling for a Royal Commission of Enquiry into the conditions of the indigenous populations in East Malaysia. Such a Commission's responsibility would be to offer realistic proposals on how indigenous identity, interests and welfare may be protected and enhanced under new laws. Evelyne Hong goes further, and claims the Forestry Departments should establish complaints bureaux in each district.[177]

In 1987, however, the Forest Ordinance for Sarawak was amended to make it a criminal offence to barricade timber roads (punishable by jail for up to two years), a move regarded by environmentalists and the Dayaks as an open attempt to repress their views. As five Penan stated from their cells after being arrested: 'Jail is for criminals. We are not criminals. We only asked for our land'.[178]

SAM is confident that a Royal Commission would find overwhelming support within the Dayak community for a new land ownership code in East Malaysia based on the principles of *adat* law. SAM and Evelyne Hong argue that *adat* law should be recognized as a system applicable to certain land areas and not simply included as a clause in another piece of legislation. In other words, *adat* law should have constitutional protection.

Such recognition would enable longhouse communities to determine the extent of timber extraction on their land. The timber industry has responded by accusing the Dayaks of either wishing to reap the benefits from timber for themselves or of wanting to stop the timber industry altogether. It is clear from SAM's studies that the Dayaks would still want a timber industry, but one under their control. This, in SAM's opinion, is the only way to create a sustainable timber industry. Harrison Gnau envisages a considerable decline in timber production, a more labour intensive industry, and an industry in which replanting and intensive forest management are compulsory.[179]

But this is a long-term goal that may take many years to realize. For the more immediate future Harrison Gnau argues that the Forestry Departments are chronically underfunded and incapable of even enforcing current legislation. The Departments need more field officers to ensure that logging companies keep within their concession areas, replant where required, and do not extract too much timber. According to Harrison, the local Dayak population would be very willing to take on the task of policing their forests, as it would provide employment in rural areas as well as ensuring that forestry laws are enforced.[180]

There is also, however, a need to review the principles underlying current methods of timber extraction. Clearly, the policy of leaving logged-over forest to recover naturally is not effective. Enrichment planting and general silviculture must be applied to these forests if they are to remain productive. As Datuk Mohammed Jabil of West Malaysia's Forest Department emphasized, in 1984, 'tropical forests take at least from 60 to 100 years to reach maturity'.[181] Only intensive management can accelerate this process, as the few experimental sites monitored by the Sarawak Forestry Department indicate. The lessons learned from these research sites must be applied in the field if East Malaysia is to sustain its timber trade. As noted earlier, silvicultural methods frequently require a significant input of labour. There is still debate among environmentalists in Malaysia regarding whether the timber industry or the state should take charge of forest rehabilitation, but all agree that such a stragegy is needed and that if implemented it would also help create more long-term employment in remote areas.

Environmental groups, such as WWF Malaysia, are concentrating their efforts at a more diplomatic level, urging the authorities to establish more national parks as the most immediate way of saving particular areas.[182] East Malaysia already has several national parks, most of which are managed extremely well. Accommodation in these parks is frequently reserved well in advance and they are regarded as a growth industry. These are good developments and should be encouraged. The current debate in East

Malaysia, however, is centred on forests outside these protected areas.

Expansion of the plantation sector is the other major threat facing longhouse communities. Sabah has much greater potential for agricultural expansion than Sarawak. Agricultural expansion need not have a detrimental effect on forests if applied sensitively, but this seems unlikely. Although most FELDA schemes are based on plantation crops, they cannot be regarded as agro-forestry projects. With some adaptations the two could be linked, but the concepts of social forestry have not been widely discussed in East Malaysia.

Within the next decade Sarawak will have to embark on replanting efforts; Sabah is already reaching that stage. The best way to ensure success in this endeavour is to involve the local population; but this is unlikely to happen under the current land ownership patterns.

The effects of shifting cultivation cannot be ignored but they do not warrant the present saliency the authorities have placed on them. There is a case for improving the efficiency of swidden agriculture in certain areas; to do this would probably prove more productive than attempting to ban the system. There is no reason to assume that timber production and swidden agriculture may not co-exist within the same forests, if both activities are seen as beneficial by the local population. In areas where plantations are proposed, an adaptation of the Burmese *tayanga* system may prove more productive than separating the two land uses. Once again this ensures the local population's continued use of the areas.

The native population must be brought into the policy making process at all levels. Real development must take into account the needs of as many people as possible. As Evelyne Hong concludes:

> Only when the rights, interests and welfare of these natives have been fully recognised and restored, can we proudly acclaim the reality of a balanced, just and integrated nation.[183]

Case study

The timber blockades of Sarawak

More than 2,000 sq. km of Sarawak's forests are logged annually.[184] Logging in the state's Fourth and Fifth Divisions is amongst the most intensive and destructive in East Malaysia. Along the Baram river alone more than 30 logging operations are working on approximately 400 sq. km of forest. Relations between the longhouse communities in the upper reaches of the Baram and Limbang rivers and the logging companies have been deteriorating since the mid 1970s.

The timber industry has profoundly disrupted the lifestyle of the Penan people. Only half of the 10,000 Penan continue to live their traditionally nomadic life style in the forests, and they are probably the last true hunter gatherers left in Asia. Most settled Penan live in government resettlement schemes. Intact forests are crucial for the survival of those who choose to live a traditional lifestyle as they plant no crops but rely on wild game, fish and edible plants. Sago, supplemented by a wide range of fruits, nuts and berries, forms the vegetable base to their diet, while boar, lizard, monkey, various birds and fish provide the major protein source.

The nomadic Penan establish a camp in an area for three to six weeks, moving on when food becomes scarce. The social groups are small, 20 to 30 individuals, and material possessions limited. Their rough, open shelters, constructed entirely from forest produce, quickly deteriorate and are reclaimed by the forest after abandonment.

The few material possessions afforded are restricted to what can be carried. Metal cooking implements, large machete-type knives (*parangs*) and a few Western consumer items, such as watches and radios are all bought by trading forest produce. Blowpipes are still in use, although rifles are more popular. Only the older Penan men continue to wear the traditional loincloth, 'T' shirts and shorts are more common. The women usually wear some form of *sarong*, a single piece of material wrapped around the body.

The nomadic lifestyle is undoubtedly hard; life expectancy is low at 40 years. For many years the government has attempted to restrict the Penan's movements and to establish them in settled villages in order to provide basic health care and education. The other side of this seemingly benevolent policy is the claim that the Penan are a threat to the development of the timber industry. In physical terms they have an absolutely minimal effect on the forests, it is their political influence that creates a challenge to the authorities. The timber industry destroys their forest environment and consequently their culture and lifestyle. The interests of the two groups are entirely incompatible.

Clearly, the Penan feel seriously threatened by the type of development to which they have been exposed. As nomads they can make no legal claims over the forest land they use because it has not been cleared; they are, therefore, trespassers on state-owned land. The Penan in the government plantation settlements live in an atmosphere of grudging acceptance rather than in hope for an improved lifestyle.

Those still in the forests have generally attempted to avoid the logging companies by moving towards the Kalimantan border. By the mid 1980s, however, logging roads extended so deep into the interior that even the most remote Penan groups could no longer avoid logging concessions. As a result there have been constant problems, with logging operations scaring away wildlife, causing the silting of rivers, killing fish and contaminating drinking water supplies. The environmental damage forms the crux of opposition to logging in these districts, but the logging companies' attitude has undoubtedly exacerbated the situation.

One example is the conflict between Limbang Trading and Along Sega, a Penan headman from Long Adang ('Long' is the local term for 'Longhouse'). The 1,000 sq. km Limbang concession is owned by Datuk James Wong, the Tourist Minister for Sarawak. The trouble started in 1985 when Limbang Trading destroyed the graves of Along Sega's parents and five other relatives. It was one of the first cases in which a more militant stand began to emerge. The logging camp manager offered Along a MS$100 (US$40) note as compensation, which Along refused. In his own words:

> I told him, even if I have to die of any cause I shall not trade the bodies and souls of my parents and relatives to save mine because our bodies, dead or alive, are not for sale. I refused the money and pleaded with him also that if you have so much money already please don't come here to take our land. But he just shook his head, laughed and replied; 'We have been licensed to work on this land. There is no such thing as your land in the forest because forest belongs only to the government. Take this money or you get nothing.' I still rejected the money.[185]

The Penan, however, are not the only tribal group to be angered by the timber industry. In 1981, 500 Kenyah from Long Apoh on the Baram river approached the Sam Ling Timber Company logging camp and demanded compensation for damage to their land. Previously they had sent a number of petitions asking the company to enter into negotiations over compensation proposals for their longhouse. All these had been ignored and when there was still no response to their suggestion of MS$40 (US$16) compensation for every ton of timber extracted they threatened to burn the camp. The Kenyah leaders were promptly arrested.[186]

Later that year 80 people from 22 longhouses descended on the Lamat logging camp demanding MS$2 (US$0.80 cents) per ton of timber extracted. The longhouses had applied for their own timber licenses a number of times but had been refused and the 68,000 ha concession had gone to Lamat.[187] Another incident occurred in the Niah area where a camp manager was stopped and forced to pay MS$7,000 (US$2,800) as compensation for damage caused by logging. The local longhouse had earlier been promised compensation, but it never arrived. Once again those involved were arrested.[188]

In 1983 the Ulu Nyalan logging camp in Niah was threatened by a small group of Iban demanding MS$100,000 (US$40,000) as compensation and MS$10 for every ton of timber extracted.[189] They threatened to burn down the camp and were arrested two days later. In October of that year several blocks of living quarters in the Batu Niah logging camp were burnt to the ground. In January 1984, 200 Iban barricaded a timber road with logs at Lubok Lalang in Sungai Medamit. They demanded MS$2m (US$790,000) in compensation from another company owned by Datuk James Wong.

They received no offers. The list of similar incidents in this part of Sarawak is long but these examples indicate that this is not a new problem; the ill-feelings have been building up for more than a decade.

In other cases, however, compensation has been agreed although the sums that change hands are clearly inadequate for the loss of resources. At Long Piah, in the Baram District, loggers drove roads through swidden fields without permission. According to the local people the sites are now useless as all the top soil has been scraped or washed away. They did not bother to take the company to court for this illegal damage on Native Customary Land, as they could only claim the maximum MS$5 per metre compensation for the damage.[190] There is a general mistrust in the justice handed out from the courts within Sarawak's Dayak community. This has built up from a number of cases in which logging companies have broken the law but received no punishment.

The law can, however, even act against tribal people attempting to stop logging on land they own. In 1985, Laeng Wan, a Kayan from Long Miri, was arrested for building a fence across a logging road leading to his land. He was charged with unlawfully restricting a trespasser from encroaching on his own land. In 1977 he had signed an agreement leasing his land for ten years to a timber company. In 1983, however, when the initial cut had been completed, the timber company moved out and was replaced by a new contractor, and logging continued without Laeng Wan's permission or any offer of compensation for the extra damage caused.[191] It was then that Laeng took matters into his own hands and built the barricade.

Due to the extremely intimate relationship between government officials and timber concessionaires, many longhouses complain that the authorities are not interested in their problems. One example, in late 1986, from Long Tepan on Ulu Tutoh, a major tributary of the Baram, illustrates this lack of concern. The Dayaks described their experiences when some government officials took the unusual step of visiting an area where complaints had emerged.

> As we are not able to write we were happy that they [government officers] came, so we told them about our problems which are mainly caused by the logging activities of Samling Timber Snd Bhd, which started operations about six years ago in Sungai Puak. They wrote all what we told them down and we were assured that they would take the necessary action to protect our land as requested. But merely two weeks after they left the bulldozers roared mercilessly around us. Then we realized it was just another empty promise from the officials.[192]

Samling Timber gained their logging rights direct from twelve longhouses by giving them MS$2,000 (approximately MS$7 per person; US$3) in return for allowing timber contractors to clear the land.[193]

SAM has a small office in Marudi, the last town up the Baram river. They have helped co-ordinate some of the complaints they receive from longhouses, giving legal advice and publicity. The co-ordinator, Harrisson Gnau, a Kayan, and his small team have been trying to defuse the situation for several years. In late 1986, conflicts between the Dayaks up-river and the logging companies were becoming so frequent that eight headmen journeyed downstream to Marudi to issue a statement through SAM. The statement to the state government concluded:

> We cannot wait any longer as every day our livelihood is continually besieged by the threatening activities of the logging companies. And if we are continually ignored we take it that you are no longer interested in our problems; and shall take appropriate actions to defend ourselves, our future generations, our land, our crops, our properties and so forth from further and continued destruction.[194]

Road blocking had been attempted before but failed because the timber companies waited until those involved had to return home. A co-ordinated blockade had never been attempted and despite it being common knowledge that each longhouse had at least one government informant, a general plan emerged.

In March 1987, 12 major logging roads were blockaded by more than 2,000 people from three ethnic groups, the Penan, Kayan and Kelabit. The Penan formed the majority although most sites were located on Native Customary Land controlled by the other groups. Nine timber companies were affected, including: Samling Timber, Limbang Trading, Wong Tong Kwong, Merlin Timber, Sarsin Lumber, Marabong Lumber and Baya Lumber. The sites formed a 150 km swathe across the upper Baram and Limbang rivers.

The authorities immediately sealed off the areas and arrested those whom they thought were instigating the trouble. Several members of SAM were charged under the Internal Security Act and held in prison for up to one month. The blockades, however, remained in place.

One primary aim of the blockades was to publicize the problems and this strategy proved to be successful. In East Malaysia, however, the national papers are directly owned by the various political parties, all of whom are involved in logging. The ruling Sarawak National Party (SNAP) claimed that outside agitators had incited the Penans and that a lawyer from Kuala Lumpur had visited the areas just before the blockades to stir up local people.

In June 1987 a delegation of Penan headmen went to Kuala Lumpur to appeal to the King and Prime Minister. They saw neither but gained considerable press coverage, and sympathy was developing abroad as international press agencies picked up on the story.

As outside support developed, the press within Sarawak began to show less tolerance. A few reports attempted to turn the blockades into an anti-development issues, claiming that SAM and other groups supporting the cause wanted to keep the Penan as museum pieces. By July the *Peoples Mirror* of Sarawak was running a general smear campaign against the Penan and the blockades. One reporter described the Penan and their lifestyle thus:

> A society without doors – a life of mere existence with no material possessions. . . . Children with phlegm-smeared faces tug to their mothers sarongs [Malaysian dress]. Sucklings and toddlers – children – could very well be their only possession and no doors can keep them safe . . . if the Penans are not ready for change now, then when will they ever be? . . . The Penans, being a very simple people are being easily swayed. The truth is that logging does not deprive them of their food and water supply.[195]

The blockades stayed in place until October 1987 when an amendment to Sarawak's Forest Ordinances made it a criminal offence – even for the land owner – to block any logging road. Forest Officers were empowered to arrest without warrant, and conviction brought a MS$6,000 (US$2,400) fine and up to two years in prison. There were 42 arrests at the blockade sites as troops were used to end the protests.

The situation that caused the blockades in this part of Sarawak has not changed. The blockades have been pulled down and a few weeks later they go up again. Throughout the campaign the conflict has been peaceful and this has helped the Dayak cause. The Penan now fear that by 1991 their last forests will be logged over.

An immense quantity of statements have emerged from the people involved and one, signed by 61 tribal leaders, clearly presents the Dayak view of their situation:

> Some people say we are against 'development' if we do not agree to move out of our land and forest. This completely misrepresents our position. Development does not mean stealing our land and forest. . . . This is not development but theft of our land, our rights and our cultural identity. Development to us means:
>
> a) recognizing our land rights in practice;
> b) putting a stop to logging in our lands and forests so that we can continue to live;
> c) introducing clean water supply, proper health facilities, better schools for our children.
>
> This kind of development we want. Why don't you give us this development and progress?[196]

Table 3.1
Comparative soil loss between virgin forest and plantations

	Soil loss (cu.m./sq.km./year)
Virgin forest	31
Small scale rubber or oil palm plantation	46
Large scale rubber or oil palm plantation	87

(N.B. Plantations are all mature)

Source: Huntington Technical Services, quoted in: Goh, K., 1983, Forest disturbance and sediment yields; paper presented at the: Regional Workshop on hydrological impacts of forestry practices and reafforestation, UPM and UNESCO, University Malaya, Kuala Lumpur.

Table 3.2
Estimated loss of certain primate species after logging between 1958 and 1975

Species	*Population in 1958*	*Population in 1975*	*% loss*
Long-tailed macaque	415,000	318,000	23%
Pig-tailed macaque	80,000	45,000	44%
Silvered leaf-monkey	6,000	4,000	33%
Dusky leaf-monkey	305,000	155,000	49%
White-handed gibbon	144,000	71,000	50%
Siamang	111,000	48,000	57%

Source: Chivers and Lane Petter (eds) quote: Khan, M., 1978, Mans impact on the primates of Peninsula Malaysia in; Recent advances in primatology vol.2: conservation, Academic Press, UK.

Table 3.3
Forest clearance by FELDA and other land development programmes

		(hectares)	
		FELDA	*Total*
1st Plan	1966–70	179,000	238,000
2nd Plan	1971–75	412,000	799,600
3rd Plan	1976–80	373,700	731,600*
4th Plan	1981–85	161,600	417,570*
5th Plan	1986–90 (projected)	175,000	286,700*

* Includes projects in East Malaysia.

Source: Government of Malaysia – various Five Year Plans.

Table 3.4
Export of major timber products from West Malaysia (1984)

Sawn Timber	73% (volume)	MS$ 647.4	million
Plywood	13%	172.1	million
Mouldings	8%	209.1	million
Logs	2%	5.4	million
Veneer	2%	18.7	million
Other	2%	(Blockboard) 15.2	million

Source: Malaysian Timber Industries Board 1985

Table 3.5
Annual log production in Sabah (millions cubic metres)

1960	2.16
1965	4.26
1970	6.56
1975	9.10
1977	12.98
1979	10.80
1980	9.06
1982	11.64
1985	10.80

Sources: 1960–1979 – FAO. Forest Resources of Tropical Asia, Rome 1981.
    1980985 – Ministry of Primary Statistics, Sarawak 1986.

Table 3.6
Annual log production by forest type in Sarawak (million cubic metres)

	Peat Swamp	Hill	Total
1970	2.70	2.00	4.70
1972	2.23	0.98	3.21
1974	2.10	0.74	2.84
1976	3.00	1.41	4.41
1978	2.84	3.14	5.98
1982	3.25	7.99	11.24
1984	3.16	8.24	11.40
1985	2.82	9.46	12.28

Sources: Forest Department of Sarawak Annual Reports.

References

1. FAO, 1981.
2. Government of Malaysia, 1986.
3. Ibid.
4. Hong, E. 1987.
5. Ministry of Primary Industries, 1985.
6. Ibid.
7. Butler, S. 1987.
8. Ibid.
9. Ibid.
10. FAO, op. cit.
11. Forest Department of Sarawak, 1985.
12. Ngau, H. et al., 1986.
13. Hatch, T. 1982.
14. Hong, E. 1987.
15. Meyer, W. 1984.
16. Ibid.
17. Butler, S. 1987.
18. *Borneo Bulletin*, 1981, 26 September, quotes Wong Leong Do.
19. Hill, P. 1982.
20. Caldecott, J. 1985.
21. Ibid.
22. WWF Malaysia, 1985.
23. FAO, op. cit.
24. Hatch, T. 1982.
25. Ibid.
26. *Borneo Bulletin*, 1981, 24 January.
27. Ibid., 26 September, quotes Wong Leong Do.
28. Ngau, H. et al., 1986.
29. *Borneo Bulletin*, 1986, 28 January.
30. Solley Wong, in *Borneo Bulletin*, 1981, 27 August.
31. *Borneo Bulletin*, 1983, January.
32. Ngau, H. et al., 1986.
33. Ibid.
34. Caldecott, J. 1985.
35. Ibid.
36. WWF Malaysia, 1985.
37. Ibid.
38. Caldecott, J. 1985.
39. 40. 41. Hong, E. 1987.
42. *New Straits Times*, 1981, 8 April.
43. Anderson, A. 1978.
44. Ibid.
45. Baram District Officer, 1981, Baram District Annual Report.
46. Hong, E. 1987.
47. Ngau, H. personal communication, February 1987.
48. Institute for Social Analysis, 1986.
49–54. Hong, E. 1987.
55. Institute for Social Analysis, 1985.
56. Ngau, H. et al., 1986.
57. Ngau, H. personal communication, February 1987.
58. Sahabat Alam Malaysia (Sarawak), 1986.

59. Hong, E. 1987.
60. Sarawak Timber Industries Board (STIDCO, 1981).
61. Sahabat Alam Malaysia, 1985.
62. 63. 64. Abang Naruddin Zainorin, 1985.
65–68. Hong, E. 1987.
69. Sarawak Museum, 1979.
70–75. Hong, E. 1987.
76. Zaidi Khaldine Zainie, 1985.
77–84. Hong, E. 1987.
85. Eckholm, E. 1976.
86. Spencer, J. 1966.
87. Grandstaff, T. 1980, quotes Watters, R.
88. Ibid.
89. Andriiesse, J. 1977.
90. Hong, E. 1987.
91. Hatch, T. and Y. Tie, 1979.
92. Hong, E. 1987.
93. Hatch, T. 1980.
94. Spencer, J. 1966.
95. Hong, E. 1987.
96. Chin See Chung, 1984.
97. Lua Buong Tiing, 1979.
98. Hong, E. 1987.
99. Ibid.
100. Eckholm, E. 1976.
101. ESCAP, 1986.
102. Evans, S. 1983.
103. Sahabat Alam Malaysia, 1987.
104. Butler, S. 1987.
105. Scott, M. 1986.
106. Ibid.
107. Zainoor Sulaiman, 1986.
108. Scott, M. 1986.
109. Forest Department of Sarawak, 1985.
110. Solley Wong, 1981.
111. Hong, E. 1987.
112. FAO, 1980.
113. Scott, M. 1986.
114. Hong, E. 1987.
115. Ibid.
116. *Peoples Mirror*, 1985, 28 September.
117. Ibid.
118. Ibid.
119. Sahabat Alam Malaysia, 1987.
120. Ibid.
121. FAO, 1981.
122. Department of Forestry, 1988.
123. Hong, E. 1987.
124. Institute for Social Analysis, 1986.
125. Meyer, W. 1984.
126. Marn, H. and W. Jonkers, 1980.
127. Department of Forestry, 1988.
128. UNDP/FAO, 1981.

129. Ibid.
130. Hong, E., 1987; and Forest Department of Sarawak, 1985.
131. *The Star* (West Malaysia) 1987, 5 September.
132. Scott, M. 1986, quotes Cassels, P.
133. Mahoney, R. 1985, quotes Massang, J.
134. Chua, D. 1986.
135. Ibid.
136. Marn, H. and W. Jonkers, 1980.
137. UNDP/FAO op. cit.
138. Hong, E. 1987.
139. Hoo, E. 1987.
140. *The Star* (West Malaysia) 1987, 5 September.
141. Butler, S. 1987.
142. Forest Department of Sarawak, 1985.
143. Hong, E. 1987.
144. Malaysian Timber Industries Board, 1985.
145. Myers, N. 1984.
146. *New Scientist*, (UK) 1982, 16 September.
147. *Asian Business*, 1981, June, quotes Datuk Harris Salleh.
148. *Asian Timber*, 1988, March.
149. Azam Aris, 1986.
150. Eads, B. 1985.
151. *Borneo Post*, 1986, 28 April, quotes Nik Mahmood.
152. Lau, S. 1984.
153. Baradan, K. 1986.
154. Ibid.
155. Lau Buong Tiing, 1980(b).
156. *Daily Express* (West Malaysia), 1986, 2 December.
157. *Borneo Bulletin*, 1983, 31 December.
158. Ibid., 1985, 27 April.
159. Hong, E. 1987.
160. Ibid.
161. Ibid.
162. FAO, 1981.
163. Hong, E. op. cit.
164. Ibid.
165. *Daily Express* (West Malaysia), 1985, 11 November.
166. Hong, E. op. cit.
167. *Sarawak Tribune*, 1981, 25 June.
168. Ibid., 1985, 16 November.
169. Hong, E., op. cit.
170. Ibid.
171. Hong, E. personal communication.
172. Hong, E. 1987.
173. Hong, E., 1987(a).
174. Hong, E., op. cit.
175. Federal Constitution of Malaysia, 1986.
176. Hong, E. 1987(a).
177. Ibid.
178. Martin Khor Kok Peng, 1989.
179. Harrison Ngau, 1986, personal communication.
180. Ibid.
181. Muhammad Jabil, 1984.

182. Rubeli, K. 1989.
183. Hong, E. op. cit.
184. Consumers Association of Penang, 1987.
185–193. Hong, E. op. cit.
194. Sahabat Alam Malaysia (Sarawak), 1986.
195. Hoo, E. 1987(b).
196. Sahabat Alam Malaysia, 1987.

4. Papua New Guinea

Introduction

Papua New Guinea (PNG) comprises the eastern half of the New Guinea island (the western half is Irian Jaya), a number of islands known collectively as New Britain and New Ireland, and the island of Bougainville to the east. The total land area of 460,000 sq. km is typified by coastal swamps and a mountainous interior.

The climate is frequently described as a wet season followed by a not-so-wet season. The average temperature exceeds 20°C with more than 2,000 mm of rainfall per year. The mountains reach 5,000 metres, and two of the world's largest rivers flow from the New Guinea interior: the Fly and the Sepik, both navigable for more than 800 km.

PNG's population of 3.2 million is increasing at 2.8% per year.[1] More than 90% of the people live in rural areas although there is considerable internal migration both to and from the towns.[2] Nearly half the rural population is found in the Highlands, separated from the coastal fringes by a natural barrier of steep mountains and dense forests. In the Highlands there is an average of 18 people per sq. km, while most coastal areas support an average of only three people per sq. km.[3]

Papua New Guinea has been inhabited for at least 30,000 years. The first people probably originated from Indonesia, Malaysia and the Philippines and it was they who first settled in the Highlands.[4] About 5,000 years ago a new wave of immigrants arrived from the Pacific islands;[5] these new immigrants stayed along the coasts and despite much mixing between the populations since then, significant cultural differences still exist between coastal and Highland people.

The population as a whole is tribal and the remoteness of many communities has led to the development of an unprecedented diversity: PNG has more than 700 distinct languages, 25% of the world's total. The diversity of cultures had led it to be described as an anthropologists' paradise.

Traditionally most tribes are animists. Christian missionaries have been very active in PNG, but despite their attempts at conversion there has been a tribal cultural revival, in part for the entertainment of tourists and in part for the people themselves

In the past some of the Highland tribes lived in a state of almost constant warfare against neighbouring tribes, usually over territorial disputes. By contrast the coastal tribes were generally less involved with organized fighting as their culture was largely based on trade.

Traditional clearance of forest for agriculture dates back at least 9,000 years.[6] The effect on the forests varies from one area to another as the basic slash and burn model also changes with location. Land ownership is traditionally based on the community inhabiting each area and individual land claims are rare. This system still applies in many areas and forms a solid foundation from which tribal groups may claim political influence.

The Spanish and Portuguese 'discovered' New Guinea in the 16th century as they roamed the region in their search for spices. The Portuguese named the entire island (including what is now Irian Jaya) *Ilhaos des Papuans*, Island of the Fuzzy Haired People; the Spanish named it *Nevau Guinea*, and the name Papua New Guinea emerged later.

The coastal swamps probably discouraged these two colonial powers from exploring inland and they both left it alone for two centuries. After the Spanish and Portuguese empires collapsed, the island was once more unclaimed by any colonial power. In 1828, the Dutch, having no idea of what they were acquiring, claimed the western half of the island (Irian Jaya) as part of Indonesia. By the late 19th century the major European colonial powers were beginning to run out of land they could claim and the Australians urged the British to make this another part of the Empire. The Germans laid claim to a large part of the northern area of what is now mainland New Guinea and the British hurriedly claimed what was left.

Thus, what is now known as Papua New Guinea, was controlled by two colonial powers. Both concentrated on opening up the few drier lowlands along the coast and establishing rubber and coconut plantations. Gold was discovered in the British sector but the major deposits were found only at the beginning of the 20th century. At the outbreak of World War One the Australians promptly claimed the German area of PNG for themselves and the British Empire.

The first large-scale gold rush was along the Bulolo river near Wau, on the east coast. Explorers had yet to penetrate the island's interior, and major dredging operations were under way before the 'hidden valleys' were discovered. By the mid 1930s Bulolo Gold Dredging Ltd., owned by the Canadian company Placer Development, had eight of the world's largest dredgers working the river. The alluvial beds were churned to a depth of 115 feet and kept more than 6,000 workers employed. The field was finally worked out in the 1960s by which time 20 miles of the river had been totally devastated.

There are five major types of forest in PNG; lowland rain forest comprising 20m ha; montane, 11m ha; swamp, 4m ha; savanna, 3m ha; and mangrove, 1m ha,[7] making an estimated total of 39m ha. These figures are projections from the last national forest survey conducted in the 1960s, but there is general agreement among relevant experts within the country that they are reasonably reliable.

The government classifies 21m ha as protective forest, on steep slopes, and 18m ha as productive.[8] The FAO estimate 33m ha of PNG's forest as 'virgin' – an exceptionally high proportion for the region.[9]

Since the late 1970s the rate of forest destruction has remained at approximately 21,000 ha per year.[10] Most clearance has been for agricultural expansion, but logging and mining are also starting to make an impact. The FAO notes that mining in particular is causing, 'massive deforestation in the mountainous areas.'[11] Before the 1980s logging was limited almost exclusively to the islands of New Britain. Large timber interests, however, are increasingly looking towards mainland New Guinea as the least exploited source of logs in the Asia-Pacific region.

By 1980, 21,000 ha of cleared forest had been replanted, mainly with mono-cultures of fast growing softwoods.[12] In that they own the land they live on, the political influence of tribal groups is unique in the region and this had undoubtedly helped reduce the rate of forest loss. PNG, however, wants to become major supplier of natural resources and sees the development of the timber industry as a key factor. At present PNG and East Malaysia are the only areas in the Asia–Pacific region still exporting logs on a large scale.

The effects of forest loss

Information on the effects of forest loss in PNG is scant. The only reasonably thorough studies have centred around the activities of the Japan New Guinea Timber (JANT) concession in the Madang area.

Environmental costs

Soil degradation: The most fertile soils are to be found in the Highland valleys. Outside these areas, except on the alluvial plains around the coastal town of Lae, and along the Fly river, most soils are unsuitable for agriculture.

Dr Saulei of PNG University claims that the timber industry is, 'accelerating erosion, weathering, and humus decomposition, and leading to the widespread formation of soils with low nutrient and absorbative capacities.'[13] No widespread surveys have yet been completed but sedimentation is clearly destroying coral reefs and mangroves that support local fishing industries. According to Dr Arthur Dahl, sedimentation is becoming 'a universal problem' throughout PNG.[14] This is partly due to deforestation but it is also severely aggravated by the scale of mining in some areas. Some of the largest open-cast mines in the world operate in the island of Bougainville.

Selective felling, the basis upon which most timber concessions operate, should ensure minimal environmental damage. Some concessions, however, for example, the one controlled by JANT in the Gogal valley, have rights to clear fell large areas. Clear felling in this area has resulted in the water table rising to the extent that semi-aquatic plants now dominate large parts of the concession. In addition, the soils have become more acidic since logging, and phosphorus levels have dropped by more than 50%.[15] For centuries, this area has supported a large tribal population, but extensive sections of the Gogal valley are now becoming unsuitable for agriculture.

Implications for wildlife: Little is known of the effects of forest loss on PNG's wildlife. Its location between the Indo–Malaya and Australian regions, and its mountain ranges, results in PNG having representatives of a wide cross section of families.

More than 1,200 tree species have been identified,[16] including some generally associated with Australia, such as Eucalyptus, as well as the dipterocarps, typically found in South-East Asia. There is no dominant family or genus in the lowland tropical forests and up to 150 species may be found in a single hectare.[17] As the altitude increases so does the dominance of non-Indo-Malayan species. Above 3,000 metres the montane forest is made up of conifers, right up to the natural tree line at just under 4,000 metres. This forest has been reduced since it dominates the highlands where a major indigenous population farms. Much of what was montane forest is now open grassland or covered in shrubs such as rhododendron.

Papua New Guinea is the only country except for Australia that has representatives from all three types of mammals; the primitive egg layers, such as ant-eaters; the marsupials, such as the possums, bandicotes and wallabies; and the placental mammals, ranging from rodents to bats;[18] the possums are highly valued for their fur as well as their meat. Of the 70 species of bats in PNG, 35 are endemic;[19] 90% of the rodents are also endemic.[20]

The country is perhaps best known for its birds, of which there are 650 species, with 500 restricted to the forests.[21] The best-known family is the Birds of Paradise. Of the 43 species found worldwide, 33 are endemic to the forests of PNG.[22] In terms of providing food, the most highly valued bird is the cassowary, a large, flightless bird similar to the Australian emu.

Forest loss will undoubtedly have a detrimental effect on much of the country's wildlife. An estimated 65% of the Papua New Guinea's endemic species of birds are restricted to untouched forest.[23] The forests also provide an environment for reptiles such as crocodiles, about 170 types of lizard and more than 100 species of snake.[24]

As most species originate in the forests it would seem logical that forest destruction is reducing their numbers, but other factors must also be taken into account: hunting for food and skins also plays a part in restricting the distribution of certain species. The timber industry is, however, frequently cited as a major cause of forest destruction and loss of species diversity; as Naru Kwapena of the PNG Department of Land Survey and Environment says:

> There is no evidence . . . that the natural tropical forest will regenerate following harvesting of some of the timber. In fact, most evidence is to the contrary; that the forest is effectively destroyed and is reduced to a very low grade secondary forest with little or no commercial value.[25]

The nature of some land development projects, such as clear felling for timber and open-cast mining, means that the effects of forest loss are extremely intensive in the areas where they occur. This has undoubtedly fuelled the present debate over land use development in PNG.

Social and economic costs
Launching tribal society into the 20th century has resulted in major social problems particularly in the urban areas. Many towns are under a dusk to dawn curfew due to the problem of 'rascals', a local term for criminals, ranging from muggers to murderers.

In rural areas tension between tribal groups has also been increasing as the mining and timber industries develop. Many tribal people find temporary work within these industries and move with the company rather than remaining in their traditional areas. Each operation will also provide a living for people supplying support services, such as growing food for the workforce. Many tribal groups are willing to lease out their lands for forestry or mining, but few envisage the subsequent influx of other tribal people as labourers and their families. Tensions frequently develop between squatters serving the needs of the timber camps and the local tribe who own the land.

Launching such societies into the cash economy has not automatically resulted in the original inhabitants receiving great social benefits. Tribes are always paid royalties for the land, but these are based on current log values, not on the loss of the forest as a resource. As a result, many tribal groups feel they have been cheated. Friends of the Earth Papua New Guinea have collected a number of testimonies that bear this out:

> Now the company has started to come and work in our area and is pulling down all the trees and spoiling absolutely everything, the water, the wildlife, the soil, it's all spoiled. Things around us are dying and finishing and our life is deteriorating.[26]

Another report from the Gogal valley illustrates the bitterness of tribal people when they realize how differently Westerners view the forests:

> You white people use sawn timber to build your houses. We Niugini [New Guinea pidgin: indiginees] use black palm for flooring. We use cane instead of nails. We use Kunai to make our roof instead of iron. Machines of the company have spoiled our black palm trees, our cane, and the dozers trampled our Kunai land. Gone is the Malou we use to make our traditional clothes for sharing our customs with the other villages. Machines have spoiled our land and our tradition. Money is no compensation.[27]

A serious consequence of the loss of access to traditional resources is the disruption of food supplies; the local population may have to buy food rather than grow or hunt for it. Freshwater fish, abundant in most areas, are frequently scarce downstream from logging or mining operations. A member of Friends of the Earth in PNG noted that despite being the landowners, tribal groups may need to sell more than one cubic metre of hardwood timber to realize the price of a small tin of fish.[28]

Growing opposition: Local opposition to logging and mining has increased considerably in the 1980s. The tactics vary from taking direct action, to acting through the courts, as in the case of Wezip against JANT (see case studies). Another tactic has been to refuse to take part in negotiations for timber rights and to produce conflicting land claims. Such delaying tactics are becoming increasingly common.

Those groups tending to favour direct action usually have logging or mining concessions already established on their land. In the Morobe Province bulldozers were pushed into the sea after negotiations between loggers and the local population broke down.[29] In 1986 logging on New Ireland, on a concession owned by Sakai Management Ltd., was brought to a standstill after local people threatened to sabotage equipment and block all roads into the forest.[30] Central government supported the tribal demand that logging be reduced, and the company was restricted to a significantly smaller concession area.

Catherine Caufield recorded an interview with a worker from Papua New Guinea Forest Products Ltd., which was a subsidiary of the British Inchcape Corporation and had had recurring problems on their Bulolo concession; as one worker recalled:

> Sometimes the government is slow with the royalties to the locals. When that happens the people just stop the logging operations. It's happened a few times. They just put a barricade across the road and inform us they don't want us around. We just have to go along with it. Sometimes they close things for weeks at a time.[31]

Opposition to replanting is also widespread amongst the rural population, and poses an unusual dilemma for those wanting to save the forests. Tribal groups fear that by losing direct control over their land for such long periods they will lose all claim over it. Michael Wood, an anthropologist studying in the Western Province explains:

> If land is acquired for such purposes, then the original landowners lose a crucial basis to their autonomy and security. In the case of follow up agricultural developments they may find themselves converted into cash crop producing peasants working small blocks while being closely controlled by state and foreign development experts.[32]

In certain areas, such as along the Madang coast and the Gazelle Peninsula, land acquisition by Europeans before independence caused severe social problems. On the Gazelle Peninsula, extensive land alienation combined with rapid population growth has created a situation that many of the Tolai people find intolerable. Nearly half their land has been alienated for cash crop estates leaving them with less than one hectare per person on which to farm.[33]

PNG, however, is the only country in this study in which tribal groups have any bargaining power with outside interests over the use of their land and development. This must be seen as a positive force, but it also shows that more complex issues need to be addressed if replanting is to be successful. These tribal landowners have little control over the wider economic forces affecting the development of PNG.

The major justification for opening up PNG's forests for timber exploitation is the promise of jobs for indigenous people. The government has been very insistent on this point when negotiating with foreign companies wishing to work in the country. Laws exist that require a company to offer work to a Papua New Guinean capable of doing a particular job before looking abroad for an employee. The policy has, however, been only partially successful.

At management level PNG's timber industry is almost exclusively expatriate. The capital as opposed to labour intensive nature of today's timber industry necessitates imports of hi-tech machinery imposing a serious drain on the PNG economy. For many logging operations, labour costs are so minimal compared to capital costs, that they have little influence over a company's balance of payments. The large profits accrue to the logging company, not its employees. In theory the local population will benefit by an increased cash flow within the local economy, but the reality is that such benefits accruing from the timber industry have probably been minimal.[34] According to the government's Department of Labour, wages are low and working conditions are dangerous in the PNG timber trade,[35] but the Department has no real power to impose its own regulations as major international logging companies frequently threaten to move out of the country and take the work with them.

Timber accounts for 10% of PNG's export earnings, a figure that is likely to increase in the 1990s.[36] How much of this actually stays within the country's economy is the subject of great debate. Logging companies receive most of the export value; the government's economic gains are in the form of various levies, royalty payments and taxes, which may be considerable, but government also has major outgoings with their reafforestation schemes. Taking these costs into account most analysts conclude that only a slight profit accrues to the government from timber revenues.[37]

Corruption in the timber trade

Since the mid 1980s the timber industry has been under close scrutiny by PNG's government because of widespread allegations of corruption. This has centred around the system of 'transfer pricing': a means of manipulating figures that costs the PNG economy millions of dollars every year.

Transfer pricing is a process whereby two companies, usually closely associated, agree a price for a product they wish to trade that bears no relation to current market values; this price may be above or below the current world market value. PNG log prices have been consistently lower than world market values; this has been achieved through a rather complex process. The largest log dealers in PNG sell their logs to major buyers from Japan, Korea and Taiwan, the price agreed is usually the current world market price for the particular wood type, for example US$66 per cubic metre. On the trade invoice, however, the buyer agrees to pay US$60 per cubic metre and the balance in cash; the cash transaction never enters the written accounts and therefore the seller pays no tax or levies on it. The buyer gains because the written prices are produced as evidence for current market values. The buyer can then approach a small timber supplier and produce evidence that the price is US$60 per cubic metre rather than the US$66 actually paid. Small timber producers can only follow the price at which the major companies are selling. According to Patrick Stephenson, a researcher based in the UK, 'there is definite evidence that a price fixing cartel of five companies, accounting for more than 62% of log exports from PNG, exists.'[38]

One company known as FMS (Hong Kong) Ltd., a subsidiary of the British giant Inchcape Corporation, was regarded as a prime suspect in trying to dominate the PNG market. The Forestry Industries Council (FIC), a government body, recently stated:

We believe that Inchcape subsidiaries, on obtaining an interest in a company, run it into near bankruptcy. They withhold trade discounts, mark up freight rates and service charges and deliberately hold down production. They later offer to absorb the so-called loses in return for higher equity in the company.[39]

This is strongly denied by FMS who claim they now make a profit, but Miscus Maraleu, chairman of the FIC, claims that, 'PNG is the only tropical hardwood forest area in the world where its operators are always near bankrupt and its price fixers are always wealthy.'[40]

The same situation emerged with the Open Bay Logging Company in East New Britain. This Japanese-owned operation had been running at a loss since their sawmill burnt down and they had to export raw logs. When the provincial government offered to take over this apparently loss-making operation and find someone willing to rebuild the mill, Open Bay went as far as persuading the Japanese government to lobby on their behalf.[41]

Although common knowledge within PNG, it was only with the emergence of the 'timber wars' that corruption within the timber trade was highlighted. Transfer pricing has been common practice in certain industries for decades, most notably the oil trade. Proof of its existence in the timber trade, however, has emerged only since the Barnett Commission report, an official government inquiry the 'timber wars', was published.

The PNG 'timber wars' developed from government attempts to establish a state marketing agency for timber exports. The FIC was given the task of ensuring that logs from PNG were realizing a realistic price. As the magazine *World Wood* commented, 'PNG prices have never risen by the same percentages as those achieved by, for example, Sabah and Sarawak.'[42] In 1985 PNG's log prices declined by more than 50%.[43]

The Barnett report noted that transfer pricing has been 'far more widespread and far more serious than previously suspected.'[44] The enquiry team issued tax assessments for several companies exceeding US$12m in unpaid revenues.[45] Previous estimates of the annual cost of transfer pricing to the PNG economy ranged from 11[46] to 30m Kina (US$11.5–31.5m.)[47]

The government can, however, find itself under considerable pressure to ignore any malpractices it uncovers. One example of this is the case of the Stettin Bay Logging Company, 75% owned by Nissho Iwai of Japan. Stettin Bay has been implicated in having invoked political influence from Japan in order to continue operating. According to Dr Grynberg of the University of Papua New Guinea:

In 1984, when two provincial forestry officers in New Ireland planned to revoke two foreign logging companies licences for non-payment of tax over the previous twelve years, the companies fought strongly against it. Their parent country also threatened to withdraw aid to PNG unless it allowed the companies to continue logging.[48]

The timber wars were largely fought on the pages of PNG's national newspapers. The Forestry Industries Association (FIA), representing companies involved in the trade, strongly denied that any of their members were involved in transfer pricing and claimed that the FIC was the wrong body to administer a state marketing agency. The Barnett report, however, uncovered enough evidence to conclude that government intervention is essential if the country's overall economy is to benefit from the timber trade.

Attempts to avoid taxes and undercut rivals within the timber trade doubtless results from the sheer greed of some individuals and consumers' demand in the timber's country of destination. Proper forest management and replanting cost money, and, as Naru Kwapena of the Department of Land Survey and Environment recently commented: 'If the end user is not prepared to pay [a realistic price] for the timber, to cover the cost of replanting the resource, then it is probably better not to sell the timber in the first place.'[49]

Development of present forest policy

During World War Two timber demand in Australia rose dramatically. To help co-ordinate exploitation of PNG's forests the Australian administration established the Department of Forestry.

Since its establishment the Forestry Department has promoted timber processing alongside timber exploitation. Under the Australian administration logging concessions were rarely granted to companies with no sawmill; it was hoped that basic processing would create more employment than would simply exporting raw logs. This policy worked in so far as local people were employed in sawmills, but it also restricted timber exploitation by local people as they could not afford a sawmill. Australian companies thus enjoyed an almost complete monopoly over the country's timber industry.[50] During the 1950s and 1960s they established claims over large parts of the interior, despite the considerable tribal population in these areas.

There have been small scale replanting programmes since the early 1900s, but they never had a significant impact on PNG's timber supplies. The first plantations were established around Madang and on New Britain.[51] Eucalyptus, native to PNG, was established in the Highlands during the 1940s, along with pine,[52] and in the latter half of that decade PNG's only hardwood plantation was established, near Port Moresby.[53]

Nevertheless, until the 1970s the country's timber industry was a rather minor part of the economic sector; in 1952, only 46,000 cubic metres of timber was produced.[54] In common with Indonesia, PNG development was heavily influenced by a report from the International Bank for Reconstruction and Development (IBRD), published in 1965.[55] The central theme, as with all IBRD reports at the time, was that in order to develop, PNG must earn foreign capital. Sectors that required low inputs and promised high returns were to be given priority and timber was near the top of the list. The report recommended exports of raw logs, as the current policy of establishing sawmills was too costly. If PNG was to enter the global market immediate implementation of this programme was essential. Consequently, the report urged, large foreign companies experienced in the timber trade should be encouraged to operate in PNG – which has since occurred.

Prior to independence, in 1975, the Constitutional Planning Committees recommended that:

> The basic concept of our society with regard to the use of natural resources is that one generation holds and uses the resources in the capacity of trustee for future generations. . . . For the sake of those who come after us, we must strictly limit the speed with which we exploit our natural resources. We must also replenish them as far as possible (for example by planting new trees after mature trees have been cut down by a timber enterprise). . . . Use of resources should be weighed carefully against the real cost to the country in terms of the damage that will be done to the whole way of life of the people living in the vicinity of a particular project, the destruction of land, rivers and wildlife in the course of the operations of, for instance, a large mining or timber enterprise.[56]

At independence, the Constitution noted:

> We declare our fourth goal to be for Papua New Guinea's natural resources and environment to be conserved and used for the collective benefit of us all, and be replenished for the benefit of future generations.

> We accordingly call for:

> 1) Wise use to be made of our natural resources and the environment in and on the land or sea bed, in the seas, under the land and in the air, in the interests of our development and in trust for future generations; and

> 2) The conservation and replenishment, for the benefit of ourselves and posterity, of the environment and its sacred, scenic, and historical qualities; and

> 3) All necessary steps be taken to give adequate protection to our valued birds, animals, fish, insects, plants and trees.[57]

This clear and unambiguous statement places an almost unique emphasis on the needs of future generations. Private and communal ownership of forests became the cornerstone of the development plans rather than the more usual state ownership of forest land. By 1986 the government owned less than 4% of PNG's forests.[58]

Forest legislation

The legislative framework for implementing such a policy was established under the 1971 Forestry (Private Dealings) Act and the 1973 Forestry Act.

The 1971 Forestry (Private Dwellings) Act aimed to ensure full land rights for clans and tribes over any forest areas they inhabit and/or use. In modern legal terms this implies full ownership rights for the group as a whole. Individual tribes may choose their own representatives to negotiate directly with timber or mining companies. Contracts with such companies must, however, be ratified by the Forestry Minister, who needs to be satisfied that: the interests of the communal group as a whole are protected; the plans do not go against the national interest; and the prospects for economic development from the project are feasible.

The Act also stipulates certain land rights that no contract may overrule, including: rights of access to all forest areas; to collect firewood; to practice traditional gardening; and freedom to hunt anywhere. Logging concessions are further disallowed from felling near villages or sacred sites; claims for protection of individual trees must also be respected by loggers.

Among the countries in this study, PNG's legislation concerning the protection of tribal land rights is the most stringent. It not only maintains full rights but contains mechanisms that attempt to ensure that tribal groups receive a fair price for their resources. These mechanisms are not always successful but it is notable that the Forestry Minister will find it extremely difficult to impose logging in an area in which the local tribe is opposed to it. Undoubtedly, this has made a major contribution to forest conservation in PNG.

The 1973 Forestry Act empowers the government to buy timber rights from tribal owners, if they are willing to sell; this does not, it should be noted, represent a form of compulsory purchase. The government may then sell the rights to a timber company and demand royalties on the timber extracted. Originally, 25% of such royalties were returned directly to the tribe or clan; recently this has been increased to 75%.

Additionally, the government can issue logging licences only if certain environmental criteria are met. These include: no felling within 20 metres of any permanent water course or within 50 metres of a river; no felling on slopes of 30° or more; no blocking of water courses to make bridges; restrictions on the disposal of sawdust waste from sawmills; and erosion control along all roads and tracks.

In 1974 the National Investment and Development Act was passed. This was a more general piece of legislation providing detailed guidelines on foreign investment agreements. It created the National Investment and

Development Authority to oversee the process and stipulate new rules as required. But because it is not specific to a particular economic sector the Act is inevitably ambiguous. It does, however, include some pertinent clauses. The technology used in any project should be as labour intensive as is economically feasible; the previous record of employer/worker relationships of any company wishing to invest in PNG should always be considered. As noted earlier, positions within the operations at all levels must first be offered to indigenous Papua New Guineans. In addition, sub-contracting should be offered to and equipment purchased through local companies.

The Environmental Planning Act was passed in 1978. This Act stipulates that all major development projects must have an environmental impact assessment (EIA) completed prior to the signing of any commercial agreement. All EIA's must be submitted to the Minister for the Environment; the developer is required to bear the costs of the research. This Act applies only to 'major' development projects but does not define the parameters of 'major'. For small operations the EIA is optional because of the administrative burden this would place on the authorities.

The inadequacies of the terms of this Planning Act have presented various problems. For example, it includes no provision for any redress in the event of non-completion or poorly researched EIAs; prosecution under the Act is possible only if damage has been recorded. The EIA was designed to prevent environmental damage but the Act can be applied only when the damage has been done. In addition, once the EIA has been submitted and accepted, it virtually absolves the developer of any responsibility for unforeseen environmental problems. Only by proving direct negligence or non-compliance with the schedule can a developer be prosecuted.

Also in 1978 the New Conservation Areas Act was passed. This enables the government to exclude certain areas from development solely for reasons of conservation. No commercial timber or logging licenses may be granted in such areas and it provides a mechanism for establishing a network of national parks.

When combined, these Acts provide the most thorough basis for forest development in the region covered in this study. They have successfully protected the forests from more recent developments, but unfortunately they do not apply to projects already underway.

There are problems, however, in implementing the regulations contained in these Acts. Almost every commentator on PNG's forests points out that there is very little scientific data on the country's ecology. In addition, there is an acute shortage of qualified personnel to research and assess EIA's, and, as a result, their value is probably limited. Despite these practical shortcomings there have been some notable victories for the environmental movement in PNG. At present, compensation negotiations are in process for the damage caused by the huge OK Tedi copper and gold mining activities in the Western (Fly) Province. In the early 1980s plans for a giant fish cannery on Manus island were halted on environmental grounds.[59]

But most logging agreements were signed before these Acts existed. These old contracts are a major source of environmental problems, but many are reaching the end of their leases and new contracts will be subject to modern laws. For the older ones, however, the comment of Dr Viner of the Taupo Research Laboratories in New Zealand is appropriate: 'once development has been established along a particular line without built-in controls for environmental protection, it is extremely difficult, if not impossible, to change it.[60]

Replanting policy

By 1985 approximately 20,000 ha of timber plantation had been established but, as one expert from the University of Papua New Guinea said: 'this does not even begin to replace the annual harvest of the logging companies.'[61]

The reason for only this relatively small area being replanted is not entirely because of inaction on the part of either government or timber companies. The establishment of timber plantations in PNG has been beset with problems from the outset, due to five major factors: susceptibility to disease; lack of estate management; omission from logging contracts; lack of funding; and, as noted earlier, resistance from tribal groups.

Monocultures of any plant are inherently susceptible to pests, particularly in the tropics. The fast-growing softwoods that dominate PNG's plantations have consistently suffered from: large-scale insect attack; fungal root rots; and a collapse in soil fertility.[62] In the early 1980s, one company, the Philippine Industry Corporation, lost 30,000 ha of Bagras trees to insect attack.[63] Increasingly large amounts of fertilizers are used on plantations as soil fertility drops due to structural damage at harvesting and the nutrient-demanding species being planted.[64] This causes a further drain on the country's economy, as chemical fertilizers must be imported.

Logging companies have been reluctant to replant; the majority of plantations have been established by the government at considerable cost to the nation's tax payers. Establishing and maintaining plantations frequently costs more than the royalties collected from the logging that necessitated the replanting in the first place. On the JANT concession in the Gogal valley, reafforestation is costing around US$180 per ha while JANT pays on average US$40 per ha in royalties.[65]

Provincial governments are responsible for replanting, but they face serious cash shortages as they receive only 25% of all royalty payments. These are in effect a tax on the timber extracted. Central government gains by imposing export duties and, indirectly, through income tax and other taxes. Provincial government forestry departments also receive funding from central government, but none is specified for replanting. These factors combine to make it unclear who should pay for replanting and maintenance.

All three parties concerned – provincial governments, central government and the timber companies – claim it is the responsibility of the other bodies. As a result, timber companies may replant areas but the bickering over who is responsible for their maintenance may take so long that the trees die from lack of care. The latest proposal to alleviate some of this confusion is to impose a local levy of two Kina (US$2.1) per cubic metre of timber produced, payable directly to provincial governments, specifically for replanting.[66]

As has already been noted, replanting also faces resistance from tribal groups who are wary of leasing out land for such necessarily long periods. In legal terms this fear is unjustified, but it is real to many groups in PNG; in some cases this has been overcome by, for example, government-sponsored plantations in the Highlands. Small-scale eucalyptus plantations have been established on alang-alang (*imperata*) grasslands where there have been local fuel shortages.[67] These fuelwood projects are the nearest thing PNG has to any form of a social forestry programme.

Present causes of forest loss

There are five major causes of forest destruction in PNG; shifting agriculture; logging; mining; plantation expansion; and road building.

Shifting agriculture

Agriculture has been practised in Papua New Guinea for more than 9,000 years.[68] For the majority of the population, traditional swidden farming is still a way of life, although there is a considerable variety of systems used.

Because PNG's plantation sector is located in the less populated lowlands, and traditional land rights are recognized, there are few landless farmers in comparison with other countries in this study. Traditional swidden farming, however, continues to expand and undoubtedly plays a role in forest destruction. The FAO estimated that in the late 1970s shifting agriculture was responsible for clearing 15,000 ha of forest annually.[69] This figure was calculated by extrapolating the average area required per person and multiplying it by the estimated population. It is not clear how much of this estimated area is freshly cleared forest or simply part of long-term field rotation. With the wide variation of farming systems and the problems of collecting data in PNG, the figure is a very rough estimate.

Population expansion accounts for some of this destruction, but there are other major factors that must be taken into account. The expansion of cropland near mines or logging sites was noted as far back as the 1930s when cabbages, tomatoes and maize were grown on a commercial basis in the Bulolo region.[70] Anthropologists also noted how the less aggressive tribes were gradually forced on to higher ground where they would have to grow food on slopes, 'so steep is seemed impossible that a footing could be obtained upon them.'[71]

Before chainsaws became more widely available, in the 1960s and 1970s, most swidden sites in the lowlands resembled forest gardens rather than cleared fields. Many tribes simply waited until the dry season and burned off the undergrowth rather than fell trees; larger trees survive such practices and thus the basic forest structure remained intact. The site is cultivated for perhaps two or three years and then abandoned. As with other traditional swidden farming systems a large variety of crops are planted; the Tsembaga, for example, cultivate more than 260 crops, frequently planting 50 on any one site.[72]

Some groups in the Highlands have developed highly intensive forms of shifting cultivation that require the removal of trees. Their small fields are frequently fenced, to keep out wild pigs, and composting as well as rotation of the fields is practised. The rotation cycle is much slower in the Highlands and many garden plots will be under cultivation for several years.[73] New gardens are generally established on open grasslands, although this is no longer always possible as the population increases. The intensive nature of this farming means that the forests do not recover the cleared garden sites, as opposed to the situation with most lowland farming systems.[74]

Another important facet of Highland culture is pig-rearing. Pigs are probably the most valued item in traditional Highland society, and many are kept as pets when young. The adults are usually left to roam free amongst the abandoned gardens, thus helping to fertilize these areas and aid their recovery.[75] Pigs are still highly regarded but their dominance as signs of wealth and prestige is slowly becoming eroded as the cash economy becomes more influential.

The population expansion – and migration as timber and mining operations move location – has meant that traditional agricultural systems are beginning to take their toll on PNG's forests. In many lowland areas the fallow periods for forest gardens are being reduced. Even in the 1930s the jungles of PNG were described as, 'partly forested, partly covered with what appears from a distance to be soft turf but in reality is coarse intractable grass, often growing to several feet high'.[76] This 'coarse intractable grass' is *imperata*, or 'alang-alang'. Regeneration of the forest in these areas has been limited as many lowland tribal groups habitually burn the grass, either to drive animals into a clearing or to send smoke messages.

There are also, however, many reports of fires being started for no apparent reason and no sense of urgency by the local population to extinguish them unless they threaten a village. North Thailand is the only other area covered in this study where this occurs. There may be superstitious reasons why these fires are left to burn but there seems no widely know reason for this.

Catherine Caufield in her book *In the Rain Forest* interviewed Jim Croft of

PNG's National Herbarium who summed up the current situation thus;

> People are running out of land now. They're moving up the slopes throughout the country but I don't think they've realised yet that it's turned sour. There is still a lot of rainforest in New Guinea. Thank God so much of it is so inaccessible.[77]

The timber industry

PNG's timber industry was operative during colonial times but expanded rapidly just prior to independence. The major expansion in the late 1960s, as noted earlier, was as a result of the Australian administration accepting the IBRD's advice – advice that provided justification for Australia's continued commercial interest in PNG's timber.[78] The major Japanese interests moved in during the early 1970s and as a result PNG's fledgling timber industry was totally dominated by foreign investors. Even now (1980s), local companies have rights to only one-fifth of PNG's total area of timber concessions.[79]

Timber production increased from approximately 300,000 cubic metres in 1969 to more than 1.7m cubic metres in 1985, mainly for export.[80] Export earnings for 1985 were US$76.5m.,[81] representing 10% of PNG's total exports.[82] Timber production is a significant but not a major sector in the economy although considerably more revenue could accrue if the corruption outlined earlier was addressed. As has already been noted, most timber exports are in the form of logs, as earlier attempts to encourage processing failed. In 1982, PNG's 58 sawmills exported 62,000 cubic metres[83] of sawn timber, by 1987 this had dropped to just 4,000 cubic metres.[84] Nevertheless, timber processing to meet domestic demand currently employs more than 5,000 people.[85]

By 1984 the government had purchased timber rights over almost 30% of the country's 'accessible' forest (4.1m ha), mostly lowland rainforest.[86]

With the constitutional declarations emphasizing that exploited resources should be, 'replenished for the benefit of future generations', PNG based its timber industry on a selective logging system. At present the only exception is JANT's clear felling operations (see case study). The government, however, has long-term plans to convert much lowland forest into rubber and oil palm plantations, but currently, with the collapse of the international markets for these commodities, there is little enthusiasm for this.

The government's eagerness to secure foreign capital frequently means that many restrictions on logging practices are rescinded. In the case of JANT, the government waived the rules on both indigenees' share holdings and on replanting.[87] The Vanimo timber concession provides another example: one of the applicants, Heturi Meja, a Philippine company, was due to obtain the concession despite having no previous experience in the industry and demanding that the government act as guarantor for the company's loans.[88] Heturi Meja openly declared they were looking for a 24% return on their investment within the first year.[89] Such a fast rate of return in a supposedly long-term industry such as forestry clearly indicates little desire to implement sustainable logging.

Heturi Meja enjoyed the full backing of the Minister of Forests and almost obtained the contract for the 268,000 ha concession. (That the Minister's personal lawyer was also the director of the PNG partner for Heturi may have influenced this support.)[90] But with a change in government and the appointment of a new Forest Minister, the company was immediately dropped as a candidate.

The Vanimo timber rights eventually went to an Australian company, Bunnings, which is currently engaged in a battle with the local government over illegal felling.[91] (See case study.)

Even when all the contracts have been satisfactorily settled, felling plans frequently go astray. One example was on the concession owned by the British timber company Inchcape, which in the 1970s and early 1980s, controlled New Guinea Timbers (now PNG Forest Products), with a major concession in the Bulolo valley. In 1982 Inchape announced they had run out of virgin forest; a situation that should not have arisen until 1994.[92] They had clearly been over-cutting but Inchcape claimed they simply increased production to meet new demands. Catherine Caufield recalled several meetings she had with company officials:

> One forester . . . called it 'pretty poor forecasting' and suggested that the company had had to take more trees than anticipated because its logging techniques were wasteful.
>
> 'We were highly selective at first,' Stan Barnes, PNG Forest Products' chief engineer and a long time employee of the company told me, 'but standards gradually dropped; we went for smaller and smaller trees as it became feasible to produce thinner veneers.'
>
> 'That's true,' Mike Callaghan, an Inchcape consultant assigned to the company said, laughing. 'Lots of these areas we have been through three or more times, in some cases five times. Each time getting a bit more desperate.'[93]

Clear evidence of the general waste of timber extracted is contained in the company's official figures that record 191,000 cubic metres cut in 1981, but only 92,000 cubic metres of produce emerging.[94]

PNG Forest Products Ltd. has been involved with replanting on the concession but this has generally been a failure because few seedlings survived. The company agreed to replant but was unwilling to maintain the seedlings. The regional government claimed it was the company's responsibility to tend the young trees, and a long debate ensued. PNG Forest Products is one of the largest companies in the forestry sector, employing around 1,800 people; it has the only plywood factory in the country and controls one of the two veneer mills. It also produces almost 500m pairs of disposable chopsticks for Japan, where it has become fashionable to use a new set at each meal.[95]

PNG's timber trade grew at the expense of its lowland rainforests. By 1987, of the total 1.7m cubic metres produced, 1.3m cubic metres were exported, more than 90% to Japan and Korea.[96]

PNG quite unjustifiably gained a reputation for producing too great a variety of timber in comparison to other exporters, as *World Wood* commented in 1986: 'Not surprisingly – and despite buyers' statements over the past twenty years – it has been found that PNG log exports are not the jumbled mixture alleged.'[97] This myth helped maintain the situation in which PNG logs were ungraded. Ungraded logs fetch a much lower price on the world timber market and this partially explains why PNG log prices have been kept so low.[98] In 1985 the government made grading of all logs for export compulsory and within two years the value of exports doubled.[99]

Japanese logging interests control 53% of all logging concessions and consume almost 70% of all timber exports.[100] This places the government in a delicate situation, as PNG could not afford to lose this major customer. Japan wants logs, and PNG is acutely aware of how foreign investment pulled out of Indonesia in the 1980s. Japanese demand for logs from PNG jumped from 290,000 cubic metres in 1983 to 746,000 cubic metres by 1987.[101]

At present PNG is facing a dilemma. On one side the timber industry is claiming that PNG is poised to become a major log exporter with, after Indonesia, the second largest forest area in the region.[102] Meanwhile, the Minister for Forests, Mr Diro claims, 'It is about time the landowners were given the benefit of their resources.'[103] These two goals may not be entirely incompatible, but experience in other timber producing areas shows there may be serious conflicts.

Mining

With its considerable mineral wealth, particularly gold and copper, mining put PNG on the world map. All mining operations in PNG are on an open-cast basis. It is less the total area of forest cleared that warrants concern than the absolute devastation caused to these sites. Most gold operations involve high pressure water blasting of the mountain side and then dredging the rivers below. The resultant visible scars produce strong responses from the people. Catherine Caufield described the present scene along 20 miles of the Eddie Creek thus:

> To look at Eddie Creek now it is hard to imagine it as once lush, unspoilt forest. . . . The miners have stripped the whole mountain sides down to bare earth and deliberately eroded them in order to wash the gold they

hope is there into the riverbed where they can sluice for it. To satisfy demands for better access to gold country the government is clearing crude roads for the few areas that are still inaccessible. The landscape is now a jumble of gravel heaps, prospectors' shacks and diverted streams. There is a sad wash of colour from the permanently bare hill sides, to the ochre of newly bulldozed roads, and the dirt brown silt-filled rivers and streams.[104]

The massive OK Tedi gold and copper mine in PNG's Western Province, bordering Indonesia, a joint venture between the American Amaco corporation and the PNG government, was producing 8,000 tons of gold ore per day in the early 1980s. Production of gold and copper ore in 1988 averaged 30,000 tons per day and it is hoped eventually to reach 70,000 tons daily.[105] The area will probably be worked out by the year 2000.

The scale of such an operation means that large access roads have to be constructed and prodigious quantities of tailings run straight into the Fly river system. At present the mine annually pours out more than 30m tons of silt, containing high concentrations of lead, complexes of cyanides, and cadmium, into the OK Tedi river system. This is due to increase to more than 55m tons when production peaks in the 1990s.[106] The company acknowledge that this would kill most fish in the river but claim stocks will survive by swimming into the tributaries. Fish from the river are an important protein source for the local people and their loss will place a greater burden on other food sources. This could result in more forest being cut down to make way for basic food crops.

Two more copper mines are scheduled for the area when OK Tedi runs out, on the Fubilan and Robertson mountains. Because of their importance to the economy all three mines are exempt from any environmental restrictions imposed under the Water Resources Bureau Act, the Environmental Planning Act or the Contaminant Act.[107]

Plantations and other causes of forest loss

Between 1965 and 1980, approximately 190,000 ha of forest around the coasts had been replaced by oil palm, cacao, rubber and coconut plantations.[108] Oil palm dominates the areas around Milne Bay and Morobe; rubber and cacao along the Sepik and throughout the Central Province.[109] Most of this is government owned land purchased before the current legislation. Research into environmental changes experienced after conversion to plantation is inconclusive but there is little reason to suspect that these will be any different from those found on Malaysian oil palm and rubber estates. The government hopes to expand this sector but requires investors to process the raw materials before export.

The only other widespread problem for PNG's forests is the expansion of the road network. In the Sepik province the Vanimo timber operations are contracted to clear at least five kilometres for the North Coast Highway annually.[110] Another major coastal road network is scheduled for the Western province. At present, however, PNG's road system is minimal. Roads can facilitate the development of local markets, helping improve the living standards of many, and to this end such a policy need not automatically be detrimental to the forests. Without proper supervision and full integration with other development strategies, however, roads could cause unforeseen problems for PNG's forests such as providing access to previously inaccessible areas and causing land slides.

There is one localized problem that is noteworthy: the large number of refugees along the Irian Jaya border. An estimated 10,000 fled Irian Jaya in 1984 as trouble flared in the region between the Free Papua Movement (OPM) and the Indonesian authorities. The United Nations is providing refugee assistance despite Indonesian claims that most of them have returned to Irian Jaya.[111] There are no estimates on how large an area of forest has been cleared in these remote locations but it may be considerable. With the upsurge in military operations in Irian Jaya during 1988, the refugee problem is likely to continue.

Papua New Guinea still has large areas of forest but all the familiar signs of environmental degradation are present. Despite the current legislation, the country finds itself in exactly the same economic trap as its neighbours in South-east Asia and to that extent has little room for complacency. It does, however, have a much firmer base for building a sustainable forestry policy than any other country considered in this report.

Forest futures

The most immediate threat to PNGs forests is the rapid expansion of the timber industry. At present timber extraction affects a larger area of forest than does the growth in population. But the population – as well as the timber industry – will expand, and the threat to the forests for this reason will undoubtedly increase in the future.

In the 1970s the government confidently claimed there was enough forest to maintain a viable timber industry for 500 years; this highly over-optimistic view has few supporters. Dr Fraser of the Institute of National Affairs claims that there will be no timber shortages till the year 2010 if present extraction rates continue.[112] Professor Frodin of the University of PNG also estimates that most commercial timber stands will be exhausted within a similar period.[113] In certain areas, such as New Ireland, timber supplies will probably be exhausted within the 1990s.[114] These predictions, however, are based on current levels of timber extraction; the proposed expansion of the timber industry will undoubtedly hasten the demise of forest resources.

The government's policy of attempting to restrict the expansion of the timber industry seems to have failed. The Turama concession covering 188,000 ha in the Gulf Province is due to start operations as soon as the environmental impact assessment is completed.[115] Concessions already active include 33,000 ha of pine stands on Manus Island, 60,000 ha on Siassi Island and a large number of smaller operations.[116] PNG sees itself as the last supplier of logs from the region when East Malaysia supplies diminish. This is a dubious goal and there is a lot of debate within PNG over the structure and direction of the timber trade.

For the 1990s it seems that PNG will continue to expand log exports rather than develop a processing sector, although there has been much talk in government circles about establishing a furniture industry. If the export of logs continues to dominate, PNG should seek agreement with East Malaysia on prices and quotas, as they are the last two log exporters in the region.

One extremely disturbing development is the government's lack of commitment to ensuring that timber companies stay within the law. In 1986 the government cut funding for the Department of the Environment and the Conservation Environmental Monitoring Unit; a retrogressive step. The Barnett Commission simply put in writing what was already public knowledge in PNG and, with its call for government intervention, implies that bodies such as the Monitoring Unit should be strengthened, not cut back.

There is now a US$2 levy on every cubic metre of timber leaving PNG; the revenue goes directly towards replanting efforts. This must be applauded but it is probably not enough and there seems to be no change in the replanting policy. Fast-growing softwoods continue to dominate replanting efforts and there is still no social forestry programme.

A novel suggestion for mixing timber extraction and conservation needs has been promoted by Dr Grynberg at the University of Papua New Guinea.[117] He proposes that forests be harvested in strips of untouched virgin areas alternating with cutting sites. The ratio would be roughly 50–50 and no logging would be allowed at any time in the virgin areas. If this were combined with 'softer' extraction methods, without the use of bulldozers, and a policy of post-logging management and enrichment planting, the results could be extremely beneficial. The cost would be higher than for present methods but it would ensure the preservation of a realistic cross section of forest types. At present, throughout PNG and South-east Asia, protected forests are restricted to steep slopes and inaccessible areas, generally with spectacular scenery, but this does not imply greater species diversity. A patchwork of productive and non-productive areas in commercially viable forests could be a workable compromise.

There is a tremendous potential within PNG for agro-forestry and the development of a minor forest produce industry. This potential is not only due to the quantity of forest still present, but also the system of land ownership, which provides some assurance to tribal groups that their wishes are heeded when forests are developed. A number of non-government organizations, most notably the Wau Ecology Centre, have been attempting to improve yields from slash and burn farming systems. There are, however, chronic shortages of funds for such projects despite some of the innovative ideas that have emerged. There is a special problem in that clan rivalries do not always help the spread of new ideas within PNG.

In conclusion, PNG still has a great deal of forest and perhaps the most viable choice of paths to take on developing their potential. This is partly due to geographical isolation but the minimal government ownership of forests cannot be ignored. There is a lot of room for improvement within the present system of resource exploitation but PNG has much to offer the region in terms of a basic model for the political control of forests. By importing some of the concepts developed in Burma (outlined in the Indonesian section), within their timber production systems PNG has a sound base for creating a sustainable future.

Case studies

1. Wood chipping in the Gogal Valley
Since its initiation in 1971, JANT's wood chipping operations have caused a storm of controversy. This operation is a useful case study because it involves the PNG government, a large multinational corporation and the local people of the Gogal Valley.

The project involves rights to clear fell more than 50,000 ha of lowland rain forest in the Madang region. The timber is converted into wood chips destined for Japan where they are processed into low quality packaging. To understand how the present situation arose it is worth noting the history of JANT's owner, the Honshu Paper Company.

JANT, an offshoot of the giant Honshu Paper Company of Japan, came into existence in 1949 when the Oji Paper Group was split up. Just prior to this period the Oji group had almost total control of the Japanese paper market but was forced to concede to government pressure against monopolies. As a result, three major paper companies emerged, Oji, Jujo and Honshu. By the early 1960s, however, the big three were starting to merge again. Towards the end of the decade they were on such close trading terms they could effectively move assets and profits among themselves.[118] At this time Oji started to look abroad for supplies, as the then company president claimed: 'Pulp resources in Japan are exhausted and the factories pollute, we cannot construct or enlarge any more in Japan.'[119] It is noteworthy that Japan has considerable softwood forests of its own but their timber is expensive because their forests are intensively managed.

Honshu has its own history of pollution problems that probably restricted expansion within Japan. In 1958 their mill on the banks of the Edo river in Japan was the target of numerous demonstrations by local fishermen complaining about the pollution it produced. The demonstrations culminated with Honshu calling in more than 1,000 riot police, precipitating a bloody confrontation between the fishermen and the authorities. The government held a full inquiry into the incident but no pressure was applied to Honshu to reduce their factory effluents.

In 1965 Honshu perfected a method of turning tropical hardwoods into wood chips. They were the first company in the world to attempt such a project; if it was successful they could gain a significant lead over their rivals.

In PNG, the Gogal Valley was originally surveyed in 1961 and the government purchased timber rights over 52,265 ha of it. The rights to selectively log the area went on sale in 1964 and 1966, but no offers were received; advertised again in 1968 it caught the attention of Honshu.

From the outset Honshu insisted upon being the dominant partner in any joint venture with a local company. This was against government policy but the authorities nevertheless capitulated and JANT was formed; the minority partner was Wewak Timbers Ltd, a local operation in the region, with a saw mill.

Only after the agreement was signed did Honshu announce they intended to clear fell rather than selectively log the area. After lengthy negotiations Honshu was finally given permission to start clear felling in 1971. But problems continued, as Honshu refused to accept that replanting was their responsibility. In 1974, JANT's Director wrote to the New Guinea Director of Forests: 'Your assumption that reafforestation is a normal part of logging operations and should be costed to the logging is totally unacceptable.'[120]

It is difficult to understand why the authorities capitulated on so many principles in order to keep Honshu in PNG. The only conclusion must be that the government regarded this as a prestige project that would launch PNG into the world timber trade. It provided an ideal situation for both parties: JANT got cheap timber, PNG a lot of publicity.

The government also hoped the cleared land could be used as a plantation. This was actively promoted despite reports from the Department of Agriculture claiming that the soils were totally unsuitable. As Professor Seddon of the University of Melbourne commented: 'Tropical soils are often infertile and poorly drained, but those of the Gogal are exceptionally so and the long term carrying capacity is probably low under any system of land use.'[121] By 'carrying capacity' Professor Seddon is referring to the intensity of agriculture that soils can support before becoming exhausted. This intensity depends on the soil itself, the farming methods applied and the number of people hoping to live off that piece of land. Hence the land has a maximum 'capacity' to effectively 'carry' a population.

Individuals within the government realized they had probably given in on too many aspects of the operation, but could not afford to lose face. By contrast Honshu had worked out a brilliant deal whereby they found it cheaper to cut and ship tropical wood chips from PNG than to use Japan's considerable softwood reserves.

By mid 1973 the wood chip mill had been established and clear felling was under way. Honshu was also aware of the potential publicity value of the world's first operation converting tropical rainforest into woodchips. The JANT promotional literature described in detail how: 'Every day one hundred various types of heavy vehicles and their operators are working and making their presence known in the green jungles of the Gogal area.'[122] They were clearing 3–4,000 ha annually and by 1984 exported more than 20,000 tons of wood chips every month.

For many years the government continued to urge JANT to replant some felled areas and eventually they won a partial victory. Honshu agreed to set up a separate company to replant limited areas. This time, however, Honshu made it clear they would abide by PNG law and remain the minority partner. Gogal Reafforestation was formed with government equity and majority share holding. But this resulted in only a few trees being planted and most of the 4,800 ha established by 1984 was through direct government replanting schemes, not Gogal Reafforestation. By this time JANT had clear felled an estimated 37,000 ha.

Despite aquiring what would be considered by most outside observers a 'very good deal', JANT seemed to be losing money. For Honshu, JANT's parent company, this had several advantages, the main one being that they paid no tax on the wood chips as they made no profit. This was achieved by claiming their costs were considerable and the price of wood chips too low.

Initial costs were undoubtedly high; JANT had to set up the mill, invest in equipment, build export facilities and so on. But JANT would have been able to estimate all these costs prior to starting operations and they should, therefore, have formed part of their costings. The wood chip price problem was a little more complex. Honshu claimed that only they were capable of processing these wood chips as no one else had the necessary technology; so JANT sold its entire harvest to Honshu. But Honshu also claimed that the process for converting the chips into pulp was extremely expensive, and consequently the raw material must be bought at a very low price. As one expert put it: 'In this context Honshu's refusal to pay higher prices for JANT's chips is a factor of corporate planning, not market forces.'[123]

The entire Honshu corporation was making minimal profits back in Japan, particularly in comparison with that of the other companies in the unofficial conglomerate. In stark contrast, however, Honshu emerges as the largest asset holder with assets amounting to more than US$1.3 billion. This was eight years after they set up the plant and most capital expenditure would have been paid off. JANT was working on the assumption that its buildings were depreciating at 5% per annum, the plant at 10% and vehicles at 20%. These are not unusual depreciation values in themselves, but if Honshu was to maintain or even increase the value of its assets, reinvestment was essential. Over this same period, however, Honshu made no significant investment in their Gogal operations.

With no reinvestment it is questionable why Honshu not only invested in the project initially but then wished to continue. In early 1984 JANT applied for and was granted timber rights for the Sogeram area, just inland from Gogal.

In short, the inevitable conclusion is that the PNG authorities have been 'taken for a ride'. As Professor Seddon puts it: 'The sum of the government's costs, although difficult to estimate, would probably exceed the sum of its returns and to that extent Papua New Guinea might indeed be said to subsidise a Japanese company.'[124]

A more comprehensive analysis is needed to estimate the effect of JANT's operations on the environment and local people. A brief outline of Gogal Valley life prior to JANT may help set the scene.

According to archaeologists the valley has been inhabited for 5,000 years. Today the population of 4,000 live in small hamlets of between 20 and 40 individuals. Hamlets are loosely allied to form the major tribal or clan groups in the area. Despite the small population the Valley can claim 21 distinct languages, which gives some indication of the independence between groups. Most people will speak at least four of them.

All land is under communal ownership and individuals may only claim use rights; these rights are inherited through the male side of the family. The present generation are custodians rather than owners, therefore when managing an area the needs of past and future generations must be considered.

Each clan has a 'head man' as a social leader; a position earned, not inherited. It is usually conferred upon the 'richest' man in the group, but here a set of criteria for wealth unique to PNG emerge. Wealth is governed by the number and extent of obligations owed to an individual. The more a person is owed, in terms of local currency or social obligations, the richer they are. The result is a system in which giving is of far greater value than receiving. In this way material objects owned by the individual are of little value unless they have been involved in some kind of social interaction. For an individual, a clay pot has no value outside its direct use, unless it is to be given away.

The basic unit of exchange is the pig. Either alive or dead they are used for all bartering transactions and ceremonies. Large numbers of pigs are generally slaughtered at the time of feasts or particular ceremonies, and the population gorges itself on pig meat, frequently leading to a stomach complaint known as 'pigbel'. The host of such events will endeavour to donate as many pigs as possible in order to increase his wealth and social standing.

The agricultural system is based on establishing forest gardens and collecting wild forest produce; crops are grown in the forest rather than on areas cleared of trees; taro and yam are the basic subsistence crops. Anthropologists have recorded more than ten varieties of yam in this Valley alone. The forest gardens and pigs are cared for by the women and the men spend most of the time hunting or gathering wild forest produce.

Earlier this century, cash crops were introduced but never became popular; the area was too remote and no local markets had been developed. As a result many cash crop trees, such as rubber, grow unattended in the forests. In this respect much of the forest could be regarded as mature secondary rather than genuine virgin forest, but there are many areas where there is no evidence of clearing, even for short periods.

When the government purchased the timber rights from the local clans in 1963, selective logging was envisaged. Compensation was based on the assumption that, if properly managed, the logging would not affect people's gardens or valuable trees and the forest would remain intact. When the plans were changed to permit clear felling, the authorities failed to develop any clear policy on how much more compensation should be paid. Eventually the system was changed to one in which the clans received a certain percentage of the royalties collected, combined with the provision of basic infrastructure.

It was hoped that JANT would take a leading role in large-scale agricultural developments in the Valley, but they were not enthusiastic and the soils were unsuitable. In an attempt to make the clear felling operations sustainable, the government initially hoped to replant 20,000 ha of the concession with fast growing softwoods. JANT showed no interest and the government target was eventually reduced to 5,000 ha.

The royalty payment system became increasingly complex as the government attempted to recoup the initial compensation payments while handing out the new production royalties. Table 4.1 illustrates this point with royalty payments becoming inconsistent and confusing. As a result the local population vented their anger on the government rather than JANT. In 1976 the people of the Gogal Valley were the first to obtain 50% of government royalties; today, as has been noted, the local population receives 75% on all concessions.

Environmental Destruction: Clear felling is carried out by chainsaw gangs backed up by bulldozers. Approximately 95% of the felled trees are used, the remainder are destroyed in the process of extraction; in order to maintain supplies for the mill, logging continues throughout the rainy season.

The devastating effect of clear felling on the ecology of the area is obvious. Compaction of the soils due to the use of heavy machinery further jeopardizes the chances of recovery, particularly during the rainy season. One local described the situation thus; 'All this machinery, bulldozers and graders . . . come in and spoil the soil. They overturn it, bringing the clay to the top and the stones, and the food will not grow well.'[125] This depletion of soil fertility has also been recorded in the few scientific studies undertaken in the area. One report noted:

> The removal of forest cover greatly reduced the phosphorus levels in the cleared areas, which were found to be 53% less than average levels in the closed forest. And in the water-logged areas the soil pH was observed to be lower than in the drier soils, indicating that the soil is acidic due to anaerobic decomposition of organic materials.[126]

Most local people claim they must leave these areas fallow for at least five years before any crops will grow. Even then yields are said to be considerably lower than before logging started.

There have also been numerous complaints that trees marked for preservation are destroyed and that, without official permission, JANT dredged the river for gravel, resulting in a general decline in fish resources.

One of the main reasons JANT was granted the concession was the promise of 1,500 jobs in the Valley, but the highest number employed was 739 in 1975. By 1980 this had dropped to 393, with an additional 84 occasional casual labourers. Only one Papua New Guinean has been promoted above assistant supervisor and that is the Industrial Relations and Personnel officer. This post is regarded by the locals as a buffer between a remote management and the general work force.

The Department of Labour have consistently challenged JANT on a number of issues including: a poor safety record, low wages, too long working hours, inadequate housing and unhygenic kitchens and toilets. JANT have not responded to the criticisms and their lethargy led one senior inspector from the department to comment, 'In my opinion the company is using the fact that their knowledge of English is limited to by-pass PNG legislation if possible.'[127]

As with the concessions throughout South-east Asia, the desecration of sacred sites has been a major source of conflict with the local people. The best-known example in PNG was the destruction of the ancient clay pit site at Zalinan.

These sacred clay pits were in the territory of the Mulgas but a number of clans had access rights. The site was protected by the female guardian spirit Kepial, who originally created it to ensure that the local people would always have a source of clay for pottery. In 1976, the site was destroyed by bulldozers.

The nearest village to the pits is Jobto, whose headman is Wezip. The villagers had been remarkably tolerant of JANT considering the scale of destruction around them, as the District Commissioner commented to JANT's Director: 'This cooperation, which is over and above what is written in the Heads of Agreement, appears to be all one way and in our opinion leaves your company wide open to severe criticism of unthinking and uncaring exploitation.'[128]

The villagers' tolerance, however, began to diminish in 1975, when they blockaded the logging roads in protest at JANT's employment policies. The government compensation payments quickly emerged as another centre for grievances and the authorities flew in a team of top officials to negotiate with the blockaders. A new royalty payment system was agreed in which the clans would receive 50% of government revenue from JANT. This was accepted conditional on a gift to the clan of video equipment to produce a film to put their case to the members of parliament in Port Moresby. At the same time, however, other clans in the valley were refusing to co-operate with land surveys the authorities were attempting.

Upon regaining access to the forests around Jobto, JANT ignored the careful markings on trees and around the site and clear felled the area. As one researcher remarked: 'To say Wezip and his clan were upset would be an understatement.'[129]

The village decided the best policy was to take JANT to a village court; an institution officially recognized by the government. The court ruled in favour of Wezip and his clan and awarded them 10,000 Kina (US$9,000) in compensation. Both the government and JANT refused to pay. The authorities attempted to negotiate the settlement but Wezip continues to demand the sum as the clans claimed that Kepial has fled the area and the quality of the clay had fallen.

JANT then wrote to the Forestry Office in Port Moresby to obtain exemption from the village courts act. In their letter they stated:

It must be remembered that there is every possibility that further actions could be brought through the village courts which will adversely affect the profitability of the company's operations. It is thought that this system was never intended to deal with matters involving foreign investment, however, it has happened and will no doubt happen again if exemption is not granted.[130]

In the 1981 general election the entire Valley voted for the opposition candidates in protest against their appeals and petitions having been ignored. Once in power, however, the local politicians took no firm action. This is not unusual as a company such as JANT has immense power in the region where they are still a major employer despite many of the promised jobs never having materialized; as one resident said: 'You don't say anything against the company if you live in Madang.'[131] The compensation payments have still not been paid.

JANT have successfully applied to fell in the Sogeram area, inland from Gogal. The Madang provincial government voted almost unanimously in favour of granting this concession to JANT rather than any rival. Even the representatives from the Gogal Valley voted in the company's favour. Just prior to the vote JANT is said to have presented the local government with a new Japanese printing press. Such gifts are common in situations like this.

In summary, despite all the legislation, a legal system that recognizes decisions by village courts, and relatively tough environmental laws, the whole apparatus can be overruled if a company has the right political connections. There is clearly a significant difference between the protection of tribal rights in the legislation and the reality in the field.

2. Vanimo forest products

During the early 1970s the central government purchased timber rights over 245,000 ha of forest in the Sepik region.[132] No suitable buyer was found for more than a decade although Heturi Meja from the Philippines (noted earlier) was one of the candidates. Heturi had in fact signed contracts with the authorities but a then new government annulled the deal.[133]

In 1984 Bunning Brothers of Perth Ltd. obtained a six-year lease over the area, in the name of Vanimo Forest Products Pty Ltd, a wholly-owned subsidiary of the Australian company. They were allowed to selectively fell and export the logs on condition that 30,000 cubic metres of timber per year was processed in the saw mill they were obliged to set up. Within one year Vanimo Forest Products (VFP) was exporting 50,000 cubic metres of raw logs from the area.[134] The concession rights are to be reviewed in 1990.

The Bunnings Brothers are very active in the forests of South-West Australia where they have built up a reputation amongst conservationists for over-cutting and poor industrial relations. They have been involved in clear felling the native Jarrah forests and replanting with pine.[135] The Australian Campaign to Save Native Forests claim that Bunnings is cutting the Jarrah trees 30% faster than they can grow back and the karri timber is extracted at 60% above present replacement rates.[136] If correct, this is clearly unsustainable.

With this background it is questionable whether Bunnings is an appropriate company to fit into the PNG policy of sustainable forestry. Central government organized the deal, not the West Sepik (Sandaun) provincial government within whose jurisdiction the site is, and which is currently demanding a review of the contract. The Province Premier, Paul Langro, wrote to the Minister of Forests:

> The Sanduan Provincial Government, as government of the landowners of the Vanimo timber concession, will seek an injunction at the National Court on the operation of the company over native land until appropriate measures are taken by both the company and the national government to ensure the safety and protection of our peoples' land and environment.[137]

This kind of opposition at provincial government level is rare. The fact that the provincial government played no part in the initial negotiations undoubtedly angered the local authorities.

At first glance all seems quite well and the company has brought some prosperity to the area. By 1986 they had exported 94,000 cubic metres of logs, 80% to Japan and Korea,[138] and the remainder to India, Hong Kong, Portugal and Singapore. These exports were worth US$5.2m of which the government claimed back US$558,000 in royalties. The company employs just over 250 people.

For the workers, however, there is little satisfaction. The local government claims to have received numerous complaints about poor working conditions, lack of medical help when injured, unhygienic housing and a host of other issues, including low pay.[139] The *Niugini News* reported local government as stating that: 'almost everything in the agreement has not been properly attended [*to*] since the signing in 1984.'[140]

In July 1986 the workers went on strike for a week, leading the local paper to describe the scene as a 'Timber siege':

The Vanimo Forest Products timber yard was yesterday under siege. And an expatriate was attacked by striking employees. A middle aged Australian was punched and kicked but not badly hurt. He had been driving a truck carrying hardwood logs to the town's wharf for export.

About 150 workers halted construction of a sawmill, then moved into the timber yard in town and rolled logs across the main driveway. "They are now in control of the whole property" said an eyewitness. "They are sitting on piles of logs and sawn timber singing and shouting".[141]

The range of grievances becomes apparent only in the light of the number of new agreements that brought the strike to an end. These included: wage increases, sick pay, annual leave entitlement, a reduction in working hours, improvements in transport and accommodation, and the company's adherence to the 1978 Employment Act.[142]

While the company's employees were in conflict with the management, so were local contractors. One local company, Concorde Plant Hire, had lengthy discussion with VTP in an attempt to obtain realistic rates for equipment hire. Vanimo Timber managed to beat the price down to well below the national average, despite the remote location of the site.[143]

To add to the pressures on Vanimo Timber, tribal landlords were also constantly in conflict with the company. As *The Times of PNG* reported in 1986: 'The ongoing battle between the landowners, developers and the government over the Vanimo timber area has reached a head yet again.'[144] At the end of October 1986 the landowners blocked all roads into the area and refused to move until their demands were met. These included: compensation for environmental damage, the landlords to own 25% of the company's shares, immediate payment of all royalties owed, including the increase announced earlier that year, and local contractors to be given preference.[145] The blockade was eventually lifted, although negotiations have since continued. The attitude of the timber trade in general was accurately summed-up by the journal *World Wood*, which referred to the 'epic proportions of the Vanimo saga' and hoped that a similar 'performance' will not occur over new concessions in PNG.[146]

The confrontation looks set to be protracted with all sides maintaining their positions. Central government and Vanimo Timbers have been relatively silent on the issues for some time. The provincial government is continuing its attempt to get the company into the courts. Paul Langro summed up his view in a recent statement in the national press:

> We cannot support and allow a foreign company which has no respect, trust and commitment to our government and its people to continue to exploit our resources without substantial benefits for our people.[147]

Table 4.1
JANT royalty payments to the government versus payments to villagers, May 1963 to June 1977 (Kina)

Date	Royalties	Villagers 25% share	Actual payments to villagers	Amount to be recouped from villagers
May 1963			50,000	
April '71			27,930	
Nov. '64 to June '74	69,954	17,488	17,679	78,121
Jan. to June '75	33,101	8,275	8,307	78,153
July to Dec. '75	49,726	12,432	13,033	78,754
Jan. to June '76	84,458	21,114	9,217	66,857
July to Dec. '76	65,275	16,319	10,000	60,538
Jan. to June '77	80,817	20,204	10,000	50,334
Totals	383,331	95,832	146,166	

Source: Office of Forests, Madang, Quoted in Colin De'Ath 1980.

References

1. Viner, A. 1984.
2. FAO, 1981.
3. Ibid.
4. Loffler, E. 1979.
5. Ibid.
6. Golson, J. 1981.
7. Saulei, S. 1986.
8. FAO, op.cit.
9. Ibid.
10. Ibid.
11. Ibid.
12. Ibid.
13. Saulei, S. 1986.
14. Dhal, A. 1984.
15. Saulei, S. 1984.
16. Kwapena, N. 1985.
17. Loffler, E. op.cit.
18. Ibid.
19. Ibid.
20. Ibid.
21. Stewart, N. 1983; and R. and V. Routley, 1980.
22. Stewart, N. 1983.
23. Routley, R. and V. 1980.
24. Lofter, E. op.cit.
25. Kwapena, N. op.cit.
26. Friends of the Earth PNG, 1984.
27. Ibid.
28. Stewart, N., op.cit.
29. Routley, R. and V. op. cit.
30. *Post Courier* (PNG) 1986, 18 March, 'New order fells a logging firm'.
31. Caufield, C. 1985.
32. Wood, M. 1985.
33. Hogbin, I. (ed.) 1973.
34. Wood, M. op.cit.
35. Saulei, S. 1986.
36. Ibid.
37. Wood, M. op.cit.
38. Stephenson, P. personal communication, November 1989.
39. Forestry Industries Council, 1987.
40. Maraleu, M. 1987.
41. Smith, A. 1984 (b)
42. *World Wood*, 1986, February, 'Trading conditions deteriorate'.
43. Ibid.
44. *Asian Timber*, 1988, May, 'Enquiry unearths PNG malpractices'.
45. Ibid.
46. Caufield, C. op.cit.
47. Diro, F. 1986.
48. Grynberg, R. et.al. 1988.
49. Kwapena, N. op.cit.
50. Wood, M. op.cit.
51. Kwapena, N. op.cit.

160   *Rainforest Politics*

52. Ibid.
53. FAO, 1981.
54. Kwapena, N. op.cit.
55. Routley, R. and V. op.cit.
56. Constitutional Planning Committee, 1973.
57. Papua New Guinea Constitution, 1974.
58. Kwapena, N. op.cit.
59. Viner, A. op.cit.
60. Ibid.
61. Grynberg, R. et al. op. cit.
62. Routley, R. and V. op.cit.
63. Caufield, C. op.cit.
64. Routley, R. and V. op.cit.
65. Caufield, C. op.cit.
66. *World Wood*. op. cit.
67. FAO, op.cit.
68. Saulei, S. 1986.
69. FAO, op.cit.
70. Caufield, C. op.cit.
71. Ibid.
72. Myers, N. 1984.
73. Loffler, E. op.cit.
74. Ibid.
75. Ibid.
76. Caufield, C. op.cit. quotes B. Blackwood.
77. Caufield, C. op.cit.
78. Wood, M. op.cit.
79. Myers, N. op.cit.
80. *World Wood*, op.cit.
81. Saulei, S. op.cit.
82. Ibid.
83. Saulei, S. op.cit. and P. Eddowes, 1988.
84. Eddowes, P. 1988.
85. Saulei, S. op.cit.
86. Ibid.
87. James, R. 1981.
88. Wood, M. op.cit.
89. Ibid.
90. Ibid.
91. Langro, P. 1986.
92. Caufield, C. op.cit.
93. Ibid.
94. Ibid.
95. Ibid.
96. Eddowes, P. op.cit.
97. *World Wood*, op.cit.
98. Ibid.
99. *World Wood*, op.cit. and Eddowes, P. op.cit.
100. Stewart, N. op.cit.
101. *PNG Post Courier*, 1984, 10 July; and Eddowes, P. op.cit.
102. Eddowes, P. op.cit.
103. Diro, T. 1986.
104. Caufield, C. op.cit.

105. Grynberg, R. et al. 1986.
106. Ibid.
107. Senge, F. 1986.
108. FAO, op.cit.
109. Saulei, S. op.cit.
110. *World Wood*, op.cit.
111. Sinclair, T. 1986.
112. Grynberg, R. et al. 1985, quotes Fraser.
113. Ibid., quotes Frodin.
114. Ibid.
115. Stephenson, P. 1988.
116. Ibid.
117. Grynberg, R. 1985.
118. *Oriental Economist*, 1969.
119. Ibid.
120. James, R. op.cit.
121. Seddon, G. op.cit.
122. Caufield, C. op.cit.
123. James, R. op.cit.
124. Seddon, G. op.cit.
125. De A'th, C. 1980.
126. Saulei, S. op.cit.
127. James, R. op.cit.
128. Ibid.
129. Ibid.
130. Ibid.
131. Friends of the Earth, PNG, 1984.
132. Kwapena, N. op.cit.
133. Wood, M. op.cit.
134. *Timberlines,* 1984.
135. *The Real Forest News*, 1981.
136. Ibid.
137. Langro, P. 1986.
138. West Sepik (Sandaun) Provincial Government, 1986.
139. *Niugini News*, 1986, 15 July.
140. Ibid.
141. *PNG Post Courier*, 1986, 31 July.
142. West Sepik (Sandaun) Provincial Government, op.cit.
143. Ibid.
144. *Times of PNG*, 1986, 31 October.
145. Ibid.
146. *World Wood*, 1986(a).
147. *PNG Post Courier*, 1986, 11 September, quotes Langro, P.

General References for JANT Case Study
DeA'th, C. 1980
James, R. 1981
Smith, A. 1984 (a and b)
Friends of the Earth PNG, 1984.

5.   The Philippines

Introduction

The Philippine archipelago comprises 7,000 islands with a land area of 30m ha, of which approximately 95% is concentrated on the eleven largest islands. Its geographical situation has created a region of vast biological variation due to its tropical location and the fact that 60% of the land is mountainous. The many small islands that rise steeply out of the sea provide a huge variety of ecological niches.

The climate, although tropical and similar to that found in its South-East Asian neighbours, is dominated by typhoons between May and November. These can cause absolute devastation along the coasts, particularly in areas where there is minimal tree cover to act as shelter from the violent winds.

Species diversity does not automatically mean ecological stability and these small islands are more easily damaged by deforestation and the subsequent land degradation than larger land masses. An example of this vulnerability is the effect of forest loss in the country's water catchment areas. The majority of the watersheds are only 100 to 150 sq. km. in area.[1] With relatively small land areas controlling the country's water regimes, deforestation even on a small scale can have very serious effects. The problems are compounded by reduced chances of natural forest regeneration because seed dispersal is hampered by the geographical isolation of many islands.

The population of 56m is expanding at 2% per year. The majority of Filipinos (the largest sector of the population) are Roman Catholics, although there are sizeable Muslim and animist cultures away from the capital island, Luzon. The Philippine economy is based on agriculture and primary products but lack of investment in rural development under the Marcos regime has resulted in a large part of the population still surviving on subsistence agriculture. In the Philippines, of all the countries covered in this book, are perhaps the largest number of farmers forced off their traditional lands. Not surprisingly this, combined with an uncontrolled timber industry, means that there is a high rate of forest destruction in the Philippines.

The Spanish arrived in the Philippines in the 16th century, and unlike the Dutch or the Portuguese, applied colonial control directly through religion. If the local population failed to comply with the Will of Christ they were regarded as savages and therefore doomed. The native population needed to be saved and for those who complied there were rewards. The discovery of gold helped sustain Spanish interest in converting the Philippines to Christianity.

Since the Spanish were more interested in gold than land, local people in political favour were given land. Land ownership was an alien concept in the Philippines before colonialism, but the advantages for those who made claims were clear. Land ownership was the next best thing to owning large quantities of gold, and an administrative system of local land-owning officials known as 'principals' emerged, originally almost always members of the clergy with a scattering of tribal leaders. In this way the Church obtained ownership over vast tracts of land through royal bequests and individual donations. A popular belief among the newly converted was that by donating land to the church one's sins would be forgiven and the route to heaven unhindered. The Spanish friars quickly emerged as the first generation of absentee landlords in the Philippines. Local farmers now had to rent the fields they had always farmed, and the pattern was set for a land-ownership distribution system that dominates the Philippines to this day.

At the end of the 19th century, with the collapse of the last vestiges of the Spanish empire, America gained control over the Philippines. The United States was generally more sophisticated in its colonial management and developed a legal system enabling them to claim any land they wanted. These regulations continue to form the legal basis for land ownership law.

After independence in 1946 the political scene became highly unstable as a succesion of generals and politicians claimed power. The turbulence eventually subsided when President Marcos came into office in the early 1970s. In 1986 the 'peoples power' revolution forced Marcos out of power and a new government was formed under Cory Aquino. The semi-fuedal system of government that emerged under Marcos is seen by many to continue to dominate Philippine society today.

Five major forest types are to be found in the Philippines: dipterocarp, pine, molave, mangrove, and moss forest. Dipterocarp make up the majority, being found from sea level up to 800 metres in the south. In the north, mainly on the island of Luzon, are the pine forests; on the northern islands too is the semi-deciduous molave forest, shedding its leaves in the dry season. Few mangroves remain, the main area is on the coast of Palawan and there are smaller patches on Luzon and Mindanao. One sub-forest type that deserves special mention is beach forest, a transition between the mangroves and the dipterocarp forest, but this has almost totally disappeared.

The post-revolution Minister for Natural Resources, Ernesto Maceda, claims that, 'of our 14 million hectares of virgin forest, Marcos allowed 12 million hectares to be ravaged by his relatives and cronies.'[2] The data base for information on the state of the Philippine forests is very poor. The Ministry of Natural Resources was regarded as one of the most corrupt departments in the Marcos government; Ernesto Maceda claims that more than 90% of Ministry employees were corrupt.[3] In short, previous government figures have been so blatantly manipulated that they are of little use when looking back at the 1970s.

The Ministry of Natural Resources divides the country into either Alienable or Disposable Land, and Forest Land, the latter being suitable only for forestry. This definition does not mean that any trees exist on what is officially forested land, simply that there should be. Alienable or Disposable Land should be agricultural land. In December 1985 the Philippine land area was classified as follows: Forest Land 14m ha; Alienable or Disposable Land 14.6m ha; Unclassified 1.3m ha.[4]

How much forest remains depends on the source of information. The Bureau of Forest Development (part of the Ministry of Natural Resources), claim that the area of forest actually increased from 10.1m ha in 1969 to 11.5m ha by 1984.[5] They also claimed that in 1986 at least 3.3m ha of virgin forest were left in the country. But independent statistics show a very different picture.

The Forest Development Centre at the University of the Philippines, using projections from 1980 data, estimated that by 1986 only 7.3m ha of forest remained.[6] Other independent studies from the University give estimates of 8.9m ha in 1974 to nine million for 1976. As these estimates are more than ten years out of date, the present forest cover is undoubtedly smaller. Delphin Ganapin, 1986 Philippine Forester of the Year, estimates total forest cover for that year as 7.3m ha of which only two million could be considered virgin.[7] He is, however, quick to point out that these figures hide the crisis in distribution of virgin forests and claims that only 'very small isolated patches are left.'[8]

Forest loss and reafforestation
The Bureau of Forest Development statistics show some remarkable coincidences in relation to deforestation. Total forest loss figures for 1982–83 were 203,905 ha and in 1983–84 total forest loss was once again 203,905 ha. Predictions on forest loss always seem to be perfect, down to the hectare, even for the conversion of virgin into secondary forest. In both 1982–83 and 1983–84, exactly 198,110 ha of virgin forest were converted.[9] It should be noted that these figures are not presented as an average over a period of years.

A recent study by the Upland Multisectoral Working Group, based in the University of the Philippines, estimates a loss of 397,000 ha of forest per year between 1972 and 1982, almost double the official figure.[10] The present rate may well be declining towards the 200,000 ha mark, but this is probably because there is less forest to cut down rather than due to a long term change in the causes for deforestation.

The plight of the mangrove forests deserves special mention. The 106,000 ha left are being destroyed at a rate of 4,000 ha per year, and more than 70,000 ha are under threat of conversion to other land uses.[11] The consequences for a region prone to typhoons could well be catastrophic to coastal communities.

The most disturbing figures are perhaps those for the loss of virgin forest. The Bureau of Forest Development under Marcos had very definite ideas on what it saw as forest development. The government's 1978–82 Five Year Plan notes:

> In the short term, log production will increase by 500,000 cubic metres per year to reach 14,000,000 cubic metres. By the early 1990s when the virgin forests of Mindanao are completely logged off, production will reach the limits of the allowable annual cut of about 13,000,000 cu.m. This will decline further to about 12 million cu.m. by mid 1990's when all Luzon virgin forests are also completely logged off.

Little wonder that according to Delphin Ganapin and his colleagues the Philippine timber industry will run out of timber during the early 1990s.[12] The repercussions of such a policy are considerable, not only for the timber industry, but also for the critical watersheds and the natural heritage of the nation as a whole.

Officially only 9,398 ha of once forested land are replanted annually, nearly all with monocultures for the timber or pulp paper industries.[13] Even using the official estimate of total forest loss (203,905 ha per year), for every tree planted, 21 are felled; the unreliability of figures suggests the ratio is even higher.

The costs of forest loss

The general effects of forest loss in the Philippines are the same as those for the other countries in this book; they are, however, intensified in many areas because of the regularity of typhoons in this part of the Pacific. In 1986, Ernesto Maceda stated that the Philippines 'now faces a real danger of poverty of natural resources. We could be Ethiopia, denuded into a desert by the year 2000 unless we act now.'[14] Perhaps an overstatement, but it certainly contains more than a core of truth.

Soil loss: In 1985 the Ministry of Natural Resources estimated that one third of the land area of the Philippines, was 'severely eroded'.[15] Thirteen provinces have 'severe erosion' over 51% to 87% of their land area; an additional 12 have between 40% and 50% of their land in a similar condition.[16] The same Ministry claims that at least 75% of the Philippines suffers from erosion problems of some kind.[17] This displaces an estimated 500m tons of top soil from the archipelago annually.[18] Erosion on this scale can lead to full scale desertification.

Most soil loss studies agree that erosion rates for grassland are around 100 tonnes per ha per year as opposed to 20–40 tonnes even under secondary or poorly stocked forest.[19] These poor rates for open grassland are typical of areas where cattle ranching is prevalent. The cost to local communities and central government has never been seriously estimated. In the rainy season, terracing, roads, bridges and even complete villages are washed away.

The watershed crisis: In 1981 the government proclaimed 39 watersheds as vital to the maintenance of the archipelago's environment. By 1986, 15 of these were considered to be unreliable water sources.[20] In these areas a familiar cycle of flash floods followed by drought became established.

The siltation of flood channels and dams compounds these problems, as the inhabitants along the Agusan River in Northern Mindanao found in 1981. Across the mouth of the Agusan River is a 200 metre spit formed by silt washing off the hills. The river was once deep enough to accommodate ocean-going ships over the very site of this spit. In the first rains of 1981 a flood wave rushed down river towards its mouth. Finding the immediate outlet closed the wave bounced back inland flooding thousands of hectares of good cropland to a depth of 22 feet. The official death toll was 283, with a further 41 persons missing; more than 14,000 were injured and the flood seriously disrupted the lives of an estimated 500,000 people in the area.[21] The local people are in little doubt that forest destruction in the river's catchment area was responsible.

Drought: In 1982 the same island experienced the worst drought ever recorded. There were major crop failures, and local people were quick to note that the worst hit areas were under cash crops or subject to extensive logging operations.[22] Little work has been carried out to discover whether or not forest clearance was the direct cause, but numerous letters in local papers testify to the popular view that logging is the main culprit. The following is a typical example:

> A decade ago Northern Mindanao was a vast vegetation of virgin forest where logging was the primary industry, but sad to say, ten years later, the once virgin forests have been transformed into barren, denuded, balding mountains. That is why in 1982 Mindanao experienced the longest drought ever recorded in its history. . . . This is what we get for cutting down our trees.[23]

The drought also prompted widespread forest fires on the island, similar to those on Borneo during the same period.

Other islands are also experiencing water shortages in the dry season, even supplies to major cities, such as Manila and Cebu, can no longer be guaranteed.[24] In some areas water tables have fallen by as much as seven feet per year according to the Local Water Utilities Administration.[25] This, they claim is also entirely due to deforestation.

Fisheries destruction: Approximately 700,000 people in the Philippines depend on fishing for their subsistence.[26] The inshore fishing industry relies on natural spawning grounds for future supplies and one source, the coral reefs, are becoming increasingly silted and useless.

Mangroves, however, are even more important to the fishermen. An estimated 60% to 80% of all commercially important marine fish caught in the Philippines spend some part of their life cycle in the mangroves.[27] Even at a macro-economic level fishing is important, accounting for 4.3% of GNP in 1981.[28]

Mangroves are being cut down at the rate of 4,100 ha per year, mostly to make way for fish farms[29] which, unlike mangroves, are privately owned and the profits limited to those able to finance such ventures.[30] Despite the capital input, these fish farms are less efficient at producing fish than natural mangroves. Almost 80% of the mangrove area has already been converted into fish farms, but they still account for less than 12% of total fish production in the Philippines.[31]

Wildlife loss: So far, more than 3,800 tree species have been identified in the Philippines' forests along with another 8,200 plant species. Combine this with at least 850 species of bird and 225 mammals, and in terms of biological diversity the islands are clearly of global importance.[32]

In common with Indonesia, the species of the Philippines are highly susceptible to extinction because many plants and animals are incapable of reaching other lands if their forest habitats are destroyed. Perhaps the most famous species on the endangered list is the Philippine Monkey-Eating Eagle, now reduced to less than 600 pairs on the island of Mindanao.[33]

Another source of wildlife loss in the Philippines is the trade in wildlife. Some animals and birds may legally be captured, but much of the trade is in order to satisfy the demand for rare species in Hong Kong and Singapore. In 1984 alone, the Bureau of Forestry Development co-ordinated the export of more than 140,000 birds, 17,000 monkeys and 380 reptiles,[34] the huge number of monkeys destined mainly for research laboratories in Europe and the United States. Total earnings from the export of monkeys were Peso 300,000 (US$16,000).[35] Of the animals officially exported, none are of endangered species, but customs and excise staff are not experts in wildlife identification, and the abundant legitimate trade enables rarer species to slip through alongside the legal exports.

Forest loss has also destabilized certain food chain systems, effectively encouraging the proliferation of pests by wiping out predators. Preliminary studies into the causes of Dengue fever (a disease fatal to humans, spread by mosquitoes) suggest a link with forest destruction.[36] Delphin Ganapin of the University of the Philippines claims that: 'Pest and disease infestations on human settlements have been found in certain cases to be directly or indirectly due to forest destruction.'[37]

Social and economic costs: The forests have become the frontier for Philippine society. They are a zone of conflict, with traditional inhabitants increasingly forced out as new populations move in. The fertile lowlands have been cleared of forest for many years, but they are now controlled by large companies and powerful individuals. These interests usually force people off the lands and into the less densely populated forests. Conflicts between forest-based tribal societies and migrants forced off their own lands have become increasingly violent in recent years. This, combined with the onslaught of the primary industries, notably timber and mining, contributed significantly to the 1986 revolution and current insurgency problems.

Tribal land rights: The reactions of many tribal people on this subject are best illustrated in their own words. The following statement is from the Kalinga-Bontoc Peace Pact Holders Association in Northern Luzon. Traditionally, the Kalinga and the Bontocs have been great rivals, but they combined to fight particular issues affecting both groups.

The government and its military criminals have acquired a notorious reputation in the mountain tribes of Bontoc and Kalinga Apayao. In the mid 1970s they tried, unsuccessfully, to construct four huge dams over the Chico river that will destroy our payaos [rice terraces], desecrate the burial grounds of our ancestors and leave us homeless; all for the benefit of transnational corporations in need of hydro-electric power.

Our brother Tingguians in Abra [province] together with the Kalinga and Bontoc people also resisted the planned deforestation of over 400,000 hectares of pineland for the Cellophil Resources Corporation, a local partner of transnational paper companies.

Our leader, Macliing Dulag, who valiantly resisted all bribes and threats made by PANAMIN [Presidential Assistant on National Minorities – government body covering tribal issues], the local government and the military, was felled by assassins' bullets in April 1980 and up till now his assassins have not been punished.

The consistency with which the government and the military have persecuted our people has taught us to be more vigilant and courageous despite exploitation and oppression. We shall face this new attempt at colonization in the same manner that we did for the Spanish, Japanese and American colonizers.[38]

It is worth noting that the Spanish and Japanese control over these mountainous areas was never strong and that the allegiance of the inhabitants to central governments in Manila has always been limited.

Table 5.1 lists the major mining and logging operations in forest areas with a significant tribal population. All these operations have been the subject of resistance of some kind, particularly during the Marcos regime, but currently too, under the Aquino 'people's power' government. Central government resource development policies rarely fulfil the aspirations of tribal groups.

For some groups, displacement from traditional lands has occurred more than once. In the early 1980s, the inhabitants of Pantabangan in central Luzon, who had already moved to facilitate a large-scale irrigation project, were again asked to move. This time their village was at the site of a large-scale World Bank-funded timber plantation project that has been criticized in a number of reports. One researcher from the Institute for Food and Development Policy in the University of California recorded a number of individual statements.

> 'Before we believed promises', explains the elderly man. 'We were ignorant and naive about what is happening to us,' his son continues, 'but this time, if the government tries to take our land, we will fight for it.' The threat is far from empty. For the people of Pantabangan are learning from the Chico [a large dam project on Luzon that has now been abandoned] victories. One of the government engineers working on the new project had already been sent an NPA [New People's Army] black ribbon – a warning to leave or else.[39]

Areas affected by mining and logging frequently become NPA strong-holds. This armed force has its roots as much in the indigenous land rights struggle as in the doctrines of Marx or Mao. The US government estimates that it comprises around 12,000 fully-armed troops, local sources claim at least 20,000.[40]

There is undoubtedly a strong communist bias within the organization, but in the words of one American:

> The NPA has grown in influence for other reasons – exploitation of tenant farmers by large landowners; government policies that limit the ability of peasants to survive independently; low pay and little work in areas dominated by the coconut, sugar and pineapple concerns; encroachment of agribusiness or military harassment.[41]

There have been conflicts between the doctrine-inspired membership and those joining to defend local land claims. A number of splinter groups have developed covering specific areas and working against specific companies; the largest is the Cordillera Peoples Liberation Army (CPLA) in Northern Luzon. In 1986 more than 15 logging companies had to abandon operations in this area due to either NPA or CPLA action. The NPA stated that their policy of attacking logging and mining interests was, 'because of the denudation of the Cordillera and Sierra Madre forests causing the destruction of crops, properties and lives by the long drought and flooding.'[42] The NPA and many local communities perceive advantages in their relationship. For the local population the NPA is often seen as a means of organizing resistance to land acquisition; and for the NPA the same issues are seen as a way of involving people in their more general struggle.

There has been a lot of publicity about right-wing counter insurgency groups, particularly on Mindanao, but despite their claims to represent local people these groups are based almost totally in the towns and it is extremely doubtful that they have any long-term influence over forest communities.

Economic losses: It is almost impossible to estimate the full costs of deforestation, not only in terms of crop losses but also involving a significant portion of the military budget, as central government attempts to control troubled areas. One study at the University of the Philippines calculated that the Philippine economy loses 35 peso (US$2) for every ton of top soil washed away.[43] With an estimated 500m tons lost nationwide every year that amounts to approximately US$927m (1988 currency rate).

The timber industry has been a major cause of the problem, and loss of future timber revenues can justifiably be included in any calculations. Between 1960 and 1984 official timber exports contributed more than US$ 3.44 billion to the economy.[44] In 1984 alone the official value of logs exported was US$350m; but supplies are now running low, and illegal logging is rampant. After the revolution the new Ministry of Natural Resources claimed that in the early 1980s, timber smuggled out of the country was up to four times that exported legally.[45]

If present timber production levels are to be maintained the Philippines will have to import logs from Malaysia in the early 1990s, according to Ernesto Sanvictores, President of the Philippine Wood Product Association.[46] Jobs are being lost as supplies dwindle: in 1982, 91,000 people were directly employed in the timber industry; by 1984 there were 83,000 and the trend continues.[47] Over-exploitation and a blatant disregard for future supplies, by legitimate as well as illegal operations, has effectively destroyed the industry's future.

The Philippines also has a significant minor forest products industry that has suffered greatly in recent years. Only a small percentage of these products enter the cash economy but large-scale operations are charged export fees on their produce. In 1984 US$137,646 in fees was paid to the Bureau of Forestry Development, indicating the existence of a significant industry.[48] These fees were almost exclusively for rattan collection, an activity that does not survive alongside destructive logging.

In short, those already in powerful positions have reaped the limited cash benefits from the destruction of the forests to the cost of the wider community. The consequent political and social upheaval is beginning to be felt by all sectors of Philippine society.

The development of present forest policy

After more than 40 years of independence the basis of the relationship between the Philippines and the West, most notably the US, has not changed. The Philippines continues to export unprocessed natural resources from which industrialized countries manufacture finished products. Despite the 1986 revolution, the attitudes of those in power remain unchanged. Before independence forests were consumed along with other natural resources, and fertile land was developed for cash crops for export. A legal system was imposed restricting access to land that traditional Philippine society regarded as a common resource. Genuine rural development has never been a priority in the Philippines.

Pre-colonial forestry: There are a large variety of forest-based tribal societies in the Philippines and consequently their farming methods vary greatly, from the pine forests in Northern Luzon to the rainforests of Mindanao. There are, however, underlying similarities, as occur with all tribal groups in the region.

For most groups the concept of individual land ownership is alien. The present generation simply holds custody of the land; the actual owners are the numerous spirits, which range from specific gods frequenting certain objects, to past and future generations. Because the spirit world frequently overlaps in both time and space with what we call the 'real world', the needs of the spirits are perceived as similar to those of people living today. Hence the spirits need a home, food and so on. The perception of forests and people is very similar to the *adat* beliefs found in East Malaysia. The forest as a whole is communally owned but individuals may claim exclusive use rights over, for example, specific trees. This concept of a right to use also applies to rice terraces, over which a family will not claim total ownership but would vigorously defend their use rights.

Many tribes, such as the Besao and Sagada in Northern Luzon, have very specific forest management traditions. The Sagadan 'Tagon' farming system involves planting trees on all idle land. A variety of traditional ceremonies ensures long-term management of the young trees across generations. A remarkable number of small woodlands can be seen in the areas where this is still practised. The system is perhaps on the periphery of more intensive agro-forestry systems in that planting trees is not central to the farming process. This should not, however, detract from the reality that many small woodlands may equal a forest. Like all successful replanting systems in Asia these are based on a strong commitment to communal efforts.

Forest management is about to turn full circle in the Philippines with many government officials today looking at pre-colonial forestry practices as the means of saving what is left. Land legislation since colonial days has, however, consistently eroded local forest management in an effort to keep people out of the forest.

Colonial forest legislation: The Land Registration Act of 1902 was originally designed to determine the extent of privately owned land. Individuals had to register land claims with the US authorities. The law was not widely publicized and, as it was written in English, few understood it. This Act initiated a period of intense land-grabbing by wealthy and well-educated individuals, and large-scale US interests.

Three years later the Public Lands Act ordained that any land not registered under the 1902 Act was 'public land'; in this context 'public' means central government, not local communities. Central government's ownership of this land resulted in many small farmers and tribal groups losing all claim to their traditional farms and forests. The Mining Law was also passed in 1905, under which all 'public lands' were freely open for exploitation and purchase by citizens of the United States and the Philippines. By this time tribal groups were becoming aware of the land ownership problems. Unlike the British in Malaysia, the US administration made no attempt to protect the interests of tribal groups. As the concept of land ownership was alien to most indigenous people they refused to involve themselves in this system; in any case, they lacked the cash with which to buy their traditional lands back from the government. US mining companies, however, did have the resources, and the Philippine timber industry developed initially to feed the demand for mine props.

In 1929, Executive Order No. 27 designated almost all the mountain areas in Northern Luzon as public parks and forest reserves, giving central government complete control over development.

One of the most notorious pieces of legislation, the Commonwealth Act, was passed in 1935. This placed severe restrictions on indigenous rights to enter forests reserved for timber. In addition, mining exploitation rights were granted only on the basis of individually registered land-ownership claims. In an attempt to restrict the size of individual claims all land registrations were limited to 1,024 ha.

The Commonwealth Act allowed for so many exceptions it was never effectively enforced. Under Marcos, influential land owners such as Alfonso

Lim gained control over 600,000 ha in North Luzon; and Colonel Marcelino Barba, Marcos's brother-in-law, managed to secure 200,000 ha, also on Luzon.[49]

The cumulative effect of these various pieces of legislation was to alienate local populations and concentrate land holding in the hands of the few. With no recognition of communal land claims, exploitation of the country's natural resources was wide open to foreign interests. The Institute for Food and Development Policy in California claim that:

> Between 1899 and 1941 the Philippines was transformed into a colonial dependency of the United States. Its foreign trade was monopolised by the U.S. and American investors achieved significant influence in practically all sectors of the economy, from export agriculture to utilities.[50]

Independence

Independence, at the end of World War Two, was followed by a period of intense political unrest. Governments changed all too frequently and social rebellion was rife; but the real seats of power remained the same. US corporate interests had tight control over production, and the landed class provided political leadership. Today, a similar state of affairs prevails; the Aquino family owns large tracts of land throughout the Philippines, and US corporate interests in the economy are still paramount.

The legal system remained almost totally unchanged until Marcos took power. One of the most astounding aspects of the Marcos regime was the massive quantity of legislation passed and the general inefficiency it created in government. Corruption became so rampant that a medieval system of government dominated, in which interpretation of the law depended upon whom you knew and who you were, rather than on what was written. Private armies flourished and central government became simply a mouthpiece for the largest landowners.

Timber became a major export sector and laws were passed to safeguard the resource from what the landlords saw as the greatest threat to forests: local people. A heavily controlled media and stifled research perpetuated the myth that tribal groups and the rural poor were wholly responsible for forest destruction. Forest legislation thus sought to restrict the activities of these two groups, a process well-established even before Marcos came to power.

In 1962 the Public Land Law gave ownership rights to occupants on 'public lands' (as laid down in the 1902 legislation) if they had occupied the land since 4 July 1945. Two years later it was amended to provide for the: 'automatic acquisition of private individual titles by national tribal minorities who have for 30 years or more, or since July 4th 1945, occupied lands of the public domain suitable for agricultural purposes.'

At first this appears to benefit tribal groups, but it only covered land under cultivation at the time and excluded all fallow areas and forest. For those groups that practised swidden agriculture it meant nothing, in so far as they had not occupied any one piece of land either since 1945 or for 30 years. Even if they had, there was the matter of proof; with no previous titles how can a tribal farmer produce proof?

For the large landholder, however, the law was very convenient, because, as individuals, the extent of public land they could own was restricted. By using false names, or 'dummies' as they became known, individuals produced 'proof' and made claims over vast areas. Vincente Madrigal, a senator under Marcos, acquired 2,793 ha of tribal land in the Cordillera mountains on Luzon in this way. Melquides Bautista, another Marcos 'crony' claimed 1,200 ha in the same mountains, as did a number of other politicians and their relatives during this period.[51]

Under Marcos, Acts became known as Presidential Decrees and, in 1974, Decree Number 410 was announced. This Decree was to run for only ten years but it is a typical example of poorly worded and weak legislation. It attempted once more to give land rights to tribal groups by defining ancestral lands as: 'areas occupied and cultivated on an open and continuous basis for the last thirty years.' A tribal group could then claim this as a community and each family would be given a five hectare plot. This, it was hoped, would quell the increasing rebellion developing amongst the Philippine tribal population.

This Decree, however, had many anomalies. Lands that could not be claimed under it included: 'forest reserves . . . watersheds and areas essential for research, recreation, wildlife or areas of great scenic beauty.' To add to these restrictions the government retained full rights to: 'establish agro-industrial projects in these areas'. Thus plantations or large-scale forestry could annul any claims. The legislation was so clumsy that even the landlords made no attempt to apply it and not one application for communal rights was made in the ten years this legislation was operative. There was little point in making an application if an area could remain government property because it had 'great scenic beauty', a highly subjective definition that could apply to most of the Philippines.

Presidential Decree 705 (The Revised Forestry Code) of 1975, however, developed the most notorious reputation amongst tribal groups. As a comprehensive policy for forestry it was not totally flawed, but certain sections were justifiably criticized. This new Code defined 'forest land' as any area either covered with trees or with a slope of more than 18%. Forest land was automatically under the public domain unless otherwise classified. Sixty percent of the Philippines is mountainous; the 18% ruling thus covered most of the country.

No provision was made for traditional land rights, even in areas where rice terraces had been established for centuries. Every year thousands of tourists visit the rice terraces in the Mountain Province in Northern Luzon. Described as the eighth wonder of the world, these terraces climb thousands of feet up the mountains and have taken centuries to construct; this is all government land and the farmers are trespassing.

Decree 705 put any forests out of bounds for the local populations. Without special permits, even hunting and gathering rights were denied. The most controversial powers, however, were those concerned with eviction from these public lands. The Decree notes: 'when public interest so requires, steps shall be taken to expropriate, cancel defective titles, reject public land applications or eject occupants.'

Unlike the laws of compulsory purchase enacted by many governments, there is no question of compensation. With the deeply corrupt government of the time, the 'public interest' frequently extended no further than the interests of local elites, as is borne out by the various punishments for breaking the forestry Code. For gathering forest produce without a permit; setting fires, as many traditional farming methods entail; and squatting on public lands, there were fines of up to US$1,000 or four years imprisonment. These are offences that many tribal people commit every day if they practise their traditional lifestyle and culture. By comparison, illegal logging, an activity that provides some powerful individuals with considerable profits and has ravaged huge areas of forest, can, if detected and proven, mean a temporary suspension or perhaps withdrawal of any timber licences an individual might own; conviction of illegal logging carried no fines or imprisonment. Many illegal logging operations have consisted of cutting on land adjacent to legitimate concession areas, in fact legitimate and illegal operations frequently work side by side. Although the penalty is relatively minor, within three months of the 1986 revolution more than 150 timber licences were revoked under this legislation. The legislation, however, continues to work against the interests of most people.

Timber specific legislation: In 1973 President Marcos announced a gradual phasing out of all log exports by 1976. Timber supplies were already low and the government decided that by exporting only processed timber more profits would remain in the Philippines. But the ban was never implemented and, in late 1975, Presidential Decree 428 brought in a 'modified selective log export scheme', which was to apply to 'deserving and responsible' loggers on a 'selective and limited' basis. This Decree effectively concentrated the industry in the hands of Marcos's allies in so far as smaller companies were refused licences. Official log export figures between 1975 and 1976 did show a decline by about one-third, to 2.3m cubic metres, but this quantity indicates no commitment to the log export ban.[52] In the latter part of the 1970s, illegal logging and timber smuggling became firmly established.

Another example of legislation passed but never enacted was the

Presidential Letter of Instruction 818. A Letter of Instruction was a personal letter from the President to individuals or an industry, whether such a document represented a law or not was never clear. Letter 818 required all concession holders to replant one hectare of open or denuded land for every hectare of forest logged. There was no real incentive to comply since there was no financial assistance and government departments failed to enforce the ruling.

The history of forest legislation in the Philippines is one of ambiguous wording, poor co-ordination and a lack of political will to enforce regulations. As with most forms of corruption and inefficiency it was the poor who suffered in an almost medieval setting of barons and a peasantry, backed up by an unjust legal system.

There was concern over forest loss during the Marcos regime but no serious attempts to discover why it was happening and who was responsible. With one forestry officer for every 4,250 ha of forest there was little incentive for loggers to abide by laws or regulations.[53]

The Bureau of Forestry Development, established under the US administration, is part of the Ministry of Natural Resources. Thus, timber, a renewable resource, is administered alongside mining rather than being allied to agricultural development.

Despite the minimal extent of forest management there were a number of replanting strategies. But these affected only relatively small areas and were never implemented on the scale needed. They are, however, noteworthy as they provide some good examples of why replanting trees does not automatically lead to forest regeneration.

Replanting schemes
As with the forestry legislation, replanting is geared towards industrial rather than social or environmental needs. Plantations are established to meet the fast-expanding woodchip industry, itself based on increased demand from Japan and Taiwan. Since the replanting requirements in Letter of Instruction 818 were never complied with, the Bureau of Forestry Development promoted plantations through its Industrial Tree Plantation Programme, established in 1981. This Programme, in emphasizing replanting open areas rather than promoting sound forestry management, is a clear example of a total misunderstanding of the causes of forest destruction.

The Programme promotes three tree species, ipil-ipil, rubber and falcatta. Ipil-ipil and falcatta are fast-growing low quality softwoods. Considerable financial incentives are offered to those taking part, but since the minimum area covered is 100 ha few small investors are involved; the government hoped the private sector would lead the replanting efforts. In the early 1980s, 80,000 ha of plantations were established, the vast majority being ipil-ipil.[54] It was hoped that the timber companies would show a lead in implementing the programme, but this has not happened. In the early 1980s timber concessions covered more than 10m ha, but of the 260 major concession holders only 82 showed any interest; despite the subsidies, it is cheaper for timber companies to cut natural forest rather than to establish plantations.[55]

Establishing 80,000 ha is better than nothing, but has this created a net gain of forest cover or has it aggravated the problem? A brief account of how the joint Agiunaldo Development Corporation and the Davao Agri-business Development Corporation project was established during the Marcos regime may give a clearer picture.[56]

This partnership established 27,000 ha of mainly ipil-ipil plantation in the Davao del Norte province on Mindanao, an area with a tribal population of around 2,000 Visayan and Ata families who had farmed the land for generations. The companies managed to 'persuade' them to leave these lands by employing a process known as 'hamleting', a method widely used throughout the Philippines to establish plantations of all kinds.

Hamleting initially involves killing some fairly prominent local leader. There is never any investigation into the murder, but the Philippine army will move into the area, allegedly to protect the local population as the authorities will lay the blame for the killing on the New Peoples Army or any local insurgent groups. The government army then gathers the people into one or two large hamlets, again allegedly for their safety, but also to isolate the rebels. A dusk to dawn curfew is usually enforced and farmers are discouraged from attending their fields.

Once established, hamlets are frequently moved, for 'security' reasons, with the result that the population becomes disorientated and their fields fall into disuse as they are frequently too far away to reach in one day. The final stage is the establishment of the plantation. By this time the local population shows little resistance to the ultimatum to either work on the plantation or remain far away from their ancestral lands.

One report by the Alternative Resource Centre in Mindanao quotes an appeal from a group of farmers on Mindanao while they were experiencing the process:

> We realise now that it is not the New Peoples Army (NPA) they are getting rid of; it is us innocent civilians! The military are hounding farmers who have begun to stand up for their rights. We are now deprived of a right to our livelihood and shelter. With our abandoned farms we are facing hunger. Many of us entertain the idea that it is not only the NPA they are interested in, but also the land we have occupied and tilled. Is it remote that they want our farms for expansion for more falcatta, banana and palm oil plantations?[57]

International pressure from human rights groups eventually forced the military to publicly abandon the hamleting system, but little has changed in more remote areas. Even when less aggressive methods are used to move farmers the net result for forests is negative: these shifted farmers have no choice but to find new forest areas to clear for cultivation. They are, in this case, a direct product of reafforestation efforts. The Visayan and Ata people have now left their traditional lands, some heading towards the towns, others further into the hills. The Philippine government has, however, also established a number of social forestry programmes.

Social forestry programmes

The first attempt at social forestry was established under the Revised Forestry Code (Presidential Decree 705) in 1975, known as the Forest Occupancy Management Project. Its aim was to involve pioneer farmers in reafforestation efforts and give them limited rights to the land they occupy.

To be eligible for the project a farmer must prove his occupancy of a site for at least five years, and renew his claim each year for the following five years. Only then is he eligible for a 'Forestry Occupance Lease', which runs for ten years with a possible extension of a further decade. Thus, a limited security of tenure is available. Leaseholders are allowed to cultivate only a certain percentage of their land; the rest is given over to tree planting. The Bureau of Forestry Development provides seedlings, technical assistance, infrastructure and marketing advice.

Superficially the Project seems viable, but few farmers take part. As with all land rights claims, there is the initial problem of proof of occupancy. The annual renewal of the lease is an added problem for the pioneer farmer far from the administrative centre of Manila. These factors, combined with an unenthusiastic central bureaucracy, have clearly militated against the project becoming properly established.

The Bureau of Forestry Development (BFD) has a longstanding National Tree Planting Programme, also established under Decree 705; within this Programme is the Communal Tree Farm Programme. Initiated in 1978, it has proved to be the most successful attempt at reafforestation. More than 25,000 ha of trees have been established, involving 13,000 families, but local interest in the programme has declined in recent years as it became clear that no land tenure is guaranteed. Once again, excessive control by central government has stifled the aspirations of local populations. The local population have no real choice on species to be planted and the project is geared towards timber production rather than establishing trees that would fulfil a multitude of purposes. As with the previous Programmes, local farmers have no choice in deciding to whom they may sell their timber. Major corporations control local markets and therefore prices. A study by the Institute of Philippine Culture on one project established under this Programme commented:

It is a good thing that the waning of interest occurred at a time when the trees had reached a certain growth stage after which they no longer need much protection and care. The sustainability of the project, none the less, became critical . . . it might prove difficult to convince people to plant again, especially since positive return from investment in the project was seen by a minority only.[58]

These programmes are far removed from what many regard as true social forestry. The words of the Alternative Resource Center in Davao, Mindanao, sum up local criticism:

Through social forestry programmes upland farmers are being required to replant logged-over lands to commercial tree crops. The very same corporate interests that profited from the original logging operations, and that failed in their obligations to replant their logged-over concession areas, are now the recipients of government loans and incentives in order that they can make more profits.

The upland farmers who in many cases have settled on these logged-over lands now find they must participate in the corporate orientated projects or else be ejected from their land. . . . The programmes did not lead to any significant socio-economic upliftment of the lives of the participants.[59]

Despite the serious shortcomings it could be claimed that there is at least some attempt at replanting. This may be true, but how large an area has actually been replanted under these programmes? A number of sites the BFD claims to have planted are covered with trees that are at least 40 to 50 years old; much older than any replanting programme. The Mountain Province in North Luzon provides the best examples of these false claims, with trees planted under the traditional farming 'tagon' system mentioned earlier. As one irate Igorot from North Luzon recently observed:

How can we be the cause of the loss of forests? We have lived here since the beginning of time and we have always drawn from the forest. The forest always remained. It was not until the time of the logging came did we lose so many trees. You ask the people in Sagada, the BFD claims they reforested that area; it was the people's ancestors who planted those trees.[60]

New policies
The 1986 revolution provided an opportunity for great change in forestry policy. The initial mood of optimism has now settled into a more pragmatic approach with few real initiatives being taken up. To date, there has been no significant shift in forestry policy, although there was a major purge of the

BFD. A remarkable amount of progress toward a more viable forestry policy was achieved simply by applying current legislation against logging companies, many of which, as noted earlier, had their licences revoked. Seizures of illegally felled logs increased dramatically after the revolution. For the whole of 1985, 1,342 cubic metres of illegally felled timber was confiscated by the authorities,[61] while within three months in the summer of 1986 the authorities seized almost 20 times that quantity.[62] In one raid alone, on the concession of Colonel Marcelino Barba (the brother-in-law of Marcos mentioned earlier who transgressed the Commonwealth Act) the authorities recovered 1,323 cubic metres of contraband logs.[63]

The most important issue of land tenureship still remains unchanged since the events of 1986. Not only has the Aquino government refused to address this crucial issue, but it has resumed military operations against those who call for land reform or who join one of the growing number of insurgent groups. The initial opening up of Philippine society to the extent that the people felt able to express their views without fear of reprisal, has once more closed, although conditions under the Aquino government have not relapsed as low as those under Marcos.

Present causes of forest destruction

Population pressure?
At the time of writing, forest destruction in the Philippines is almost exclusively in the mountains as very little lowland forest remains. Since the 1960s, these upland areas have seen a major growth in population. This, combined with an irresponsible timber industry, has led to the present sorry state of the forests.

For many years population growth was canvassed as the root cause of the depletion of forests in the Philippines. The basic statistics seem to support this view: a population of 56m with an annual growth rate of 2.5%.[64] But this expansion has not been evenly distributed; the uplands show a much higher growth rate than most other areas. This fact came as a severe shock to the Bureau of Forestry Development (BFD), the body administering most of the Philippine uplands. In the mid-1980s a population survey revealed that the upland population was around 14m, not the four million they had been assuming.[65] Commenting on the results of this survey, the Agrarian Reform Institute notes: 'the result, which shows that about 29% of the total population are currently residing in the uplands, indicates that the official estimate is in error by a factor of at least ten.'[66]

Natural population expansion cannot account for these figures. Infant mortality rates are higher in these remote areas than the national average and there is no tradition of people having larger families here than elsewhere in the country. The only reasonable conclusion is that there has been extensive migration into the uplands. The BFD's astonishment at the actual population figures indicates how remote they were from the forests they supposedly administered. Any development programme is rendered almost obsolete by the disparity between the assumed and the real population figures.

Studies show that this new upland population is almost wholly comprised of landless poor, forced out of their traditional homes by absentee landlords or agribusiness development projects. Numerous studies note that this 'economic' land pressure leads to social tensions and a lack of employment possibilities in the fertile lowlands.[67] With no other means of support the choice is either to move into the forests or scrape a living in the major cities.

While lowland development has been geared solely towards the export economy, upland development has been almost non-existent. Dr Kummar of the Forestry Department in the University of the Philippines notes:

> The most salient feature of upland development has been the government's complete lack of control over it and its lack of political will to impose equitable and environmentally sound regulations on those involved. In short: upland development is actually a reflection of uneven Philippine development in general.[68]

This view is reflected in the widespread poverty in the Philippines as a whole. According to the World Bank, in the early 1970s, agricultural production increased by 5% per year, yet the number of rural families living below the official poverty line also increased, from 48% in 1971 to 55% in 1985.[69] This trend continued into the late 1980s and is more sharply emphasized in the upland areas. The inadequacy of lowland development has played an equally crucial role in forest destruction as has the underdevelopment of the uplands themselves.

Agribusiness exporting the best soils
In the Philippines are more than three million tenant farmers; one of the highest tenancy rates in South-East Asia.[70] Over the country as a whole more than 30% of the total cultivated land area is given over to export crops;[71] the situation on the southern island of Mindanao provides some good examples.

The Davao del Norte region of Mindanao, which in historical terms was the most populated agricultural area, has the best soils on the island. In 1970 the area under banana plantations on Mindanao was a few hundred hectares; by 1980 this had increased to more than 25,000 ha,[72] of which more than 92% is in the fertile Davao del Norte area.[73] Three large estates dominate production: Dole with 9,000 ha; Del Monte with 6,600 ha; and United Fruits with 4,500 ha.[74] The plantation sector provides few jobs, and working conditions are frequently appalling. If bananas become less popular on the world markets, the work force will be the first to feel the effects. Sugar production on the islands of Palawan and Negros provide typical examples of how developments in the US sugar substitute industry can destroy an economy, and forests, in the tropics.

The island of Palawan, with a large upland population of shifted farmers, is losing 20,000 ha of forest each year.[75] There is a significant timber industry but shifting farmers also play a major role in forest loss. The farmers are there because they have no access to the lowlands, despite the large tracts of idle land in these areas. Fertile soils are all controlled by absentee landlords, caught out by the collapse of the world sugar market with the emergence of alternative sweeteners. They laid off their work force but wish to retain control of the land in the event of the markets picking up some day or a new cash crop emerging. Ironically, one of the most widely used sweeteners responsible for the steep decline in natural sugar demand originated from a rainforest plant.

In Negros, itself dependent on the sugar cane trade, a similar situation exists. Here, reports claim that incidences of starvation occur regularly, while almost two-thirds of the land given over to sugar lies idle.[76] The power of the *haciendero*, or landowner, is total: all buildings, roads, water supplies, tools and land rights, are at his mercy. A sugar worker's dependence is almost complete as he will almost certainly be in debt to the *haciendero* and may expect perhaps only 180 days work each year. A Japanese report provides a fair description of the situation on Negros:

> If you plant food to eat anywhere on his [the *haciendero's*] property – and everything is his property – he takes it out with his bulldozer. If you join the union he drives you out of the hacienda [estate] sometimes by taking the roof off your house in the rainy season; he can do that; it's his house. If you persist the danger gets worse. Some of the bigger haciendaros have private armies . . . dozens of union organisers have been found floating in the river or in shallow graves.[77]

The choices for poor farmers are few and it is little wonder so many head into the forests. An increasing number are joining the New Peoples Army (NPA) which now regards Negros as one of its strongholds.

Transmigration programmes
Not all migration into the Philippine forest is spontaneous. The government runs a significant transmigration scheme. Government sponsored migration in the Philippines dates back to the beginning of this century. The lowlands of Luzon suddenly became overcrowded following the Land Registration Act (1902) and, as a means of diluting political unrest, landless farmers were given free passage to Mindanao. This had an added political bonus of setting

Catholic Filipinos against the Muslim rebels on Mindanao, thus ensuring divisions within the population.

Successive governments kept the migration programme operating and in the the 1970s found a new advantage. Generally, migrants' affinity to the land they farmed was less than that of indigenous populations. This made it relatively easy to move migrants on from land wanted by the plantation sector. The Marcos regime expanded the programme under Presidential Proclamation 2282, which designated 1.5m ha of denuded forest land as 'agricultural and settlement lands'. In this way the landless poor were to help with the reafforestation programme.

The reality, however, was a programme of incompetence and corruption. As one expert explained:

> The areas proclaimed were not only unsuited for agriculture and settlement, but were found to overlap existing pasture lease agreements; timber licence agreements; all forms of licences and permits issued by the Bureau of Forestry Development and other agencies; reafforestation projects; national parks; critical watershed reservations; bodies of water; and other committed areas where occupancy is prohibited.[78]

Despite the stated aim of attempting to revitalize denuded lands, a pattern emerged whereby areas selected for settlement tended to have harvestable timber stands.[79] This provided a good excuse to clear fell valuable stands of timber under the guise of providing land for the landless.

Since the revolution the programme has been temporarily suspended while the administrative chaos is sorted out. Conflicts still occur between migrants and local indigenous populations. The most notable example is the Quirino Nueva Ecija project covering 40,000 ha of the Conwap Valley in Mindanao. A large tribal population inhabited this area before the project was initiated.

Large-scale dam projects

Schemes for the construction of large-scale dams have been a major cause of farmers being moved from their lands. The Philippines has great potential for hydroelectric power and in the late 1970s the Marcos regime proposed the construction of more than 40 huge dams. International development agencies vigorously promoted large-scale dams, regarding them as the ideal energy source for developing countries. For Marcos and his 'cronies' this was an opportunity to acquire major building contracts.

Dams, however, are based in valleys, the uplands' main agricultural areas, with considerable populations that must be displaced if dams are to be constructed. The people so displaced usually move to higher ground where the forest would normally be left intact; dams thus can create deforestation problems.

The most controversial dam was the proposed Chico River project (see Case Studies), which directly or indirectly would have displaced an estimated 100,000 people and, as a result, local resistance was fierce. Another example is the Cotabato-Agusan River Basin Development project on Mindanao, which proposes a total of 17 dams. The two most advanced in the planning process will destroy 1,400 ha of agricultural land and force the relocation of 5,000 T'bolis.[80] The proposed Tandog-Tago dam in Northern Mindanao will displace at least 3,000 families.[81] In total the six dams proposed for the Pulangri river basin will displace an estimated 54,000 people.[82] Small dams have proved vital for development in many areas of the world but dams on this scale create a myriad of problems. These are outlined in more detail in the Thailand case study of the Nam Choan dam.

The relocated farmer

The end product of all these developments is the relocated farmer. The Philippines has a significant population of *traditional* shifting farmers who practise swidden agriculture. The relocated farmers, however, as they attempt to survive in what to them is a hostile environment, usually practise a crude copy of the traditional swidden systems known as *kaingin* farming. It should be noted that many of its exponents do not even have an agricultural background. Many mining jobs were lost in Northern Luzon in the 1970s and in consequence significant numbers of those without work turned for the first time to farming, simply in order to survive. By 1984 in the Philippines as a whole there were more than 4.5m people living below the official poverty line, with an annual income of less than US$150 per family.[83]

Poverty and ignorance, above all else, are responsible for the bad farming techniques that dominate certain areas. Swidden farming systems properly carried out have been shown not only to be less destructive to the environment but also more productive in terms of crop yields.

A brief description of these two main forest farming systems found in the mountains will serve to highlight the problems associated with *kaingin* farming.[84] Both systems involve clearing trees and burning the resultant debris. The burning returns a limited quantity of nutrients to the soils and helps maintain the pH balance; but here the similarities stop.

The traditional swidden techniques in the Philippines are essentially the same as those practised in East Malaysia and Indonesia. The Philippine tribal people plant an exceptionally large variety of rice strains: there may be up to 15 varieties within a few hectares of land. The Hanunoo tribes cultivate 430 different crops, frequently intercropping 40 species at any one time.[85] In contrast *kaingin* farmers tend to plant a single species crop, which is thus open to attacks by pests and disease and the potential loss of the whole crop.

One comparative study of the two systems on Mindanao found no visible signs of erosion on traditional swidden sites with a slope of 60°; but *kaingin* sites frequently showed serious erosion problems even on 15° slopes.[86]

A major factor in the swidden system's sustainability is that sites are left fallow after two to four years of cultivation; that is, before crop yields decline. Most *kaingin* farmers, however, do not change sites until crop yields have virtually ceased. The soil is thus exhausted and its future capacity to support anything more than extremely low density grazing is threatened. The fertility of the soil is further depleted by *kaingin* farmers constantly burning the land at the end of each harvest in order to clear weeds. Swidden, because the different crops are harvested on a continuous cycle, requires constant weeding by hand, not burning.

Regular burning not only bakes the soils but also kills tree seedlings. A longer land-use cycle then develops as rough grasslands evolve. The Philippines has developed a taste for US style fast food beefburgers. To meet this demand, cattle ranching on abandoned *kaingin* sites has become common. Although beef yields from such sites are extremely low, grazing can be continued on these very poor quality grasslands for up to 30 years. After this time the soils cannot even support this extremely low intensity useage. There has been no research on the recovery time for these overused lands.

For too long Philippine planners and foresters have blamed shifting cultivators for forest destruction. The *kaingin* system is without doubt harmful to the environment, but to simply condemn those who practise it does not solve the problem. This destructive farming system is a direct result of poor development policies, responsibility for which rests with the very people who blame poor farmers for forest destruction. With no land tenure, *kaingin* farmers have little incentive for long-term investment in the land. Single crops are planted because that is what 'modern' Western farmers do. *Kaingin* farmers harvest one crop at a time, leaving soils totally exposed between crops, because that is what mono-cropping requires. These farming techniques are promoted by the authorities in the large estates; the landless simply copy the idea without understanding, or being taught to understand, its full impact. Furthermore, lowland farmers frequently regard the traditional swidden system as backward and out-dated precisely because it is practised by tribal people.

The 'Green Revolution' of the 1960s promoted high-yield rice varieties, mono-cropping, widespread use of fertilizers and pesticides and a general specialization in farming. The net result was to further devalue swidden farming because it was based on a diverse and integrated cropping system. Recently, however, there has been renewed interest and understanding of the traditional farming systems in the Philippines, which, if it continues, bodes well for the future.

Fuelwood crisis

In some areas a combination of factors has led to fuelwood shortages. Fuelwood gathering, usually of tree branches, tends to affect forest cover only when wood resources are either severely depleted or are near major cities. For the poor, wood fuel is essential for both cooking and for warmth. In 1980 an estimated 26m cubic metres of wood fuel was consumed in the Philippines.[87] The official estimate for domestic timber consumption, that is, from felled trees, for the same year was four million cubic metres.[88] This apparently significant difference led to a few calls of 'crisis', but the comparison is hardly viable: one cubic metre of small branches can be replaced much more quickly than an equal volume of solid timber. Many trees can tolerate the removal of branches, but none can survive total felling, which is what the timber industry requires.

To date, the role of fuelwood gatherers in forest destruction has been somewhat overstated. Consumption of fuelwood in the future, estimated to be 106m cubic metres by the late 1990s does, however, give cause for concern.[89]

But this figure is only a prediction, and a number of factors could change the picture. For example, alternative fuel sources could be developed or the efficiency of wood-burning ovens could be increased. Future sources would also be relatively easy to ensure with widespread planting and social forestry projects. A tropical environment has perhaps the greatest potential for producing wood suitable for fuel anywhere on earth. The return on investment for fuelwood is also much faster than that for timber. At present, however, fuelwood gathering cannot be regarded as a major cause of forest destruction in the Philippines.

The timber industry

The Philippines' timber industry has affected thousands of square kilometres of forest. Over-cutting, illegal logging, log smuggling and general corruption within the industry has resulted in the present collapse of the trade. As with Malaysia and other countries in the region, the Philippines has at most ten years' supply of timber before it will need to become a net importer to meet domestic demand.[90]

Timber and mining have been closely related since colonial days and a considerable number of US companies continue to have influence in these sectors; table 5.2 lists some of the largest, including Georgia Pacific and Weyerhauser. In the late 1970s these interests could expect a 25% to 30% return on their investment within one year, through various subsidies, tax benefits and the considerable profits a company could make by exploiting the forests and making no reinvestment for their future.

Underlying this was the 'strategy' on forests outlined in the government's own five year plans; a typical extract was noted in the introduction to this chapter. Since the 1986 revolution the system of obtaining licences and control over the timber industry has changed significantly. Here, it is useful to briefly outline the old system in order to show how the present situation arose.

Timber licences: During the Marcos regime there were two ways to obtain a timber concession: either by knowing the President, or knowing someone in the Wood Industries Development Board. Officially, the criteria upon which the Board based its choice of companies were, past performance, internal structure and capability in this field; if these were considered satisfactory a licence was issued. The price was a fee of one peso (US 5 cents) per hectare per year plus a tax of 1.5 peso (US 8 cents) paid for every cubic metre of timber harvested.

The profit margin can only be described as massive. Dipterocarp forest operations were extracting an average 80 to 100 cubic metres of timber per hectare.[91] At 1980 prices, raw logs for export were selling for around US$100 per cubic metre, which amounts to approximately US$8,000 worth of timber per hectare. A rough equation of fee costs per hectare would run: logging fee, US 5 cents; tax on timber, US 8 cents; value of timber extracted, US$8,000. Even taking account of machinery and labour costs the profits are considerable.

With the potentiality of such wide profit margins rivalry to acquire licences was fierce; companies were willing to fund considerable bribes to secure concessions and still be guaranteed a large profit. Cases of past bribery within the forestry department began to emerge after the revolution. In June 1986, four employees of the Wood Industries Development Board were found guilty of issuing fake concession licences; although no money was directly attributed to the issuance of these licences, abuse of power within the Department was obvious. One licence gave access to more than 100,000 cubic metres of high quality standing timber (1,000 ha concession) worth an estimated US$800,000 as export logs.[92]

Concession holders even tried to avoid payment of the negligible taxes and fees. In 1986, Pamplona and Tagat Industries, the major companies controlled by Alfonso Lim, a friend of the Marcos family who held rights over 600,000 ha of the Cagayan province, were accused of having failed to pay concession fees since 1975 and of owing the government more than one million peso (US$53,000) in unpaid taxes. By 1986 they had logged over 1,360 ha while replanting just 99 of them.[93]

Such conduct not only results in a loss of revenue to the public purse, but a lack of long-term investment in forestry. In the new system now applicable, the concession is granted to the highest bidder, above a minimum price, which is considerably more than the previous 1.5 peso per hectare. Nevertheless, forest management methods employed during the Marcos period still dominate.

Timber extraction methods[94]
The two most commercially valuable forest types in the Philippines are the
northern pine forests and the dipterocarp forests of the south. Extraction
methods and silvicultural practices obviously vary from one area to another
but the Bureau of Forestry Development claim they all follow a basic
guideline.

Dipterocarp forestry: Officially, as with all the other countries in the region,
forests are harvested on a sustained yield basis using selective felling
techniques. Since the early 1970s the most intensive timber extraction rates
in the world have occurred in the Philippines. This is carried out within what
is known as the Basilan Working Cycle.

In this Cycle, all mature and over-mature trees are selectively felled and
the forest left for 35 to 45 years to recover before repeating the process, but
this recovery period is rarely adhered to. The Western Mindanao Lumber
Company, who selectively logged their concession between 1953 and 1955,
provides a fairly typical example of disregarding the fallow period. They
took out an average of 150 cubic metres of timber per hectare. In 1969, just
15 years later, they selectively logged the same area, extracting a further 120
cubic metres per hectare; so far they have not returned to the area for
another crop. It is highly unlikely that these forests can produce this quantity
of timber on a sustainable basis. The FAO described the Philippines as:
'the country where logging intensity is the highest and cannot be assimilated
to a simple "creaming" as in most other tropical countries.'[95]

Because the terrain in the Philippines is so mountainous, timber
extraction methods are dominated by the 'high lead' system. Bulldozers and
skidder tracks, like those used in Malaysia and Indonesia, are relatively rare
outside the island of Palawan and parts of Mindanao. 'High leading'
involves dragging logs out of the forest with high tension steel cables.
Strategically placed spar trees form pivots along ridges overlooking the
cutting sites and logs are dragged up to them. This is a costly method and
there is debate over the extent of damage it causes to forests in comparison
to skidding techniques. While a smaller area is completely cleared of trees
the high lead method can reach areas inaccessible to bulldozers. Loggers are
thus able to work on extremely steep, fragile slopes and the logs are still
dragged along the forest floor. The FAO notes that on average, 31% of the
land surface is stripped of vegetation in Philippine logging operations.[96]

After extraction the forest needs some kind of enrichment planting and
silvicultural treatment. But because costs would thus be increased beyond
what the logging companies are willing to pay, such treatment is rarely
applied.

Pine forestry: In these forests, totally dominated by pines, almost every tree
will be harvestable, thus creating a great temptation to clear-fell areas.

These forests can, however, recover slightly faster than the dipterocarp forests, which means the cycle for cutting is shorter.

Timber is extracted using the 'skyline' method, which is very similar to the 'high lead' method, except that cables are strung from ridge to ridge and logs suspended from them. This is also an expensive system but causes comparatively little environmental damage.

Forests are then left to recover for a 30 to 40 year period. Regeneration relies on the 'seed tree' method: trees with favourable characteristics are often used as a 'mother' and left standing. These trees naturally reseed the area after logging and this can be regarded as a method of enrichment planting. But regeneration and management of the forest is left to nature.

To a great extent, however, these methods exist in theory only. Since the mid-1970s illegal logging and log smuggling have dominated the Philippine timber industry. These activities occur in both kinds of forest and are frequently found taking place alongside legitimate concessions.

Illegal logging and log smuggling

In 1984 the Bureau of Forest Development officially recognized 189 major sawmills in the country; in 1985 it detected 175 of these handling illegally felled timber.[97] Of these, the Bureau recommended that the licences of only four mills were to be suspended or revoked. Sawmills work very closely with the concession holders and, because illegal timber is not distinguished from legitimately felled logs, detecting illegal operations is difficult. The revolution brought in a much less tolerant administration; of the 157 major concession licences active in 1985, 150 were revoked within three months of the revolution.

Most illegally felled logs did not even reach the saw-mills, but were exported in their raw state. Concession holders were by no means the only groups felling timber; heavily armed, independent operators were also common. The authorities were remarkably impotent when it came to tackling the illegal operations; in the words of one forestry officer in Mindanao during the mid 1980s:

> What would you do as a forestry officer manning an isolated road block if a dozen armed men pushed the barrels of their rifles down your nose and politely requested you let their log laden trucks through? If you resisted you would die.[98]

In 1986, one reporter interviewed Democrito Plaza, an ex-governor of Northern Mindanao, who, with his family, still controlled 90,000 ha of timber concession in Northern Mindanao.[99] He expressed the following, then typical, view of the situation in the timber industry:

> You must understand how we do things in the Philippines and how hard

it is to impose law and order. What can a politician do when one of his friends is in trouble but to help him? This is a problem that plagues not only us but every politician; right up to the president [Marcos].[100]

Despite the revolution and the subsequent revocation of most concession licences,[10] such attitudes still persist.

Log smuggling could be regarded as occurring only as isolated incidents, but it reached such a scale that the figures for smuggled logs appeared in Philippine log export records. The Philippines' two main markets for logs, legal and illegal, are Japan and Taiwan. The trade figures for exports to Japan reveal some interesting anomalies: between 1981 and 1983, 1.47m cubic metres of logs were officially exported to Japan. Japan's import figures covering the same period, however, register 3.55m cubic metres of Philippine logs having entered the country.[102] The extent of disparity between these two figures can be illustrated by the fact that it is equal to twice the volume of Wembley football stadium (in London, England). Table 5.3 lists some of the major Japanese trading houses that import timber from the Philippines. The post-revolution Minister for Natural Resources, Ernesto Maceda, estimated that between 1978 and 1986, logs to the value of approximately 2.4m peso (US$127,000) were smuggled out of the country annually.[103]

In 1985 Marcos established a task force to identify the major flows of capital out of the country. Log smuggling was investigated and the task force identified ten ships involved, and the companies that supplied them.[104] The companies' logging licences were temporarily revoked; reportedly, two weeks later, these companies were conducting business as usual.[105] The complicity of foreign trading companies cannot be ignored as in 1985 smuggled logs were reportedly selling at 30% to 40% below current market values.[106]

The effectiveness of the new administration at eradicating such problems will not become clear for a few years. In August 1986 President Aquino announced a total log export ban.

Timber exports[107]

Logs dominated timber exports prior to the present ban; more than 70% went to Japan. Although official export figures are available they are clearly of little use except for indicating the main destinations of timber. Tables 5.4 and 5.5 provide details of exports by species, destination and form (logs or plywood). Approximately 10% of exported logs were destined for Taiwan, a major producer of plywood.

Plywood production in the Philippines has undoubtedly increased since the log export ban, but figures are not yet available. The major markets for Philippine plywood, the UK, US, and Hong Kong, are, however, likely to remain unchanged. In 1984, Japan, with its own plywood industry, imported just 151 cubic metres of plywood from the Philippines.

There is a strong argument for increased processing in the light of export values. Average prices of timber exported from the Philippines in 1984 are provided in table 5.6.

Plywood shows the greatest increase in value when processing raw logs, but it is doubtful if the Philippines can make an impact on the world market in view of Indonesia's current domination. The government has proposed importing logs from Malaysia to feed its own plywood industry, which is a rather fanciful means of propping up an export trade, but it may provide for the inevitable growth in the domestic plywood market. The ban on log exports is undoubtedly regarded as a turning point in the country's timber industry. At present no clear pattern is developing in the Philippine timber trade and, with the political instability of the provinces reaching the major cities, developments hang in the balance. The heyday of the Philippine timber trade has, however, clearly ended.

Forest futures

Since the 1986 revolution there has been a major shift in forestry planning. The purging of the Bureau for Forest Development, a tough line on concession abuse, and the ban on log exports will have lasting effects on Philippine forests. In 1987 the government began to offer rewards for information on illegal logging; informers would receive 30% of the value of any illegally felled logs that were intercepted after a tip-off. Timber concession holders must now place a deposit equivalent to the replanting costs for every hectare they log; if they themselves replant the area the deposit is returned. There seem to be no binding restrictions on what tree species they plant and this may foreshadow a major problem. A company may harvest mahogany, for example, and replant with eucalyptus, and that is a long way from sustainable forestry.

One major change in the Philippine political scene has been the role played by non-government organizations (NGOs). Before the 1986 revolution most NGOs spent their resources trying to oust the Marcos regime, seeing corruption in government as the root of the country's social and environmental problems. Today, however, they have more freedom to air their views and thus a slightly greater chance of influencing government policy.

A major replanting programme has begun, aiming to plant 100,000 ha of trees each year up to the year 2000.[108] It is encouraging that only 36% of these are to be for timber production; at last the social function of trees has been officially acknowledged! Apart from this 36%, 31% is for fuelwood, 18% for protective and other use forest, and 15% for pulpwood production. Early in 1988 the Ministry of Natural Resources secured loans totalling

US$100m from the Asian Development Bank and a further US$50m from Japan for this programme.[109] The government, aware of public concern about environmental issues, organized a major publicity campaign before the programme was fully designed. Most notably, those groups not directly involved at the initial stages were tribal organizations and small farmers. Possibly this was due to their association with the NPA and other rebel groups that the Aquino administration still regards as a threat. A central theme of the programme is, however, the provision of 'stewardship contracts' for shifting farmers. These contracts are to be renewable only every 25 years, and may be handed on from generation to generation.

Replanting is co-ordinated and implemented through the NGO sector and the Catholic Church as, according to Celso Roque, Under-secretary for Research at the Ministry for the Environment: 'This government has shown it cannot reafforest.'[110] It is acknowledged that these replanting programmes are no substitute for saving the forests but they do fulfil some immediate environmental needs.

This programme is a positive development and will go a long way toward relieving pressure on Philippine forests, but does it go far enough? In 1981 the University of the Philippines produced a 'People's Forests Programme'[111] designed to save Philippine forests. This Programme was based on land tenureship reform, full involvement of local populations and direct financing, not loans; land reform was identified as the key task. The present government continues to avoid this issue, particularly in so far as the fertile lowlands are concerned. The Programme was extremely forthright on the need for a directly financed non-loan system for small farmers, in order to pay for projects as, however well-intentioned, some projects do fail, and if this happens under a loan system, local people would be burdened with debts they were unable to pay. The principle of participation of the local population in all projects that affect them has, however, been taken up in the government's current plans, and this provides the greatest hope for their replanting efforts.

In the Philippines, underdevelopment has played a major role in forest destruction. The total lack of infrastructure and services in poor, rural areas and the centralization of the economy in Manila, has meant that local economies remain undeveloped and vulnerable to external markets. It is towards the domestic and regional market place that the Philippines could guide its development policy. The country's involvement in global markets has contributed very little to the well-being of the rural poor. Above all, some sense of stability in rural areas is needed; large plantations fail to provide this because of ill-thought-out creation and mismanagement.

The limited resources available could be more beneficial if aimed at the shifted farmer population. There are a number of extremely small projects directed towards this group: on the island of Cebu a US organization, World Neighbours, is working with displaced farmers in the mountains, on a project to stop soil erosion and improve productivity, as well as seeking land titles for those involved.[112] This education project, initially led by a foreign director, has since been taken over by local people. Seminars were conducted on basic contouring techniques and inter-cropping with trees; a communal labour group was established in which participants gave up one day each week to work on terrace building. By late 1987, five years after the project's initiation, approximately 750 farmers were involved. One of the largest capital investments for equipment was the slide projector, which contributed significantly to the seminar programme. Of course, compared to the scale of the problem, this is a minor project, but it indicates that huge capital investment is not always necessary.

Many of the tribal groups have been remarkably well-organized when opposing over-exploitation of their lands; the Chico dam protests provide a good example. If the social cohesion of these tribal groups is maintained they are a highly independent people. This is often seen as a threat, but if given greater control over their lands these tribal groups have much to offer, particularly in caring for the forests.

But to achieve this general development the redistribution of land ownership is essential in many areas, and that is unlikely to take place for some time in the Philippines. The possibility of local control over timber exploitation, however, looks more hopeful. As the resource diminishes, extraction costs increase and the operations become less attractive to foreign investors. In the 1980s a significant proportion of the foreign timber companies active in the Philippines have moved out, mainly to East Malaysia and the Amazon. Control over domestic timber demand and promotion of the processing sector are the current government aims.

Minor forest produce, such as rattans, oils and so on, contribute little to the Philippine economy at present. There is undoubtedly potential in this area as these markets are relatively undeveloped. Exploitation of these products is, however, dependent on a more highly developed transport system. To date, central government has paid little attention to the role minor forest produce could play in the economy. The Philippines receives much development aid, and development of the exploitation of these products is one facet of the economy that would benefit greatly from more investment.

Perhaps all that can be said at the present time is that the political future of the Philippines is unpredictable and so, consequently, are its rural development policies and the fate of its forests.

Case studies*

The Cellophil Resource Corporation

In 1972 the first jeeps marked 'Cellophil' were seen in the Abra Province in the Cordillera mountain range on Luzon. This would have passed unnoticed except that they were accompanied by the notorious Malacanay Palace Guard – Marcos's personal security troops. Unknown to the local population they were surveying the area for timber resources. In October 1973 and March 1974 two sister companies, the Cellophil Resources Corporation and the Cellulose Processing Corporation, were granted exclusive timber rights over 198,795 ha of this mountain range; two company names were used in order to bypass the limit on land holdings, and for tax purposes.

Company background: The companies were so closely linked that their ownership structure can be regarded as one. In the early 1970s they were controlled by the Herdi Group (70%) and a number of foreign multinationals (30%). The latter were dominated by three Japanese companies: Mitsubishi Rayon; Daical; and Marubeni. But the Herdi Group, wholly owned by Hermino Disini, brother-in-law to Emelda Marcos, effectively ran the company.

Before marrying into the Marcos family, Hermino Disini had been a not particularly successful business man. Within eight years of his marriage, the Herdi Group owned more than 30 companies dealing in a huge range of products, from a complete monopoly on the cigarette filter trade to being a major insurance company.

Disini was quite frank about his relationship with the President and his views on development. In an interview with *Business Day* in 1978 he said:

> We went into pioneering industries because we wanted to do our share in the economic development of the country. It is an admitted fact that the President and I are very close friends and this personal relationship has made us aware of our responsibility in helping the government speed up industrialisation and development of the economy in God-forsaken places.

These areas are perhaps better described as 'government forsaken'. Within the boundaries of the concession were 150,000 tribal people, mainly Tinggians – a proud and strongly independent people. They were to be brought into the 20th century by performing paid work in the pulp factory and as logging crews. The plan was to build the pulp mill and selectively fell

---

* Based on local tribal leaflets produced at the time and personal interviews. Most sources wish to remain anonymous for security reasons, even after the 1986 revolution.

the pine forests, using the Tineg river as the main transport route for logs. Local interest was first noted when the company began taking sample cuts and making more detailed surveys.

The campaigns: By 1977 preliminary extraction was underway and the Tinggian tribes made a formal request to the company and regional government that their: 'tribal grazing lands, communal forests, fallow agricultural lands and critical watersheds were excluded from the logging areas.' The request was flatly refused.

Cellophil then went on the offensive. A massive publicity campaign was launched involving: seminars to 'educate' local leaders; a 'provincial cultural renaissance' with singing, dancing, writing and painting contests; and the provision of free medicines, food and sports equipment for the local population. The other side of the Cellophil campaign was a sharp escalation of military harassment against any local leaders who still opposed the plans. Town mayors who commented adversely on the development were replaced by military personnel.

The other main centre of organized resistance was the Catholic Church, a powerful institution in the Philippines. Most church leaders had to leave the area because their safety could not be guaranteed. It was at this time that Father Conrado Balweg fled to join the New Peoples Army; he is now a legendary figure throughout the Philippines.

The Tinggians were not the only people affected and a peace pact was formed with other tribes in the area. In September 1978 a meeting was held between the various tribal leaders, local government officials and representatives from the Bureau for Forestry Development, the Philippine Constabulary, and employees of Cellophil. No agreement was reached but the tribal leaders produced a resolution explaining why they opposed the plans. This resolution provides an insight into the tribal view of such development policies:

> *Economic dislocation:* Cellophil Resources Corporation (CRC) has intruded into our ancestral lands using resources there and thus denying us our very source of livelihood that has been ours since time immemorial. Concerning the promises that CRC will duly compensate the dislocated farmers: the Tinggians point to the plight of farmers in Mudiit and Gaddani, who demanded and failed to receive payment for lands forcibly taken from them.

> *Political tyranny:* CRC did not properly consult us on its concrete plans before it started its activities. CRC connived to deceive tribal leaders as well as coerce the people to stamp out resistance.

> *Cultural uprooting:* The entering of CRC undermines tribal unity and

harmony. It will destroy our most cherished traditions, undermining and violating the Tinggian concepts and custom laws on property, indigenous use of resources and communism.

Despite the opposition logging went ahead. To some extent local hostility was a minor problem compared to the technical difficulties Cellophil were facing. The team of foreign advisers had planned on floating the logs down to the mills, but they had failed to see whether these logs would actually float; they didn't. Furthermore, the pulp produced fell below the standards required for export.

The mill, which cost the Herdi Group more than two billion peso (US$105.8m) to build was never fully operational. In 1973 Marcos had announced his ban on log exports, but Cellophil, with its political connections, was one of the 'deserving and responsible' companies eligible for exemption. By the mid-1970s Cellophil was the major log exporter in the Cordilleras; but the Corporation still had financial problems and in 1978 Disini persuaded the government to take control of the company.

Local resistance, at first sporadic, escalated towards the end of the 1970s as, undoubtedly due to the increasing use of troops to quell local resistance, support for the NPA grew. This armed opposition severely restricted the areas in which Cellophil could be active. Government troops were used to protect logging site personnel and thus much smaller areas were harvested. In an attempt to recover costs Cellophil started to clear-fell the pine. This further incensed the local population and more joined the NPA or the newly formed Cordillera People's Liberation Army (CPLA) in which Father Conrado Balweg was a key figure.

By 1984 Cellophil's cost to the government was five million peso (US$265,000) per month to keep open, and in June of that year the mill was finally closed. It is noteworthy that total public expenditure for the entire Abra Province was just ten million peso (US$530,000) for the whole of 1984. By late 1985 the remaining staff were unable to continue logging due to NPA and CPLA pressure, and the project collapsed. After the revolution it was rumoured that Aquino had offered the complete operation to Father Conrado Balweg, who at present is with the CPLA; so far he has not taken up the option.

Almost every aspect of Cellophil's operation was a complete failure. In 1984, even the provincial governor commented on the irony of this squandering of resources:

> If the company's initial investment of 2 billion Peso, and its accumulated losses since it started operations, had been used in support of small scale projects like irrigation systems, cottage industries, agricultural productivity, social health and services; the [local] government would have touched and improved the lives of all its more than 160,000 inhabitants.

The Chico river dam
The area affected by the proposals for this project was by no means all forested, but the cumulative effects of mass eviction and loss of farmland make the Chico dam a good case study of the development of shifted farmers.

Northern Luzon is very mountainous and has great potential for hydroelectric power. The Philippines has very little oil and imports vast quantities. The potential hazards of depending on imported energy sources had engaged the government's attention since the mid-1960s, when the notion of building dams on the Chico river first emerged. Not until the 1972 oil price crisis, however, were any feasibility studies carried out.

A German consultancy, Lameyer International Gmbh, in partnership with the Engineering and Development Corporation of the Philippines, undertook the study and identified four main dam sites. They also proposed an additional irrigation project that would make the whole package more economical. Lameyer recommended additional feasibility research to assess the project's potential environmental and social impacts. The government ignored this recommendation and went ahead with a full-scale proposal.

Proposed sites of Chico river dams:
Chico 1: Sabangan: Mountain Province, 100 megawatt (MW).
Chico 2: Saganda: Mountain Province, 360 MW.
Chico 3: Basao: Kalinga-Apayao, 100 MW.
Chico 4: Tomiangan: Kalinga-Apayao, 450 MW.
Total power potential: 1,010 MW.

It was envisaged that the dams would provide enough power to pave the way for development in the whole of northern Luzon, but the proposed sites were the main population centres for these regions, and in order to carry out the project a total of 65,000 Bontocs and 75,000 Kalingas would have to move. The subsequent shift in population out of the valleys would cause a major demographic change in a region where the traditional population is strongly territorial. The tribal population foresaw serious social unrest if this occurred, but this social upheaval was regarded as a relatively minor problem by central government. The authorities seemed genuinely surprised that there was any resistance to their proposals.

The government's case for construction of the dams was put by the National Power Corporation of the Philippines. The then Chairman, Gabriel Itchon, issued a statement listing the advantages of the project:

1) The project will increase food production and there is no gainsaying its importance in our country, with its population growth and our region, with its rice prospects.

2) . . . transform the energy from the Chico river into electric energy, and the benefits generated by the project will grow larger as the supply of imported oil becomes more expensive and increasingly uncertain.

3) . . . contribute to the economics of extending the Luzon grid to the Cagayan Valley and the resulting supply of cheaper electricity 24 hours per day that is so essential to industry, trade, health and education.

4) . . . provide the means of arresting the decline in the culture of the tribes that will be affected by the project; and more generally, for uplifting their living standards.

Significantly, the irrigation scheme for the Cayagan Valley would cater for the needs of large plantations rather than small farmers. Both President Marcos and his then Defence Minister, Juan Enrile, owned large tracts of land in this valley. Because the Chico 2 dam was to be the water source for this project its construction was given priority. The World Bank had been approached and had shown interest in the project, but were still considering it in the early 1980s. If all had gone according to plan this first dam would have been completed by 1982.

Local opposition: From the time of the announcement of the plans the various tribal groups threatened by the dams decided to act together. In the mid 1970s Peace Pacts were arranged so that all inter-tribal disputes were suspended until the Chico dam proposals were abandoned.

Survey work on Chico 2 started in 1974. The local Bontoc tribe's resistance was immediate and imaginative. They started with peaceful demonstrations, petitions, public rallies and such like. At one point the local women stopped survey teams from entering the area by disrobing and refusing to move from the road; despite some visitors' image of the Philippines, the women are remarkably modest. The soldiers refused to arrest the women because they found the situation very embarrassing and potentially dangerous; arresting half-dressed women could involve them in an explosive situation with husbands and boy friends.

Such demonstrations were widely reported in the press. A delegation from the Bontoc tribe even obtained an audience with the President, only to be told they were too sentimental. The Catholic church became involved at this stage and helped co-ordinate publicity for the cause.

Opposition was based around the loss of good agricultural land, the destruction of local communities and the lack of consultation with the people most affected. The tribal people estimated that more than 1,200 stone-walled rice terraces and a further 2,500 ha of coffee and fruit trees would be destroyed. The land to be flooded was producing crops worth more than 13m peso (US$690,000) in 1972 and the people had no faith in the government providing compensation for this loss. They were also angered at the loss of hunting and fishing grounds.

In addition the forced relocation of a culture whose religious beliefs and political systems are based on communal management of the land would further destabilize the area. The Peace Pacts that had kept these mountains relatively free from inter-tribal conflicts would be nullified. A large proportion of local communities would lose all political influence within the tribal political system because they would no longer be living on the land of their ancestors.

The government claimed they had completed a cost-benefit analysis for the projects that took such factors into account and the ratio was in favour of the dams. But this study was never produced in public, and full-scale surveys began before the World Bank had made any formal response to the request for funding. This is unusual for a project of this scale: Chico 4 was to cost US$500–600m for construction alone.

In the face of such strong resistance to Chico 2, it was proposed instead to complete Chico 4 first. The government clearly hoped the Kalinga would not oppose the projects with the same tenacity as had the Bontocs; they badly misjudged the situation. In late 1975 the Presidential Assistant on National Minorities (PANAMIN) was brought in to help the National Power Corporation (NPC) implement the surveys. But the situation deteriorated rapidly while the authorities tried both soft and strong hand tactics. PANAMIN used bribery in an effort to split the opposition, as well as the provision of scholarships for colleges in Manila. But the names of most scholarship recipients turned out to be fictitious and the stunt did little to gain people's confidence in this government body supposedly delegated to help tribal interests. In December 1975 PANAMIN took a number of the tribal leaders to Manila on the pretext of a meeting with the authorities. On their return to the province the leaders claimed they were forced to sign blank sheets of paper that later appeared as declarations of support for the projects.

By 1976 resistance was becoming more direct. Government troops were enforcing a dusk to dawn curfew and demonstrations had become more frequent and violent. The NPC survey team camps were regularly destroyed. On the fourth occasion this occurred 250 Kalinga completely dismantled the camp and carried the pieces overnight to the nearest Philippine Constabulary base, 24 km away at Bulanao.

PANAMIN could no longer control the situation and successively tougher troops were flown in to quell resistance. By 1978 the Chico 4 project area had become a NPA stronghold. Normally, the murder of one tribesman by members of another tribe would develop into a major family conflict; this traditional law was temporarily annulled and the Peace Pacts strengthened to the extent that anyone found working for the NPC could be killed with impunity: the deceased's relatives no longer had a right to avenge the killing. As a result the NPC was forced to employ labour from outside the area.

The region had become ungovernable and, by 1980, more than 100 deaths, including government officials and troops, NPC personnel, NPA guerrillas and local civilians, were directly attributable to the Chico 4 project. In April 1980, a turning point was reached with the assassination of Macliing Dulag, a popular local leader and outspoken opponent of the dam, who died of multiple bullet wounds in his own home. The authorities obviously hoped this would dampen resistance, but precisely the opposite occurred.

Government tactics then changed to simply trying to maintain control over the area and postpone the project. No further survey work was carried out for a number of years, and in late 1986 President Aquino formally announced that the government had abandoned the entire programme.

The area is still a NPA stronghold but relatively peaceful. It is developing a major tourist industry, which will probably be far more beneficial, by way of providing the region with jobs and infrastructure, than would the dams. As the tourist industry increases the provision of electric power will become a problem, but small-scale hydro dams may prove a viable proposition.

In many ways this is a success story for local resistance and it has provided inspiration to other tribal groups in South-East Asia. In reality, however, it was a totally irresponsible waste of government resources. If the costs of maintaining troops in the region had instead been put into infrastructural development the lives of all the people would undoubtedly have improved. The conflict should also be seen in the wider context of events in other areas of the Cordilleras, such as the Cellophil case. Both examples clearly illustrate that development projects can hope to be successful only if the local people want them.

Table 5.1
Major mining and logging operations affecting national minorities

Area	No. Mining Companies	No. Logging Companies
LUZON		
Benquet – Mt Province	8	4
Kalinga	4	2
Abra	1	2
Ifuago		1
Isabela		14
Nueva Vizcaya		8
Quirino		5
MINDANAO		
Surigao del Norte	4	
Surigao del Sur		7
Agusan del Norte	1	16
Agusan del Sur		6
Davao del Norte	3	1
Bukidnon		13
Laneo del Norte		2
Laneo del Sur		1
Misamis del Norte	1	
Zamboanga del Norte	1	

Source: The Philippines; Authoritarian government, multinationals and ancestral lands. The Anti-Slavery Society London 1983.

Table 5.2
Major American logging interests in the Philippines

Local Co. (subsidiary)	U.S. Owner (parent)
Lianga Bay	Georgia Pacific Corp.
Findlay Millar Co.	Findlay Millar Co.
Zamboanga Wood Products	Boise-Cascade Corp.
Paper & Industrial Corp. of the Philippines	International Paper Andres Soriano & Associated Companies
Bislig Bay Lumber	International Paper Andres & Soriano
Basilan Lumber Co.	Weyerhaeuser Corp.

Table 5.3
Major Japanese trading companies dealing with Philippine timbers

	Volume (cu.m.)	
Company	1985	1982
Nisso Iwai	92,527	297,793
Marubeni	29,001	28,708
Yautaka Mokuzai	23,621	91,707
Mitsui Bussan	16,408	44,810
Mitsubushi Shoji	15,100	25,424
C. Ito	11,081	14,020
Sumitomo Ringyo	10,000	42,586
Meiwa Sangyo	4,500	82,921
Yuasa Sangyo	4,275	33,897

Source: Japan Tropical Forest Action Network – Tokyo 1987.

Table 5.4
Lumber exports by species and country 1984

Country	Luan	Others	Total
Japan	135,350	27,022	162,372
UK	144,770	271	145,041
EEC (Excl. UK)	81,606	305	81,911
USA	59,647	979	60,626
Australia	25,619	1,939	27,558
Hong Kong	13,046	316	13,362
Others	46,574	2,400	48,974
Total	506,612	33,232	539,844

Source: Bureau for Forest Development – 1986.

Table 5.5
Log, plywood and other timber products exports

Country	Logs	Plywood	Others (Mainly wood waste – kilos)
Japan	603,738	163	381,088
Korea	98,653	2,141	360,378
Taiwan	97,214	7,107	1,050,291
France	34,780	2,448	—
Hong Kong	—	60,441	2,400,000
USA	—	77,800	—
UK	—	73,419	—
Others	8,637	26,355	82,920
Totals	*843,022*	*249,874*	*4,274,677*

Source: Bureau for Forest Development. 1986.

Table 5.6
Average export prices for timber produce (1984)

Logs	US$ 102 per cu.m.
Lumber	US$ 199 cu.m.
Plywood	US$ 231 cu.m.
Veneer	US$ 199 per cu.m.

Source: Philippine Forestry Statistics – 1984 – BFD. Manila.

References

1. Ganapin, D., 1986(a).
2. *News Herald* (Manila), 27 May, 1986.
3. Ganapin, D., 1986(a).
4. Bala, V., 1986.
5. Revila, A., 1984.
6. Ganapin, D., 1986(a).
7. Ibid.
8. Ibid.
9. Bureau of Forest Development, 1984.
10. Ganapin, D., 1986(a).
11. Ibid.
12. Ibid.
13. Ibid.
14. Madela, E., 1986.
15. Bureau of Forestry Development, 1986.
16. *Depthnews*, 1986.
17. Bureau of Forestry Development, 1986.
18. Ibid.
19. Revilla, A., 1985.
20. Upland Multisectoral Policy Group, 1986.
21. Sahabat Alam Malaysia (SAM), 1983.
22. Alunan Glong, 1986.
23. Vega, V., 1986.
24. Ganapin, D., 1986(a).
25. Ibid.
26. Ibid.
27. Ibid.
28. Bureau of Fisheries, 1981.
29. Ganapin, D., 1986(a).
30. Ibid.
31. Ibid.
32. Ibid.
33. Snow, J. 1984.
34. Ganapin, D. 1986(a).
35. Bureau of Forestry Development, 1986.
36. Ganapin, D. personal communication, 1986.
37. Ganapin, D. 1986(a).
38. Bello, W. et. al. (eds) 1982.
39. Ibid.
40. Goodno, J. 1986.
41. Ibid.
42. *The Malaya* (Manila), 1986, 31 July.
43. Ganapin, D., 1986(a).
44. Ibid.
45. Ibid.
46. *Sarawak Tribune*, 1986, 7 July.

47. Bureau of Forestry Development, 1986.
48. Ibid.
49. Alunan, M. 1986.
50. Bello, W. et. al. (eds), 1982.
51. Ganapin, D. 1986(b).
52. Bureau of Forestry Development, 1986.
53. Agaloos, B. 1983.
54. Freese, P. and T.O'Brien, 1983.
58. Aguilar, F. 1982.
59. Freese, P. and T.O'Brien, 1983.
60. Agbayani, R. 1984.
61. Bureau of Forestry Development, 1986.
62. *Daily Express* (Manila) 1986, 1 March.
63. Lobo, F. 1986.
64. United Nations
65. Upland Multisectoral Policy Working Group, 1986.
66. Cruz, T. 1985.
67. Anderson, J. 1974.
68. Kummer, D. no date.
69. Bellow, W. et. al. (eds) 1982.
70. Ibid.
71. Ibid.
72. Third World Studies Programme, 1983.
73. Ibid.
74. Ibid.
75. Ganapin, D. 1986(a).
76. Limis, D. 1986.
77. Ibid.
78. Basa, V. op.cit.
79. Ibid.
80. Ganapin, D. 1986(b).
81. Ibid.
82. Ibid.
83. Bureau of Forest Development, 1984.
84. Appropriate Technology Centre, 1984.
85. Myers, N. 1984.
86. Olofson, no date.
87. Revilla, A. op.cit.
88. Ibid.
89. Philippine Institute for Development Studies, 1984.
90. Ganapin, D. 1986(a).
91. Agaloos, B. op.cit.
92. *Daily Enquirer* (Manila) 1986, 1 May.
93. *The Malaya* (Manila) 1986, 20 July.
94. Agaloos, B. op.cit.
95. FAO, 1981.
96. Ibid., 1979.
97. Bureau of Forestry Development, 1986.
98. Snow, J. op.cit.
99. Ibid.

100. Ibid.
101. *The Malaya* (Manila) 1986, 22 May.
102. Alunan, M. 1986.
103. Ganapin, D. 1986(a).
104. Alunan, M. op.cit.
105. Ibid.
106. Ibid.
107. Bureau of Forestry Development, 1986.
108. *Manila Bullitin*, 1986, 15 August.
109. Mackenzie, D. 1988.
110. Ibid.
111. Revilla, A. 1985.
112. Gradwolh, J. et.al. 1988.

6.   Thailand

Introduction

Thailand occupies approximately 514,000 sq. km of continental South-East Asia and shares borders with Malaysia, Burma, Laos and Cambodia; geographically it comprises five major regions: the northern highlands; the west and the north-east hills; the central plains; and a southern peninsular. The climate is strongly influenced by the monsoons, which contribute to the creation of forest types quite different from those in the other countries of this region.

The population, estimated as 52m, is expanding at the rate of 1.6% per year.[1] This is a low population expansion rate in Asian terms, but that 87% of the population still live in rural areas and relatively few people are moving into the cities,[2] undoubtedly contributes to the demand for the creation of more farmland at the expense of the forests. The Thai urban economy is totally dominated by the industrial chaos of Bangkok, 59 times larger than the country's second city, Chang Mai, in the north.[3]

Rice and rubber form the base of the national economy; tin also makes a major contribution to exports. In the early part of the 20th century forest produce was the main export but this now accounts for only 1.8% of the GNP.

Culturally Thailand is strongly Buddhist. There are considerable Chinese and tribal populations, but not on the scale of those found in neighbouring Malaysia. There are also numerous refugees along the Cambodian and Laos borders, but in terms of the country as a whole they have little influence.

Thailand's written history dates back to the lowland rice cultures of the south and central regions which have been established for more than 2,000 years. This was the first of many waves of agricultural expansion that continue today. In the 18th and 19th centuries expansion into the forests accelerated considerably with the implementation of large scale drainage and irrigation schemes. Throughout this period Thailand's main exports were forest produce, ranging from teak to tiger skins.

Thailand was never colonized, principally due to a policy of deftly playing off one European power against another. Foreign companies were, however, sold rights to trade or exploit resources, and the government imposed duties on exports. Established in the latter half of the 19th century, this system dominated the trade in teak until the last wholly foreign-owned timber operation left in 1960.

Forest resources and destruction rates: Official figures claim that 115,000 sq. km of forest still remains, approximately 22% of the total land area.[4] The main forest types are: tropical rain forest; dry dipterocarp; dry evergreen; mixed deciduous; pine and mangrove forest. The FAO, however, estimate that at least 40% of the country's broad-leaf forests (everything except the pines) have been heavily over-cut and are in a poor condition.[5] This applies particularly to the mixed deciduous forests with their high proportion of teak.

Thailand is currently losing its forests at the rate of more than 8,000 sq. km per year. Table 6.1 illustrates the extent of loss since 1961.

Few virgin forests remain and, until 1989, they were the main site for the timber industry. At present there is a complete ban on all logging in Thailand, a drastic step that indicates the scale of the country's problems. But, as an FAO report noted, logging is only one problem:

> Where there is logging, shifting cultivation follows fairly rapidly, in such a way that it can be considered that there is never a significant area of logged-over forest: in other words, deforestation in this category [shifting cultivation] is approximately equal to the areas of undisturbed forests logged-over during the corresponding period.[6]

This sequence of events is typical for the region as a whole, but because of Thailand's expanding rural population, is more widespread than in other countries.

Replanting: Thailand has initiated more replanting programmes than other countries in the region, probably because it has lost proportionally more forest than most. The majority of replanting is geared towards the industrial sector in the form of large-scale, softwood plantations. This is starting to change, but so far social forestry projects cover a much smaller area than do commercial plantations. Financial restraints have resulted in a reduction in replanting efforts since 1980. Replanting has, therefore, had little effect on overall forest cover despite the scale of some of the commercial schemes. On average, 800 sq. km were planted each year between 1979 and 1984.[7] Replanting thus covered less than 8% of the forest lost annually. A promising development, however, is the major upsurge in Thailand's environmental movement since the mid 1980s.

As Thai forests are in an advanced form of decay the problems of deforestation are correspondingly more acute, and debate over what should be done, more heated. As Thailand was never colonized responsibility for these problems is perceived as largely domestic rather than solely that of outside forces: a view that promotes greater willingness to accept personal responsibility for the direction Thai development has taken.

The effects of deforestation

Environmental impacts

Soil erosion: More than 170,000 sq. km of Thailand is affected by soil erosion, 140,000 of which is classified as 'severe', according to research from Kasestart University in Bangkok.[8] Erosion problems occur in every region.

Studies from the Northern region found that the annual soil loss in areas of undisturbed forest was approximately 28 tons per square kilometre, while in deforested areas it was between 1,400 and 10,000 tons.[9] In the late 1970s, research into the sediment load on the huge Mekong river found it to be carrying 500 tons of soil for every square kilometre in its catchment area.[10]

This soil loss is beginning to affect crop yields in certain areas. Thin, old and generally infertile laterite soils dominate the north-east, which until recently was covered by tropical dry forest. Today the trees have gone, to be replaced by cassava. Between 1960 and 1982, as erosion increased, average crop yields dropped by more than 15% despite higher inputs of fertilizers and pesticides.[11] In total an estimated 4.4m ha of upland crops have been planted on soils that, according to one report, are totally 'unsuitable for agriculture'.[12]

Only in the central rice-growing plains has the government started to take action to reclaim soil fertility. This, the 'rice-bowl' for much of South-East Asia, is under the control of large landlords. The soils here are becoming increasingly acidic and the government proposes to improve and rehabilitate 123,000 ha.[13] Soil degradation has also led to an increase in Thailand's *alang-alang* grasslands which, by the early 1980s, already covered more than 20,000 sq. km.[14]

Erosion has also reduced the effective lifespan of Thailand's innumerable waterways, irrigation channels and dams; within eight years of the Bumipol dam reservoir's construction, the dam's lifespan had been halved due to sedimentation.[15] Sediment, gathering in the Gulf of Thailand, is also causing problems in fish spawning grounds and blocking major river mouths.

Breaking down of the water cycle: The magazine *Asian Agribusiness*, reviewing Thailand's agricultural performance in 1984 commented that: 'While 1982–83 was the year of the drought for most Thai farmers . . . 1983–84 can unquestionably be called the year of flood.'[16] In 1984 serious flooding occurred in 60 of Thailand's 72 provinces, destroying an estimated 640,000 ha of commercial crops, [17] and Bangkok experienced its worst floods of the 20th century, prompting a massive flood-relief project to protect the capital from the Chao Phraya river. Rather than regenerate the eroded slopes in the upper reaches of the river catchment the government is planning a 120 km flood-relief canal and dike to surround Bangkok, at an estimated cost of at least 20 billion *bhat* (US$ 800m). If this project is implemented Bangkok is again destined to become a walled city.

In November 1988, as a direct result of logging, the most serious floods on record for southern Thailand killed 460 people, left hundreds 'missing',[18] and rendered 70,000 homeless; damage to property was estimated to exceed US$ 40m.[19] In early 1989, as a result of this disaster, the authorities imposed a complete ban on logging.

Little research has been undertaken on widespread changes in the water cycle and the effect on weather patterns. Farmers in the north-east claim that the dry season lasts two months longer than it did 30 years ago; evidence emerging from a number of smaller studies support this, but there is no definite confirmation.[20] Research on the dry deciduous forests in the north found that on average 50% of rain falling on the forest is returned to the atmosphere through evapo-transpiration from the trees.[21] No nationwide study has been carried out but clearly Thai forests are a major source of atmospheric water for many areas. It is therefore reasonable to assume that in common with other countries in this region, rainfall in Thailand's deforested areas has probably decreased.

Wildlife loss: Thailand is unique in that it forms a geographical bridge between the Chinese, Malay and Burmese sub-regions. As a result it has a wide variety of species, although it can claim few of them exclusively, but it does have significant populations of some of the region's rarest fauna and flora.

Thailand is home to an estimated 870 bird species and 263 mammals, including 94 species of bats. In common with elsewhere in the region the large-cat population has decreased severely over the years; currently, Thailand's tiger population is estimated to be fewer than 500. Even the more common elephant is under threat: records just prior to World War Two estimated the wild elephant population to run into tens of thousands; today between 2,400 and 4,000 elephants survive in the wild and fewer than ten of the country's protected areas can claim herds of more than 100.[22] Species even closer to extinction include the Thai crocodile, the mouse deer and the kouprey, a large herbivore similar to an elk, of which fewer than 200 remain.[23] Thailand also has a small population of Sumatran rhino, an indication of the wide natural distribution of this species. The Sarus crane, another native of Thailand, has not been sighted for 20 years.[24] No sightings for many years does not necessarily mean a species is extinct. For example, Gurney's pitta, a small forest bird, was classified as extinct, there having been no sightings for 34 years, but in July 1986 a pair was spotted in the south of the country.[25] The area where they were found was due to be felled by a logging company but because of the sighting it has been saved.

Forest destruction has by no means been the sole cause of wildlife loss in Thailand, there has always been a vigorous trade in wildlife produce. Many of the items banned by the CITES convention, to which Thailand is a signatory, are openly available in Bangkok. Thailand is undoubtedly a major supplier to the markets in Singapore and Hong Kong.

Social and economic costs
Despite occupying little more than 19% of the land area, forests continue to play a vital role in the economy of many rural areas. The official estimation that forest produce contributes as little as 1.8% of GNP has been challenged from many sources; Norman Myers, for example, estimates that forest produce accounts for nearer 7% of GNP.[26] A study from Northern Thailand found that natural forests continue to provide most villages with their building materials, fuel and a variety of minor forest produce, even in national parks and wildlife sanctuaries.[27]

Social conflicts: Because forests still contribute to the welfare of those who live in or near them rivalries over their use are common. Unlike in Malaysia or Indonesia, however, conflicts arise mainly between the government and small farmers; only in the north is there a significant tribal population affected by forest loss. There is little adherence to forestry legislation at the ground level in Thailand as both groups involved, the authorities and the farmers, show little respect for one another. With rebel armies present along most of its borders Thailand has major internal security problems.

In the north, the Karen tribe is highly organized and has a significant armed force calling for self-rule. At one time much of the funding for this army came from the opium crop. Government policy has been to wean tribal farmers away from producing opium and to grow other cash crops. The opium poppy, however, provided a reasonable cash income for the amount of work and area of land required, whereas other crops frequently failed to provide the same income for an equivalent area; consequently, for a village to maintain its income, more forests must be cleared.

The opium trade continues, but the Karen army, now restricted mainly to Burma, have turned to illegal logging and controlling border traffic to sustain their cash supplies. In 1985 the authorities imprisoned more than 5,000 log poachers in the northern region alone.[28] The authorities' attempts to stamp out illegal logging is already costing lives; more than 40 forest officers have been killed trying to protect what is left of the country's timber.[29] Illegal logging is not restricted to rebel tribesmen but, according to recent reports, also involves local and even national politicians.[30]

In the north, however, the scale of illegal logging is due more to a difference in political ideology than simply the greed of a few individuals cutting timber for their own gain. In other parts of the country there has been remarkably little conflict over land rights and forest issues.

Economic losses: Thailand, once the world's largest producer of teak, is now a net importer.[31] Annual timber production has been declining since the mid 1970s to the present three million cubic metres.[32] Today, more than one million cubic metres is imported annually to serve domestic demand.[33] Imports of timber are likely to increase as the logging ban restricts supplies of domestic wood.[34]

This ban will have a dramatic impact on what remains of the timber processing industries, where an estimated 47,000 jobs will be lost, as imported timber is much more expensive, despite the government's reduction of import duties on logs from 7% to 1%.[35] Timber processors, however, cannot always be regarded as innocent victims of the illegal logging operators. Many sawmills knowingly processed illegally felled timber, so to a certain extent, the current timber industry has been built on a non-sustainable resource.

In harsh financial terms, the need to import timber is costing the Thai economy more each year. Even in 1983 the timber industry had an import deficit of more than US$9m.[36] The country now imports 16% of its timber needs.[37]

Replanting the forests will also prove to be a great drain on the Thai economy. The cost of the Green Esarn Plan, a massive replanting programme, will exceed US$800m.[38] Even with such vast sums invested success is not guaranteed, as the Plan is facing widespread hostility from local populations. In short, the overall cost of forest destruction in Thailand has only just begun.

Development of present forest policy

The financial value of forest produce has been recognized for centuries. Forest legislation, however, has developed only since the early part of the 20th century. Thai teak production, which peaked around 1907, was dominated by foreign companies.[39]

In the 1930s the railways opened up the north and north-east of Thailand to the export economy. Prior to 1920, little rice from the north went down to Bangkok, but by 1930 approximately 10% of rice passing through the port was from that region.[40] After World War Two, other cash crops began to appear and what forest the timber industry left was quickly cleared for *kenaf* (a fibrous plant used like jute) and later cassava. The 9,000 ha of *kenaf* in 1952 was, by 1965, increased to more than 420,000 ha.[41]

Throughout the 20th century, central government enacted various items of forestry legislation, but rural development policy was left in the hands of individual ministries. The result was a confusing patchwork of laws, frequently in contradiction with more general development policy.

Forest legislation
In 1896 the Royal Forestry Department was established and, within two years, two Acts were passed: the Preservation of Forests; and the Teak Tree Preservation Acts; both designed to save valuable timber species. In 1913 these were repealed by the Preservation of Forests Act, which established the present administrative structure for forest management. General preservation of timber supplies, however, continued to be the major goal of forest legislation.

In 1941, just prior to Thailand's involvement in World War Two, the Forest Act was passed. The first forest classifications system was laid down, with Productive and Protective forest. This was the first official recognition that forests played a protective role in the environment. Critics, however, see this as an administrative Act that simply increased the number of restricted species and fines for breaking the law.

The problems facing shifting farmers were recognized early in Thailand and in 1953 the Social Justice Land Reform Act was passed, in an attempt to provide land tenureship for landless farmers. This remarkably radical and enlightened piece of legislation, however, was rarely implemented due to opposition within government.

The first Wildlife Sanctuaries and Non-hunting Areas were established under the 1960 Wild Animal Reservation and Protection Act. This was geared towards species preservation rather than ecosystem maintenance, although it prohibited private land-ownership as well as a wide range of activities, including interfering with trees, cutting any vegetation, and grazing animals; access to these areas was limited. Hunting, for permit holders, is allowed in Wildlife Sanctuaries but completely banned on Non-hunting Areas. Transgression of this Act can result in remarkably severe penalties of two year gaol sentences and fines of up to US$1,000. In legal terms, the Non-hunting Areas are the most protected forests in Thailand, although implementing the Act in remote locations has proved to be difficult. By 1984, 64 Wildlife Sanctuaries and Non-hunting Areas had been established covering 5,656 and 2,526 sq. km respectively.

In 1961, to facilitate the development of a national park network, the National Parks Act was passed. Except that people were allowed to enter, restrictions for national parks are the same as those for Wildlife and Non-hunting Areas. Management is by the Royal Forestry Department, but administration and policy is decided by the National Parks Commission. National Parks can be established only by Royal Decree, a lengthy process but one that is equally difficult to annul. At present there are 49 national parks covering 2.5m ha. Some of these are immensely popular with the Thai public but, in common with other protected areas, the authorities encounter problems when trying to implement farming and hunting restrictions in the more remote areas.

One of the more innovative projects attempting to protect these areas from such problems is in the Khao Yai National Park in the Central Region. With help from the WWF and the IUCN the Forestry Department is implementing an integrated development plan for settlers within, and adjacent to, the park.[42] This pilot project centres around the village of Ban Sap Tai, where the villagers are being provided with general infrastructure and technical assistance to improve farm yields. The greatest innovation has been the establishment of a local credit bank. Local money-lenders were charging interest well in excess of 50% and farmers found themselves increasingly in debt, which was forcing them to clear more forest to grow cash crops in order to pay their debts. The credit co-operative, known as the Environmental Protection Society, provides loans at 12% interest on the understanding that farmers do not intrude into the Park. One difficulty is that eligibility for participation in the plan is dependent upon a farmer having land rights. Apart from this aspect, however, small credit co-operatives could prove to be invaluable for relieving the pressure on farmers to grow cash crops to pay off debts.

The most general forest legislation is the National Forest Reserves Act, passed in 1964, which established a system of Forest Reserves with restrictions similar to those in National Parks. The major differences are that management is controlled by an individual committee for each area and that various government departments can issue a wide range of permits. Local populations have grazing rights, but may settle only with a residence permit. These areas, however, can be deregulated relatively easily and therefore do not guarantee a secure future for forests.

Current forest policy
A major criticism of Thailand's forest legislation is that it is concerned more with administrative systems than with developing a coherent policy. The current crisis in forestry, however, owes more to general rural development policy than to forest legislation.

Thailand's development programmes are organized in five-year plans. The First Plan (1961–66) recommended the maintenance of forest cover over 50% of the country. This was to be achieved by encouraging the private timber sector to replant concessions, and through the protection of specific areas, such as wildlife reserves and national parks.

By the Second Plan (1967–71) the government began to realize the scale of the deforestation problem. A target of 22,400 ha of reafforestation was proposed, with the Forest Industries Organisation (a government quango), and the state-owned Thai Plywood Company, taking the lead. The first forest village programme was established as a means of involving local people in reafforestation efforts, but the species planted were to meet the needs of the timber industry rather than those of the local population. The programme made little impact on the rate of forest loss across the country as a whole. During the same period planting trees to protect watershed areas was started.

The Third Plan (1971–76) accepted the failure of its predecessor and proposed the establishment of 37,200 ha of plantations over the five years. Considering that more than 500,000 ha of forest was being cleared annually during this period, the replanting programme was totally inadequate. In 1973 a more vigorous step was taken when Royal Decree No. 33 banned the export of all high-value, hardwood logs, including teak. The role in forest destruction played by the rural poor and the expansion of cash crops, however, continued to be ignored.

The Fourth Plan (1977–82) increased plantation expectations to 80,000 ha, but still for timber production. The role of the shifting farmer was at last recognized and 'occupational rights' were issued to many landless farmers; this gave them cultivation and grazing rights but no firm tenureship. The ban on log exports was extended to include sawn timber, as it was a simple matter for timber smugglers to saw logs. During the Fifth Plan (1982–87) a 'National Forestry Policy' was being developed, which was partially adopted in October 1987.

The National Forestry Policy aims to replant and expand the present forest area until 40% of Thailand is once more forested. One-third of this would be conservation or protected forest, the remainder commercial forest. This is to be achieved by a massive awareness campaign combined with enforcing regulations on the timber industry and promoting replanting at all levels of society. At current replanting rates it will take the Forestry Department an estimated 200 years to replant this area and the authorities are therefore relying heavily on investment by the private sector.[43]

To reduce forest destruction rates the authorities began taking strong measures against illegal logging. Many timber operators lost their licences, and corruption within the forestry department was reduced as mass transfers of personnel were imposed.[44] The total ban on commercial logging imposed in 1989 was partially due to the lack of progress in trying to 'clean up' the timber industry.

The 'occupational rights' programme is now being expanded as a means of encouraging landless farmers to stop clearing forests to plant crops. By 1988 these rights had been conferred on some 1.2m landless families, linked, for most of them, to the social replanting programmes.[45]

The policy takes a rather classical approach to the problem with an emphasis on large-scale planting and only limited promotion of social forestry. It is surprising that so much emphasis is placed on investment by the private sector when this has been tried since the 1960s and has clearly failed. As one analyst put it: 'The National Forestry Policy and Sixth Five year plan are full of generalities but short on specific incentives.'[46]

Even with the new policy there are major problems that need to be addressed if the government is to have any chance of saving the country's forests. The influential Thai Development Research Institute claims that government strategies are relatively ineffectual due to: inadequate co-operation between departments; an obsolete legal framework; poor land-use planning; and the absence of an effective enforcement programme.[47]

The replanting programmes initiated by the authorities have had little influence over the general rate of forest destruction but they are outlined here as some have great potential, if government plans for expansion are realized.

Replanting programmes

By the mid 1980s approximately 4.8m ha of forest had been replanted;[48] Table 6.2 illustrates the mix of the programmes so far.

Timber plantations: Three major institutions dominate this sector: the Royal Forestry Department (RFD); the Forestry Industries Organization (FIO); and the Thai Plywood Company. By 1982 the RFD had established 394,000 ha of plantations, the FIO 50,000 ha and Thai Plywood 2,700 ha.[49]

The programme established by the RFD involves three major objectives: environmental protection; industrial production; and enrichment planting for logged-over forest. To cover this range of functions they have included 88 different tree species. The largest area has been planted with eucalyptus, for industrial production. The programme's success has been limited, as the RFD admit: 'In the ten year period 1970–80, only one third of the 60,000 hectares replanted could be considered fully established. The rest was destroyed by fire and degraded by farmers.'[50] Illegal logging has also taken a toll, bringing survival rates on some plantations down to 10%.[51]

The low survival rates reflect a general lack of investment from central government. In 1984 the RFD had hoped to establish 48,000 ha of plantation but their funding allowed for only 19,000 ha.[52] New financial commitments were announced in 1988 and hopefully this will enable a full programme to be initiated.[53] For environmentalists this investment has proved to be a mixed blessing as commercial plantations continue to be dominated by eucalyptus, a tree that has faced widespread criticism throughout Asia. All three institutions are, however, also involved in social forestry projects, which have a much greater potential for addressing the fundamental reasons for forest destruction.

Forest villages: These programmes have taken an integrated approach with as much emphasis on relieving rural poverty as on reafforestation. The first projects were started under the National Land Allotment Committee in 1956. Since then all the major agencies have been involved in one or more of the following projects: Integrated water management project (1965); Forest villages programme (FIO and Thai Plywood) (1967); Forest villages programme (RFD) (1975); People's voluntary tree planting programme (1978); Village woodlot (fuelwood) programme (1981).

1)   Thai Plywood and FIO Forest Villages: Most programmes employ the Burmese *taungya* system of interplanting commercial tree species with subsistence crops, resulting in a village surrounded by a timber plantation combined with crops that also provide food for the local population. Each village is limited to 100 families.

The annual rate of tree-planting is 160 ha, and this rate is maintained until sufficient trees have been planted to ensure a continuous supply of the chosen timber. For teak trees to reach maturity the full programme requires 60 years; that is, 9,600 ha of teak will need to be planted in order to maintain a sustainable annual supply of 160 ha of harvestable trees. Softwood species need 20 or 30 years to mature, therefore a smaller area may be planted.

Each family is allocated 1.6 ha each year on which to grow crops and plant trees. The intercropping continues for three years, after which the first 1.6 ha site is left untouched to enable the trees to mature. Each family also has 0.16 ha under permanent cultivation as a kitchen garden.

These projects are successful because they take account of the needs of the local population. The trees remain the property of the FIO or Thai Plywood but villagers receive cash bonuses for every tree in their care that reaches maturity. By the early 1980s most families were earning approximately US$700 per year from cash crops and bonuses, a considerably higher figure than the average Thai rural income.[54] The FIO and Thai Plywood also provide infrastructure, such as schools and medical care, as well as roads, which provide access to the market economy, enabling villagers to earn cash from their food crops if they wish.

Land ownership is still retained by the institution involved, a policy that may cause future problems. It was originally hoped that 2,000 such villages would be set up to replant 32,000 ha, mainly under fast growing softwoods. The project started well, with 26 villages established by 1981, but by 1987 this had increased to only 35.[55] Direct government funding has since been withdrawn, before one full cycle of the timber crop has been completed, in the hope that the private sector will follow their lead. Although the government has given large commitments to other replanting efforts, the withdrawal of direct funding seems rather short-sighted as these villages are spearheading afforestation in Thailand. Many private investors will be examining how successful these schemes are before investing in similar projects.

2)   Royal Forest Department Villages: Although the aim of these is very similar to that of the FIO villages – producing timber – the approach differs in that the area to be rehabilitated is determined less according to the demand for timber than the scale of deforestation in the area. RFD villages

are larger, involving 250–300 families on average, and unlike FIO and Thai Plywood villages, the participants are always native to the area to be replanted. Thus, those who have cut the original forests are involved in replanting them.

The RFD gathers the volunteer families, often from scattered, pioneer communities, into a central 'village' area where each family has rights over 2.4 ha of crop land. The initial goal is to replant at least 20% of the area in the total scheme at a rate of at least 160 ha per year. Each family is responsible for the upkeep of one particular replanted area, thus seeing the process through from beginning to end. Only two members from each family are directly employed in the project, and only 30 families are represented for every 160 ha block. Those directly involved are guaranteed regular wages on a local scale. A variety of incentives are also offered for producing good quality timber, but the trees remain the property of the RFD.

By 1985 the RFD had established 75 villages and they are generally considered to be a positive development. The most important factor has been that the participants themselves regard the projects as successful and their living standards as having improved.[56] This programme is due to be expanded as the experience gained will be integrated with the government's US$800m Green Esarn Plan.[57]

Thailand's experience of forest village projects has undoubtedly been of great value. The other programmes mentioned are either more specialized – for example woodlots – or have taken a less integrated and sustained approach, such as the People's Voluntary Tree Planting Programme. The villages are a further illustration that despite the fact that local farmers have largely contributed to the problem, they can also contribute substantially to its solution.

Present causes of forest destruction

The Thai authorities claim that the rate of forest destruction in the late 1980s has been lower than for many years. In terms of area this is true, but this apparently encouraging trend is due more to a lack of forest to cut than to a changed attitude towards forests. Lowland farmers, moving into the hills to produce both subsistence and cash crops, are currently clearing the largest area of forest. The timber industry still plays an important role in forest loss, but despite widespread illegal felling the blanket ban on logging will reduce its impact. Government-controlled development programmes, such as large dam construction and the security road programme have, however, aggravated the problem further.

Agricultural expansion and population growth

Rural population expansion and the promotion of cash crops for export are the underlying causes of demand for new land. Of Thailand's 52m people 43m inhabit the rural areas.[58] As the population grows, large numbers of people will be either seeking farming land or moving into the cities. According to Dr Shlomo Angel, a UN adviser on human settlement patterns:

> Between 1961 and 1982 the rural population grew by 19 million people. About four million were absorbed by Bangkok, other urban areas, and government sponsored schemes. So where did the other 15 million go?[59]

The answer, he claims, is the forest.

Approximately 24.4m ha are under cultivation in Thailand, but only 3.7m ha carry legal land titles.[60] In the mid 1980s an estimated 330,000 ha of forest were being cleared each year to make way for crops.[61] Dr Bhumibhamom notes that: 'Production [of crops] since 1960 has been directly correlated to the enlargement of the deforested area.'[62] But there is more to this than simply an expanding population trying to feed itself, as the Ministry of Agriculture and Co-operatives notes:

> Agriculture in the squatter area is clearly commercialized as opposed to subsistence . . . on average, upland farmers growing commodities for export have higher incomes than the rain fed farmers in the valleys.[63]

The government faces a dilemma because those clearing the forests are contributing to the export economy. Agricultural exports account for more than 60% of Thailand's foreign earnings and the authorities have no wish to alienate such a productive, if unofficial, industry.[64] As a result, although the RFD designates vast areas as protected forest, there is scant chance of enforcement.

One reason why farmers in these freshly cleared areas enjoy a higher standard of living is that they no longer pay rent, unlike in the central, 'rice bowl' region, where of the 4.6m ha farmed, 4.1m are worked by tenant farmers. [65] Table 6.3 shows that the proportion of tenant farmers is lower in other parts of the country, but nevertheless illustrates that the most fertile areas are controlled by relatively few individuals. The problem is far less acute than in many parts of the Philippines, but the same underlying trend is clear.

It may be the landless who actually cut down the trees, but the large landowners' role can be considerably more direct than that of simply shifting the peasant farmer. In the South there are many cases of sugar-cane landlords actually paying landless farmers to cut down forests.[66] The landlord then disregards these peasant farmers for three to five years, during which time the tree stumps will have rotted and the area can then be ploughed. Leaving the peasant farmer to his own devices for this period also means that the landowner is not closely implicated in the initial deforestation process. At the end of the three to five years the landlord makes a claim over this deforested but 'unclaimed' land; the then once more landless farmer moves on to cut another area of forest. This devious system enables the large landlord to seem remote from the deforestation problem while in fact playing a central role. Timber companies have used similar methods.[67]

In the northern region the situation is in some ways similar; the role of the rural poor is by no means innocuous, but the damage they inflict is frequently exaggerated. Dr Ramitanondh, in a recent UN report said: 'the people who have done far more harm to the forests of northern Thailand were, and continue to be, those who occupy the medium to high socio-economic strata.'[68]

The development of Thailand's cassava export trade is illustrative of the variety of people who are putting pressure on the country's forests. It is worth looking at this trade in some detail because this crop is produced almost entirely for export to the industrialized nations.

The cassava connection: Cassava was introduced to Thailand on a large scale in the 1960s. This tough root crop will grow on a wide variety of soils and is to be found in most areas where rice cultivation is limited. After its introduction, the government quickly promoted it as the most valuable cash crop, and large cassava estates developed in the east and central areas of the country. Once cassava became established, the Eastern Province suffered a period of its most rapid forest loss: forest cover fell from 41% in 1973 to 21% by 1982.[69]

Forest loss in the north-east has been 3.5% per year since the 1970s.[70] Today, 60% of this agricultural land is under cassava.[71] Growers here, however, are small pioneer farmers, frequently squatters, not large estate owners. Cassava rapidly emerged as the most popular cash crop when the European Economic Community's (EEC) demand for it as cattle feed grew.

At present Thailand exports at least 5.5m tons of cassava to the EEC each year. In 1982, exports to this market alone exceeded eight million tons.[72] Naturally, the Thais do not wish to lose the EEC's custom, and in order to satisfy this, forest clearance by squatter farmers is frequently ignored. But this uncontrolled growth provides no long-term solution for either the Thai economy or its environment; cassava crop yields have been decreasing despite increased inputs of fertilizers and pesticides.[73] The north-east is rapidly becoming semi-arid territory and has become the centre of government efforts to replant the forests.

Ironically, the production of cassava feeds a trade cycle that finally ends back in Thailand. The EEC's cassava imports are used mainly as cattle feed, contributing to an excessive production of milk, much of which is dried and then dumped on Third World markets. 'Dutch Lady' brand dried milk is available throughout South-East Asia, where for many years it was promoted as better for babies than human milk. Thus, the profits from cassava may be spent on dried milk for Thai babies.

The hill tribe problem

Responsibility for forest destruction has been imputed largely to the hill tribes of Northern Thailand. Newspaper headlines concentrate excessive attention on these tribes' contribution to the problem. The north does have serious deforestation problems, but so does the rest of Thailand, as a recent UN report noted:

> In the central region the swiddenists turned the reserved and unreserved forests into permanent fields of sugar cane, cassava and maize. In the North Eastern region, the swiddenists turned thousands of hectares of dry evergreen and dry dipterocarp forest into permanent fields of kenaf, maize, cassava and upland rice. In the southern region they also changed thousands of hectares of dense tropical evergreen forests into permanent rubber plantation areas.[74]

The north, however, has quite specific forest problems that are worth examining in some detail.

The region as a whole has probably around 5,000 sq. km under some kind of shifting cultivation cycle.[75] Dr Sriburi of Chulalongkorn University estimates that the tribes clear between 300 and 400 sq. km of forest each year.[76] In contrast, the National Security Chief for Thailand was recently quoted as estimating that they were clearing 1,600 sq. km of forest annually.[77] The major problem is that in attempting to identify who is responsible for forest loss there is a tendency to classify all the tribal groups as a single entity, and to blame them, when the responsibility may lie with other social groups. In certain areas of the north, the lowland Thai population is very active in forest clearance; the Thai media rarely mention their contribution to the problem. The hill tribes are by no means blameless, but neither are they the sole cause of Thailand's forest problems.

Table 6.4 outlines the major tribal groups present in the area and the nature of their agricultural system. In the north three distinct types of traditional farming methods are practised. The following classification is based on the work of Chapman, Sabasri and Kunstadter in their book *Farmers in the Forest*, one of the most thorough studies of traditional farming in the region.

- Short cultivation, short fallow: generally practised by the lowland Thai farmers and rarely found above 400 metres. These are often secondary farming sites used by farmers who have land holdings in the valleys.

Rice, vegetables, maize and beans are the major crops. Few cash crops are grown as the wet rice paddy in the valley provides the family income. The generally rapid rotation of the land for fallow periods leaves the soils little or no time to recover between planting. The forest rarely regenerates, even to a secondary stage, and rough scrub eventually dominates. In short, this is a typical form of destructive shifting agriculture practised by few traditional tribal farmers.

• Short cultivation, long fallow: practised by the most established upland farmers in the region, the Karen and Lua tribes. Cultivation is for one year and the farmer then abandons the fields before soil fertility and crop yields drop. Given a choice, the tribes will return to an abandoned plot only after ten years, but today this recovery period is shorter due to a combination of population pressure and encroachment by lowland farmers. The Karen, by far the largest tribal group in northern Thailand, have attracted much critiscism because of this farming system. One of the most common arguments employed is that they use more land than is necessary. The short cultivation period means sites are changed frequently and, therefore, new areas must be as frequently cleared. But this is a misapprehension because the Karen prefer secondary forest sites, thus, over a ten to 20 year period, the area of virgin land used is usually minimal.

Forest cover is always maintained along the ridges and near rivers. There is also a significant area of sacred forest near the villages. In contrast to the methods used by lowland farmers in the region, when traditional Karen clear the forest, fires are set carefully and kept under control. A complex system of inter-cropping helps prevent soil erosion; for example the Lua cultivate 75 food crops, 21 medicinal plants and 27 plants for decorative or ceremonial purposes.[79]

A major factor for the success of this system is that it is practised in the most fertile upland zone. The Karen and the Lua have been established in the area for several centuries and hence are well-adapted to the environment. They avoid the higher ground, above 1,000 metres, and it is here that the more recently arrived tribes have settled.

• Long cultivation, very low fallow: is found over the 1,000 metre mark and is practised by the Lahu, Lisu, Meo and Akha tribes. The major difference from the Karen and Lua systems is that the land is cultivated until crop yields drop; that is after four or five years, by which time the soil's fertility has collapsed. The area is then abandoned for as long as possible, which today may be no more than four or five years. Staple crops are rice and maize, the main cash crop is the opium poppy, which needs relatively fertile soils, preferably freshly cleared forest. For the grower it is an attractive crop commanding a comparatively high price with a regular and expanding market.

Thailand's opium boom occurred in the 1970s. In 1970 the authorities estimated that northern Thailand produced 150 tons of the drug.[80] For the small farmer, payments from the opium war-lords were frequently more reliable than development funding from the government. Lack of development in the region undoubtedly made opium the most popular means of earning cash.

International government campaigns against the trade have made a strong impression on the poppy growers. By 1985 the authorities estimated that only 35 tons came out of the area.[81] The anti-opium campaigns funded by the US have contributed to this success; but they were also responsible for damaging large areas of forest by, at one point, attempting to spray the poppy fields from the air with 'agent orange', a highly toxic defoliant. But because the opium fields were small and isolated, the spray frequently over-ran the target, resulting in the destruction of large areas of forest, which were replaced by bamboo. The narrow leaves of bamboo are relatively impervious to this broad leaf defoliant.

In total, an estimated 70% of the forests above the 800 metre mark have been cleared in the northern region.[82] Responsibility for this is laid mainly on the tribal groups, but underdevelopment is an equally culpable factor. With no other opportunities to enter the cash economy it is hardly surprising that tribal people grow the only crop that fetches a good price in the region. These remote hill tribes received more in the way of economic development from the growth in the US market for heroin than they did from the development departments in Bangkok. When the income from opium was threatened, thus undermining the area's cash economy, the insurgency problem increased. The main Karen army units, despite having retreated into north-eastern Burma, continue to be active in the north of Thailand and along the borders.

There was a change in development emphasis during the 1980s. Criticism of tribal people in the region has not diminished, but at least some positive steps are being taken about development in the area.

Present tribal development policy
In 1976 the government produced a declaration on tribal development designed to 'integrate' the tribes into the Thai economy while maintaining their cultural independence.[83] The strategy had three major points; to promote economic growth by introducing new crops and cultivation techniques; to rehabilitate the existing deforested areas through agroforestry and general reafforestation schemes; and to substitute the opium poppy with other cash crops.

Superficially, the policy looks viable, but more than 15 major agencies are involved in its implementation, with each organization or agency having its own priorities, resulting in projects frequently overlapping.[84] One example, the King's Royal Project, just outside Chang Mai, promotes the cultivation of market garden produce by tribal groups. As far as the tribal people are concerned, this project has been a success, but the Forestry Department is less pleased, as a recent article noted:

> Encouraged by the Royal Project to plant vegetables and flowers the hill tribes practice slash and burn agriculture. And attracted by the good life brought about by the Kings Project, or assistance from other government agencies on Doi Inthanon [National Park and Thailand's most holy mountain] hill tribesmen from other areas have migrated to the national park.[85]

There has been no major shift in the management of these programmes. The goal of developing the local economy makes sense, but its current implementation, in common with much forestry policy, is hampered by poor co-ordination.

Fuelwood consumption

Fuelwood users fall into two major categories; industrial charcoal and tobacco producers; and domestic consumers. It is almost impossible to estimate the quantity of fuel consumed in the domestic sector. Current estimates put the total (domestic and industrial) annual consumption at 73m cubic metres, but this at best is a very rough estimate.[86]

The quantity of charcoal produced today is unknown, but it is a flourishing trade. At present the major official source of charcoal are the mangroves, providing more than one million cubic metres of charcoal per year.[87] On average it takes eight kilos of wood to produce one kilo of charcoal; the pressure on Thai forests is therefore considerable.[88]

A similar situation prevails in Thailand's tobacco industry; 44,000 ha are currently under this crop, mainly in small holdings.[89] It has been estimated that timber from one hectare of forest is required to cure tobacco produced from one hectare of land.[90] Thailand's tobacco industry consumes prodigious quantities of wood: it is still used as fuel by 67% of tobacco curing plants.[91] Thailand's growing trade in tobacco, of which 65% is exported, thus places a further burden on its forests.[92]

Rural development policy

Roads: The expansion of any transport network frequently opens up previously inaccessible forest areas. By the late 1970s few areas of Thailand were remote from the highway system. This in itself could be regarded as an inevitable part of the development process. In Thailand, however, road construction goes hand-in-hand with the eradication of insurgency groups; many roads are constructed for security rather than local development needs.

Many new security roads, which rarely appear on maps, lead to areas where farmers are actively encouraged to clear land only recently reclaimed from rebel forces. The office of Accelerated Rural Development (ARD) is responsible for road construction and development in regions with insurgency problems. The government classifies 56 of Thailand's 72 Provinces as areas requiring work by the ARD.[93] Meanwhile, the Royal Forestry Department is trying to keep farmers out of the forest, but apparently security issues override environmental considerations. Eventually, problems due to deforestation may well create their own security problems, in which case the two departments will have to work together. At present, however, old rivalries are likely to persist; a situation only the politicians can solve.

Large dam projects: Thailand, with its long history of irrigation and canal construction, has developed a major dam-building industry. For example, some of the largest dams constructed so far include: Bhumibol, 318 sq. km; Khao Leam, 353 sq. km; Sirikit, 260 sq. km; Sirindhorn, 292 sq. km; Srinagarind, 419 sq. km; and Ubolratana, 410 sq. km.

The surface area gives little indication of how much forest may be destroyed. As Dr Nart Tuntawiroon and Dr Poonsab Samootsakorn of Mahidol University note: 'The building of dams . . . sets off an uncontrollable chain reaction of destruction which eventually destroys far more forest than the area which is drowned by a dam's reservoir.'[94] The proposed Nam Choan dam, (see case studies) on the upper reaches of the Kwai River, aroused particularly strong opposition in Thailand. The damage that can be inflicted by dams on the surrounding forest is well illustrated, in this case by the scale of illegal logging after survey roads were constructed.

Resettlement programmes: The government has initiated a number of resettlement programmes in forest areas. These projects cover more than one million hectares, although how much forest was cleared to accommodate them is not clear. General development policies undoubtedly affect a large area of forest, but these Thai resettlement projects cannot be considered on the same scale as transmigration programmes in Indonesia or Malaysia.

Four main categories of resettlement projects are operated by the government: general aid; flood victim; marginal populations; and political relocations.[95] General aid projects, aimed at relieving rural and urban poverty by relocation, represent the largest category, with 30 sites covering 740,000 ha. Flood victim projects relocate people from areas flooded by dams; eight of these cover a total 197,803 ha. The marginal population programme, occupying 194,552 ha aims to move people out of rebel-controlled areas and to provide them with basic development needs elsewhere, thus isolating the rebels. The political relocation programme is closely linked to the ARD road construction policy noted earlier; the present five sites cover 31,000 ha.

The timber industry

The total ban on logging may be seen as a somewhat drastic measure, but it is reasonable in view of the state of Thailand's timber industry. The scale of illegal logging and the administrative chaos in respect of legitimate operations, rendered the industry almost uncontrollable. As one influential Thai journalist put it in 1986: 'Forest destruction by hill tribes and landless farmers has been rampant, it's true, but these are no match to the destruction by illegal loggers.'[96]

Official figures on the industry were frequently unreliable or blatantly out of date. In 1985, while the RFD still registered 196,000 sq. km of Thailand as under timber concessions, although many of these were inactive, they also claimed that only 115,000 sq. km of forest remained in the country.[97]

By the mid 1980s, while officially most timber concessions were inactive, it has since become clear that many continued to extract timber. This continued production was geared towards meeting domestic demand rather than an export market. In 1985 the RFD claimed that domestic timber consumption had declined by 40% since 1979, which is highly unlikely.[98] The trade figures for timber entering and leaving Thailand were also similarly unreliable, showing excessive fluctuations from year to year, as Table 6.5 shows.

In 1988, before the logging ban, Thailand was already importing an estimated one million cubic metres of timber annually, a figure that is expected to increase three-fold when the ban became fully operative.[99]

The Thai timber industry provides a clear example of how voluntary restraint rather than firmly implemented regulation can have disastrous consequences. Before the ban the industry traded in 180 different species, providing a wider resource base than that of most of its neighbours.[100] But firm regulations on how extraction should take place were absent, and even adherence to the concept of sustainable forestry was never enforced. As a result, clear felling was much more common than in other countries. The tacit philosophy guiding Thai timber production has been to clear-fell natural forest and at some later date to establish plantations to sustain future supplies. To date less than 90,000 ha of logged forest have had the benefit of any level of enrichment planting.[101]

Extraction methods employed in many legitimate operations, however, were far less environmentally damaging than those elsewhere in South-East Asia. This was primarily due to the widespread use of elephants, rather than heavy machinery, to pull out logs; almost 2,000 elephants are working in the Thai timber industry.[102] Elephants have a number of advantages over bulldozers; they are cheap to buy and maintain, they work on local fuel sources and do not need expensive foreign spare parts. Environmentally, too, elephants are far more efficient. They can pull logs along relatively small tracks, disturbing a minimal number of surrounding trees and, unlike bulldozers, they do not churn up the soils. They can also work on steeper slopes and an operator has enough control over them to ensure they step over individual saplings, thus protecting the next generation of trees.

Thailand is now training elephants for work in the forests of Java and Sumatra. Thailand and Burma were the only countries in the region to use elephants on a regular basis.

In all other aspects, however, Thai timber policy has been ineffectual in preventing deforestation. The timber industry will now be reliant on the commercial plantation sector, which is obviously due for rapid expansion.

Plantations: Thailand's replanting policy has been mainly one of afforestation; that is, planting trees on land that has been deforested for at least 50 years; most commercial replanting is thus not near the deforestation front line. Two major timber plantation types have been developed; fast-growing softwoods and teak.

Thailand's fast-growing industrial plantations are to accommodate a swiftly increasing demand for paper, wood chips and charcoal; in 1983 charcoal exports totalled 70m kg.[103] The plantation sector is dominated by eucalyptus, despite RFD claims that it regularly plants 88 different species. Eucalyptus will continue to form the basis of reafforestation efforts, with major international companies, such as the British-Dutch company Shell, becoming involved in this type of plantation.[104]

There is a strong case against the use of this family of trees for afforestation and it has become Asia's most controversial tree. In India, where opposition to eucalyptus plantations is strongest, local people have destroyed millions of seedlings.[105] It is a combination of the tree's ecological impact and the politics of establishing such plantations that has aroused such passions. Eucalyptus grows exceptionally fast, but to achieve this it consumes prodigious quantities of water. In many cases in India it has been responsible for lowering water tables and depriving farmland of water supplies. In addition, it provides poor shade and is thus unsuitable for inter-planting with food crops. These trees have also developed a reputation for producing too many toxins in their leaf litter to enable other plants to grow beneath them; a problem compounded by the fact that they continually drop leaves throughout the year. Eucalyptus is, therefore, of little use in agro-forestry.

How many farmers may have been moved off squatted land in order to establish these plantations is not clear. The largest wood chip producer in the country, Yuan Heng Lee Wood Industry Co. Ltd, has established more than 1,600 ha of eucalyptus, and planned a further 4,800 ha by 1990.[106] The general manager was recently quoted as claiming: 'We only launch our plantations in non-farming areas and no farmers would sell fertile land to us for that purpose.'[107] Possibly, but how many squatter farmers are in a position to 'sell' their land? Considering that large areas of the north-east are planted with crops, despite their unsuitability for permanent agriculture, these 'non-farming' areas may house significant populations. A similar state of affairs applies to the Shell plantations, which will dwarf any previous projects and cover 20,000 ha, to produce woodchips for export to Japan and South Korea.[108]

To some extent the government sees eucalyptus planting as an emergency measure, to be succeeded by longer-term teak production. If this actually happens the strategy is understandable, but the temptation to retain eucalyptus plantations, once the first crop has been taken, rather than progress to teak, may prove too strong. At present, however, the Thais are acutely aware of the need to attract commercial investment into tree planting, and eucalyptus plantations seem the only way.

Teak plantations fall into two major categories; social forestry projects (already dealt with) and commercial-scale teak plantations, run by provincial forestry companies in which the government's Forest Industries Organisation (FIO) holds 51% of the shares. The FIO obtains most of its income from the fees collected from logging companies in each Province.

These companies are concerned not only with timber production, but also the implementation of many watershed rehabilitation projects. They claim to plant 26 species to cover their needs but have found teak to be the best multi-purpose tree. Teak plantations are worked on a 30-year cycle, although with recent developments in the processing sector some claim the cycle can be reduced to 20 years, which in terms of investment makes teak almost comparable to eucalyptus or conifers.

Plantations of this kind have had a limited success, but the survival rate up to harvesting falls short of that under social forestry projects. Thailand's commercial teak plantations may be more highly developed than most in South-East Asia, but they have experienced problems similar to those in other countries: pest attacks and local peoples' resistance. In so far as producing timber, however, the success of Thailand's commercial teak plantations has been sufficient to provide log poachers with a significant source of income.

Commercial teak plantations may have contributed to the reafforestation efforts so desperately needed in Thailand, but even combined with a logging ban in natural forest, the effect on deforestation is limited. If the National Forestry Policy is to become a reality, a major effort is essential in order to end illegal logging.

Illegal logging

Since the late 1970s illegal logging has become highly organized. As Professor Suraphol Sudara of the Siam Environment Club commented: 'Money talks very big and very loud in forestry in Thailand.'[109]

The scale of operations is incredible. Already, in the late 1970s, sawmills were producing 6.5m cubic metres of timber annually from a legal annual production of 2.5m cubic metres.[110] In the 1980s the RFD conveniently stopped publishing the sawmills' production figures.

By the early 1980s parts of the north and north-east were experiencing poachers hijacking freight trains to transport contraband timber. The logs were loaded on, at gunpoint, and freighted to the outskirts of Bangkok, which is surrounded by sawmills desperate for timber to process. In 1983 the rail workers went on strike until the rail company dropped charges brought against drivers who had been hijacked.[111] Even the head of Thailand's railway system admitted little could be done to counter such highly organized crime.

Today, many illegal logs are transported by road. Since 1986, with the appointment of Harn Linanond as Minister for Agriculture and Cooperatives, raids by the authorities have become more frequent. More than 50,000 cubic metres of illegally felled timber were seized by the authorities in the early 1980s, although this is clearly only a small portion of what has been taken from the forests.[112] The following examples reported in the national press during 1986 give some idea of the scale of the problem: May, police seized what they described as a 'huge quantity of illegally processed teak and teak logs' being carried in a convoy of more than ten trucks in the north-west region.[113] In September more than 240 teak logs and 800 teak planks were found in two raids near Tak along the Burmese border.[114] By November, satellite photographs of the forest around the proposed Nam Choan showed what the *Bangkok Post* described as:

> Vast areas . . . laid to waste . . . Gangs, including villagers backed by influential merchants and corrupt officials have been cutting trees and bamboo on 10,000 rai [1,600 hectares] for three years.

The authorities found more than 13 previously unknown truck routes leading out of the area.[115] Officially this entire area is a national park. In December, more than 1,000 teak logs were found near Tak, in the north-east, but no arrests were made.[116]

There have been many accusations that local government officials are involved in the trade, but few convictions are brought against the organizers. Smaller-scale operations lack the political clout to bribe officials, so more ingenious methods are used to by-pass the laws. One method popular in the north is to manipulate the right to fell timber for local house construction. In the early 1980s houses with two-foot thick solid teak floors and walls began to appear; huge, solid beams were always used, even if they supported nothing. The timber buyer would then come along and buy the house, not the timber. Thus the law forbidding felling timber except for domestic construction was not broken.[117]

The state of the processing sector in Thailand is further confused by large quantities of illegally felled logs arriving from Burma. A climax was reached in 1986 when the 'Burmese logging scandal' led to the resignation of the Commerce Minister, Surat Osathanugrah.[118] He had given two companies permission to process 80,000 cubic metres of unregistered Burmese teak logs; all Burmese logs exported are numbered, unregistered logs could therefore only be illegally felled. The main source of such timber is the border region, controlled in parts by the rebel Karen army. In effect, the Minister had virtually implied that, at least for these two companies, to process logs supplied by rebel groups in Burma, presented no problem. This did not go down well with the Burmese government, which is also trying to eliminate log smuggling. It was also argued that to permit the handling of these logs would set a precedent, allowing companies to process illegally felled timber from any country thus undermining reafforestation efforts throughout the region.

That a Minister was forced to resign over this issue shows the current determination to end illegal logging. But despite the assertion by Sanan Kachornprasart, Minister for Agriculture, that, 'as long as this government is in power the forests will be closed to logging' the problems will continue if illegal felling is not brought under control. Clearly, however, the logging ban is a good starting point.

Forest futures

Some environmentalists in Thailand claim that there is no longer a deforestation problem, there is simply no forest to deforest. This, perhaps a cynical viewpoint, has an element of truth. Thailand has much more replanting to do than other countries in the region, and the late 1980s have seen a distinct change of attitude within the country; deforestation is now one of the key issues in Thai politics. The adoption of the National Forest Policy has done much to improve politicians' understanding of the problems involved, but will it prove to be a success? The forestry department at Kasestart University in Bangkok, produced the original draft policy,[119] but the present National Forest Policy, although commendable as a genuine attempt to address the problem from a number of angles, is less far-reaching.

In broad terms, this Policy reflects the original proposals, with an emphasis on large-scale plantations as the way to reafforest the country. The original draft policy, however, placed strong emphasis on a fully integrated approach to agricultural development and forestry in general. The major points of these original proposals were as follows:

● Forest Area: to eventually cover 40% of the country, of which approximately half was to be protected. Current policy includes the 40% forest cover, but only one-third of this to be designated protective forest.

- Land Zonation: to define proper, overall land classifications, not for forested land alone.
- Protective Forest: any land with a slope of 35° or more to be classified as protective forest. A total ban on timber extraction and very limited use by shifting cultivators would help maintain these slopes.
- Shifting Cultivation: crop yields should be improved so that more food can be produced from a smaller area. There is still much debate over whether shifting cultivation should be banned or developed into a more sustainable form. The goal, however, is to relieve poverty in the uplands by nurturing sustainable agriculture.
- Loans: provide cheap loans for small farmers to help develop local economies and investment in the land. The Thai Small Farmers Bank partially fills this role, but its influence on the very poorest sectors could be improved.
- Timber Management: continue to improve silvicultural techniques and general management by improving co-ordination between the various bodies involved. There is still a lack of co-ordination between ministries.
- Forest Law: reduce the areas of protected forest where there are no trees. This would liberate these sites, enabling other agencies to develop sustainable farming, rather than the RFD constantly attempting to keep people out of these areas.
- Relationship with other resources: when considering any policy on the exploitation of natural resources, other government bodies should be obliged to co-ordinate with the RFD.

The draft proposals, however, failed to highlight social forestry efforts that were already established and could be built upon. This is surprising as the forest village programmes have generally been a great success.

Case studies

A village history from the north-east: Ban Ngio
This case study, based on an unpublished thesis by S. Subhadhira and M. Samart of the Regional Development Institute at Khon Kaen University, provides a typical history of forest destruction in north-eastern Thailand.

The earliest records of habitation in the area of Ban Ngio go back only as far as 1865. The area was inhabited in prehistoric times – artefacts from 2,500 years ago have been found – but no evidence of habitation between these periods seem to exist.

This upland region was covered with dry dipterocarp forest and generally sandy, shallow soils. The area now occupied by the village was known originally as 'Kok Luang' or Thick Knoll. Two distinct historical periods divide the social, economic and environmental developments in the area: the pre- and post-railway periods.

Pre-railway

Superficially, the village life-style before the railway (pre-1929) seems romantically simple. The reality was probably very different, in view of the hardship and dangers faced in living in a remote part of Thailand at that time.

Ban Ngio was an agricultural village growing subsistence crops, including rice, maize, sugar-cane, cotton and tobacco. Most other essentials came from the forest, not only timber but herbs, soap from the *knee mod* tree, and tree bark which was burnt on the fields as a fertilizer; game also figured in the daily diet.

A cash income was derived from selling buffalo. Each family owned 20 to 30, which were allowed to wander the forest and required little attention; every year a number were driven to market in central Thailand. A similar practice was common throughout the north-east and villages would combine to send their cattle to market. This simple lifestyle was perceived as adequate; as one elder said: 'there were wild pigs and wild cows and the villagers were never short of food.'

The social structure was based on a democratic system with an elected village headman and a religious leader. Election to these positions was based on personal attributes; but a leader could be voted out of office over a single issue at any time. The function of these leaders was to settle internal disputes and to represent their village at the external level.

Land ownership was regarded as good security but was not a sign of absolute wealth. Cleared land could be owned; inheritance passed through daughters; and the forest was regarded as common property. At this stage in the village history there was an abundance of fertile land, and rivalry over this resource was minimal. Labour was not specialized, everybody did a bit of everything. Most of the larger tasks were carried out communally and the concept of paying a wage for the time spent was totally alien. Then, in 1934, the Korat to Nonkai railway was completed.

The railway

With the arrival of the railway the remote north-east of Thailand was opened up for the first time and a chain of events that was to transform the region was set in motion. The effects on the forest were two-fold: the construction and fuelling of the railway consumed large quantities of timber; and the area became exposed to the international cash economy.

The railway passed within one kilometre of the village and a station, known as Ban Rot Fai, was built. A market quickly developed at this stopping point as the demand for forest produce was booming. Timber, wild animal skins, plants, herbs and charcoal were all traded on an ever increasing scale. At one point the village was producing five railcar loads of charcoal for Bangkok each day. In 1937 the first sawmill was established in the village and within a few years Ban Ngio could claim two sawmills, a tobacco-curing factory, an opium den and a large number of shops. Trade was almost totally based on forest produce.

Entry into the cash economy altered social values considerably. First, labour became a saleable commodity as villagers hired themselves out to the sawmill or tobacco factory. The first casualties of these new values were the communal tasks such as house-building and harvesting. Land began to become scarce as the population increased and a small cash value developed on private fields. This value was based primarily on the cost of subsistence crops the land could produce rather than on its potential to produce cash crops for profit. Buffalo were still traded; they now went to market by train, but the numbers sent were decreasing. The electoral system for village leaders, however, remained intact.

Cash crops: Towards the end of World War Two, cotton was in great demand and many villagers began to grow this crop. The post-war period saw the most rapid growth of Ban Ngio, from 100 households in 1944 to 230 by 1952.

The first major cash crop, however, was *kenaf*, introduced into the village in 1947, and which throughout the 1950s spread across the whole region. In 1951 Thailand had 9,900 ha under *kenaf* and by 1966, 420,000 ha.

As demand grew so did the villagers' efforts to produce the crop. Land suddenly became a valuable commodity and its price rose dramatically, from around 10 *bhat* to more than 2,000 *bhat* per *rai*. This led to forest being regarded as a liability – compared to the income from *kenaf*, it was unproductive. Today the villagers refer to this period as *papa baan* or 'flattened forest'. The rate of deforestation was a new experience for the local population, and *kenaf* completely dominated the village, even to the exclusion of growing subsistence crops.

This wholesale forest clearance rapidly depleted the quantity of game as well as the trade in buffalo. Nevertheless, throughout this period, villagers' welfare improved. But the new traders at Ban Rot Fai profited considerably more from these new developments; Ban Rot Fai had become a typical frontier boom town.

Within the village a new, rigid hierarchy developed, based on land ownership or cash wealth. This brought about a change in the power basis as land became concentrated in the hands of a few. Leadership contests became based less on personal attributes than in terms of vote-buying. The role of leaders had changed: they now represented and interpreted outside interests. To have political influence also meant having a major financial advantage; buying votes is still acceptable within the village.

The decline of Ban Rot Fai: By the early 1960s, the market at Ban Rot Fai had begun to decline as it was based on a rapid, rather than a stable, growth economy. There was a new frontier further north and traders were moving towards these areas. In 1964 a major armed robbery cleared Ban Rot Fai of cash and many traders took fright and moved out. In 1967 the world market for *kenaf* collapsed and the village lost its main cash income.

For a time water melon was cultivated on ex-*kenaf* land. But this crop soon proved to be too fragile and to require a greater investment than *kenaf* and therefore never became a popular crop. Rice for export was also grown, but yields were low and the trade was dominated by other regions; consequently, rice-growing was never able to provide a reliable income.

By the late 1960s forests were restricted to hills that could not support cash crops. The sawmills were still operating, although at a much slower pace than before. During this period the timber industry was the only major threat to forests in the area. The late 1960s was also a period of migration from the village following the collapse of the Ban Rot Fai market. The wealthier families that remained set themselves up as merchants, replacing those that had left, and were thus in a position to reap the maximum benefits when the cassava boom took off.

Cassava: As a hardy root crop cassava could grow on very poor, thin soils, and thus opened up the possibility of cultivating marginal land. The good quality land around the village was already being farmed. Government legislation made cutting down of forest illegal, but connections with the right officials could ensure no trouble with the authorities. Wealthier families were thus able to expand their agricultural claims over what had previously been regarded as common land. By the late 1970s cassava had replaced the last remnants of forest in the area.

There can be little doubt that growing cassava improved the living standards of most villagers. It has, however, taken over as the sole source of cash for Ban Ngio; there is no longer either a sawmill or tobacco-curing plant in the area. Subsistence crops are still grown, but all other produce has to be brought in from outside.

Conclusions: In general, living standards in Ban Ngio have improved, but the domination of cassava leaves the economic base of the village open to the wild fluctuations international markets are frequently subject to; the collapse of the *kenaf* market typifies this potentiality.

The effects of forest loss have influenced the entire north-east region, with climatic changes and increased soil erosion. At present, cassava has largely minimized the economic effects of this environmental degradation because it will flourish where few other crops could. But if this market were to fail it is highly unlikely that another crop could be found that would grow in such harsh conditions.

The history of Ban Ngio exemplifies how the provision of new transport routes can not only change the landscape, but also the entire social structure of a region. Whether these changes will, in the long-term, be seen as beneficial or not is impossible to predict. For the forests they have been disastrous; but the local people have benefited by improved living standards. The sustainability of the present economic base, however, depends on a wide variety of mainly external factors over which Ban Ngio has little control.

2. The Nam Choan dam

Thailand's rapidly expanding economy is placing new demands for energy on the country's electricity authority. With the oil price crisis of the early 1970s and the country's reliance on imported oil, energy became a major issue. There had been much discussion of diversification of energy sources and at one time hydroelectric power seemed to have great potential. In 1966, 64% of Thailand's electricity was produced by dams, but demand increased so rapidly that by 1980, with ten major dams in operation, hydroelectric power provided less than 10%.

Against this background the Electricity Generating Authority of Thailand (EGAT) started a programme to harness the power of the Mae Klong river in the west of the country. EGAT's policy was apparently one of construction before public consultation, in so far as the Chao Nane dam, the first of three for the Mae Klong basin, was completed while the public inquiry was still in progress. Independent analysis of EGAT's environmental impact assessment found it to be both inaccurate and incomplete.[120] Starved of water supply while the dam reservoir was filling, the lower reaches of the river became saline as sea water intruded. Thousands of hectares of coconut and lychee plantations were destroyed and EGAT was forced to provide compensation.

The second dam in the basin was at Kao Laem along the Kwai Noi, a major tributary of the Mae Klong. As before, construction was hastily pushed forward despite opposition. This dam was regarded as a major technical triumph as it was located along a geographical fault line. Thailand's best known environmentalist at the time, Dr Nart Tuntawiroon of Mahidol University in Bangkok, commented: 'A triumph for what; ingenuity or stupidity?'

One of his major criticisms was that the huge volume of water would create earth tremors in this region which could conceivably destroy the dam itself. The dam still stands, but in 1983 a series of earth tremors did occur. The epicentre, however, was not the Kao Laem, but another major reservoir, the Chao Nane. Third in the programme was the Nam Choan dam. This dam has not yet been built, but it provides an ideal illustration of the arguments for and against building large dams in South-East Asia.

The Nam Choan dam was to be the largest of the three, with a height of almost 200 metres, forming a reservoir covering 223 sq. km, and flooding approximately 148 sq. km of virgin forest. In 1982, EGAT estimated the dam would cost in excess of US$520m, most of which they hoped would be loaned by the World Bank.

EGAT followed their previous policy of avoiding publicity for this project. In March 1982 they began to renovate an old track to the proposed site through the Tung Yai Wildlife Reserve. This access road was already under construction when the Reserve's director, Phairot Suranaban, discovered it on a routine patrol. Mr Suranaban, justifiably angry as he had received no information about the proposal, brought the road to the public attention. Only then did EGAT announce their plans for the Nam Choan dam.

A public outcry quickly developed, with students from 14 universities taking a lead. This forced EGAT to publicize their reasons for constructing a dam that would flood one of the country's best and healthiest forests. Two months after Mr Suranaban had discovered the road the debate became so heated that the government banned all groups and individuals from making any public statements to the media on the issue.

In October 1982 the government held a special Cabinet meeting to discuss the dam proposals. One of the few non-Cabinet memebers invited to voice their opinion was Dr Nart Tuntawiroon who, at the time, was Dean of the Faculty of Environment and Resource Studies at Mahidol University. He had studied civil electrical engineering and for many years had supported the development of hydroelectric power, and thus had a most creditable background for an understanding of all aspects of the scheme.

EGAT put forward their standard case for proposing to construct the dam, which, according to Dr Tuntawiroon, can be summarized as follows:

1. The electricity is badly needed to continue Thailand's development.
2. The dam will help farmers by providing irrigation and alleviating flooding.
3. The area of forest flooded is insignificant compared to total forest destruction in Thailand.
4. The project has the support of independent foreign consultants.
5. EGAT has already invested heavily in the project.
6. Foreign loans have been secured for the project. Failure to proceed with the project means those loans may well be withdrawn.

Dr Tuntawiroon was not impressed with EGAT's arguments and found a significant number of inconsistencies in their case. He first questioned the 'need' for the dam. Hydroelectricity is generally used to provide the 'base load' for meeting demand. This demand or load comes from heavy industry, which requires a constant source of electric power. 'Peak load' demand is mainly from the domestic sector, particularly around meal times when everybody is cooking or using domestic appliances. This is met by the expensive oil-fired power stations because they are more controllable and generation can be increased or decreased with minimal effort; for dams this is technically difficult.

According to Dr Tuntawiroon, by the late 1970s EGAT was using hydroelectric power to provide much of the peak load. This fact was confirmed when the droughts in 1980 forced EGAT to control peak demand because their reservoirs were so low; to achieve this the government banned all television transmissions between 6 and 8 pm each day. Thus, the intended purpose of hydroelectricity had been changed despite its unsuitability as a source of peak demand electricity. EGAT had not made clear the type of electricity demand this new dam was intended to supply.

Rainfall and dams: The generating potential of the dam was heavily dependent on rainfall predictions for the catchment area. Dr Tuntawiroon claimed that EGAT's data on rainfall could be out by 400%. As a result there was no certainty that the water behind the dam would be high enough at the appropriate time.

EGAT also claimed that the reservoir would irrigate more than 380,000 ha of farmland in the area; a common argument used to promote the idea of a multi purpose dam. It assumes, however, that the demand for electricity will coincide with local farmers' demand for water, but this is not always the case. In the dry season farmers will want as much irrigation water as possible. Conversely, EGAT will need to retain the water in the reservoir in order to continue generating electricity and, if their aim is to provide for peak demand, a maximum quantity of water will be needed in the reservoir. Who gets priority, small farmers or the urban consumers? The reverse is also applicable: when water is plentiful it simply passes through relief channels or over the top of the dam. Farmers will thus not be relieved from flooding as the dam wall is unlikely to be high enough to fully retain flood waters. The large scale dam programme thus loses its 'multipurpose' rationale: the local farmer is provided with water when he already has plenty, but deprived of it when he needs it most.

This, in fact, was the state of affairs in 1979, when droughts affected the farmers in the central region. EGAT held back water in its reservoirs to supply peak demand electricity, while crops were dying. A furious row broke out and the arguments of the Ministry of Agriculture and Co-operatives eventually prevailed on the grounds that the country would lose more money from a crop failure than by cutting peak demand electricity.

Pricing the project: Opponents of the dam also claimed that EGAT's analysis of the total cost was greatly over simplified. The feasibility studies accounted for only the costs of construction and running maintenance; no other liabilities figured. The value of crop land to be flooded, or assessment of compensation for farmers downstream who would be deprived of water for at least two years while the reservoir filled, were not mentioned.

In addition, the Thai Fisheries Department claim that dams trap nutrients that would normally be present further downstream. As a result of the construction of the Maer Klong dam stocks of the much prized giant freshwater prawn have been decimated due to a lack of essential nutrients.

Perhaps the greatest case against the Nam Choan dam is its location on intact forest. The intrinsic value of this area increases year by year as Thailand's forests are cleared. EGAT's report calculated that they would need to clear 12 sq. km of forest to accommodate the people relocated by the scheme; no other deforestation figures were given, apart from those flooded. But this can be regarded as the minimal forest area destroyed, as became clear in 1986. As mentioned earlier, illegal logging at the dam site cleared 1,600 ha of virgin forest when only one minor track had been constructed into the area. What would be the result if a network of roads and tracks were constructed?

Poor survey work: One of Dr Tuntawiroon's key arguments against EGAT was that their study and proposals had not been well researched. EGAT claimed that the area was of no archaeological interest and possessed no mineral deposits; to counteract this claim Dr Tuntawiroon led several expeditions into the area. They found sites of major archaeological significance from the Pleistocene period. The primitive stone tools found were similar to those found at the *Pithecanthropus pekenesis* site just outside Peking in China, and those on the *Pithecanthropus erectus* site on Java. This Thai site provided a link, indicating a possible Pleistocene migration through Thailand. For anthropologists studying the very earliest developments of humans, the sites in China and Java are amongst the most significant areas in the world, and Dr Tuntawiroon's discovery was of international importance.

The same expedition found what they claimed were significant deposits of lignite coal in the area. Whether or not this was a commercially viable deposit is of no significance in this argument; at issue was the fact that EGAT had failed to survey the area properly, if at all. In conclusion Dr Tuntawiroon stated that: 'I found so many things wrong with the data and calculations in EGAT's feasibility report: sufficient to discredit the whole thing.'

The government committee was given 90 days in which to consider the project after the arguments were heard. No announcement was made and it seemed that the project had been shelved.

On the 22 November 1984 Dr Tuntawiroon and his wife were gunned down while working in Mahidol University. To date no individuals have been brought to trial for this double murder, but within Thailand it is widely believed that it was linked to Dr Tuntawiroon's opposition to the Nam Choan dam.

In June 1986 EGAT attempted to resurrect the Nam Choan project under a different name: the 'Upper Quae Yai Development Project'. EGAT were aware that a new government Cabinet had been formed and hoped that, with this new name, approval for the dam would slip through. The environmental lobby was, however, well organized and a public debate soon developed. In September 1987 the government appointed the Thienchai committee to produce a full report on the proposals. In March 1988 the government voted unanimously to 'shelve' the project indefinitely, following the committee's conclusions that: 'Too little is known about the environmental impact to justify building the Nam Choan at this stage.'

This case study typifies not only the manner in which large scale development proposals are imposed on people, but also the nature of the environmental movement in Thailand at the time. This one dam provoked intense opposition, yet there is little long term interest in the environment. Most wildlife or environmental groups have a very small membership and limited grass-roots support. That has changed for the better in the late 1980s, but compared to neighbouring Malaysia, environmental concern still lacks consistent support from the general public. This case study also demonstrates that until a project is formally abandoned it may be resurrected at any time.

Table 6.1
Forest area in Thailand

	Sq.Km.	*% of land area*
1961	273,628	53.33
1973	221,707	43.21
1978	175,224	34.15
1982	156,600	30.52
1985	115,194	22.45*

Source: Forestry Statistics of Thailand: Royal Forestry Department 1983.

* National Statistics Office: Bangkok 1985.

Table 6.2
Annual forest replanting by objective (square km)

	Prior to 1978	1979	1980	1981	1982	1983	*1984
Afforestation	982	205	371	145	89	90	90
Watershed Rehabilitation	336	119	129	118	56	56	50
Reforestation	304	158	169	149	48	48	52
Timber Concession reforestation	307	137	140	111	125	129	132
Total	1,929	619	809	523	318	323	324

Totals by objective

Afforestation	1,972
Watershed rehabilitation	864
Reforestation	928
Timber concession reforestation	1,081

Total area of land replanted up till 1985: 4,845 square kilmetres.

Source: Forestry Statistics of Thailand 1983; Royal Forestry Department, Bangkok 1984.

* National Statistical Office, Bangkok 1985.

Table 6.3
Total landed households, farmland and rented farmland by region

Region	Total landed households (thousands)	Total farmland (million rai)	Total rented farmland (million rai)
Central	829	29.1	26
North East	1,786	50.1	4
South	627	13.8	5
North	1,163	26.0	15

Source: Min. of Agriculture and Co-ops - 1981 – Agricultural Statistics in brief - Crop year 1980-81 – Bangkok.

Table 6.4
Tribal population and land use by tribe in Northern Thailand

	Number		Land Use (%)		
Tribe	Villages	Pop'n (1,000)	Perm'nt	Rotating	Abandon'g
Karen	1,701	199	41	59	0
Hmong, Meo	142	43	2	—	98
Yao, Iu Mien	108	24	7	21	72
Akah, Ikaw, Ekaw	136	20	3	—	97
Lisu	101	17	19	45	37
lahu, Mussuh	290	35	12	3	85
lua	45	10	13	87	—
Htin	47	20	—	93	7
khamu	27	6	10	89	1
Lowland Migrant Farmers	—	—	19	45	37

Total tribal Popn. 376,000 in 2,597 villages.

Source: Tribal Research Centre - 1979 – Chang Mai University – Chang Mai Northern Thailand.

Table 6.5
Teak production and trade for Thailand (cubic metres)

	1979	1980	1982	1983
Production (000 cu.m.)	3,100	2,500	1,800	1,800
Imports (cu.m.)	5,174	304	816	7,189
Exports (cu.m.)	6,407	3	1	zero

Source: *Royal Forestry Department* – Forestry Statistics for 1983.

References

1. United Nations, 1982.
2. Ibid.
3. Ibid.
4. Royal Forestry Department, 1985.
5. FAO, 1981.
6. Ibid.
7. Bhumibhamon, S. 1986.
8. Ibid.
9. Myers, N. 1984.
10. Burns, W. 1986.
11. Bhumibhamon, S. 1986.
12. Burns, W. 1986.
13. FAO, 1981.
14. Ibid.
15. Johnson, A. 1984.
16. Ibid.
17. *Timber Trades Journal*, 1989, 4 February.
18. Ibid., 14 January.
19. Bhumibhamon, S. 1986.
20. Ibid.
21. Rao, R. 1986.
22. Kemf, E. 1986.
23. Gabhir, R. 1986.
24. *Bangkok Post*, 1986, 21 July.
25. Myers, N. 1981.
26. Bhumibhamon, S. 1986.
27. *The Nation*, 1986, 4 January.
28. *Timber Trades Journal*, 1989, 21 January.
29. Ibid.
30. Bhumibhamon, S. 1986.
31. *Timber Trades Journal*, 1989, 4 February.
32. Ibid.
33. Ibid.
34. Ibid.
35. Royal Forestry Department, 1985.
36. *Timber Trades Journal*, 1989, 21 January.
37. Ibid.
38. FAO, 1985.
39. Ibid.
40. Subhadhira, S. and M. Samart, 1984.
41. Burns, W. op.cit.
42. Sricharatchanya, P. 1987.
43. Ibid.
44. Ibid.
45. Ibid.
46. Ibid.
47. Bhumibhamon, S. 1986.
48. Sharma, Y. 1984.
49. Ibid.
50. FAO, 1981.
51. Borsok, R. 1984.

52. *Timber Trades Journal*, 1989, 21 January.
53. Gradwohl, J. et. al., 1988.
54. Ibid.
55. Mukhopadhyay, S. (ed) 1985.
56. *Timber Trades Journal*, 1989, 21 January.
57. Angel, S. 1985.
58. Thongtham, N. 1984.
59. Sricharatchanya, P. 1987.
60. Thongtham, N. 1984.
61. Bhumibhamon, S. 1986.
62. Agricultural Reform Office, 1980.
63. Johnson, A. 1984.
64. Agricultural Reform Office, op.cit.
65. Scholz, V. 1986.
66. Sricharatchanya, P. 1987.
67. Ramitanondh, S. 1985.
68. Royal Forestry Department, 1985.
69. FAO, 1981.
70. Duangpatra, P. 1983.
71. Myers, N. 1986.
72. Duangpatra, P. 1983.
73. UNESCO, 1983.
74. Sriburi, T. 1986.
75. Ibid.
76. *Bangkok Post*, 1986, 16 July.
77. Chapman, E. et. al. (eds), 1978.
78. Myers, N. 1984.
79. Chapman, E. et. al. (eds) 1978.
80. *Bangkok Post*, 1986, 16 July.
81. Myers, N. 1984.
82. Sriburi, T. 1986.
83. UNESCO, 1983.
84. Thongtham, N. 1986.
85. Bhumibhamon, S. 1986.
86. Christensen, B. 1979.
87. Myers, N. 1984.
88. Ramitanhondh, S. 1985.
89. Muller, M. 1978.
90. Ramitanhondh, S. 1985.
91. Ibid.
92. Howe, J. and P. Richards, (eds) 1984.
93. Goldsmith, E. and N. Hildyard, (eds) 1986.
94. Bhumibhamon, S. 1986.
95. Normita, 1986.
96. Royal Forestry Department, 1985.
97. Ibid.
98. *Timber Trades Journal*, 1989, 4 February.
99. Bhumibhamon, S. 1986.
100. Ibid.
101. Ibid.
102. Royal Forestry Department, 1985.
103. Friends of the Earth (UK) 1988.
104. Asia Pacific Peoples Environmental Network, 1984.

105. *The Nation*, 1986, 11 December.
106. Ibid.
107. Friends of the Earth (UK) 1988.
108. Borsuk, R. 1984.
109. Myers, N. 1984.
110. Borsuk, R. 1984.
111. Sricharatchanya, P. 1987.
112. *Bangkok Post*, 1986, 6 May.
113. Ibid., 4 September.
114. Ibid., 20 November.
115. Ibid., December.
116. *The Nation*, 1986, 8 September.
117. Pannee Kornkij, 1986.
118. Bhumibhamon, S. 1986.
119. Ibid.
120. Tuntawiroon, N. 1984.

7. Common Factors: A Regional View

The rate of forest clearance and degradation on a regional scale is fearsome. Even according to official figures, more than 25,000 sq. km of forest are totally cleared each year, plus an equally large area damaged by the timber industry. The consequences of this destruction are the same throughout the tropics; only the scale varies between countries.

Why is this happening? Despite considerable differences in culture and political systems across the region, the foregoing individual country studies, particularly in their historical and legislative aspects, show remarkably little variation.

Setting the scene

As populations increase and with it the demand for land, a degree of forest destruction is inevitable, but clearance of these vast areas is due less to population growth than to political and economic decisions introduced during colonial times. Apart from Thailand, all the countries studied in this book experienced colonial administrations, trapped for decades, sometimes centuries, in a grossly exploitative relationship with Western powers. Colonies were primarily established to exploit a country's natural resources and create new markets for finished produce; that a range of problems would arise from such relationships is hardly surprising. Deforestation in South-East Asia is very much a 20th century phenomenon, its widespread initiation frequently coinciding with the height of colonial influence.

In each of these countries the early 20th century saw the development of new but essentially similar legal frameworks that conferred upon central governments immense power and control over land ownership. These laws reflected a Western concept of land ownership and political control: land ownership was the root of Western wealth. The pattern of land management was therefore based on this alien Western concept rather than on the traditional Eastern one of land as a communal resource.

This pattern is reflected in the way forestry departments were established. In almost every country covered in this book forestry departments began to replant trees 50 or more years ago, yet very little has been achieved to avert forest destruction. To argue that forestry departments should have foreseen the present crisis is an oversimplification.

That almost invariably, forestry departments are part of a larger body, such as the Ministry of Primary Industries in Malaysia, or the Ministry of Agriculture and Co-operatives in Thailand, indicates their general low standing in their governments' priorities; all suffer chronic shortages of finance. Thus a vicious circle is set in motion: forestry departments are seen as ineffective, which further undermines their status and funding, and renders them even less effective. Responsibility for the present condition of forests cannot, therefore, be imputed entirely to forest departments. They operate within government frameworks that approach the environment as individual units – agriculture, mining, forestry – not as an integrated whole. Each department is concerned with its own specific interests even though all may be acting on the same piece of land. In this way contradictions in government policy begin to emerge. There are ample instances of these in the region: in Thailand the military is opening up new security roads and encouraging farmers to settle along them, while the forestry department attempts to restrict access to these same forested areas. Some of the worst examples are in the Philippines where many 'agricultural settlement lands' were totally unsuitable for agriculture. Even today there is minimal official recognition of the cumulative effects one land development policy may have on another. This compartmentalization is a cornerstone of Western scientific philosophy, and perhaps the present administrative chaos could have been largely avoided if an Eastern approach, based on philosophies emphasizing the whole rather than its components, had been adopted.

Ironically, forest departments have generally taken a far more integrated approach to the problem of forest loss than have governments as a whole. Even before the development of Western ecological theory the relationships between forest cover and the water balance, soil erosion, and so on were well understood. Colonial administrations invariably classified forests under different functions as those suitable for clearance and those that should remain as protective areas. But frequently these were little more than theoretical divisions imposed by authorities whose own record showed them to be unsuitable managers. The major colonizers in the region were the British and Dutch. The British arguably had the greatest influence over the region as a whole and this analysis therefore concentrates on British colonialism.

Many texts note how, to the newly arrived colonial powers, South-East Asia's forests must have seemed infinite; but the same could have been said of British forests 300 years previously, yet by the 19th century these had been almost totally cleared.

Creating dependence

In the West, trees obstructed what was regarded as agricultural development; in short, the enclosure of common land and the extraction of maximum cash profit from it. Thus, despite tropical forests being undoubtedly amongst the most productive ecosystems on earth, they were not individually owned and, therefore, created little wealth in Western terms. The British saw social groupings, and consequently land ownership, on only two levels: the individual, whose supposed freedom had to be retained, and the nation state, the entire population. In Britain this had manifested itself in the persistent erosion of communally owned land during the mass enclosures of the 18th century. Common ownership of land was regarded as a threat to the ruling classes in Europe, not only in their colonies.

In South-East Asia, however, the basic unit of traditional society was the community. Control of land was as important to traditional Asian society as it was to the Western colonialists, but solely for the community as a whole. By refusing to recognize communal land ownership the Europeans effectively annulled any traditional claims to power. This process was extended to banning traditional farming methods, thus denying the local population the right to grow their own food in their own way. Common access to natural resources and traditional swidden farming techniques do not accord with colonial economic and political systems.

For the colonial economist, the traditional Eastern concept of forest use meant that too many people had access to these resources, resulting in a reasonably equitable distribution of wealth throughout society; as common property, forests facilitated economic independence from the colonial power. Areas that are highly productive for the community as a whole create little cash revenue either for individuals or governments. To this day, only forests that provide timber are termed 'productive'; clean water, abundant wildlife and a stable environment are equally tangible forest products, but the benefits accruing from these are difficult to restrict and therefore no individual can lay exclusive claim to any profit they may generate. In short, to achieve great personal wealth from a resource that anyone was free to exploit was difficult if not impossible.

Traditional swidden agriculture within forested areas evolved to meet the needs of the local economy, not to provide raw materials for export. Along with forests this system represented independence and provided nothing for the colonial economy.

Forests to hide in

The colonialists' problems with forest also had other dimensions. It is relatively easy to claim ownership of a field or cleared land as these have well-defined boundaries and are defensible against intruders; but forest boundaries are less easily defined and to restrict access is difficult.

Additionally, forests are easy to hide in and, from the point of national security, control has always been a problem for centralized government. The forests of South-East Asia were, and still are, the strongholds of rebel armies. Colonization led inevitably to the creation of rebel armies, not only because the European invasion and general oppression provoked a rebellious response, but also because of the establishment of the nation state, or of countries. The colonial powers had little idea of the dominant cultures in the areas over which they claimed sovereignty, consequently some bizarre geographical combinations were designated as separate countries. For example, Sumatra and West Malaysia have much in common, yet they are in different countries; Irian Jaya has far more in common with Papua New Guinea than with Java; and Sabah is historically much closer to the southern Philippines than Peninsula Malaysia. The pockets of cultural minorities created by these ill thought-out combinations were frequently involved in internal political struggles.

The long-term solution for the Europeans was to claim all the forests as their own, thus eliminating the boundary problems. A more subtle attempt at political control has evolved since independence. Minor forest produce industries, traditionally a major source of economic independence in the more remote areas, have been subject to the onslaught of modern timber extraction. The timber industry has become increasingly capital intensive and, therefore, more easily controlled by those with access to cash. This has been a major factor in enabling central governments to deny control of forest resources to the local community. The result is that where there is a significant logging industry there is almost no minor forest production by the local population. Access to and exploitation of minor forest produce continues to represent a high degree of economic, and subsequently political, independence.

For the colonialists, the difficulties in maintaining security and in concentrating the wealth derived from minor forest produce persuaded them that forests were not a viable economic proposition, except for timber production or clearance. Total forest clearance, however, was and is almost exclusively due to cash crop expansion. Cash crops either replaced forest directly, as in Malaysia with the rubber and oil palm plantations or, as in the Philippines, created a large number of landless farmers, leading them to migrate into the forests after large estate owners had appropriated the best quality land. Government transmigration programmes to relieve the sudden 'overcrowding' that developed as farm land was snatched from under the peasantry's feet, are not a new phenomenon in South-East Asia. The combination of cash crop expansion to meet colonial demands and the accrual of high quality agricultural land by a small minority contributed to the creation of one of today's major desecrators of tropical forests: the displaced, shifted, or landless farmer.

This colonial thinking and means of organizing land development profoundly influenced certain sectors of Asian society. The notion that land accrual meant power quickly took root, and individuals who co-operated with the colonial powers found themselves forming a new social elite. Most of this new breed of Asians was Western-educated and consequently shared their teachers' values and goals. This process set the stage for the neocolonial economies that today dominate most of the Third World. Because these newly independent governments were frequently comprised of 'Westernized' individuals, their approach to development policy continued to be based on a Western world view.

Neocolonialism and foreign investment

Post-independence governments thus had much in common with their colonial predecessors. The departmental structure of central governments remained essentially the same, as did their roles in the development process. Despite the new Constitutions, all of which displayed concern for the environment and the eradication of poverty, recognition of the hard economic realities these countries faced quickly superseded any more idealistic goals. Above all,the influx of foreign capital became the centre of any development plans. Capital would enable a country to industrialize; this was how Europe and the US became rich, why not Malaysia or the Philippines?

Industrialization was regarded as the salvation of the Third World: a means by which living standards for all would be raised, while simultaneously maintaining the political status quo. Third World governments realized that the industrial world's wealth is generated from the processing and production of finished goods, rather than the export of raw materials, hence the need to industrialize. To develop this capability, however, required money, and that could come only from foreign trade and investment. By the early 1960s the Third World scramble for foreign investment was on.

There has been significant industrialization in some countries in the region, South Korea and Malaysia for example, but the process has not resulted in the hoped for success. In fact, Asia, and the Third World in general, can never attain the West's current levels of consumerism and industrialization because there are insufficient natural resources for the entire population of this planet to indulge in such lavish lifestyles. The Third World cannot invade other countries and exploit their natural resources as did the colonial powers. A major problem is that the industrialized economies continue to increase their consumption of raw materials rather than improve the efficiency of their use. Many Third World governments have followed this lead and some individuals – usually politicians or their associates – have done very well for themselves. At the ground level, however, the situation has hardly changed, and in many cases has worsened. The new elite effectively milked the lands in much the same way as did their colonial predecessors, but this time under the banner of 'development'. This resulted from the promotion of a major fallacy: that to increase production in the cash economy would automatically improve the living standards of all. Most of the poor in South-East Asia have minimal contact with the cash economy; mechanisms to redistribute wealth from the common good, such as taxes to pay for hospitals, schools and so on, remain woefully undeveloped. As a result, there is no 'trickle down' of wealth from the rich to the poor in South-East Asia.

The Philippines provides one of the clearest examples of the warped development that typifies neocolonial economies. Agricultural production has increased alongside the number of families living below the poverty line. Pressure for the exploitation and clearance of forests became even greater. Cash crop land expanded ever more rapidly and the timber industry was promoted as an almost 'free' means for a country to acquire wealth.

Producing cash crops for export has been taken to an extreme extent in several countries, forcing the importation of produce that could easily be grown at home. Malaysia, for example, imports large quantities of rice and fruit, while most of its land is taken up by oil palm and rubber for export. A similar situation is exemplified in Thailand's need to import teak.

The crucial questions for those who support the notion that to increase the gross amount of cash in the economy will secure development are: did this policy generate the money? and, was there long-term investment in industries appropriate to Asia? After all, industrialization was the goal, the scramble for foreign capital by exporting raw materials was only a temporary measure towards that end. The short answer was, and still is, no. Investment capital from multinational corporations flooded in to take advantage of the considerable tax incentives these countries provided. Corporate investments, however, frequently return to the parent company, and with minimal taxation in many Third World countries, and a cheap labour force, handsome profits were easily made. Multinational corporations invested in a vast range of industries, effectively establishing an influence over whole economies, not only certain industries. Today, it is estimated that multinational corporations control 60% of all international trade. In the Philippines, these companies were almost exclusively from the United States, her old colonial power; in Papua New Guinea, where less than 20% of the logging concession area is controlled by local companies, they are based in Australia and Britain; and in Indonesia, they are Japanese. Even in Malaysia, where business ownership restrictions require a majority of local shareholders, most logging companies have foreign 'advisers' who undoubtedly influence company policy.

Foreign investment need not automatically imply mismanagement, underpricing and a net loss for the producing country, but this has frequently been the case. From the beginning, however, Third World economies attempting to enter the industrial world were at a great disadvantage. Their industrial development was deliberately impeded during the colonial period when they produced only raw materials and had no manufacturing industry. Since independence, any processing sectors that may have provided employment found themselves up against stiff import tariffs wherever they tried to sell. Even if a country managed to develop an industrial processing sector it could sell its produce only at extremely low prices because it had to undercut the trade tariffs. Low prices are frequently achieved by paying grossly inadequate wages and ignoring any safety regulations that may reduce output. The industrial dream worked well for management and central government, but not for the population as a whole. Long-term investment and the processing of natural resources has been discouraged in favour of a mining approach that continues to export raw materials to this day.

The present structure of the region's timber industry accords perfectly with this general model: it is always capital intensive, usually under foreign control, and is based almost entirely on raw material exports; the initiation of any processing of the product is promptly faced with severe tariffs. After Indonesia managed to break into the Japanese plywood market by selling below cost price, plywood markets became highly unstable. Unstable markets are a further disincentive to long-term investment.

Building the debts
By the 1970s it became clear to many Asian governments that their foreign corporate investment policy for industrial development was not working; it provided few jobs and, if profits were to stay in Asia, business needed to be under local control. The new tactic was to borrow money from such institutions as the World Bank and Western merchant banks. This gave Third World governments direct control over their investments; but all loans are subject to interest charges.

The Third World is now required to pay off huge loans, recently estimated to be US$ three trillion (million, million), with crippling interest rates. The irony is that although the new government investments may enable developing countries to produce finished products, little else has changed from the colonial days. External markets for finished products remain closed, and the multinationals are consolidating their influence over production and pricing. Consequently, even after decades of independence, raw material exports continue to form the backbone of most Third World economies.

At present these economies are in a trap: they can only pay off their huge debts with unprocessed or raw materials, and, because they cannot change their products, they must continue to sell more of the same. Palm oil, rubber, timber, rice, and sugar, for example, are land-based; in order to increase production more land is needed – and that comes from the forest. The debt crisis developed in the 1980s alongside the rapid expansion of farmland in many Third World countries. In 1980 t' e cumulative debt of the six countries examined in this book exceeded US\$ 33 billion, by 1985 this had increased to US\$ 65 billion. Servicing these debts averaged more than 18% of their gross national product, consequently it was necessary to produce more and more raw materials to maintain their economies. The process accelerated throughout the 1980s; for example, by 1986, the Philippines alone had external debts in excess of US\$ 28 billion.

The result has been the development of highly unstable world markets as everybody tried to undercut prices in order to sell. According to the UN Congress on Trade and Development (UNCTAD), the average price index of primary products exported from the Third World fell by 28% between 1960 and 1986. By 1989, the average price of these raw materials (excluding oil) was 30% lower than in 1979. It is virtually impossible to improve the living standard of an expanding population if the value of the goods they produce keeps falling. A variety of international trade agreements have been established in an attempt to alleviate some of these problems (these are outlined later). Low market prices, however, continue to hamper the development of unions and civil rights in the Third World, thus maintaining low wages and poor working conditions. All this influences the decision a small farmer must make when faced with eviction in order to make way for export crops: to move into the city or into the forest?

The multilateral development agencies are a key component of the present world economic order. Despite, originally, being established to help alleviate poverty in the Third World, there have been accusations that many of their projects have exacerbated the divisions between rich and poor nations. Their powers to instruct governments how to run their countries are limited, but they can refuse or propose loans capable of maintaining or toppling a government. They also produce reports that have an incalculable influence over general development policy.

Development aid and agencies

The basic concept of aid may be ideologically sound, yet the severe restrictions frequently imposed by donors effectively make much aid a tool for maintaining the international status quo. The result has been schemes involving inappropriate technology that can be built only with the donor countries' expertise and equipment, regardless of local needs and aspirations. More money is spent on foreign advisers in the Indonesian transmigration programme than on health care and education for the migrants themselves. Some aid, however, is less geared towards maintaining the status quo, and in recent years many aid agencies have attempted to rectify their performance in this respect. The British and US governments employ the most pernicious forms of 'aid with strings', while most European governments have dramatically improved their aid programmes over the 1980s. But aid is a much smaller factor in controlling Third World economies than the general conditions of trade noted above.

In the 1980s many large development agencies were strongly criticized for the effects of their projects on the Third World's forests and the people who live in them. In 1985, John Spears of the World Bank estimated that less than 1% of multilateral development banks' total investments in the Third World contributed to forest conservation and management. The vast majority of agricultural aid has been utilized for short-term food production and emergency food relief. The following analysis focuses on the World Bank as the largest single agency of this type. The approach of this institution, however, is by no means unique, having much in common with other development agencies such as the FAO and the Asian Development Bank. The criticism has not gone unheard and these agencies now claim to place greater emphasis on environmental issues than previously.

Criticisms of such agencies regarding their forestry policies fall into three main categories:

1)   Providing aid or loans for agricultural development projects that force local farmers off their land, for example, cash crop expansion and irrigation schemes in the northern Philippines; or unsustainable agricultural expansion into forests, as in the Indonesian transmigration programme.

2)   Promoting aid or loans that encourage direct over-exploitation of forests for timber or paper pulp. These would include the IBRD's advice in the 1950s and 1960s recommending rapid expansion of the timber industry as a quick way to earn foreign income. It may also include replanting or rehabilitation programmes that absolve private timber companies of responsibility to manage forests after they have been exploited. The Malaysian Forest Rehabilitation programme is an example.

3)   Providing funds for progammes that aim to replace 'natural' forest with timber plantations of eucalyptus and pine – trees that provide few benefits for the local populations, frequently undermine land rights for local communities, and do little to maintain biological diversity.

It is not suggested that these institutions are driven by a desire to destroy tropical forests, in fact the opposite is probably true. The problems are in the way they are structured and how they target their loans.

The World Bank
The World Bank (originally the International Bank for Reconstruction and Development (IBRD)) was established in 1944 along with the International Monetary Fund (IMF), with a rather vague concept of providing money to aid development. IMF loans are generally for short-term economic crises as opposed to the World Bank's longer-term investments. As a result, the

World Bank is perhaps the most influential loan agency in the Third World. The other main international banking agency active in the Third World is the International Development Agency (IDA), established in 1960, at the request of Third World countries, to provide loans at nominal rates of interest for the very poorest countries; most World Bank loans, in contrast, carry commercial interest rates.

Possibly the World Bank's (hereinafter referred to as the Bank) greatest influence stems not from its ability to provide major funding but from its 'Country Planning Papers'. These detailed studies of a country's economy define development priorities that, in the Bank's opinion, should be taken into account by the government concerned. The World Bank is above all a *bank*, interested in secure loans and a good return on investment. Its role in the development process is therefore motivated largely by its internal ethos rather than altruism. Consequently, what is good for the Bank need not necessarily be good for the general development of the country receiving the loan. Aiming investment at maintaining the international status quo and supporting donor nations' domestic industries cannot be ruled out as a major objective of Bank policy.

Based in the US, the Bank's head is traditionally an American, and its fundamental policy is one of industrial growth using Western models; in other words, it promotes a Western ideal of economic growth. Almost 150 governments are members, but all major policy is agreed under a general voting system in which the number of each country's votes is proportional to its contributions to the Bank. Consequently, the US controls more than 20% of the vote, Japan and the United Kingdom around 6% each and France a little over 5%. The cumulative votes of the five countries examined in this book are approximately 2.5%. The most important and knowledgeable voice on Third World problems – that of the people who live there – is thus barely heard in the Bank.

Governments that receive funding usually propose a project, carry out a feasibility study, and then apply to the Bank. Third World governments are aware that funding is more likely to be granted if the project they propose falls within the target areas identified by the Country Planning Papers; the influence of these papers cannot be over-emphasized.

All aspects of Asian life, however, not only the priority areas, are affected directly or indirectly by these projects. Every project has social and environmental consequences that all too often are the subject of scant analysis by the Bank. Some major assumptions are made by the Bank and similar institutions about a host government's degree of concern for the people most affected by a project; government interests and those of the people they govern do not always coincide. As a recent IIED paper noted: 'It is an unfortunate but inescapable fact that not all borrowers [from the World Bank] place sufficient importance on the well-being of the poorest of their citizens.'

But what are the sources of information for these Country Planning Papers? The Bank produces the final Paper, but are its sources reliable and unbiased? The confidentiality of these Papers makes it difficult to identify sources, although they are probably based on government data. As the individual country profiles in this book have illustrated, government figures are not always reliable and are sometimes blatantly manipulated. Lack of technical expertise to establish the facts is, in most cases, not a valid excuse. There is no way of assessing exactly how many figures have been 'massaged' in order that unscrupulous politicians or contractors may profit from Bank-funded projects.

Should the Bank and other international institutions rely totally on official information sources? Even if a government genuinely cares about the social costs involved in certain projects, their anxiety to obtain foreign investment capital may be so desperate that potential problems are understated in order to secure the loan.

The IMF is undoubtedly another source of information for some of the Bank's ventures. In 1988, Davison Budhoo, an economist with the IMF for more than twelve years, who specialized in the economies of Caribbean and Latin America, commented in the *Ecologist*:

> We manipulated, blatantly and systematically, certain key statistical indices so as to put ourselves in a position where we could make very false pronouncements about [the] economic and financial performance of that country.

One means of counteracting such data problems is for the Bank to broaden its sources of information; to employ a wider source of information would not jeopardize any loan for a sound project proposal. For example, information from NGOs working at the grass-roots level, particularly when researching projects' social implications, is invaluable. Day to day contact with the people likely to be affected is perhaps the only effective way to assess a project's impact, and NGOs are ideally placed to provide such information. At the very least they can contribute an alternative view that would help establish a balanced discussion.

It is unreasonable to expect the Bank or any other development agency to end corruption in Asian politics, but they could stop funding it. It could be argued that if the Bank refuses loans on the grounds of corruption the people to suffer will be mainly the poor. But corruption can lead to the creation of projects that are clearly inappropriate to the poor in the country concerned. The Chico dam saga in the Philippines provided a good example. The Bank never provided the loan, but it was still on the government's agenda right up to the revolution; the Bank made no effort to discourage the government's proposals.

Another aspect of large-scale funding also needs recognition. Refusal to fund projects on political grounds is probably quite frequent; Vietnam and Cambodia are perhaps the most widely known examples. There is no direct evidence to support this, but the political interests of those most influential in the Bank must increase the probability of loan decisions being strongly influenced by political objectives.

As has been suggested, Third World governments undoubtedly gear project proposals towards schemes they consider are likely to attract funding, often regardless of their real development needs. This might explain why the Bank has never consistently provided for, or even been asked to provide, large-scale funding for some of the excellent social forestry programmes found in the region. Large-scale commercial timber plantations, which accommodate the Western approach to forest management, however, receive considerable funding from the Bank.

If the ultimate aim of the Bank and host governments is to improve Third World peoples' living standards, then precedence must be given to the environmental and social impacts of a project rather than to simply ensure a financial return on investment. The record shows that this has rarely been the case, but perhaps attitudes are beginning to change in this respect.

Whatever the cause, many environmental and social problems that have arisen as a result of Bank-funded projects could have been anticipated had the proposals been properly analysed. But, until recently, only six out of a total Bank staff exceeding 6,000, were employed in its environmental department, making adequate analysis of a project's implications almost impossible. The Bank funds several hundred projects at any one time, many based on changes in land use; according to informed estimates, the environmental department has approximately three days in which to analyse each project. The Bank now claims to have undergone fundamental changes in policy-making and has expanded the environmental department, but many environmentalists remain sceptical; they claim there is still no indication that the Bank will make fundamental changes in its voting structures or in the parameters of its economic development criteria for projects. If a comprehensive environmental analysis is produced which suggests the project could prove to be a disaster, old political allegiances may still dominate. This assertion has been supported by Catherine Watson, who worked in the Bank's Department of Environmental Affairs and was reported, in the *Ecologist*, to have stated: 'Project staff treated us like scourges. As far as they were concerned, we were trouble.' The Department, she said, was just:

a token office within the Bank . . . When our proposals were accepted it was because they enhanced the progressive image of the Bank and cost the Bank little. When our proposals threatened the future of a project, or had major implications for Bank practice, they and we were dismissed as unrealistic and impractical.

It is from this background that current approaches to saving the forests have emerged. Obviously, however, the immensity of the problem is such that, despite their poor record, it would be foolish to consider excluding such agencies from aiding the recovery process. Furthermore, as many of their policies have helped create the present problems they may be able to provide the framework for a solution. The facts remain that: these agencies command considerable respect within most of the Third World governments; they form the most comprehensive inter-governmental forum present today; and they are more open to new ideas than many of the oppressive governments with which they have to work.

Tackling deforestation

National parks

For many years the establishment of national parks was seen as adequate protection for the world's forests. It is now clear that to protect a few areas as national parks will have little influence on the rate of forest destruction across South-East Asia as a whole. However successfully a government may establish a policy for national parks, they will cover only a small percentage of any country's forest area. All parks or reserves are based on the idea of policing the forests, even if this is performed in an enlightened manner. To delineate a park on a map is easy, but to protect it at ground level is not. From a logistics point of view, it is quite impossible to deploy enough people to patrol every square kilometre of forest in the Third World; that is why this study has given little weight to national parks. Nevertheless, they have an important role to play in the conservation process and, in fact, there have been significant developments in this field as the system of simply sealing-off these areas has declined.

Some organizations, particularly the International Union for the Conservation of Nature (IUCN), have provided enlightened investment and have been instrumental in establishing the network of globally important 'super parks' known as World Heritage Sites. Some IUCN projects have been criticized because they remove local populations from core areas of some of their parks, but as an institution the IUCN has been less heavy-handed than many of its counterparts. There is, however, insufficient international funding for many of these projects.

In the Third World, national parks may take up land that has great timber or agricultural potential, whereas in the West, most national parks are based on land for which there are no other major claims; as soon as one is suggested, the legislation protecting these areas is frequently by-passed. What justification has the rich industrial West to expect poor countries voluntarily to exclude people from vast areas of their land? Neither should Third World countries be expected to bear the costs of establishing and managing national parks. A compensation system is needed if World Heritage Sites are not to impose a further burden on the already stretched economies of the Third World.

To date, the tropical timber industry has played a major role in creating the present problems, and a small minority of individuals have made a great deal of money out of wholesale forest destruction. Calls for the industry to set aside just one percent of its annual profits to help develop the World Heritage Site network have received a positive response, in principle, but so far nothing has emerged in practice. Long-term investment in national parks and World Heritage Sites by the Bank and other institutions could be recouped from an efficient and sustainable tropical timber industry.

In summary, areas of international importance should be maintained by international finance funding environmentally sensitive development that meets the needs of the local populations, both within and adjacent to a park's boundaries. It has become increasingly clear that only when the local population are fully involved in planning, implementation, and management of national parks can they survive. Only if the management of national parks and World Heritage Sites is guided by this criteria will they make any significant impact on deforestation in the Third World.

Large-scale plantations

Since the late 1970s large-scale plantations have been seen as the saviour of South-East Asia's forests. Most agencies regarded them as environmentally beneficial in that they did establish trees. But the country studies in this book show that large-scale plantations may actually contribute to forest destruction; in many cases forest has actually been cut down to accommodate plantations. In addition, as the Thailand study illustrates, the type of trees chosen can place heavy demands on the soil and water in these areas. Large-scale plantations' contribution to protecting the environment is now widely questioned by environmentalists throughout Asia. Timber plantations also face significant technical problems; the exceptions, as noted earlier, have been based on the Burmese *tayanga* system. Outside Burma, however, this system of timber production from agro-forestry is limited, although there are signs that its application is increasing.

The rapid expansion of softwood plantations has satisfied some of the growing demand from the region's paper industry, but plantations are frequently promoted as the means to maintain the timber trade. This is an unlikely proposition because fast-growing, low quality softwoods are no substitute for tropical hardwoods. Eucalyptus can never replace the current markets for meranti, luan or mahogany. Even with full processing, the export value of these softwoods would probably be lower than that of present raw hardwood timbers.

It may be argued that eucalyptus or the acacia families will still contribute significantly to exports as there is an international trade in paper pulp and low quality softwoods. But almost every country in the Third World is planting the same kind of trees; therefore, any potential international trade in eucalyptus will, within a few years, be swamped by the sheer volume of this one timber type, resulting in the price of an already low grade product falling even lower. The scale of demand from the industrialized countries, which already have considerable supplies of fast-growing softwoods, is also questionable. Clearly, major replanting schemes are essential, but large-scale plantations are not the answer if the aim is to maintain the region's forests. The need for a more integrated approach has become obvious, and many development analysts are moving towards that goal.

These fundamental problems of approach, however, continue to manifest themselves in the most recent strategy to save the world's tropical forests. In 1985 the World Bank, in conjunction with the World Resources Institute, the FAO and the UNDP, launched a 'Tropical Forest Action Plan'.

The Tropical Forest Action Plan
This Plan calls for a US$ 8 billion programme of investment to promote: reafforestation; protection of watersheds; fuelwood and agro-forestry; and the establishment of national parks. More than one-quarter of this budget will be devoted to improving the efficiency of industrial timber production. The Plan acknowledges the social role of forests and mentions land reform, but only as peripheral measures. In essence it promotes a high-finance, high-tech approach involving large-scale replanting schemes of non-native species.

Despite the criticism that follows, the Plan deserves credit for its dismissal of the usual excuse that more research is required before action is taken. Its introduction notes that:

> Lack of knowledge is no longer a barrier to action; the real obstacle is the lack of political, financial and institutional support to apply the solutions.

The planned solutions are, however, based on the authors' analyses of the causes of forest destruction. In the World Resources Institute's initial Call for Action publication, on which the Action Plan is based, the authors claim: 'it is the rural poor themselves who are the primary agents of destruction as they clear forests for agricultural land, fuelwood and other necessities.' This rather shallow analysis that dominates the Plan's agenda has little support amongst many people involved with Third World development. As James Nations and Daniel Komer of the Centre for Human Ecology in Austin, Texas, in discussing deforestation in Central America put it:

> To blame colonizing peasants for uprooting tribal people and burning

the rain forest is tantamount to blaming soldiers for causing war. Peasant colonists carry out much of the deforestation in Central America, but they are mere pawns in a general's game.

This point is recognized by the Plan, but only in a rather vague statement on page 24, outlining strategies to save forests for conservation purposes:

> Local populations may be the principal agents of destruction, but in most cases they are only responding to outside pressure. If those pressures can be eased or removed, the immediate threat to the forests will be reduced. Force or legal compulsion is no answer; the solution lies in working with local people and in responding to their needs as well as those for conservation.

'Outside pressure' is mentioned, but not seen as one of the basic causes of the problem, perhaps because those responsible for this external pressure, the rich and powerful in both the industrialized and developing countries, are the same people whom the Plan hopes to influence. There is also a strong possibility that the same institutions that compiled this Action Plan themselves helped create these 'outside forces'.

Very noticeably, the Plan's 'Forest-based industries' section is devoted almost exclusively to timber and paper pulp production. Five of the eight examples of successful projects cited supply these industries. The development of minor forest produce industries is covered under the 'Conservation' section, implying that those engaged in these activities should not be given access to forests open for logging.

In the absence of any challenge to the political status quo that governs most forest areas, the Plan can be regarded as contributing to maintaining the present situation. Adoption of the Plan in its present form would imply that current political control over the forests has worldwide endorsement via the United Nations. Local populations fighting to control their resources would thus be faced with a government able to refuse to implement such measures as land reform, and still claim they were co-operating with the UN to save tropical forests.

Many NGOs involved in environment and development have rejected the Plan as it stands. Despite the rhetoric about the involvement of NGOs and the voluntary sector, no attempt was made to obtain their views when compiling the initial drafts of the Plan. This emerges clearly in the Plan's diagram, 'How to implement the Plan.' Five major points are noted, with arrows indicating a sequence of events. The final point: 'Involve local groups and non-government organizations in the above process', appears almost as a afterthought. The first point reads: 'Review forestry sector to devise or update a national forestry development plan.' Why were NGOs and local groups not involved in this initial process? The local population should have the right to influence any development plan before being asked to implement it.

In 1986 the Bank *et al.* hurriedly arranged a series of meetings with NGOs in all the major tropical regions in an attempt to win their support, without which the Plan would be severely restricted. Reactions ranged from a resigned acceptance to firm opposition, much of which is based not only on the Plan itself but on the past record of Bank-funded projects. In short, many NGOs trust neither the Bank nor its associates.

Developing trust

Over the years many forest dwelling societies in remoter regions have developed a deep distrust of their central governments and the big international institutions closely associated with these governments. The Bank has undermined its own credibility by working under conditions of almost obsessive secrecy; even the Country Planning Papers are classified as confidential. This strategy has proved to be a mixed blessing: while on the one hand the Bank could claim that its opponents were ill-informed, on the other it suggests it had something to hide.

The Bank's credibility has been further undermined by its supposed policy on forest development and tribal people. In 1982, its policy on tribal people was launched in a document, 'Economic Development and Tribal Peoples: Human Ecological Considerations', designed to allay fears that the rights of tribal groups affected by Bank-funded projects would be eroded. It included some quite unambiguous statements, such as: 'The Bank will not support projects on tribal lands, or that will affect tribal lands, unless the tribal society is in agreement with the objectives of the project.' Neither would it support a project that, 'denies then extinguishes ethnic diversity' which it recognizes as 'a form of extinction'.

These statements generated problems, as certain projects contravened their intent and in 1986, one of the Bank's leading lawyers told the International Labour Organization (ILO) in Geneva that: 'The published policies are not those it [the Bank] observes.' The Bank thus maintained the funding of such projects as the Indonesian transmigration programme, despite the Indonesian government's admission that: 'the different ethnic groups will in the long run disappear'. In 1986 a confidential Operational Manual Statement was leaked, outlining the Bank's 'real' policy. In contrast to the original text in 'Economic Development and Tribal People' it notes:

> In those cases where environmental and/or social changes promoted through development projects may create undesired effects for tribal people, the project should be designed so as to prevent or mitigate such effects.

In other words, projects go ahead, whatever the attitude of tribal people involved, although some aspects of the project may be changed to meet their needs.

Implementation of this policy also contravenes certain international agreements. Article Two of the UN resolutions from the International Conference on Civil and Political Rights states: 'In no case may a people be deprived of its own means of subsistence'. The ILO also recognizes the rights of tribal people to collective ownership of traditional lands and outlines a guide to compensation due in cases of loss of such lands. In almost every country in South-East Asia the Bank has funded a project that has contravened one of these international agreements.

There is, however, little chance of imposing such agreements on signatory governments as domestic policy interests always dominate international commitments. But it is precisely because the Bank is an international organization that it has a stronger obligation to comply with international agreements. If the Tropical Forest Action Plan is to be implemented it must adhere to international agreements, or it can no longer claim to be a worldwide strategy working towards the resolution of a global problem.

A contradiction in funding

Ensuring that the guidelines laid down by the Bank and other similar institutions are closely adhered to may prevent particular projects receiving international funding. But a more fundamental contradiction in the realization of the aims of Bank funding is emerging. Many Bank-supported projects have not only been environmentally damaging, but have provided an opportunity for individual contractors to reap financial gains, for example, the Indonesian transmigration programme and some of the irrigation projects in the Philippines. Some projects funded have not only done little to alleviate forest destruction but have actively promoted it. The Bank is then asked to fund rehabilitation programmes in an attempt to alleviate problems that have largely been caused by a previous project! Once again, the Indonesian Transmigration programme provides examples.

The internationally-funded forest rehabilitation programmes in Malaysia illustrate a similar process. Malaysia is currently receiving loans from the Asian Development Bank (itself closely linked to the World Bank) to aid its forest rehabilitation programme. The government, using public funds to secure and accommodate the loan, replants logged-over areas while the private timber industry, the initiator of the problem, pays nothing. In effect, the Malaysian government has been caught in a trap whereby public money must pay for the damage inflicted on the forests by private companies. There is every indication that once these forests have been rehabilitated, contracts for felling will be granted to private companies, who will once more reap the benefits from the timber. In this way institutions such as the Asian Development Bank are, in effect, subsidizing the timber industry in South-East Asia. The Forest Occupancy Management project in the Philippines is another example of public funding used to subsidize the timber industry: farmers obtained funding to plant trees conditional upon them planting only species the large timber corporations want.

For the Bank and other major institutions to tackle these fundamental problems a new set of criteria for assessing the success of projects must be developed – new criteria that must give far greater prominence to social and environmental factors.

The change of perspective is possible within the major aid agencies; development agencies were initiated as a means of co-ordinating international humanitarian aims, but this is not so with the major lending banks. The World Bank, as has been noted, was established with the rather vague aim of providing funds for development, but even this tenuous link with humanitarian aims does not apply to the other Western banks. The violent demonstrations that occurred outside the World Bank and IMF meeting in Germany in late 1988, indicate that the industrial nations are strongly convinced that the social and environmental impacts of international aid funding should take precedence over economic goals. Whether the lending banks respond to the pressure remains to be seen.

An Alternative Tropical Forest Action Plan
In 1987, the World Rainforest Movement, a coalition of major Third World and Western environmental groups, together with the journal *The Ecologist*, proposed an alternative strategy to save the forests. Broadly, this strategy identifies four major interrelated components that need to be changed: ending the debt crisis; reforming trade patterns; halting environmentally destructive development projects; and land ownership reform. Together these would create a new criteria for development. These proposals are not intended as a blue-print for saving the forest but aim to present a framework for discussion.

Dealing with the debt crisis: Already many countries have defaulted on major debts and many more seem likely to follow. Several Western banks, notably Citicorp from the United States, accept that these debts will never be paid and have made provisions for defaulting. Rather than simply writing-off these debts some environmental groups have developed a strategy whereby they can be exchanged for conserving particularly important forest areas. Two major debt-for-conservation swaps have been carried out: in Bolivia, Central America, where a US$650,000 debt was written off in exchange for the establishment of a 1.5m ha rainforest reserve; a similar agreement has been reached with the Costa Rican government. As yet there have been no similar suggestions from South-East Asia.

This possible solution to the Third World's problem could also be applied to researching and developing minor forest product industries and the establishment of small-scale social forestry projects. By 'writing-off' debts in this way investment within a country's economy could be redirected towards socially responsible projects. The concept could be developed, but it needs to be defined unambiguously in order to ensure that a new form of environmental colonialism imposed by the Western banks does not emerge.

In more general terms, freed of these debts South-East Asia could increase investments in domestic industries and sustainable development. Investment in processing forest products and forest management has generally been minimal due to two major factors: 1) the ecological cycle of producing timber bears no relation to the economic cycles through which it is traded; and, 2) unfair tariff systems.

Sustainable timber production requires long-term investment, which could be encouraged by a stable international timber market. How such a stabilization could be achieved depends on a wide variety of factors, including international trade patterns. Reforming the current trade imbalance between the Third World and the industrialized nations forms the second part of the Alternative Tropical Forest Action Plan.

Trade patterns: There are two major theories on how Third World commodity prices are reached: they are either 'supply led' or 'demand led'. The 'supply led' argument claims that the most important factor affecting the price of a raw commodity is the variation in supply. Over-produce, and the price falls; under-produce, and the price rises. For the world's timber markets, Third World tropical timber production exceeds current demand and consequently the price of timber has fallen. The argument accepts that demand for timber may fluctuate, but claims that suppliers should react to these changes. If suppliers are able to achieve this, a balance can be reached, thus, excluding other factors, a relatively stable trade price should evolve. Third World timber producers are said to be unwilling to adapt to these fluctuations in demand, and as a result either over- or under-produce.

Many Third World economists regard this analysis as simplistic, especially when applied to forest produce. Members of the Third World Network, for example, believe it is based on the view of a producer of finished products, not raw materials. They claim that market prices are determined by what the consumer is willing to pay, that is, the market price is 'demand led'. The market price may have little or no relevance to the actual production cost of the timber. In short, they claim Western consumers are unwilling to pay the true cost for tropical timber, which would include replanting and forest management.

An industrial producer can decrease or accelerate production almost at the touch of a button. But, due to the very nature of the product, the sustainable tropical timber producer must employ much longer-term planning, as the growth rate of trees is extremely difficult to change.

Economic and ecological balance sheets: Sustainable forestry may be regarded as an ecological economy with a ledger balance sheet; the currency considered in terms of energy, nutrients and biological productivity rather than money. To be sustainable, the inputs and produce must balance, in the same way that a cash economy must balance revenue sales with costs. Despite considerable advances in silviculture and forest management, however, the ecological economy is clearly less adaptable than the market economy, as is unmistakably demonstrated by comparing the time scales of market fluctuations and forests' ecological recovery rates. The market economy cannot wait for the trees to grow and, as a result, producing countries, desperate for cash, must somehow ensure they can meet any future peaks in demand if they are to retain their markets. As it is almost impossible to predict when the next peak in demand may occur, a producer lacking an excess pool of timber to ship out at the whim of the buyer, is branded as unreliable. This fundamental dilemma is common to most Third World governments. In short, it is impossible for Third World timber producers to develop sustainable forestry in isolation from their customers; a co-operative effort is needed. The problem is further exacerbated by the fact that in many areas timber extraction is seasonal; consumer demand for timber does not coincide with the wet and dry seasons' rhythm.

International commodity agreements: In the West and Japan, protectionism of the timber processing industries is extremely strong. Any significant timber processing industry is invariably accompanied by tariffs operating against foreign imports of that same product. This is partly in order to avoid unemployment; an issue most governments feel is worth defending. In the West, however, there has been a swing towards the concept of free trade based on the ideologies of the free market system. The aim of the international commodity agreements outlined below is to reduce these tariffs and increase the power of free market forces. While Western leaders vigorously promote this concept, the operations of some of these agreements show a distinct bias in the type of commodities Western governments consider should be freely traded.

General Agreement on Trade and Tariffs (GATT): GATT was established in 1947, through the United Nations, with the ultimate goal of reaching a world of free trade with no or very few trade barriers. GATT signatories, including many Third World countries, agree to provide equal market access to all other signatory nations. Promoting free trade is seen by signatories as a means of increasing trade as it reduces the price of many goods. To reach this goal tariffs are gradually reduced on all products, including raw materials. But as far as Third World raw commodity producers are concerned, the benefit of this approach is limited, because the Agreement fails to recognize the disadvantages faced by the Third World. The equality, in free trade terms, may help maintain the current economic relationship between signatory countries as industrialized nations are already at an advantage when producing finished products. Any reduction in import tariffs for finished produce from the Third World is subject to reciprocal reductions for finished produce from industrial nations entering the Third World signatories' economy. In the long term GATT will help free trade, but at present it does little to develop processing industries in the Third World.

The Generalised System of Preferences (GSP): The GSP is set within the framework of UNCTAD. Under this system industrialized consumer countries grant tariff reductions, on a non-reciprocal basis, for certain produce from the Third World. These individual agreements between nations can thus help Third World countries develop foreign markets for their produce and processing sectors. Superficially these agreements seem altruistic on the part of industrialized signatories, but this is not always so. Taking the EEC as an example, various countries from South-East Asia can export, duty free, a quota of tropical hardwood products each year under the GSP. The EEC sets overall quotas, but they need not be equally distributed to every country in the Community. The size of the tariff-free quota allocated to individual EEC countries depends upon whether or not the product is challenging a major domestic industry.

The restrictions on tropical plywood imports to the EEC provide a good example of how protectionism can still prevail within a GSP agreement. The agreement's quota system allows each Community country to import, tariff-free, a fixed quantity of tropical plywood. Because the United Kingdom has almost no domestic plywood industry it gets by far the largest share of the EEC quota – imports of Far Eastern plywood are not regarded as a threat to British industry. But France and Italy have major plywood industries, based on their imports of tropical logs; they are allocated only 0.3% and 0.8% respectively of the total EEC quota of duty-free plywood. For France, this tariff-free quota totals 250 cubic metres imported from the world's top six producers each year. If South-East Asia wishes to increase exports of plywood to France over and above this quota, it will be subject to the full French tariff.

Francois Nectoux and Nigel Dudley of Earth Resources Research neatly summarized the situation:

> If a Third World country manages to develop a modern industry, it is right and proper, in the eyes of the European policy makers, to prevent it reaping the benefits of its effort on the European market.

EEC trade tariffs on timber produce are, however, considerably lower than those imposed by Japan and the US, both of which have large domestic plywood processing industries to protect. In 1982 the UNCTAD Secretariat noted that in these two countries:

> Barriers to market entry as a result of tariff duties imposed on processed products are in fact much higher than nominal rates would suggest. Effective protection, which takes into account tariff escalation, can be estimated for Japan at roughly more than twice the nominal fee for plywood, or 40%, and nearly three times for sawnwood, or 30%.

The tropical timber trade's inherent problems are compounded by a distinct lack of communication between producers and consumers. As long ago as the mid-1970s there were proposals within UNCTAD to form an international body to help co-ordinate the trade in tropical timber. Eventually, in 1985, 41 countries ratified the International Tropical Timber Agreement (ITTA), which established a system of consultation and co-operation between the major producer and consumer countries. The ITTA is administered by the International Tropical Timber Organisation (ITTO).

The International Tropical Timber Agreement: The ITTA is of particular importance because it is the only international commodity Agreement that includes conservation as a major objective, noting in its preamble that it:

> Recognis[es] the importance of, and the need for, proper and effective conservation and development of tropical forests with a view to ensuring their optimum utilisation while maintaining the ecological balance of the regions concerned and the biosphere [and that the ITTA should] encourage the development of national policies aimed at sustainable utilisation and conservation of tropical forests and their genetic resources and at maintaining ecological balance in the regions concerned.

Whether or not this will be acted upon remains to be seen. The voting structure within the Agreement encourages sustainable use of forests in that votes are proportional to a range of factors, including the total area of forest, the size of the timber trade, and so on; thus countries which conserve their forest resources are not penalized in terms of their voting strength on the grounds that they do not export large quantities of timber.

The ITTO has, so far, not been very active. It took two years to decide that its secretariat should be in Yokohama, Japan. Its most significant development has been to establish a special projects fund to help research into forestry development. It does, however, provide an invaluable international forum for all those involved in every aspect of the tropical timber trade: previously there had been surprisingly little exchange of information at this level. The ITTO also provides an environment in which foresters can sit alongside those more directly involved in government policies and trade. These regular meetings will inevitably lead to a closer understanding between all involved in the industry. Foresters will realize that their proposals have political implications; trade ministers will acquire a greater understanding of the dilemmas facing timber producers.

Another important aspect is that, for the first time, all the world's tropical timber producers, who have traditionally been great rivals, can gather under one roof. This may not lead to a reduction in rivalries, but it does at least provide the environment out of which a cartel, similar to that for the major oil producers, may emerge between tropical timber producers. Probably only through such a collective strategy may producers be able to influence the international tropical timber markets.

A log export ban: One possible outcome of producers meeting may be a ban in log exports from South-East Asia, or even all producer nations. The future of the timber industry in South-East Asia will be strongly influenced by whether the Malaysian and Papua New Guinea governments continue to export logs. By early 1990 a log export ban was under consideration by the Malaysian Federal government, but this is meeting much resistance from the East Malaysian states.

It is generally accepted that the timber industry's exploitation of forests would decrease if the profit margin from the timber cut could be increased. Processing timber into finished products dramatically enhances its value, therefore fewer forests would need to be cut to maintain current profit margins enjoyed by the trade in logs. Conversely, however, it could be argued that to increase the value of timber in this way would create an even greater incentive for illegal logging. Both arguments have credence, but timber processing requires investment in sawmills and factories. This makes the operation less mobile and generally less attractive to the timber poacher.

It may be argued that to ban log exports helps only those countries with a well-developed domestic demand for timber. In this view, major international buyers will obtain their logs from other sources, and any economy that operates a ban will therefore lose custom. This scenario, however, presumes that Western consumer nations will be able to buy logs elsewhere. A cartel between tropical timber producing nations could reduce that option. There is little sign that the industrialized nations will lose their desire for tropical timber because they can no longer buy logs. Without co-ordinated action, however, there will be little incentive for areas with small domestic timber markets, such as Sarawak in East Malaysia, to stop exporting logs.

Timber trade problems and the debt crisis partly explain why the industry has to work at maximum speed using highly destructive extraction methods. Abandoning these methods and developing sustainable forestry, however, requires more than adjustments within the international timber trade; it must be linked with developments in other fields, notably rural development policy and land reform. The third strategy in the Alternative Tropical Forest Action Plan is to halt international funding for destructive rural development projects.

Destructive development projects: All projects that necessitate clearing large areas of tropical forest, particularly virgin forest, need to be reviewed. This does not mean that all projects that affect forest areas must be abandoned, but that reassessment under new social and ecological criteria is essential.

A major assumption in current forestry projects, including replanting schemes, is that the outcome is the same whether the forest is managed collectively, privately or through a multinational corporation. The proposals for many replanting programmes go no further than that trees need to be planted and that forests should be sustainably managed. The social context is frequently ignored.

In most rural areas of Asia, the extraction and distribution of forest produce operates under two separate economies: subsistence and market. Both are active in most areas, but the majority of the rural poor receive little or no benefit from the market economy. Many rural development projects aim to replace the subsistence economy with a market economy; this is frequently cited as 'development', but development for whom?

Only by meeting the needs of both economies will development projects attain their stated goal of sustainable forestry. Development agencies should avoid projects that are likely to have a detrimental effect on the subsistence economy. Whilst no one should be denied access to the cash economy, the most basic needs of the population must be ensured before a surplus is produced for cash.

The more successful reafforestation projects have adopted such an approach. The Burmese *tayanga* system may plant fewer trees than some of the vast commercial estates in Thailand but, primarily due to the social organization of the replanting process, the Burmese trees have a much better chance of survival. The present Tropical Forest Action Plan fails to recognize the importance of the social aspects of replanting and assumes that to plant trees for the market economy will automatically aid the subsistence economy; whereas market economies frequently destroy subsistence economies. The Burmese *tayanga* system, however, illustrates that the two economies can be developed side by side without one overriding the other.

In short, all development projects in forest areas should be based on the social imperative of restoring people's rights to maintain their life-supporting base, before the demands of the market economy are met. The sole means to apply this philosophy in all areas is through land ownership reform.

Land reform: The issue of land reform seems to have been purposefully avoided by development agencies, the World Bank and Third World governments, but this is a political raw nerve in Asia that can no longer be ignored. A major obstacle to land reform is that, due to the inequitable distribution of land ownership, a few powerful individuals in the Third World, who usually have strong ties with government, have amassed personal fortunes from the current situation. Most development agencies disregard the issue in order to avoid antagonizing the authorities with whom they must work. A more cynical view on why development agencies may not promote land reform is that, if put into practice, the cost of Third World produce to Western consumers would be increased. This is in part because current prices are kept artificially low by Third World producers paying extremely low wages and making very little long term investment in the land.

Control of land and resources may be organized in a variety of ways: under outright, permanent, individual ownership; permanent ownership by a community; free access and use rights may be granted to individuals or a community by a land owner; or rented out to an individual or group by the owner. There are, obviously, a variety of permutations possible in this model.

Currently, the predominant patterns in much of South-East Asia are either: state ownership, under which individuals or very occasionally, communities, may be granted free or rented access rights; or individual ownership. In most countries, the best quality agricultural land is owned by a few individuals or companies, and the state owns the rest.

This pattern of land ownership has led to the creation of the landless farmer, cited by many governments and development agencies as the main perpetrator of deforestation. The landless farmer is, however, largely a political refugee rather than the result of too many people in too small an area. Landlessness does not imply an insufficiency of land to support a population, but a denial of access to, or ownership rights over, land.

There are three major reasons why land reform should receive priority: 1) the need to provide adequate land for the subsistence economy, as outlined earlier; 2) the probable inability of industrial sectors to provide enough employment to absorb the projected growth in population; and 3) traditional forest dwelling societies' wealth of knowledge and experience, properly harnessed, would be an invaluable asset in developing sustainable forestry systems.

Many development analysts now realize the value of the environmental and agricultural knowledge held by all traditional farmers in the tropics, not only those in forest areas. But the ability of these farmers to practise sustainable agriculture is frequently restricted to the areas particular groups have traditionally farmed. Nevertheless, these traditional farming systems have much to contribute to the development of sustainable agriculture throughout South-East Asia, and knowledge of these techniques must not be lost.

Giving the land back to the landless, however, would not automatically end forest destruction. Even with land titles, many farmers who have been forced into forested areas would continue to clear trees because they have no experience of farming in the forests. The knowledge of traditional forest-dwelling societies must also be sought and harnessed in order to provide the technical expertise essential for sustained use of forest areas.

Only individual governments can implement a land reform system. Obviously, powerful landowners would oppose such reform as it would undermine their status. The common arguments used against land reform are: the economy would collapse; it is impractical; and it is based on communist ideals. These criticisms arise more from fear of losing power than rational consideration.

What might result if land reform became a reality? The following is based on tackling the deforestation problem in the three major agricultural land types present in any tropical country: high-grade farmland far from the forest; marginal farmland on the forest edge; and farming within the forest itself. All three areas form a continuum of any land use, and development policy should, therefore, be fully integrated; here, however, it is convenient to deal separately with each land-use type.

High-grade farmland: Originally, almost all these areas were centres of population, but at present most farmers who traditionally cultivated this land are denied access to it as it is currently occupied by large estates producing cash crops. Redistribution of land titles would involve splitting these estates into smaller individually or communally-owned farming units.

In the Third World, not only are small-scale intensive farms able to meet the needs of the subsistence economy more effectively than large estates, but they also make greater use of the available resources and thus reduce dependence on expensive imports. In addition, unlike large estates, small farms are labour, not capital intensive, and thus provide greater employment.

Small-scale forestry projects could be initiated within such a new land distribution system. As these areas have been cultivated for many years, the need to replant large areas of forest to protect the immediate environment is not as urgent as in more recently deforested areas. Small but numerous plots of trees could be established to provide a full range of products, such as fuel, fodder, and food, some of which could service both the cash and subsistence economies. Local control of species grown and areas to be planted must be retained, because the farmers have the greatest knowledge of what the local environment can sustain. Non-local participation in the reafforestation process should be limited to the provision of initial capital – donated, not loaned. These small woodlands could be managed either as individually or collectively owned plots; the crucial factor being that whichever system is adopted, it must be socially acceptable to the people involved.

Obviously the implementation of such a policy would be a huge, complex operation. There would no doubt be problems in ensuring that current owners are not allowed to manipulate the policy in order to retain land, as well as ensuring that redistribution was equitable. A major problem, however, would be to secure international funding to facilitate such change. International lending and development agencies have enthusiastically provided funding for such grandiose projects as large dams, but will they come forward with the cash for a more controversial approach? It would be a major change of focus in their funding objectives; a change that at this time it is impossible to predict will, or will not, take place. Probably the most difficult obstacle to such proposals would, however, be the host governments themselves.

One result of such a programme would be a major shift of population back to the more fertile lowlands. But this alone would not entirely relieve landless farmers' pressure on the forests.

Marginal land on the forest edge: It should be emphasized that a flexible approach is needed when defining areas that are marginal land or full forest.

With proper management, farming on marginal lands, which will continue to be a fact of life in many areas as the population of South-East Asia increases, could be considerably less damaging than at present. The combined research of ecologists and anthropologists has confirmed that many traditional swidden cultivation systems are both highly productive and also conserve forests; a fact that may have been revealed much sooner if an intensive analysis of traditional farming across the region had been undertaken earlier. It is hardly coincidental that tribal groups in Papua New Guinea, the Philippines, Indonesia, and Malaysia have developed similar, environmentally-sound farming systems; modern, Western-style farming on recently cleared forest land has, however, frequently proved to be disastrous.

A new approach to farming these areas would need to be developed. To implement such drastic change the authorities must ensure the full co-operation of the local population. The starting point should involve providing farmers with legal claims to the land they cultivate, thus ensuring their long-term interest in the area. This is especially pertinent in these particular areas because tree planting should be central to the farming system and, therefore, planning has to be on a long time-scale.

The development of a co-ordinated management system would be necessary in order to promote the three major forest types that need to be established: 1) agricultural forests, where field-based agriculture is combined with agro-forestry for timber and other forest produce; 2) productive forests, where tree cover is maintained and minor forest produce and timber are developed; and 3) protective forests, on steep slopes, where only a limited variety of minor forest industries may be practised. Once established, however, there would be an overlap in function and area between these forest types. For example, all forested areas are environmentally protective, and both protective and productive forest may be exploited for a range of produce, timber extraction defining the difference between the two. One universal principle, however, must be that no forest may be cleared to accommodate any replanting project.

Central to development in the marginal lands should be that trees and forests are close by and easily accessible to the farmers. One advantage of the Burmese *tayanga* system is the farmers' perception of a close link between the health and abundance of the food crops and the condition of the forests in which they are planted. Agro-forestry should be practised in all replanted areas, possibly including protective forest zones.

In agricultural forests the land would form a patchwork of small fields and forest, similar to many swidden systems already established. A rotation system would help reduce dependence on imported fertilizers; land left fallow could be planted with as wide a variety of native trees as possible. Local people should be permitted to sell timber that is felled as a result of clearing swidden sites, thus to a limited agree, swidden forests could contribute to timber production. But the primary function of these agricultural forests should remain as soil-retention and food-production areas. A general principle that might be considered is that replanted or semi-natural forest should cover at least 50% of the land surface.

Individual farming plots could either be owned outright or held under long leases. Long-term interest in the area's trees and fallow land would be perceived to have value in so far as their potential contribution to a family's welfare is concerned, although there may still be a temptation to clear all the land for crops. Planning restrictions similar to those imposed on developments in the West might provide limited support for the scheme by ensuring that farmers do not totally clear their areas of trees; but this may prove difficult to enforce. Secure, clearly defined land titles would help enforcement, but the main impetus must clearly come from external economic incentives not to clear trees.

An alternative to individual land ownership might reflect traditional *adat* systems, with ownership of land vested in the community. This would require an unambiguous definition of what constitutes a 'community' in each country; obviously such a group should not extend to the nation state. Within such a system individual families living within the community could receive 'use' rights over specific areas of cleared land, including fallow areas; these rights to be forfeited by any family which left the community. In both systems, use or ownership rights apply equally to all land including the forest and fallow areas.

Productive forests could be established in areas unsuitable for permanent or swidden agriculture. The management of these areas could also be based on the *adat* system whereby ownership of the forest rests with the community but use rights are granted to individuals. Unlike at present, however, timber would be only one of many materials to emerge from productive forests; a wide variety of tree species should therefore be established. If the timber industry is active in these areas it must ensure that extraction methods do not damage other trees. Certain slow-growing trees could provide a base for crops such as rattan, interspersed with faster-growing hardwoods that would ensure a significant economic return within a generation.

A new approach to environmentally protective forests is essential, one that ensures permanent tree cover. In areas where trees need to be re-established, less intensive agro-forestry systems may be applied. Low impact minor forest product industries should be developed in established protective forest to ensure that a ban on logging and clearance for agriculture is adhered to. Planting groves of fruit and other productive trees should be actively encouraged, thus making the forest a valuable resource. In all areas preference must be given to native trees; exotic species such as eucalyptus should be used only sparingly, in the absence of any other option.

In the forest: In these areas there has been relatively little forest clearance by shifted farmers, and land reform here would perhaps be the easiest sector to administer. With the exception of Papua New Guinea, forests are almost totally controlled by central government so redistribution would involve only one major body.

Most tribal groups still lay claim to particular forest areas despite lack of official recognition. In addition, the social structure for organizing land development is already present in the form of *adat* law.

Recognition of *adat* law would facilitate the elimination of many internal problems tribal groups have encountered. In East Malaysia, for example, individual tribal leaders have made claims over areas of communal forest and then sold the land to timber companies. This has been possible only because the authorities refuse to recognize decisions taken by village co··. :s which either nullify these claims or depose the tribal leader. *Adat* law can deal effectively with such abuse of power because it is a system based on communal rights. The recognition of the *adat* system in South-East Asia is supported by the UN International Conference on Civil and Political Rights, which declared that:

> All people have the right to self determination. By virtue of that right they freely determine their political status and freely pursue their economic, social and cultural development.

Tribal groups, according to most anthropologists, are a distinct people and not simply a sub-group of mainstream society. They have their own languages, cultures and social structures, all of which differ significantly from the dominant cultures.

Legislation could be developed to give legal protection over land issues for the group or community as a whole. In legal terms, ownership could extend to past, present and future members of the community. Ownership rights would need to include all land used by the community and everything that grows on that land or is found beneath its surface. In effect this would result in timber and mining rights for tribal communities.

The exclusion of tribal groups from development projects is well documented. Without the security of owning land, tribal groups have no means of ensuring their inclusion in development proposals. For example, forests are being exploited faster than at any time in the past and yet only in Papua New Guinea, where land rights for forest dwellers are recognized, do tribal people derive any benefits from the exploitation of their lands. Can the claim by many authorities that forests are being developed for the benefit of people in these remote areas be justified when the people themselves are rarely consulted? How can failure to consult those whose entire life-style may be disrupted by some project contribute to their development?

The strongest argument in favour of tribal land rights, however, is that it comes from the tribes themselves. Throughout South-East Asia the demand for land rights has been the same. Tribal groups are not opposed to development, but obviously they want to influence what happens to them and their land. This demand is hardly unreasonable but rather a contribution to a more balanced form of development. As the previous chapters have shown, for tribal groups, development means providing them with a choice of life-style rather than relegation to work on plantations or becoming urban squatters.

The strongest opposition to tribal land rights has come from politicians and businessmen involved with the timber and mining industries. They frequently claim that: the forests belong to the nation as a whole, not just those who live in them; they require orderly and systematic management, and local inhabitants are incapable of this; and that development for people in these remote areas can be provided only by exploiting the forests for timber. The national control over a national asset argument does not stand up to closer scrutiny, as benefits from forest exploitation have frequently extended no further than an urban political elite.

The case that only the timber industry can manage the forests efficiently is equally unfounded, particularly in view of the industry's poor record in the past. The method of obtaining timber licences, for example, can hardly be judged fair or orderly. The argument also fails to explain how the present crisis arose. If forest destruction is the work of tribal groups, why are they still living in the forest? If tribal agricultural systems are as destructive as some claim, the trees would have been cleared generations ago.

The claim that tribal land rights would retard development is equally unfounded. The argument implies that a community loses its right to development if it controls what happens on its land.

The economics of reformed lowlands

By splitting the large estates into smaller units, individual farmers will have a greater choice over what they grow on their land. Farmers in most parts of the world first ensure that they have enough subsistence crops before producing a surplus for market. The development of infrastructure will influence which crops are grown in any region. If access to ports was highly developed, farmers may choose to grow crops for export; in other locations they may depend more on local economies.

In the short-term the national economy would lose income from cash crop exports; but this may be counteracted by two consequential developments: 1) small farms would not be so heavily reliant on imported fertilizers and machinery as are the large estates. There would therefore be a decrease in imports of these materials, which necessitate a major flow of cash out of the country and into the coffers of Western business; 2) cash flows within the country's economy would be stimulated as wealth became more equitably distributed. The wealth amassed by the large landowners is rarely kept or reinvested in the country of origin; it usually resides in European bank accounts or property investment in the more affluent parts of the world, providing an escape route if the political climate changes. A multitude of small farmers, producing cash crops for local as well as international markets, would retain capital in their respective countries.

Redistribution of land ownership, and consequently wealth, would not necessarily improve the servicing of foreign debts, but the present system is also incapable of this. Under a system similar to that outlined above, local populations would be more able to support themselves. The viability of cash crop production in smaller units, using local technologies and dividing profits between a large number of small farmers, would also do much to reduce demand for new farmland in forested areas.

Economics of reformed marginal lands

Rehabilitation of the environment in these areas by establishing agro-forestry systems would, initially, be a major drain on a country's economy, but within approximately 30 years significant economic gains could be achieved. With proper management, the forests that already survive could be exploited for minor forest produce, but not for logging.

A range of government financial incentives would be needed to encourage farmers to develop minor forest produce industries as their main source of income, rather than to clear forest for cash crops. Investment by government and development agencies should, therefore, be channelled in the same direction, with the provision of processing and distribution facilities for such produce. It could be argued that the profit incentive to clear forests on these marginal lands will remain if the forest is a communal resource, but there is a clear distinction between communal ownership and a more general, state ownership, in which the local population has no direct interest. All forest in these marginal areas should be managed privately or communally, not by the central government. This would help ensure that unscrupulous individuals are unlikely to plant crops in these areas, as individuals or the community in the vicinity would have legal claim over its ownership.

By basing agriculture in these areas on agro-forestry or traditional swidden systems, the methods used will be totally new to many of the farmers involved. The strong influence of traditional forest agriculture in this system will create its own problems, as tribal groups are consistently regarded as the lowest class of people in Asian society; consequently, many migrant farmers would probably dismiss these agricultural systems simply because of old prejudices. A major education programme is therefore necessary: old ideas can be promoted as new innovations, with the right approach. That most Third World communities regard Western ideas and methods as more advanced and successful could, ironically, prove to be useful: an education campaign combining Westerners and tribal peoples could be very influential. Obviously this would be no substitute for breaking down social prejudices between migrant farmers and tribal groups, but it may help the process.

Economics of a reformed forest
There can be little doubt that the tropical timber industry would become much less active in South-East Asia. Tribal groups recognize the value of tropical timbers, but also believe that timber exploitation should no longer dominate forest development.

In East Malaysia, tribal communities envisage a low-key timber industry: using locally appropriate technology; labour not capital intensive; and controlling a locally based processing industry. Tribal groups see replanting and forest management as crucial to the survival of their culture as well as to their economy and environment.

Because of this deeply-rooted commitment that combines cultural and economic survival with the environment, the possibility of developing a sustainable timber industry would be stronger if local forest dwellers controlled forests. Most tribal peoples' deep veneration for forests, and the multitude of spirits that inhabit them, should not be underestimated. Many of the bitterest conflicts between tribal groups and loggers have been provoked by loggers destroying religiously significant sites.

On a national level, loss of income from current timber exports could be more than equalled by the development of minor forest product industries. Norman Myers goes into some detail on his vision of tropical forests as industrial complexes in his book *The Primary Source*. Forests, he argues, could almost be regarded as industrial estates with industries based on 'phytochemical' rather than petrochemcial production; in other words, plants rather than oil could form the industrial base. Myers estimates that one in six tropical forest plants (15,000 species) are of some value to humankind.

Collection of these raw materials may not provide a great income in itself, but with basic processing the financial returns could be considerable. Certain kinds of forest produce, mainly the waxes, resins and low bulk items, increase greatly in value with basic processing. These industrial complexes could have small processing plants in or near the forests, thus reducing transport costs for the raw materials and providing rural employment as an alternative to cutting down more forest. But such an industrial system would be viable only if general infrastructure was developed concurrently, as the produce needs collection and distribution networks. The potential for such development, however, cannot be overstated.

A major capital input is required to establish numerous small projects. Attempts to encourage private sector investment in reafforestation have failed in most countries and it is unlikely that this sector would be willing to invest in minor forest produce industries. Government and foreign development aid should be directed towards this option. As noted in the Indonesian study, minor forest produce is a boom industry.

These proposals may seem complex, but the forest environment is itself complex. The Alternative Tropical Forest Action Plan is a workable alternative to current development policies for the forests. To approach environmental problems as a series of discrete compartments is no longer viable; integrated and co-operative endeavours by all concerned are needed. There are no easy answers and the final stage in the process for change – creating the political will – is perhaps the most difficult to achieve.

People destroy forests; people can stop the destruction. Political awareness of the problem is developing, from small tribal villages up to the World Bank. Even within forestry departments there is an acceptance of the need to reform forest politics. To overtly oppose the present political control of forests can, however, cost an employee his or her job. To develop an awareness of the problem in those not directly involved in forestry is vital, but at present trees are being felled faster than the general awareness is developing. The political process must be accelerated.

Creating the political will

A political will is not a static concept; the West's rapidly increasing anxiety over the health of the planet is a relevant example. All major political parties in the West are asserting their concern for the environment, despite their previously poor records on these issues. The problem of tropical forest destruction is central to the health of the planet, and international action, regardless of political ideology, is clearly essential.

All nations are becoming ever more intricately linked in one another's affairs. International trade presupposes that foreign companies, individuals and governments will have interests in other countries. This interdependence is at all levels: from the multilateral development banks to the promotion of pop culture: Michael Jackson and Pepsi Cola are immensely popular throughout South-East Asia.

Foreign influence in what is considered to be a country's domestic policy is far more pervasive than governments admit. Advising and encouraging development along a certain path will, to many, seem simply a subtle way of influencing another nation's politics; but, as the previous pages have shown, this kind of influence is acceptable to many Third World governments. Ideas from the industrialized nations do, even if indirectly, affect Third World politics. For example, coverage of environmental issues in the Third World media is frequently based on reports in Western newspapers (although the process is not generally reciprocated). Cynics claim that such reports divert attention from domestic problems; others argue that it is a form of ridiculing the West by showing that 'we in Asia have no such problems'. Officials in Asia commonly tell an audience that the forests in Asia are in good condition while those in Europe and the US are dying of acid rain. In the early 1970s, however, these same politicians had probably never heard of acid rain, or seen the environment as a political issue.

The environmental movement has developed three strategies within which it promotes its cause: 1) to fund specific projects such as nature reserves and poverty alleviation schemes; 2) to educate future decision-makers in environmental concerns; 3) by dynamic campaigns to exert direct pressure on politicians and industry towards changing their thinking. The application of these strategies varies from country to country.

The specific projects approach has been covered in the previous chapters. The education of future decision-makers is, however, a long-term objective that eventually will have a more beneficial effect on development problems. The majority of current Third World politicians have at some time worked or studied in the West, and have probably been strongly influenced by the attitudes of their teachers. Until the late 1970s many Third World overseas students studied subjects that had little relevance to the situation in their home country. This has, however, changed as the number of courses designed specifically for Third World circumstances increases. But many of these courses are still taught within a Western frame of reference that stoutly resists an integrated approach to development.

The process of transferring ideas and creating the current political climate, however, is not limited to the academic field. Much of the pressure exerted on Western governments to take note of environmental issues originates from the more dynamic campaigning methods developed since the early 1970s. In the West, Greenpeace, Friends of the Earth and similar groups have the support of significant proportions of the population. Greenpeace is perhaps the best known group which has become extremely efficient at creating news. Groups involved with tropical forest issues, using high-profile media campaigning techniques, include Worldwide Fund for Nature (WWF), Friends of the Earth International, the Rainforest Action Network and the World Rainforest Movement. There are also a large number of smaller, national organizations.

Political pressure from such groups is not limited to publicity exercises. Direct lobbying of politicians and influencing consumer demand is also employed. Friends of the Earth in the UK identified tropical timber as a major source of the deforestation problem, and now actively encourage consumers to boycott all tropical hardwoods from non-sustainable sources. This poses a direct threat to the timber industry and to politicians in tropical timber-producing countries. The effect of the boycott has been limited, but it still retains the possibility of inflicting serious damage to a producer's economy. Direct economic pressure is perhaps the most potent weapon for changing the views of today's decision-makers.

Most Third World pressure groups must be cautious about any public statements they make regarding development issues; few governments will tolerate repeated criticism. Government authorities unjustifiably accuse conservation groups in Asia of being anti-development and working against the national interest. Nevertheless, since the late 1970s the Third World has seen a similar growth in pressure groups and non-government organizations. Most have taken a different approach to tackling environmental problems. Many Western environmental groups developed from single issue campaigns such as whaling, or nuclear power. In South-East Asia, however, most groups cover as wide a range of environmental issues as possible. Groups such as Sahabat Alam Malaysia (SAM) and members of the Asia Pacific Peoples Environmental Network base campaigns on the problems faced by particular communities. Environmental problems are initially identified by their effect on the local population. This spatial definition for campaigning requires a much more integrated approach than that taken by most Western environmentalists, and it could be seen as a more sophisticated means of tackling environmental problems. Both styles have their merits.

An important aspect of environmental organizations in both the Third World and the West is that most have some form of membership which enables the general public to become involved. This is more popular in the West where people have had enough money to join a group or give donations. Sahabat Alam Malaysia does not base its work on servicing a membership, as most of the people it seeks to help could not afford to join. The similarity between all these organizations is, however, that their approach involves contacting large numbers of people, and as a result politicians have begun to show an interest in their views. The common philosophy behind this is quite simple: the greater the number of people involved, the more likely are politicians to realize the potential votes in these issues, and hence act on them. Clearly this approach is beginning to work.

Most environmental pressure groups, particularly those in the Third World, are chronically short of funds. They may be able to bring issues to the attention of the public and politicians but they lack the finances to implement their proposals. For practical action an alliance is needed between the voluntary sector, central governments, and development agencies at all levels.

The crux of this argument is that the problem of tropical deforestation is of sufficient importance and urgency to warrant an immediate end to political in-fighting and rivalry. Unless political ideologies can be bridged in order to prevent the occurrence of perhaps the greatest environmental disaster to face the human race, the 20th century will undoubtedly go down in history as a dark age.

A final comment

This book is intended to pose as many questions as it attempts to answer. The changes suggested are aimed at creating debate rather than proffered as the one solution. More data is needed in some areas, but there is enough evidence to warrant immediate action to halt the present scale of forest destruction.

Nevertheless, the present decimation of the tropical forest should not be regarded in isolation but rather as a symptom of the general problems associated with development, which is why a holistic approach to tackling these problems is needed. Life on earth can survive and evolve without humankind and we are simply one, probably temporary, occupant. Only by accepting this view is there any chance that enough forest will survive into the next millennium to ensure the health of the planet and all that depend on it.

Unless this book stimulates a desire to help stop the destruction of tropical forest it has failed in its purpose. To this end, in addition to a grasp of information and 'facts' there is an acute and universal need to exercise wisdom, tolerance and compassion.

What can the ordinary person do?
1) Join a campaigning organization – see the list at the end of this text, which, although incomplete, includes some of the major groups campaigning on this and other development issues.

2) Those already active within local social or political groups should ensure that environmental issues appear on their agenda. The environment covers the entire globe, from conditions on a factory floor in London or Bangkok, to the forests of Borneo. A poor environment affects the potential of all humans in it, wherever the location.

3) The final and most profound change therefore must come from individuals. Politics and the survival of the environment cannot be separated. It is the non-political consumer who fills the coffers of the Philippine sugar barons. Environmental and development problems are not perpetuated by political greed alone, they are also created through complacency and ignorance. City-dwellers in the industrialized nations have not become less reliant on the environment for their everyday needs; they see only the end product of an industrial process and tend to forget what supports that process. What does a rubber or mahogany tree look like, and where do you see their products?

By finding the answer to such questions the consumer has the option of choice. It is not the timber from the forests or the fruit from plantations that is bad, but the system under which they are produced.

One option is to find an alternative source. This is one way in which governments who make an effort to meet the needs of their people may be rewarded on the international markets. Such efforts must be encouraged by consumers asking for these products and increasing demand, thus helping those countries that make a positive step towards creating a sustainable future.

In the end, however, it is pointless to tell the Third World to stand on its own two feet when we in the West continue to stand on their hands.

1.) Join a campaigning organization

Organizations Involved with Rainforest Issues

Australia

Rainforest Information Centre
PO Box 368
Lizmore
New South Wales

Tasmanian Wilderness Society
129 Bathurst St
Hobart
Tasmania 7000

Friends of the Earth
366 Smith St
Collingwood
Victoria 3066

India

Research Foundation for Science Technology and Natural Resource Policy
105 Rajpur Rd
Dehra Dun 248001
North India

Indonesia

WHALI
Ji Suryopranto 8
Jakarta Pusat
Indonesia

Malaysia

Sahabat Alam Malaysia
43 Salween Road
Penang 10050
Malaysia

Papua New Guinea

Friends of the Earth
PO Box 554
Konedobu
PNG

Wau Ecology Centre
Wau
PNG

Philippines

Episcopal Commission on Tribal Filipinos
Room 15
Cap Buildings
372 Cabildo St
Intramuros
Manila

UK

Friends of the Earth
26–28 Underwood St
London N1 7JQ

Survival International
310 Edgware Rd
London W2 1DY

Worldwide Fund for Nature
Panda House
Godalming
Surrey

International Institute for Environment and Development
3 Endsleigh St
London WC1H 0DD

United States of America

Rainforest Action Network
300 Broadway
Suite 28
San Francisco
CA 94133

Friends of the Earth
1045 Sansome Street
San Francisco
CA 9411

Bibliography

Abang Naruddin Zainorin (1985) 'The status of logging safety and accident prevention in Sarawak'. Paper presented to seminar on occupational safety in the logging industry in Sarawak, 19–20 August, STIDC, Kuching, Sarawak.

Adittondro, G. (1979) 'The Jungles are Awakening'. *Kogui No.22 Jishu Koza*. Tokyo, Japan.

————(1986) 'Transmigration in Irian Jaya'. *Open House for Development*. April, Amsterdam.

————(no date) 'Forest Wealth: Exploitation in Indonesia'. *Asian Environmental Newsletter*. Sahabat Alam Malaysia (SAM).

Agaloos, B. (1983) 'Silvicultural and logging systems in the Philippines'. Paper presented to the First Asian Forestry Conference, Bureau for Forest Development, Manila.

Agbayani, R. (1984) 'Injustice against man'. *Tribal Forum*, Sept./Oct. Episcopal Commission on Tribal Filipinos, Manila.

Agricultural Reform Office (1980) 'Land areas development projects'. Ministry of Agriculture and Cooperatives, Thailand.

Aguilar, F. (1982) 'Social Forestry for Upland Development.' Institute for Philippine Culture, Ateno de Manila University, Philippines.

Alken, R., and C. Leigh (1985) 'On the declining fauna of Peninsula Malaysia in the post colonial period'. *Ambio* (Sweden) Vol. 14, No. 1.

Alunan, G. (1986) 'Letters to the Editor'. *The Malaya* (Manila) 30 July.

Alunan, M (1986) 'Blamed for Forest Destruction'. *Daily Yomuri* (Tokyo) 27 April.

AMPO (1980) 'Indonesia', Vol. 12, No.4. Pacific-Asia Resource Centre, Tokyo.

Anderson, A. (1978) 'Nutrition of Kayan and Kenyah children in the middle Baram river'. *Sarawak Gazette*, 30 November.

Anderson, J. (1974) *Social strategies in population change: Village data from Central Luzon*. University of California Press. USA.

Andriesse, J. (1977) 'Nutrient level changes during a 20 year shifting cultivation cycle in Sarawak'. Paper presented to the International Society of Soil Science Conference on Classification and Management of Tropical Soils. Kuala Lumpur.

Angel, S. (1985) 'Where have all the people gone?'. Paper presented to the UN seminar on Planning for Settlement in Rural Regions'. Nairobi, Kenya.

Asia Pacific Peoples Environmental Network (1984) 'Eucalyptus: The controversy continues'. *The Ecologist* (UK) Vol. 14, No. 4.

Appropriate Technology Center (1984) 'Data base on shifting cultivation, agroforestry and social forestry'. Appropriate Technology Center for Rural Development, Manila.

Arndt, H. (1983) 'Transmigration: Achievements, Problems, Prospects'. *Bulletin of Indonesian Economic Studies*, Vol. XIX, No.3. Australian National University, Canberra.

Astbury, S. (1984) 'Agriculture in Indonesia'. *Asian Agribusiness* (UK) Vol. 1, No.5. International Trade Publications.

Azam Aris (1985) 'Local timber industry faces one of its toughest times'. *Malaysian Business Times*, 25 December.

———(1986) 'Time to deregulate local timber industry'. *New Straits Times* (Malaysia), 11 August.

Baharuddin Ghazali (1983) 'Peninsular Malaysia's timber industry in perspective'. Paper presented to the Malaysian Timber Marketing Conference, Ministry of Primary Industries.

Baradan, K. (1986) 'Sabah Foundation MS$170m. in the red'. *The Star* (Malaysia), 20 February.

Basa, V. (1986) 'Forest Land Use statistics and issues in the Philippines'. Paper presented to the Land Use Seminar, University of the Philippines at Los Banos.

Bellow, W. et al (eds) (1982) *Development debacle: The World Bank in the Philippines*, Institute for Food and Development Policy. University of California Press, USA.

Bhumibhamon, S. (1986) 'The environmental and socio-economic aspects of tropical deforestation: Thailand'. Department of Forestry, Kasestart University, Bangkok.

Bird, E., and O. Owgkosongo (1981) 'Indonesia Losing and Gaining Coastal Land'. *Work in Progress*. UN University, Tokyo, Japan.

Bonner, R. (1988) 'Reporter at Large'. *The New Yorker* (USA) 13 June.

Borsok, R. (1984) 'Vanishing forests expose Thailand's economy'. *Asian Wall Street Journal*, 30 January.

Bureau of Fisheries (Philippines) (1981) *Fishery Statistics of the Philippines*, Vol. 31. Ministry of Natural Resources, Philippines.

Bureau of Forest Development (Philippines) (1984) *The Environmental and Social Aspects of Deforestation in Asia and the Pacific: Philippines*. Ministry of Natural Resources, Philippines.

———(1986) Philippine Forestry Statistics: 1984. Ministry of Natural Resources, Philippines.

Burns, W. (1986) 'A cry in defence of the environment'. *Bangkok Post* (Thailand) 24 June.

Butler, S. (1987) 'Battle to save Sabah's Forests'. *Financial Times* (UK) 16 April.

Caldecott, J. (1985) 'Letter from Long Lellang'. *Far Eastern Economic Review* (Hong Kong) 26 September.

Caufield, C. (1985) *In the Rainforest*. A. Knopfe, New York, USA.

Centre Technique Forestier Tropical (1983) *Regional study for the commercialisation of timber resources in the Asean region.* Association for South East Asian Nations. Paris, France.

Chapmen, E. et al (eds) (1978) *Farmers in the Forest*. University of Hawaii Press, Honolulu, Hawaii.

Ching See Chung (1984) 'Agriculture and subsistence in a lowland rainforest Kenyah community'. Unpublished Ph.D. dissertation. Yale University, USA.

Chirapanda, S., and W. Tamrongtanyalak (1981) *Landlessness in Central Thailand*. Agricultural Land Reform Office, Bangkok.

Christensen, B. (1979) *Mangrove Forest Resources and their Management in Asia and the Far East*. FAO, Bangkok.

Chua, D.K.H. (1986) 'Forest engineering; its role in the management of the mixed dipterocarp forest of Sarawak'. Paper presented to the 9th Malaysia Forestry Conference. Kuching, Malaysia, October.

Colchester, M. (1986a) 'Unity and Diversity'. *The Ecologist* (UK) Vol. 16, Nos.2/3.

——— (1986b) 'The Struggle for Land'. *The Ecologist* (UK) Vol. 16, Nos.2/3.

Consumers Association of Penang (1979) Papers presented to the Conference on the State of the Environment. Penang, Malaysia.

——— (1987) 'Sarawak Blockades'. *Utasan Konsumer* (Malaysia) July.

Cruz, T. (1985) *Population pressure and migration in the Philippine Upland Communities*. Agrarian Reform Institute Occasional Paper No.13, Manila.

De Ath, C. (1980) 'The Throwaway People'. *Monograph* 13, Institute of Applied Economic and Social Research, Konedobu (PNG).

Depthnews (1986) 'Soil erosion affects 75% of Republic of Philippines Land Area'. *Metro News* (Manila) January.

Dhal, A. (1984) 'Oceania's most pressing environmental concerns'. *Ambio* (Sweden) Vol. 13. No.5–6.

Diro, T. (1986) 'Landowners get 75% timber cut'. *PNG Post Courier*, 24 March.

Duangpatra, P. (1983) 'Characteristics and potential productivities of some major cassava soils in Thailand'. Paper presented to the Fourth International Forum on Soil Taxonomy. Department of Land Development, Thailand.

Eads, B. (1985) 'Mighty timber blight', *The Guardian* (UK) 28 August.

Eckholm, E. (1976) *Losing ground*. World Watch Institute and United Nations Environment Programme (UNEP)/W.W. Norton. New York, USA.

——— (1979) 'Planting for the future: Forestry for human needs'. *World Watch Papers* No.26. February. World Watch Institute, New York, USA.

Eddowes, P. (1988) 'PNG steps forward as key log source'. *Timber Trades Journal* (UK) 27 August.

Endicot, K. (1982) 'The effects of logging on the Batek of Malaysia'. *Cultural Survival Quarterly* (UK) No.2.

Evans, S. (1983) 'Letters to the Editor'. *New Straits Times* (Malaysia) 14 March.

Flynn, R. (1978) 'The Sumatran rhino in Endau Rompin park'. *Malayan Naturalist*, January. Malayan Naturalist Society, Kuala Lumpur, Malaysia.

Federal Land Development Agency (Malaysia) (1956) Minutes of first meeting. FELDA, Kuala Lumpur, 8 August.

FAO (1979) 'The effects of logging and treatment on the mixed dipterocarp forests of South East Asia'. FAO, Rome, Italy.

——— (1980) 'Economic data for forestry planning in Sarawak'. UN Development Programme and FAO for the Forest Deparment of Sarawak,

Kuching, Malaysia.

———— (1981) *Forest Resources of Tropical Asia*. FAO. Rome, Italy.

———— (1985) 'Socio-economic benefits for social forestry; for whom?' FAO, Rome, Italy.

———— (1986) 'Promotion of Public Awareness for the consideration of forestry resources'. Environmental and Social Committee for Asia and the Pacific (ESCAP) meeting on the Environment and Socio-economic aspects of deforestation. FAO, Regional Office Bangkok, Thailand.

Forestry Department of Malaysia (1984) *Annual Report*. Ministry of Primary Industries. Kuala Lumpur, Malaysia.

———— (1988) 'Forestry in Malaysia'. Ministry of Primary Industries. Kuala Lumpur, Malaysia.

Friends of the Earth (PNG) (1984) 'Invaluable forests exchanged for worthless paper goods'. *FoE PNG Newsletter*, Lae, PNG.

Friends of the Earth (UK) (1988) Unpublished internal memo: Summary review on Shell company proposal project in Chantanaburi Province, Thailand.

Freese, P., and T. O'Brien (1983) *Forests, Trees and People*. Alternative Resource Center, Mindanao, Philippines.

Gabhir, R. (1986) 'Thailand's disappearing wildlife'. *The Nation* (Thailand) 20 June.

Ganapin, D. (1986a) 'Forest Resources and the Timber Trade in the Philippines'. Paper presented to the Regional Conference on Forest Resource Crisis in the Third World. SAM, Penang, Malaysia.

———— (1986b) 'Philippine Ethnic Minorities'. Paper presented to the Regional Conference on Forest Resource Crisis in the Third World. SAM, Penang, Malaysia.

Gnau, H. et al (1986) 'Malaysian timber Exploitation For Whom?' Paper presented to the Regional Conference on Forest Resource Crisis in the Third World. SAM, Penang, Malaysia.

Goh Kim Chum (1979) 'Rainfall trends and fluctuations in Peninsular Malaysia and other water resource implications'. Paper presented to the International Conference on Climate and History, University of East Anglia, UK.

———— (1983) 'Forest disturbance, runoff process and sediment yield'. Paper presented to the Regional Workshop on the Hydrological Impacts of Forestry Practices and Reafforestation. University of Malaya and UNESCO, Kuala Lumpur, Malaysia.

Goldsmith, E. and N. Hildyard (eds) (1986) *Social and Environmental Effects of Large Scale Dams*. Vol. 2. Wadebridge Ecology Centre. Cornwall, UK.

Golson, J. (1981) 'New Guinea agricultural history: a case study'. In Denoon, D. and C. Snowden (eds) *A History of Agriculture in PNG*. Institute of PNG Studies, Port Moresby, PNG.

Goodland, R. (1981) 'Indonesia's Environmental Progress in Economic Development'. Office of Environmental Affairs, World Bank, USA.

Goodno, J. (1986) 'Opposition mounts in the Philippines'. *Unte Reader*, February/March, Minnesota, USA.

Gradwohl, J. et al (1988) *Saving the Tropical Forest*. Earthscan, UK.

Grandstaff, T. (1980) 'Shifting conservation in Northern Thailand'. *Resource systems theory and methodology series*. No. 3. UN University, Tokyo, Japan.

Grynberg, R. (1985) 'Reafforestation; another empty promise?' *PNG Post Courier*, 2 December.

―――― (1986) 'An ecological disaster in the making?' *Times of PNG*, 15 March.

Grynberg, R. et al (1988) 'Transfer pricing and malpractice in the PNG log export industry'. *Journal of Interdisciplinary Economics*, Vol. 2. A.B. Academic Publishers, UK.

Guppy, N. (1984) 'Tropical Deforestation – a Global View'. *Foreign Affairs* (UK) Spring.

Hafield, E. (1986) Testimony before the Sub-Committee of Foreign Operations of the Senate Committee on Appropriations. SKEPHI, Jakarta, Indonesia.

Hanbury-Tenison, R. (1975) *Pattern of Peoples*. Survival International, UK.

Hatch, T. (1980) 'Shifting Cultivation in Sarawak, past, present and future'. In Furtado, J (ed.) *Tropical Ecology and Development*. Proceedings of the 5th International Symposium on Tropical Ecology, 16–21 April. International Society of Tropical Ecology, Kuala Lumpur, Malaysia.

―――― (1982) 'Shifting cultivation in Sarawak; a review'. Technical Paper No.8, Department of Agriculture, Sarawak, Malaysia.

Hatch, T. and Y. Tie (1979) 'Shifting cultivation in Sarawak and its effect on soil fertility'. Paper presented at the 6th Meeting on Standardisation of Soil and Plant Analysis in Malaysia. Society of Agricultural Scientists, Sabah.

Hayter, T. (1985) *The Creation of World Poverty*. Pluto Press, UK.

Heenuman, H (1983) 'The Future of Tropical Forest in Indonesia'. Paper presented to the Symposium on the Future of Tropical Rainforest in Southeast Asia. International Union for the Conservation of Nature (Malaysia).

Hill, P. (1982) 'Sinking feeling on a tedious river trip'. *Borneo Bulletin* (Malaysia) 30 October.

Hogbin, I. (ed.) (1973) *Anthropology in Papua New Guinea*. Melbourne University Press, Australia.

Hong, E. (1987) *Natives of Sarawak*. Institute Masyarakat, Penang, Malaysia.

Hoo, E. (1987) 'What logging really is; the inside story'. *Peoples Mirror* (Malaysia) 5 September.

Hood Saleh (1984) 'Orang Asli perceptions of the Malay world'. *Ilmu Masyarakat* (Malaysia) No.6.

Howe. J. and Richards. P. (eds) (1984) 'Rural Roads and Poverty Alleviation'. Intermediate Technology Publictions, UK.

Indonesia, Government of, and International Institute for Environment and Development, (GOI and IIED) (1985) *Forest Policies in Indonesia*. International Institute for Environment and Development, UK.

Institute for Social Analysis (1986) *Logging in Sarawak, the Belaga Experience*. Institute for Social Analsysis, Sarawak Study Group, Petaling Jaya, Malaysia.

James, R. (1981) 'Japanese paper companies come to PNG'. *AMPO* (Japan) Vol. 13, No.4. Pacific Asia Resource Centre, Tokyo.

Jhamtani, H. and E. Hafield (1986) 'Forest Resources in Indonesia'. Paper presented to the Regional Conference on Forest Resource Crisis in the Third World, Penang, September. SAM, Malaysia.

Jin Eong Ong (1982) 'Mangroves and Aquaculture in Malaysia'. *Ambio* (Sweden) Vol. 11, No.5.

Johnson, A. (1984) 'Thailand: Mixed prospects for agricultural development'. *Asian Agribusiness* (UK) Vol. 1, No.2.

Johnson, B. (1985) *Migrants to Disaster?* Earthscan, UK.

Karim, G. (ed.) (1986) *Information Malaysia*. Berita Publications, Malaysia.

Kartawinata, K. (no date) 'The Environmental Consequences of Tree Removal from the Forests in Indonesia'. National Biological Institute, Bogor, Java, Indonesia.

Kartawinata, K. et al (1981) 'The Impact of Man on a Tropical Forest in Indonesia'. *Ambio* (Sweden) Vol. 10, No.23.

Kemf, E. (1986) 'New hope for the Kouprey?'. *The Nation* (Thailand) 4 June.

Kew Bong Heang (1982) 'Conservation status of the Malaysian Fauna'. *Malayan Naturalist*, May, Malayan Naturalist Society, Selangor, Malaysia.

Khan, M. (1978) 'Man's impact on the primates of Peninsular Malaysia'. In Chivers and Lane-Peters (eds) *Recent Advances in Primatology*, Vol 2. Academic Press, UK.

Khoo, G. (1977) 'What's with this rain?'. *New Straits Times* (Malaysia), 5 June.

Kummer, D. (no date) 'Upland degradation and attempts at upland development in the Philippines'. Forestry Development Centre Policy Paper No.12. University of the Philippines.

Kwapena, N. (1985) 'Tropical rainforests and plantation forestry in PNG'. *The Environmentalist* (Switzerland) Vol. 5 Supplement 10, Sequoia.

Langro, P. (1986a) Personal communication with the Minister for Forests. 7 October, PNG.

—— (1986b) Personal communication with the Campaign to Save Native Forests. Western Australia. 26 October.

Lau Buong Tiing (1979) 'The effects of shifting cultivation on sustained yield management for Sarawak'. *Malaysian Forester* (Malaysia) Vol. 42, No.4.

Lau, K. (1984) 'Four sued for MS$35m.' *Sarawak Tribune* (Malaysia) 13 June.

Lennertz, R. and K. Panzer (1983) 'Preliminary Assessment of the Drought and Forest fire damage in Kalimantan Timor'. German Agency for Technical Cooperation, West Germany.

Leong Khee Seon (1983) Paper presented to the National Workshop on Underutilized Timbers. Malaysian Timber Industries Board.

Li Dun Jen (1982) *British Malaysia: an Economic Analysis*. Institute for Social Analysis, Kuala Lumpur, Malaysia.

Lim Ching Hing (1978) 'Quick before the valley goes'. *Malay Mail* (Malaysia) 1 February.

Lim, K.H. and M. Osman (1984) '41 major sawmills in Kelantan may close in May'. *New Straits Times* (Malaysia) 13 April.

Limis, D. (1986) 'Starving in Sugarland: a visit to Negros'. *AMPO* (Japan) Vol. 18, No.1. Pacific Asia Resource Centre, Tokyo.

Lobo, F. (1986) 'P2.7m. logs seized in raid'. *Manila Bullitin*, (Philippines) 13 March.

Loffler, E. (1979) *Papua New Guinea*. Hutchinson (Australia).

Mackenzie, D. (1988) 'Uphill battle to save Filipino trees'. *New Scientist* (UK) 30 June.

Mackie, C. (1984) *The Lessons behind East Kalimantan's Forest Fires*. Rutgers University Press, New Jersey, USA.

Madela, E. (1986) 'Forests Crisis'. *Manila Bullitin* (Philippines) 15 August.
Mahoney, R. (1985) 'Malaysia's fast vanishing forests'. *Borneo Bullitin* (Malaysia) 11 June.
Malaysia, Government of (1966) First Malaysia Plan (1966–70). Kuala Lumpur.
—— (1981) Fourth Malaysia Plan (1981–85). Kuala Lumpur.
—— (1986) Fifth Malaysia Plan (1986–90). Kuala Lumpur.
Malaysian Timber Industries Board (1983) 'Timber consumption patterns in Peninsular Malaysia 1983'. Ministry of Primary Industries, Malaysia.
—— (1985) 'Timber market profile: Japan'. Ministry of Primary Industries, Malaysia.
Maraleu, M. (1987) 'F.I.C. Notice to F.I.A. members'. *The Times* (PNG).
Meyer, W. (1984) Unpublished document. Kentucky University, USA.
Marn, H. and W. Jonkers (1980) 'Logging damage in tropical high forest'. In Srivastaua, P. et al (eds) *Tropical Forests; Source of Energy Through Optimisation and Diversification.* Proceedings of the International Forestry Seminar, Selangor, November 1980. Forestry Department of West Malaysia.
Ministry of Primary Industries (Malaysia) (1984) Department of Forestry: *Annual Report*.
—— (1985) 'Forestry in Malaysia' (promotional booklet). Department of Forestry, Malaysia.
Mohd Sham Bin Kasim (1986) *Nutritional status of the children of various Orang Asli communities in Malaysia.* University Kebangsaan, Malaysia.
Mukhopadhyay, S. (ed.) (1985) 'Case studies in poverty programmes in Asia'. Asia Pacific Development Centre, Kuala Lumpur, Malaysia.
Muller, M. (1978) *Tomorrow's Epidemic.* War on Want, UK.
Myers, N. (1980) 'Multinational Timber Corporations and Tropical Moist Forests'. *Newsletter of the Council for Economic Priorities*, September. New York, USA.
—— (1984) *The Primary Source.* W. Norton, UK.
—— (1986) 'Economics and Ecology in the International Arena'. *Ambio* (Sweden) Vol. 15, No.5.
Narinder Kaur (1985) 'Food Production in a Developing Country; The Malaysian Experience'. *The Ecologist* (UK) Vol. 15, No.5/6.
Nash, S. and A. Nash (1985) 'Elephants in Indonesia'. *WWF Monthly Report,* Project Number 1777, December. Gland, Switzerland.
'Normita' (1986) 'Nature notebook'. *Bangkok Post* (Thailand) 28 December.
Norzita Samad (1986) 'Signs indicate a limited recovery'. *The Star* (Malaysia) 14 July.
Olofson (No date) 'Adaptive strategies and change in swidden based societies'. Forest Research Institute, Lagunna, Philippines.
Osborne, R. (1985) 'Limited Success or Grandoise Failure?' Briefing Paper, May, Australian Council for Overseas Aid. Canberra, Australia.
Otten, M. (1986) 'Transmigration: from Poverty to Bare Subsistence'. *The Ecologist* (UK) Vol. 16, Nos.2/3.
Pannee Konkij (1986) 'Opposition moves on Burma log imports'. *Bangkok Post* (Thailand) 21 September.
PNG Consitutional Planning Committee (1973) Final Report. Government of Papua New Guinea.

Papua New Guinea Constitution (1975) Quoted in Instprofitive and Legislative Framework for Forestry Management in the ESCAP region. Proceedings of the Expert Group Meeting on the Environmental and Social Aspects of Tropical Deforestation, ESCAP, 1986. UN Regional Secretariat, Thailand.

Plumwood, V. and R. Routley (1982) 'World Rainforest Destruction'. *The Ecologist* (UK) Vol. 12, No.1.

Poore, D. (1984) 'Conservation: Major Issues'. International Institute for Environment and Development (IIED), UK.

Pushparajah, E. (1985) 'Development induced erosion and flash floods in Malaysia'. *The Ecologist* (UK) Vol. 15, No.1/2.

Rajaswary, I. and H. Rohiman (1986) 'FELDA at the crossroads'. *The Star* (Malaysia) 14 December.

Ramayah, J. (1977) 'Logging's the cause'. *Sunday Mail* (Malaysia) 14 August.

Ramitanondh, S. (1985) 'Socio-economic benefits from social forestry: For whom?' in, *Community Forestry: Socio-economic Aspects*. FAO, Rome, Italy.

Rao, R. (1986) 'Asian elephants fight for survival'. *The Nation* (Thailand) 20 April.

Repeto, R. (1986) 'Soil Loss and Population Pressure on Java'. *Ambio* (Sweden) Vol. 15, No.1.

Revila, A. (1984) 'Forest Land Management in the Context of National Land Use'. Philippine Institute for Development Studies. Working Paper No. 84-02-1984, University of the Philippines.

———— (1985) Paper presented to the Seminar on the Fifty Year Forestry Development Programme in the Philippines. Forestry Development Centre, University of the Philippines.

Rokiah Talib (1986) 'The politics of land development in Malaysia'. Quoted in Rajeswaary, I., and H. Rohiman (1986).

Romm, J. (1980) 'Forest Development in Indonesia and the Productive Transformation of Capital'. Department of Forestry Occasional Papers, University of California, USA.

Routley, R. and V. Routley (1980) 'Destructive Forestry in Melanesia and Australia'. *The Ecologist* (UK) Vol. 10, No.1.

Royal Forestry Department (Thailand) (1985) Forestry Statistics of Thailand for 1984. Ministry of Agriculture and Cooperatives, Thailand.

Sahabat Alam Malaysia (SAM) (1982) *State of the Malaysian Environment: Development Without Destruction*. SAM, Penang, Malaysia.

———— (1983) 'Fostering Deforestation'. *Environmental News Digest*, No.4, SAM, Penang, Malaysia.

———— (1985) *Sura Sam*. Autumn, SAM, Penang, Malaysia.

———— (1987) 'Sarawak Blockades'. Information sheet, SAM, Penang, Malaysia.

———— (Sarawak) (1986) Public Statement on the Timber Industry. November, Marudi, Sarawak, Malaysia.

Sarawak, Forestry Department of (1985) *Annual Report*. Kuching, Malaysia.

Sarawak Museum (1979) *Batang Ai Hydro-electric Project*. Report No.1, July, Kuching, Malaysia.

Sarawak Timber Industry Development Corporation (STIDC) (1981) 'Notes on forest industry safety and accident prevention in Sarawak'. 15 April, Malaysia.

Saulei, S. (1984) 'Natural regeneration following clear-fell logging in the Gogal valley'. *Ambio*, (Sweden) Vol. 13, Nos.5–6.

—— (1986) 'Forest resource development crisis in PNG'. Paper presented to the Regional Conference on Forest Resource Crisis in the Third World. SAM, Penang, Malaysia.

Scholz, V. (1986) 'A Regional Overview'. Paper presented to the Expert Group Meeting on the Environmental and Socio-economic Aspects of Tropical Deforestation. January, ESCAP, Bangkok, Thailand.

Scott, M. (1986) 'Southeast Asia's forests: lost for the trees'. *Far Eastern Economic Review* (Hong Kong) 10 April.

Secrett, C. (1986) 'The Environmental Impact of Transmigration'. *The Ecologist*, (UK) Vol. 16, No.2/3.

Seddon, G. (1984) 'Logging in the Gogal Valley'. *Ambio*, (Sweden) Vol. 13, No.5/6.

Senge, F. (1986) 'Environmental Watchdog Chained Up'. *The Times* (PNG) 8 March.

Shallow, P. (1956) 'Riverflow in the Cameroon Highlands'. *Hydro-electric Technical Bullitin* No.3. Central Electricity Board, Kuala Lumpur, Malaysia.

Shamsul Bahrin et al (1986) 'Taking a second look at the Jengha Triangle'. University of Malaya. Quoted in Rajeswary, I. and H. Rohiman (1986).

Sharma, Y. (1984) 'Landless Thai farmers make use of forest land'. *Malay Business Times* (Malaysia) 8 August.

Shelton, N. (1983) 'Good-bye to Malaysian Wildlife'. *Defenders* (USA) December/January.

—— (1985) 'Logging verses the natural habitat in the survival of tropical forests'. *Ambio* (Sweden) Vol. 14, No.1.

SKEPHI (1985) 'The Human perspective of Tropical Forests'. Paper presented to the Rainforest Action Network Conference, November, San Francisco, USA.

Smith, A. (1984a) 'When the axe fell'. *The Times* (PNG) 23 February.

—— (1984b) 'Timber profits fall to outside interests'. *The Times* (PNG) 1 March.

—— (1984c) 'A change of resource'. *The Times* (PNG) 1 March.

Snow, J. (1984) 'Timber'. *Asia Magazine* (Hong Kong) 20 May.

Soenarso, R. and Sampe Radja (1979) *Duta Rimba* (Indonesia) Vol. 5/35, Forest Research Institute, Bogor.

Soedjarwo (Dr) (1985) 'Future of Tropical rain Forests in Indonesia'. *The Environmentalist* (Switzerland) Vol. 5, No.10, Sequoia.

Solley Wong (1981) 'Treat it as an emergency'. *Borneo Bullitin* (Malaysia) 27 August.

Sothi Rachagan and Shamsul Bahrin (1983) 'Development without destruction'. *The Planter* (Malaysia) No. 59. Incorporated Society of Planters, Kuala Lumpur.

Spencer, J. (1966) *Shifting Cultivation in Southeastern Asia*. University of California Press, USA.

Sriburi, T. (1986) 'Forest resource crisis in Thailand'. Paper presented to the Regional Conference on Forest Resource Crisis in the Third World. SAM, Penang, Malaysia.

Sricharachanya, P. (1987) 'Jungle warfare'. *Far Eastern Economic Review* (Hong Kong) 17 September.

Stephenson, P. (1988) 'The PNG Timber Trade'. Unpublished thesis for Plymouth Polytechnic, Department of Environmental Sciences, UK.

Stewart, N. (1983) 'Tropical forests: PNG'. Unpublished correspondence with Friends of the Earth (UK).

Subhadhira, S. and M. Samart (1984) 'A Thai village history: Ban Ngio'. Unpublished thesis, Khon Kaen University, Thailand.

Syed Abu Bakar (1984) 'Logging to a fury'. *Malaysian Business Times* (Malaysia) 16 June.

Tan Sri Rama Lyer (1983) Paper presented to the National Workshop on Underutilized Timbers. Malaysian Timber Industries Board, Malaysia.

Third World Studies Programme (1983) *The Political Economy of Philippine Commodities*. Third World Studies Center, University of the Philippines at Quezon City, Manila, Philippines.

Thongtham, N. (1984) 'Missing millions took to the forest'. *Bangkok Post* (Thailand) 24 November.

——— (1986) 'Strawberry fields forever'. *Daily News* (Sri Lanka) 23 January.

Tuntawiroon, N. (1984) 'Thailand's Dam Building Programme', in Goldsmith E. and N. Hildyard (eds) (1986).

United Nations Development Programme (UNDP)/FAO (1981) *Hill Forest Silviculture for Sarawak*. Forest Department of Sarawak, Malaysia.

UNESCO (1983) *Swidden Cultivation in Asia*, Vol. 2. UNESCO Regional Office, Bangkok, Thailand.

——— (1986) Instiutive and Legislative Framework for Forestry Management in the ESCAP Region. Proceedings of the Expert Group Meeting on the Environmental and Socio-economic Aspects of Tropical Deforestation. UNESCO Regional Office, Bangkok, Thailand.

United Nations (UN) (1982) *Comparative Study on Migration, Urbanisation and Development in the ESCAP Region, Vol 5: Thailand*. UN Secretariat, Bangkok, Thailand.

United Planting Association of Malaya (1983) *Annual Report*. Kuala Lumpur, Malaysia.

Upland Multisectoral Policy Group (1986) 'Policy Imperatives in Upland Management for National Recovery' (Policy Paper). University of the Philippines at Los Banos, Philippines.

Vega, V. (1986) 'Rampant denudation of Philippine forests'. *Sarawak Tribune* (Malaysia) 27 October.

Viner, A. (1984) 'Environmental protection in PNG'. *Ambio* (Sweden) Vol. 13, No.5/6.

Warner, K. (1988) 'Markets'. *Timber Trades Journal* (UK) 26 November.

West Sepik (Sanduan) Provincial Government (PNG) (1986) Policy Submission No. ?/86, For members of the National Executive Council, Vanimo Timber Project, PNG.

Wheller, T. (1985) *South-east Asia on a Shoestring*. Lonely Planet, Australia.

Wienstock, J. (1979) *Land Tenure Practices of the Swidden Cultivations of Borneo*. Master's Thesis, published by Cornell University, USA.

Wood, M. (1985) 'Desperate options'. *Chain Reaction*, No.14. (May), Friends of the Earth (Australia).

World Bank (1984) *Environmental Policies and Procedures of the World Bank.* Office of Environmental and Scientific Affairs, projects Policy Department, World Bank, New York, USA.

—— (1985) Staff Appraisal Report; *Indonesia: Transmigration Project.* World Bank, New York, USA.

World Wildlife Fund (WWF) (1980) *Saving Siberut; A Conservation Plan for the Government of Indonesia.* WWF Indonesia, Bogar, Java, Indonesia.

—— (1984) *Yearbook 1983/84.* WWF International, Gland, Switzerland.

—— (Malaysia) (1985) 'Proposals for a Conservation Strategy for Sarawak'. WWF Malaysia, Kuala Lumpur, Malaysia.

Yong Chai Ting (1984) 'Compensatory Plantations in Peninsular Malaysia'. Paper presented to the Seminar on Forest Plantation Development in Malaysia. July, Forest Department of Sabah, Kota Kinabalu, Malaysia.

Zaidi Khaldine Zainie (1985) 'Land tenure systems in Sarawak'. *Sarawak Gazette* (Malaysia) July.

Zainoor Sulaiman (1986) 'Sabah enjoying good spell in sawn timber trade'. *Sarawak Tribune* (Malaysia) 7 July.

Newspaper References

Asian Timber, 'Enquiry into malpractices', May 1988.

Asiaweek, 'Wound in the world', Hong Kong, 13 July 1984.

—— 'How to move millions: and how not to', 4 May 1986.

Bangkok Post, 'Illegal teak seized', Thailand, 6 May 1986.

—— 'Hilltribesmen blamed for forest . . .', 16 July 1986.

—— 'Thailand's rarest bird tracked down', 21 July 1986.

—— 'Joint team raid illegal timber operations', 4 September 1986.

—— 'Rangers to combat sanctuary poaching', 20 November 1986.

—— 'Forestry police seize teak logs worth Bhat 8 M.', 10 December 1986.

Daily Enquirer (Manila), 1 May 1986.

Daily Express (Manila), 1 March 1986.

Far Eastern Economic Review, 'More a matter of policy than one of population', 7 February 1985.

Jakarta Post, 'Transmigration', 5 July 1985.

—— 'Cases of corruption in transmigration', 11 January 1986.

Sunday Mail (Malaysia), 'Flood: Don't just wait', 17 October 1977.

The Malaya (Manila), 22 May 1986.

—— 20 July 1986.

—— 31 July 1986.

Malaysian Business Times, 'Slump affects Johore timber sector', 29 November 1985.

—— 'Finalize proposed forestry estate', 15 September 1986.

Manila Bulletin, 'Forest Problems Noted', 15 August 1986.

The Nation (Thailand) 'Log poaching suspects crowding northern jails', 4 January 1986.

—— 'New tactics used to smuggle wood', 8 September 1986.
—— 'Eucalyptus chips for foreign markets soon', 11 December 1986.
New Straits Times, (Malaysia), Editorial, 11 April 1977.
—— 'Kedah freezes issue of saw mill licences', 8 December 1983.
—— 'Flood havoc in two states', 2 December 1986.
New Straits Times on Sunday, (Malaysia), 'Water projects to cost MS$100 million', 6 April 1986.
News Herald (Manila), 27 May 1986.
Niugini News, 15 July 1986.
Oriental Economist, 'Japanese paper giants move', January 1969.
Post Courier (PNG), 10 July 1984.
—— 'New order fells logging firm', 18 March 1986.
—— 'Timber siege', 31 July 1986.
—— 'Timber firm faces province's wrath', 11 September 1986.
The Real Forest News, 'Our disappearing forests', Campaign to save native forests, Western Australia, 1981.
Sarawak Tribune, 'Philippines may import logs after August', 7 July 1986.
—— 'Indonesia bans export of raw rattan', 11 October 1986.
The Star (Malaysia), 'January palm oil to decline', 27 February 1986.
—— 'Recession: 30 sawmills close shop', 28 March 1986.
—— 'Flood damage to farmers', 15 May and 25 May 1986.
—— 'Floods cause MS$10 million damage' and 'Mada the rainmaker', 8 December 1986.
—— 'Late planting may cause MS$100 m. loss', 9 December 1986.
Timberlines, (UK), 'New operation at vanimo', Spring 1984.
Timber Trades Journal, 'Thailand takes tough line', 14 January 1989.
—— 'Thailand's grief seeks culprit', 21 January 1989.
—— 'Logging ban spreads', 4 February 1989.
Timber Trade Review, Editorial, Volume 13. No. 3, 1984.
The Times (PNG), 'Villagers block vanimo timber', 31 October 1986.
World Wood, 'Trading conditions deteriorate', February 1986.
—— 'Manus island; Development or not?', February 1986.

Index

Marcos regime, 162, 169, 183, 187, 191
marginal land, 272; reform of, 276-7
meat, wild, availability of, 86, 101
mechanisation of felling, 153
Meja, Heturi, 143-4, 156
Melayu peoples, 54
meranti tree, 18, 64
Merlin Timber company, 119
Meyer, W., 105
migration patterns, 181
milk, dried, 221
mining, 8, 145-6, 169, 176, 186, t201, 275
Mining Law (1905) (Philippines), 172
Mitsubishi company, 16, 34
Mitsui company, 16
Moggie, Datuk Leo, 108
Mohamed, Datuk Patanggi Taib, 104
Mohamed, Nik, 109
molave forest, 163
monkeys, threat to, 54, 86, 167
monocultures, 140
moratorium on logging, 113
multinational companies, 3, 15, 250
Myers, Norman, 34, 211, 277

National Forest Reserves Act (1964)
   (Thailand), 214
National Forestry Act (1984) (Malaysia),
   62, 63
National Forestry Policy (Malaysia), 71,
   72
National Investment and Development
   Act (1974) (Papua New Guinea), 138
National Land Council (Malaysia), 60, 62
national parks, 12, 13-15, 114, 183, 257-8,
   259; Gunung Leuser, 6; Taman
   Negara, 55, 62, 72
National Parks Act (1961) (Thailand), 213
National Parks Act (1980) (Malaysia), 62
National Power Corporation
   (Philippines), 197, 199
Nations, James, 259
Nectoux, François, 266
Negritos peoples, 54
neocolonialism, 249-51
New Conservation Areas Act (1978)
   (Papua New Guinea), 139
New Economic Policy (West Malaysia), 47
New Guinea Timber company, 144
New People's Army (NPA) (Philippines),
   169-70, 177, 182, 192, 196, 200
Nisshe Iawi company, 135
North Borneo Company, 81, 83, 106

oil palm, 46, 50, 62, 65, 66, 250, 251;
   plantations, 143, 146, 248
oil resources, 10

Oji Paper Company, 149
OK Tedi mine, 139, 146
Open Bay Logging Company, 135
open-cast mining, 145
Operation Clean Sweep (Irian Jaya), 26
opium, 48, 233; growing, 222-3
opposition to logging, 132
Orang Asli peoples, 54, 58, 59, 60, 71;
   resettlement of, 55
Orang-utan, threat to, 5
Osathanugrah, Surat, 230
ownership, land, 98, 99, 149, 217, 232,
   245, 247; as alien concept, 163, 171;
   communal, 152, 247; reform of, 269
Oxford Forestry Institute, 13

Pairin, Datuk Joseph, 103
Pampona company, 187
Pancasila philosophy, 9, 17
Papua New Guinea, 8, 127-58, 248, 250,
   268, 272, 274, 275
Papua New Guinea Forest Products
   company, 132
Peace Pacts (Philippines), 199
Penan people, 115-22
pepper growing, 29, 100
Perum Perhutari Corporation, 14
pesticides, 14, 22, 185, 209, 220
pests, attacks by, 140, 168, 184
Philippine Wood Product Association,
   170
Philippines, 162-203, 246, 248, 250, 253,
   255, 262, 272
Philippines migrant labour, 91
phytochemical production, 278
pig as unit of exchange, 152
pig-rearing, 142
pine, 3, 136, 163, 188-9, 195, 208, 253
Placer Development company, 128
plantations, 33, 146-7, 177, 227-8, 258-9;
   establishment of, 226
Plaza, Democrito, 189
plywood, 15, 20-1, 108, 145, 190-1, 251,
   266; prices of, 21
poaching of logs, 56, 110, 211, 229
political will, creation of, 278-81
Poore, Duncan, 4
population growth, 46; and forest loss, 180
Population Resettlement programmes, 12
Portuguese colonialism, 1, 128
Preservation of Forests Act (1896)
   (Thailand), 213
prostitution, 8, 88
Public Land Law (1962) (Philippines), 173
Public Lands Act (1905) (Philippines), 172

Rahman, Norlia Abdul, 90